TOWARD
A
PLANNED
SOCIETY

TOWARD A PLANNED SOCIETY

From Roosevelt to Nixon

Otis L. Graham, Jr.

New York
OXFORD UNIVERSITY PRESS
1976

Published for the Center of Technology Assessment and Resource Policy,
Department of Engineering-Economic Systems, Stanford University.

To John T. McAlister, Jr.
and
Ann, Annie, and Wade

Contents

"We were not commissioned to lead the people into some new land of promise, but to retrace our recent wanderings, to indicate and interpret our ways and rates of change, to provide maps of progress, make observations of danger zones, point out hopeful roads of advance, helpful in finding a more intelligent course in the next phase of our progress."

President's Research Committee on
Social Trends, *Recent Social Trends
in the United States* (1933)

"If to do were as easy as to know what were good to do, chapels had been churches, and poor men's cottages prince's palaces."

Merchant of Venice, I, Scene 2

"Can we forestall ruin by reform? If we wait to be forced by events we shall be astounded to find how much more radical they are than our utopias."

Wealth and Commonwealth,
Henry Demarest Lloyd

Introduction

In 1972 I was asked by a group of scholars at Stanford University to participate in a series of seminars on something called "national growth policy." My own work on planning in the 1930s, they hoped, might allow me to provide some of the necessary background for the study of their subject. The exchange was to be unfair. I took to them some inconclusive and (as it turned out) poorly aimed remarks on the planning experiences of the 1930s. Their contribution to my own education was vastly greater. I heard the phrase "national growth policy" for the first time, learned that President Richard Nixon, in his 1970 State of the Union Address, had said:

> . . . For the past thirty years our population has been growing and shifting. The result is exemplified in vast areas of rural America emptying out of people and of promise—a third of our counties lost population in the sixties.
> . . . The violent and decayed central cities of our great metropolitan complexes are the most conspicuous area of failure in American life today.
> . . . I propose that before these problems become insoluble, the nation develop a *national growth policy*.
> . . . If we seize our growth as a challenge we can make the 1970s an historic period when by conscious choise we transformed our land into what we want it to become.

Other revelations followed. The Nixon administration, upon close examination, turned out to have been engaged on several fronts in an apparent even if undeclared effort to enhance the government's planning capacities. Planning was again in the air, as it had been in the 1930s.

But this time there seemed no general discussion of the planning concept, no public acceptance of a new planning system that appeared to be evolving. The people in the 1960s and 1970s who were extensively involved with bits and pieces of the planning idea did not recognize that the work of the 1930s had been resumed. They thought of planning in the spirit of Christopher Marlowe's comment that it had been a long time ago and in another country, and besides the wench was dead.

So I resolved to write a historical account of planning in the United States from the depression decade, when it was thought to have been tried and rejected, to the 1970s when it emerged as a shaping influence in American life. Such a study, at first thought, promised to be brief. By the usual definitions of national planning, America has either had no experience with it at all, or at most witnessed a truncated episode of it under Roosevelt's NRA in 1933-35, and in a different form during World War II. Yet like other subjects the matter of planning turns out upon inspection to be more complex than first thought. Taken as an idea, planning has a substantial history even if no American has ever seen it here in full flower. Planning has component parts, intellectual and institutional. If these are partially provided, enhanced, better understood, to that extent the society approaches planning. At a certain point, people see that planning is almost here, and they had better decide whether they want it or not. That is where Americans have arrived by the 1970s.

What do we mean by planning? I shall let the American idea of planning define itself through historical narrative. But the elements we deal with are persistent enough, and might be tentatively stated. Planning assumes that modern industrial society requires public intervention to achieve national goals; assumes that such intervention must touch all fundamental social developments; must be goal-oriented, and effectively coordinated at the center; must be anticipatory rather than characterized by ad hoc solutions and timing dictated by crisis. Our history will help us to expand on these phrases.

What follows is a brief historical study of the idea and practice of national planning in twentieth-century America, with some speculations upon the forms which our eventual accommodation to that idea may take. I argue that liberal planning as explored by the New Deal generation has been revived and re-cast by many hands while the Democrats were led by Kennedy-Johnson-Humphrey-McGovern. This broad rediscovery of the planning idea is only now being perceived for what it is. A second vitally important development in the evolution toward planning took place during the Presidency of Richard M. Nixon, when a conservative form of planning was vigorously and imaginatively explored. We seem on the eve of a workable consensus that the time has come to plan, and to openly debate the many choices that the planning framework permits. In making these choices, whether to plan and how to do it, our own history is more illuminating than the experience of those other societies which come to mind when planning is discussed. The New Dealers located a set of strategic points where the society and its direction might be influenced: not only the gross size of the economy, but natural resources, including especially energy and land-use, population distribution, manpower, public credit, science and technology, incomes. Turning policies into national Policy in these areas has been the unfinished work of both liberals and conservatives as the problems of social management became so acute in the mid-1960s and after. In addition to locating these strategic points of contact—to which a later generation would only add population size—Franklin Roosevelt and the New Dealers began work on some of the institutional innovations necessary to provide a planning capacity: executive branch reorganization, a central planning board, science and technology assessment, economic and social accounting, political democratization. The search for all of these has been resumed in recent years.

I am acutely aware of the deficiencies of this attempt to narrate and analyze the history of American planning. The planning ethos has worked its way deep into American life via two institutions in particular, the city planning aspect of urban government, and the large corporation. Books have been written on both subjects, and I have made only the briefest reference to them. Regional planning is another part of the story of the planning idea, but is a subject which would intolerably enlarge this study if it were explored. Anyone seriously interested in planning must acknowledge the importance of economic theory, especially macroeconomic modeling. It is a wondrous subject; I have left it to others. Likewise the mysteries of input-output analysis, and linear programming, analytic techniques which have entered the world since FDR's time and to some undetermined degree weakened the conviction that Man can never understand society well enough to manage it.

All of these are subjects for other books, other authors. One final subject that I did not include in this brief study that belongs in any complete examination of the idea of a planned society is the prospect for international planning. When we understand that we are one society and accept what this implies, we will look to the interrelationships of things, and commence learning to plan our future. And then we will be ready for the next step, the recognition that our crisis leaps over borders, that we are one world. The Japanese, planning since the 1950s, had learned enough by their seventh plan to make one of their four official national goals "the enhancement of international cooperation." Perhaps we may also find our own way in that general direction.

Preface

Countless people have helped me. The Bibliography and the
Notes list some of them. In Washington, James Thornton of Senator Humphrey's staff, formerly with Orville Freeman in the Department of Agriculture, qualifies as the prime mover of the
growth policy movement; he and Bruce Johnson of OMB, formerly of Senator Hartke's staff, gave me invaluable aid. I was
much helped by ideas and information offered by Ken Khachigian
of the National Goals Research Staff; Herbert Stein, Chairman of
the Council of Economic Advisors; Congressman Jerry Litton;
Senator John Culver; Norman Beckman and Susan Harding of
the Congressional Research Service; Ellis Mottur of Senator Kennedy's staff. I am grateful to John Ehrlichman, Daniel P. Moynihan, and Kenneth Cole for interviews. Albert Lepawsky, Morton
Borden, Samuel F. Wells and Richard Polenberg read portions
of the manuscript, and Thomas Cronin, John McAlister, James
Sundquist, and James Thornton read it all. To the latter four
especially I am deeply indebted. Adele Wilson and Wendy Yager
were imaginative and resourceful research assistants, and I could
not have finished without typing help from Nancy Florence, Chris
Johnson, Mary Menzies, and the History Department staff at
UCSB, headed by Helen Nordhoff.

James M. Banner, Ralph Widner, and Paul Sweet called my

attention to numerous developments I might have missed. John O'Keefe encouraged me at a critical moment, and Allen and Karen Sears gave well-timed support. My brother, Fred P. Graham, restrained his natural skepticism, and arranged an interview with John Ehrlichman when that gentleman was preoccupied with other things. It is pleasant also to thank the National Endowment for the Humanities for a grant in 1972-73, the resourceful librarians of the UCSB library, the Fund for New Priorities in America, and not least the Center for the Study of Democratic Institutions and its prime mover, Robert M. Hutchins.

A conference was held on a late draft of the book in Washington, July 10, 1975, hosted by the Department of Engineering-Economic Systems, Stanford University, assisted by the Alfred P. Sloan Foundation. George Agree, Thomas Cotton, Edward Dale, Dennis Dugan, Eli Jacobs, Louis Lehrman, William Linvill, Charles Manatt, Ernest Manuel, John Pierson, and Christopher Roosevelt gave candid and informed criticism.

Rexford G. Tugwell, through his life and writings, has taught us all much more than we were willing to learn about how to make a better America. He supplied me with both inspiration and admonition. Of the former there is no need to speak. Text and notes to this book tell of that debt. Of the latter, I must record a remark he made in the winter of 1975 when I described the evolving book to him. "You are getting into a swamp!" Of course he was right. He had been in that area for a lifetime, illuminating the dark and firming the ground.

More than anyone else, John T. McAlister nurtured this project. Authors are expected to accept responsibility for their errors, and this I now do. But John McAlister is responsible for the fact that this book was perpetrated at all. If it is helpful, to him goes a primary credit.

I have never written anything that was not supported in fundamental ways and improved in both style and content because Ann Zemke Graham was with me. This book is no exception.

O. L. G., Jr.

August 1975
Santa Barbara, Calif.

TOWARD
A
PLANNED
SOCIETY

The 1930s: Roosevelt and the Planning Idea

It was not Franklin Roosevelt, but the Great Depression, that brought the Planning idea to the front of American political life in the 1930s. And so we begin with the depression and its relentless pressure upon accepted methods of national governance.

2

The year 1929 opened upon a pleasing prospect. A new president with unsurpassed economic experience now stood at the head of an expansive society. The population was rising (would reach 121 million by 1929), and this was a national objective in those days as well as a sign of a better future. The national income climbed in that year to $104 billion. There were other material and cultural achievements, too many to number.

More important than immediate levels of progress was the apparent fact of systemic strength. The violent economic cycles of the late nineteenth century had apparently been put behind us by the economic and political reforms of the pre-war reform era, or by technological advance, or both. Enterprise seemed now nicely balanced and blended with social responsibility. The marketplace allocated resources, rewarded initiatives and genius, chastened carelessness and poor judgment. Individuals were free to become rich, or to fail, and this brought out the best in them, to society's benefit. But sufficient public authority stood on guard against the darker side of human nature. Should capitalists attempt monopoly or fraud, there were the Sherman and Clayton acts and a barricade of regulatory agencies monitoring business practice. Immigration laws in 1921 and 1924 completed federal control of the threat of destabilizing population influxes; tariffs guarded against destabilizing foreign competition. Treasury agents protected the public against alcoholic beverages. These and other public laws and regulatory interventions appeared fully adequate to most citizens. Outside their purview, individuals were free to chart their own futures, and thus the nation's destiny. The result, plain to see, was an outpouring of energy, productivity, innovation, economic and population growth. Who would not be bullish on America in the first year of the Presidency of the Great Engineer, Herbert Hoover?

Then toward the end of summer 1929 there began an economic downturn which was soon accelerated by a string of stock market disasters. It would be eleven years later, in 1940, that the country would again reach the per capita incomes of 1929. This decade of economic agony became known here and the world over —for it was worldwide—as the Great Depression. Economic collapse gave to that era its characteristic qualities of class conflict, of social and political crisis, of reform. The first four years saw an almost unrelieved decline from the level of well-being which had been reached on the eve of the stock market crash. With only a brief plateau in 1931, economic production spiralled down to a floor of $56 billion in the year 1933, and the cold winter months of 1932–33 were marked by economic activity so sluggish that even this total would not have been reached without improvement in the summer. By 1933 the national product was cut in half, and a quarter of the labor force could find no work.

These years were Hoover's testing ground, not only for his political leadership and character, but also for his ideas about the proper relationship of the national government to the rest of society. He was judged at the end to have failed that test, and his ideas absorbed the same punishment he received as an individual. In both cases, there was explicit rejection and banishment. This may not have been entirely just, as Hoover argued to the end. He had operated as President in a minefield of obstructions which prevented a consistent trial for his ideas. This interesting question is left to other books. The important thing here is that Hoover's way of coping with depression was marked down in history as a failure, and there necessarily followed a time of experimentation which was the seedtime of our own era.

Hoover is a more respected figure now than in 1933, and years after. This is not merely because, as he told Earl Warren, he "outlived the bastards," but because careful historical scholarship and a lengthening perspective have brought into view both the basic consistency of his approach to questions of political economy, and the reformist thrust of his ideas which was blunted by circumstances. Hoover believed American capitalism to be a social organization superior to all others, both in economic performance and in guaranteeing individual liberty and development. He never considered fundamental alterations of that system. Yet he was a reformer of a mild sort. His eight years as secretary of commerce saw him exert intellectual and administrative pressure upon public and private sectors to rationalize their operations. To abbreviate his social goals, Hoover envisioned governmental leadership of capitalist institutions toward economies of size, standardization, cooperation, and internal rationalization. All of this was to be voluntary. As secretary of commerce he was vigorous in sponsoring trade associations through which corporations could move beyond blind competition to industry-wide stabilization. Trade associations did in fact flourish in the 1920s, but Hoover was not satisfied with these little gains. When he became President he still thought the economy marred by flaws, and saw an important governmental role in removing them. He intended to press the great industrialists (in a friendly spirit) to end competitive abuses, pay decent wages, adopt modern data-gathering and research methods, and cooperate in dampening excessive swings in investment. All of this pressure would of course have been in the form of moral suasion. Hoover was not fond of legislation, or at ease with coercion. But he was far from the passive figure he has been pictured. His ideas represented the enlightened conservatism of the day, the fostering of economic concentration and modernization through government-business cooperation.

The depression struck before he had been in office a full year, and Hoover never had an opportunity to display the economic reforms he might have urged upon American capitalism. The depression created obvious problems of investor confidence, and Hoover thought himself forced by the circumstances to speak against novelty and reform rather than for it. He was a mild reformer whose reforming instincts were muzzled by the onset of bad times (which he thought originated in Europe), bringing conditions in which he dared not disturb the owners of capital.

And so he turned his considerable energies toward governmental leadership, while confining himself to that narrow zone where capitalist nervous systems would tolerate the governmental presence. He called numerous conferences to bolster morale, appealed for sustained production and wage levels. He spurred the private organization of relief services. All of this required much exertion. Hoover was no Coolidge, taking naps in the afternoon and predicting that nine of ten problems coming down the road would run in the ditch if you ignored them. He was no Andrew Mellon, the secretary of the treasury who urged standing aside and letting the depression run its natural course, with the words "liquidate labor, liquidate stocks, liquidate the farmers, liquidate real estate." No, Hoover worked long days, and in the effort to bolster confidence he predicted too many upturns that did not materialize, eroding his credibility and whetting an edge of despair to the public mood. A brief economic rally in the autumn of 1931 was ended by an Austrian bank failure which spread to other countries, and gloom returned.

From every political quarter the demand for new and effective governmental action began to increase—although today we are astonished at how much the public of 1929–33 would take without an uprising. Hoover's energies toward the end of his administration went principally toward staving off proposals he thought damaging to business confidence and ominous for the American free enterprise system. These included Senator Wagner's bill for direct federal relief to the unemployed, or various calls for expansion of the money supply. In these innocuous measures Hoover and others saw a subversion of the work ethic, an opening of Pandora's box of threats to the treasury. The work ethic was in little danger, but Hoover was right that a mob of subsidy-seeking interest groups was gathering at congressional doors. Farmers forced a grain-buying program in 1929, businessmen secured the Reconstruction Finance Corporation to give loans to banks and railroads in 1932. Who knew when less legitimate and formerly powerless groups, such as the unemployed, might find some way to pull themselves together and press *their* demands upon the government? Deep grumbling could be heard in the *lumpenproletariat,* and the federal treasury and printing presses seemed vulnerable to radicalism as the depression stretched out into its third, then its fourth year.

The election of 1932 found Hoover at the end of his ability to devise more assurances, even to feign confidence. He had explored the policy options of the center as best he could, and under the pressure of mounting demands for federal action had emerged as a defender of the crippled system as it was, when all along he had nurtured modest reform ambitions. Faced with reform suggestions too radical for his temperament, Hoover went on the defensive, deciding that eternal constitutional verities and economic principles were worth more than a quick recovery brought about through expediency. He waited it out, and the electorate threw him out. The day he left office, on March 2, 1933, a quarter of the work force was unemployed, some Americans were literally starving, and the net profits of business enterprise were negative for the second year in a row.

3

Turning from Hoover and his counsels of patient endurance, the electorate voted in the other party, despite the fact that neither the Democrats' history nor their candidate for the Presidency promised anything very clear or new as a remedy for economic collapse. The restlessness and rebelliousness of the American people were greater than the November 1932 vote suggested. Many informed people warned that explosive sentiments lay under the sullen apathy of that autumn. There would be action in 1933, they thought, one way or the other. But what strategy might those in charge of the national government follow when confronted with an economy deeply sick, deflated to half its normal size?

Cranks and one-idea men were everywhere, purveying urgent tracts, buttonholing and even convincing an occasional congressman. The native American monetary fixers were most prominent, predicting instant recovery if the government would only mint silver at the old Bryanite ratio, or issue a mass of greenbacks, or move to 100 per cent reserve banking. These inflationists were actually probing an important part of the anatomy of collapse. And in addition to being instinctively right that the money supply was important (although they treated their truth as The Truth), they were not very radical. They thought that one big monetary injection would save capitalism, a message that was not believed. They might well have stressed more than they did the assurance that inflation would leave property and power pretty much where they had been in the good old days so recently fled. But drastic monetary remedies frightened most people in responsible positions, and would never get a real trial. Hoover resisted inflation tenaciously, and his successor defeated it by grudging and insignificant concessions. With monetary remedies deeply suspect, especially in the East, and with Hoover's policies discredited, American conservatism had little to offer to a nation desperate for new recovery strategies.

American radicalism was intellectually much better prepared for crisis leadership. Socialists and Communists were eager to implement their central idea, replacing capitalism with public ownership. There were shelves full of tracts and street corners busy with orators outlining the various and differing details of

the socialist alternative. Considering the unemployment rolls
and general suffering, it is astonishing how little public impact
such theories had. Truly radical alternatives had little political
following even at the low point of the depression. Later on,
radical approaches would gather strength, but at the pivot of the
depression, in 1932–33, they were not considered where national
policy was made.

The collapse of Hoover's administration was instead an opening and call for help to the liberal-progressive tradition. What
were its resources? For more than fifty years, progressive intellectuals such as Lester Frank Ward, Richard T. Ely, John
Dewey, Walter Lippmann, Herbert Croly, Charles Van Hise,
and others had taught the necessity in a modern era of public intervention to guide social evolution. They had long since dissolved the old chains of laissez-faire belief, had provided texts
for public regulation of capitalist enterprise. Spurred by their
ideas, as well as by widespread social problems in urbanizing
America, a wave of progressive reformers had busied themselves
in the years prior to World War I with the renovation of American society. Under progressive prodding, cities had made efforts
to throw off inept and corrupt governments, regulate public
utilities, control the discharge of wastes, improve living conditions in slums. States enlarged their regulatory duties in the
areas of conservation, transportation, and labor legislation. No
millennium had been achieved, but twenty or more years of reform exertion did seem to leave cities and states a bit more
orderly and consciously directed than in the turbulent 1890s, out
of whose troubles reform had grown. At the national level,
Presidents Theodore Roosevelt and Woodrow Wilson had
pressed for a more active government, and secured new authority
in the areas of railroad regulation, anti-trust policy, banking
regulation, and conservation. They stood as models for executive
activism and leadership, a ready inspiration and resource for
those wrestling with the Great Depression. Below these towering
figures the progressive era had mobilized an entire class of men
and women who saw the need for a managed society—business-

men, lawyers, and other citizens ready for occasional public service with the newly invigorated governments of America, as well as the rising "new middle class," in Robert Wiebe's phrase, the sanitation engineers, statisticians, economists, welfare professionals, public health officers, and university-based social scientists who were eager for policy roles in the job of social regulation. These reformers had produced a current of self-correctional fervor and a confidence in social intervention that was not spent when the reform era was ended by the war. It had touched the lives of all those of leadership age in the 1930s, and it would assist those who wished to break with the fatalism that had settled in under the unhappy Hoover.

Yet there were important ambiguities and schisms in the liberal reform heritage as it arrived at the early 1930s. One face of reform had been moralistic and emotional, nostalgic for small-town and small-business values. The other aspired to a more scientific and pragmatic approach to social problem-solving, was managerial by temperament, accepted large institutions as the inevitable framework in which progress must be pursued. These contrasting tendencies were rarely perfectly embodied in individual men or causes, never in political parties. Pre-war reform was complex, contradictory, shifting in its intellectual and emotional makeup. But the division between the "modernist" and the "traditionalist" impulses, to use John Braeman's terms, was roughly embodied in the careers of Theodore Roosevelt and Woodrow Wilson. Roosevelt inclined toward continuous governmental regulation and management of the society, with large corporations secure in the center. But Wilson was sympathetic with governmental intervention to break up concentrations of economic power and reinvigorate the marketplace. Beyond this he saw little need for and much danger in the growth of governmental bureaucracies for permanent regulation. A political leader or movement in the 1930s which turned to the reform tradition would find these two broad social theories contending for dominance. Thus contemporary liberalism, underneath its "can do" spirit and faith in social intervention, offered a divided and confusing counsel.

4

The "usable past" for desperate men in 1933 contained one other experience, the mobilization for war in 1917-18. In many ways the war offered more guidance for addressing the problems of Depression than the generation of dispersed reforms that had gone before. Sudden involvement in global war forced the first American attempt at economic and social control on anything like a national scale and comprehensive basis. For the first time, the word "planning" was heard as observers attempted to describe the new degree of social control which war had brought.

Nothing like it had ever been attempted in America. For approximately sixteen months the national government commanded the major economic and manpower resources of the country, recruited, trained, and supplied an expeditionary army along with arming the allies. The Food Administration stimulated the production of selected products through purchases at high prices, restriction of civilian consumption, and the occasional coercion of producers with the threat of a newly enacted federal licensing power. The Shipping Board took control of all shipping over 2500 tons and established government shipyards to increase the size of the merchant fleet. The Railroad Administration operated the nation's railroads as a unit, breaking through a traffic bottleneck that had existed in early 1917 as private roads carrying the orders of uncoordinated government agencies had become hopelessly snarled. The Selective Service moved 4 million young men (16 per cent of the male labor force) into the armed services, where they were housed, trained, and deployed at stations around the country and in France. The Fuel Administration instituted coal rationing and rationalized coal marketing to minimize crosshauls. The Committee on Public Information manipulated public opinion. The War Finance Corporation lent money to munitions manufacturers. The Capital Issues Committee passed on new securities.

It was obvious from the beginning that the government's wartime powers must have some central coordination, although the intricacies of this assignment were beyond the experience of contemporaries. At first, President Wilson relied upon the Council of National Defense, but it was a large committee with no clear authority or leadership, and was superseded in the summer of 1917 by the War Industries Board. It was this agency, reorganized in 1918 and placed under the chairmanship of Bernard Baruch, which finally established an acceptable degree of order in economic mobilization. The board replaced the marketplace where large industry was concerned, utilizing persuasion and mild threats to gain acceptable prices, adjustment of competing claims for scarce resources, and priorities in military contracting. American production was remarkable in quantity, and contributed conspicuously to Germany's defeat. The WIB was dissolved within weeks after the Armistice, and was not caught in the fratricidal struggles of demobilization. It left with a high reputation for industrial planning, enhanced by its chairman Baruch, a man of great political sensitivity and a gift for self-dramatization.

The result of this intense sixteen-month experience was to have a profound effect upon the minds of contemporaries, and through them upon the political economy of the 1930s. Let us distinguish between reality and contemporary perceptions. In fact, the WIB never secured unified control of war mobilization. It lacked control over industrial prices, which Wilson gave to a separate price-fixing committee, and over transportation, which remained with the Railroad Administration. Baruch and his colleagues were unsure of their legal authority to coerce recalcitrant industrialists, and in any event preferred conciliation and compromise. Within the WIB bureaucracy, moreover, there were as many contradictions and different paths as in the complex society outside. In the words of a recent brilliant study, the WIB was "a bundle of paradoxes where decentralization vied with centralization, competition with combination, individualism with integration, freedom with coercion."[1]

But this was not known to the public. Baruch effectively obscured his agency's shortcomings by persuading Congress to dismantle it six weeks after the Armistice, on January 1, 1919, before the problems of demobilization could lay open the weaknesses of the government's economic controls. What stuck with contemporaries, and came down in memory, was a well-coordinated mobilization under government direction, with the WIB as the nerve center. The experience left an indelible imprint upon the minds of important groups. Both public managers and businessmen learned what could be achieved, in the way of rapid and full production, when the national economy was considered as a unit and directed toward agreed ends by the agencies of government. Anyone could see the advantages of centralized purchasing and standardized operations, as many of the irrationalities of the raw young industrial order were smoothed out under the temporary rule of federal administrators (themselves often businessmen serving the government, some at $1.00 a year). And many of the wastes were invisible. While it is impossible to estimate the impact of war mobilization upon the thinking of the general public, we know that the experience was seminal for the American policy-making elite. For the lawyers, businessmen, economists, social workers, statisticians, engineers, and others who staffed the bustling mobilization agencies, World War I was a revelation in the advantages of an economy managed through government-business cooperation.

The attitude of businessmen toward wartime controls was especially interesting, and prophetic. While business always had many points of view, it was businessmen, chiefly spearheaded by the young Chamber of Commerce, who had mounted pressure on Wilson to replace the listless CND with a strongly centralized operation. As the end of the war approached, Baruch learned that important segments of business opinion were fearful of the abrupt end of controls, and were ready for the extension of stabilization measures at least some way into the conversion period. Heads of Baruch's commodity sections argued unsuccessfully against his decision to ask that WIB be discharged at the end of 1918. When a depression seemed imminent in the spring of 1919, a group of businessmen joined with Secretary of Commerce William Redfield to establish an industrial board within the government. It would convene industrial conferences for the purpose of arranging industry-wide price reductions on an orderly basis. The board hoped that the announcement of new and somewhat lower price schedules would reassure the public, stabilize the market, and lead to renewed buying.

It is difficult to escape the label "liberalism" for this appeal for the peacetime expansion of government's stabilizing role, even though it came chiefly from capitalist sources. But if this was a brand of liberalism, so was Wilson's suspicion of exactly this sort of governmental function. He had signed much regulatory legislation, had helped build federal power in the area of anti-trust activity, central banking, and elsewhere. But he had a long record of opposition where positive government was concerned. He suspected great concentrations of power within the government as he did in the economy, and designed the WIB at first as a weak agency which might nonetheless mollify those who wanted a central munitions agency with commanding powers. Even after granting Baruch exceptional powers in May 1918, Wilson kept coordinating authority fragmented. It was his decision to place price-fixing, rail and shipping beyond WIB's control. He resisted the coalition of businessmen and bureaucrats in late 1918 who urged the agency's continuation. Even Baruch wanted some of the WIB's standardization and conservation duties shifted in peacetime to the Department of Commerce, and suggested the continuation of the small Central Bureau of Planning and Statistics that the war produced. Wilson dismantled it all, announcing his commitment to move at once from emergency arrangements to constitutional and regular ones. A bill in the Senate would have given the President a reconversion planning staff, but he opposed that also. The machinery of planning and control did not long survive hostilities. Wilson sailed for Europe in December 1918, and upon his return in the spring he realized that the fledgling Industrial Board set up behind his back was involved in illegal price-fixing. The board was terminated.

There were no efforts to reverse the President and retain some of the apparatus of wartime control. One exception was the Railroad Administration, which organized labor struggled without success to preserve. The economy expanded after the war, and the only mass protest in the country was a Red Scare, a social convulsion which businessmen found quite tolerable. Most liberals were disappointed at Wilson's negative approach to the role of government in the last months of his administration, and felt that important opportunities had been lost to advance social justice. But by 1921 Wilson was out of office, replaced by a president even less interested in active government. Through the 1920s American national government remained in form much as it had been prior to 1917; and in spirit it revealed nothing like the earlier energy for social correction. The war left little institutional trace, and in many ways contributed to the exhaustion of social activism. The little group of public officials and businessmen who hoped for the continuation of some form of government economic stabilization was no match for the forces of individualism and apathy. Yet the experience of war mobilization had left an indelible imprint, and many who lived through it would turn their minds to this model in the national emergency of the 1930s.

5

As the shattering months of economic decline piled one upon another under Hoover, one heard more and more frequently of the virtues of wartime "planning." This was a word one had not often heard, except from stray socialists or unsettled journalists who punctuated the 1920s with errant reminders of a brief, better time. The depression raised up the word. Between 1930 and 1933, George B. Galloway counted six major legislative proposals for "some sort of central planning body," their sponsors ranging from liberals like Senator LaFollette (1931) to the Chamber of Commerce's Henry I. Harriman.[2] Galloway counted nine other "private" plans which attracted national attention, from people such as the historian Charles A. Beard (1931); economic writer Stuart Chase (1931); and labor leader Matthew Woll (1931). John L. Lewis of the United Mine Workers called for planning under a national economic council in 1933, and he was joined by Sidney Hillman of the clothing workers. Gerard Swope of General Electric had been talking along similar lines since 1931.

To people who relied upon reflex rather than examination of the evidence, the idea of planning, "social" or "national" or "economic" or whatever it was called, seemed a Left-wing idea. Indeed, the use of the word usually brought Russia to mind. And it is true that some who placed their hopes on planning had either been to Russia or become admirers of its full employment and social solidarity from a distance. "Why should the Russians have all the fun of remaking a world?" demanded planning-oriented economic writer Stuart Chase in 1932.[3] But the inspiration of the U.S.S.R. was thinly rooted, and soon slipped away to free the idea of planning for serious discussion. For those using the word were not proposing the importation of the Russian system. Indeed, they were not all on the far left. Socialists advocated planning, to be sure, men like Norman Thomas, who had little popular audience, and John Dewey, who commanded unusual respect among intellectuals. And so did quasi-socialists like Paul Douglas, economist and political activist at the University of Chicago. But many of those calling for planning were liberals like Father John A. Ryan, or the *New Republic*'s George Soule or the writer Stuart Chase. Both Chase and Soule authored books in 1932 (Soule's was called *A Planned Society*) calling for a system of planning in which the nationalization of industry was somewhat ambiguously regarded as an occasionally useful but not entirely necessary condition for a planned economy. Charles Beard was one of the few intellectuals converted to planning by the depression who went so far as to borrow from the U.S.S.R. the idea of a five-year plan, which he proposed, along with a national planning board, in 1931. But often a formal plan was thought unnecessary, socialization of industry optional or even unwise. The planning idea was plastic and flexible, and fuzzy at the edges always, but it was put forward in a decidedly American way, as a cooperative, open, democratic way of collectively responding to the obvious imbalance between productivity and purchasing power.

The central thrust was usually clear enough. Individual self-interest had reigned unchecked under old style American capitalism, and had brought on a crash and four years of wrenching depression. The economy must be fundamentally altered through political means, the State setting up permanent instruments of collective control to balance purchasing power with productivity. The American Left did not think much coercion would be necessary. Controls would be democratic, rational, and cooperatively established and modified, with all major groups participating, as in the World War I experience. The inevitability of collectivism seemed so obvious that there was little thought of violence, or expropriation, or civil war. We would move toward planning the American way, through persuasion, and through the established political system—considering Hoover's record, this meant through the Democratic party if possible, a third party if necessary.

But planning was not a concept owned by the Left. Healthy profits had been made during the war period when business had been closely controlled by government, and there had been a welcome degree of standardization introduced through the gentle coercion of the War Industries Board. Many businessmen were impressed with the advantages of doing business under government supervision as against competing in the chaos of the marketplace where reasonable cooperation was so unlikely. Hugh Johnson, a Moline Plow Corporation executive who worked under Baruch in the WIB, wrote in 1918:

> No one will contend that there can ever be any peacetime necessity or reason for such close-held control over industry as was practiced during the war. . . . Still the great lessons remain: efficiency is attainable only by cooperation; . . . industry is susceptible of such regulatory control as would prevent the abuses aimed at by the Sherman Act and yet attain the efficiency of cooperation without impairing the advantages of individual initiative.

"What is needed is a statute," he went on, legalizing trade association activities leading toward industrial cooperation. But Johnson was not proposing the mere passage of a law setting aside the anti-trust acts. "A mechanism is required, an organization set up on a different theory than any permanent organization we now know . . ." so that the government would possess the capacity to act not as a "policeman . . . but a cooperator, an adjuster, a friend."[4] He envisioned a planning board made up of representatives from basic industries, passing upon prices, wages, plans for investment, trade practices.

The depression revived such ideas. To some businessmen the problem of overproduction could not be solved without government cartelization. A leading voice for planning was General Electric's Gerard Swope, who called for planned production through trade associations under loose supervision, in a speech in September 1931. Henry I. Harriman of the Chamber of Commerce endorsed Swope's general idea before a Senate hearing in 1932, where Senator LaFollette's proposal for a national economic council was being debated. Whatever planning was— and none of its proponents, either among the radicals or the businessmen, were very clear about exactly what was involved— it was now being talked about across the political spectrum. "Not long ago," wrote James G. Smith of Princeton, ". . . economic planning connotated socialism or communism." More recently, "wily capitalists," the "liberal Democratic Party," and finally "staunch Republicans" are extolling its virtues.

> What is the meaning of this change? . . . Now we have everybody, or nearly everybody, vigorously favoring it. . . . What has . . . happened . . . is that it has been taken up as a fad; and . . . no one really knows what exactly he is favoring, or what really is meant by economic planning. . . . We are all 100% in favor of economic planning when we do the planning.[5]

The vagueness of the idea may have unsettled a Princeton economist, but it conferred on planning a great political advantage. The notion of a cooperative, rational, collective management of economic affairs to end the depression touched strands in the pre-war reform experience, and also recalled the unity and productivity of wartime. The lack of precision as to the exact forms and interactions of planning allowed these vague associations to be made, even though the analogy between planning of any type in 1933 and the progressive or wartime experiences was bound to be misleading. Interest groups normally hostile to any suggestion of government direction of the national economy were close to desperation by the end of 1932, and allowed themselves to remember what they had gained during the short war experience. With the forms of planning unspecified in the general chatter, with writers and publicists differing on or obscuring the details, planning attracted people of all ideological tendencies.

So long as planning was only talk, there would continue to be this broad, amorphous, and fragile agreement that it had many merits in the fourth year of depression. Hoover's government by summer of 1932 had drifted into a baffled passivity, and all around the administration there rose up a great clamor for action. In this clamor the idea of planning was a major note, and the idea of government intervention to establish more social control of economic life was by far the dominating element. When planning was proposed, it produced no fierce and organized opposition. Coming together in Washington to plan for recovery had a reasonable sound to it.

To these advantages in the desperate search for remedies in 1932, planning soon added another—the advocacy of the governor of New York and Democratic candidate for President, Franklin Delano Roosevelt.

6

Roosevelt was not a likely sympathizer with any idea that had a radical sound. Descended from an old, wealthy Hudson River family, educated at the best private schools in the East, he had been a mild progressive in the New York State legislature and a capable governor since 1928. The Eastern banker-industrialist faction of his party and the Southern wing were not alarmed at his nomination for President in the summer of 1932. Roosevelt was a loyal party man, and if anything seemed less bold than the situation required. Walter Lippmann pronounced him a pleasant man with no important qualifications for the Presidency, and a Harvard classmate, Brand Whitlock, judged Roosevelt "a nice fellow and a gentleman, . . . but I doubt seriously whether he has got the requisite grit and backbone for what is going to be a gruelling task."[6]

But 1932 was a year in which Franklin Roosevelt began to talk about planning, publicly and well before he was nominated. In an article in *Survey* in early February 1932, the New York governor claimed a long interest in city planning, called planning "the way of the future," and hopefully guessed that "perhaps the day is not far distant when planning will become a part of the national policy of this country."[7] The article offered little illumination of what planning was, as Roosevelt's examples were few and somewhat confused, having to do with the need to plan so that milk would not be shipped from one region to another when it could just as well be procured nearer the market, or to plan to get people out of the cities to the healthful outdoors. But his hospitality to the idea was evident, and however innocuous his conception of it in early 1932, it was still a novel concept for American national politics.

That spring Roosevelt sensed the need for a staff of policy advisers, and through his law partner Samuel Rosenman he recruited three Columbia University professors who volunteered to write his speeches, prepare position papers, and clarify his thoughts. They were the core of a group which was later augmented by a pair of Senators and a journalist or two, and called the "Brains Trust." The academics were Raymond Moley, Adolf A. Berle, and Rexford G. Tugwell. They had not formerly known each other, and were picked at random—but each of them was talking of the need for planning in the spring of 1932.

They became Roosevelt's tutors, encouraging his inclination toward comprehensive social management. It is now clear that

Roosevelt was never under the intellectual domination of any of the Brains Trust or anyone else. It is also clear that the Brains Trust did not agree on what planning meant. There is no need to go deeply into these distinctions. Roosevelt, with the Columbia group now supplying much of his speech material, began to talk more like a planner. In a Jefferson Day speech he gave on April 18, he expressed admiration for a Jefferson somewhat unfamiliar to the Virginian's admirers, a man who stressed the universality of the national interest and who concentrated men's thoughts upon "the shared common life" rather than the predicament of individuals. In that address Roosevelt spoke for "a true concert of interests" rather than class rule. "In this sense I favor economic planning, not for this period alone but for our needs for a long time to come."[8] And at Oglethorpe University, in Georgia, he spoke approvingly of the need for social experimentation, and used the words "collectivism" and "planning."

Random utterances, these occasional forays into collectivist terrain, invariably vague about details and hedged by qualifications. And after Roosevelt was nominated his campaign had no clear central theme, certainly not planning. At the Commonwealth Club in San Francisco he delivered an imposing speech advocating greatly expanded public control of private property and private economic development, and he spoke of planning in agriculture at Topeka. But most of his speeches not only said nothing about planning, but were remarkably platitudinous and conservative for a country in which unemployment was climbing above 20% and the GNP dipping toward $60 billion. Roosevelt spoke of federal relief, expanded public works, and the virtues of public electric power, but these were liberal ideas of considerable popularity. He also talked a lot about the need to balance the budget and return the government to safe hands.

But Hoover's sensitive ear had detected the planning instinct, the social engineer, in his evasive rival. He was alerted in part by certain alien tones in Roosevelt's rhetoric, and presumably also by recalling that Roosevelt had always admired his Uncle Theodore's vigorous approach to the Presidency. Hoover warned that the Democratic candidate was a planner and a radical, inclined toward experiments in active government that people would find shocking. But he either did not convince many people, or they were ready in November of 1932 for almost anything new.

Hoover greatly exaggerated the radicalism of Roosevelt and the men around him, including the much-feared Tugwell, who as a young man had pledged to "make America over." But he was not entirely mistaken about the new President. FDR was a flexible politician with few fixed opinions, but he did have certain intellectual predispositions which abutted through his caution, his pragmatism, his instinct to compromise now for a gain later. Beyond being a Christian and a Democrat, to which he gladly confessed, Roosevelt was something of a nut about conservation, was strongly biased toward rural life, was inclined to come down on the side of the underdog with some indignation when he noticed particularly flagrant forms of exploitation. But more important for our purposes, he was, I believe, an instinctive collectivist. This was his friend Rex Tugwell's word, and Roosevelt himself never used it. But by 1932 it seems clear that his absorption of the conservation outlook had matured, under the pressure of economic disaster and the reinforcement of the Columbia professors, into an organic view of society which assumed the need for continuous public intervention to compensate for imbalances that were not inherently self-correcting.

One can best appreciate this persistent element in Roosevelt's thought by simply reading through his public papers for the 1930s, or his press conferences. Two brief examples may suggest the underpinnings of his managerial instincts. "There was a time," he told the Young Democratic clubs in 1934, "when the formula for success was the simple admonition to have a stout heart and willing hands. . . . But . . . today we can no longer escape into virgin territory; we must master our environment."[9] By 1935 everyone knew that FDR meant the social environment. When sending the Tennessee Valley Authority proposal to Congress in 1933, he said:

Many hard lessons have taught us the human waste that results from lack of planning. Here and there a few wise cities and counties have looked ahead and planned. But our nation has "just grown." It is time to extend planning to a wider field.[10]

The argument here is not that Roosevelt had a secret but conscious self-identification as a "planner," or that his collectivism was guided by some preconceived vision of what America would look like when he and his friends were finished. Rather that he assumed deep inside that private development produced periodic imbalances, both between human groups and between man and nature—social injustices, economic irrationalities, environmental damage. And he further believed it was the permanent duty of modern government to exert its managerial hand in widespread places to regulate, compensate, and control, protecting the public interest and ensuring stability along with progress. Because this was so fundamental to his outlook, the idea of national planning would take root in corners of his administration, would flourish in public debate (to the infinite fright of conservatives), and in the first few months would come close to being the new administration's central strategy.

7

There was an interval between FDR's election and inauguration, four long months between November 1932 and March 1933. The weather was bitter cold, and the depression had relentlessly worsened. A banking crisis began to gather destructive force in late February, and on inauguration weekend every bank in the nation was shut. The depression had resisted Hoover's every policy, had not responded to his patience. Confidence in the natural recuperative powers of the economy had vanished. Something new must be tried, or even the vast reservoirs of loyalty and acquiescence of the American people would run dry. Even revolution could not be discounted, some observers warned.

Roosevelt was not at first prepared with a coherent recovery strategy. He had not, that is, planned what he would do. His inaugural address was heartening in the firmness of his jaw, the ringing timbre of his voice. But it was mostly mush, such as the phrase about nothing to fear but fear itself, and the economic analysis was inane. The rulers of exchange had fled the temple, he said, because of incompetence and stubbornness. We needed "action, and action now," to "move as a trained and loyal army willing to sacrifice for the good of a common discipline."[11]

Out of what intellectual and political materials might he forge a new strategy? Hoover's Presidency, one would have thought, had discredited forever the idea that a balanced budget (or, talk of a balanced budget; Hoover never balanced it) and the bolstering of business confidence by presidential boosterism were adequate remedies. There were conservatives in Roosevelt's party—there was a bit of Hoover in FDR anyway—and he would try a bit of that bottle of medicine from time to time. But appealing to businessmen to invest and cutting the federal budget would be minor strains, overwhelmed and unacknowledged. The idea of fiscal stimulation through a deliberate deficit, the general strategy associated with John Maynard Keynes, had no substantial following among economists, financial wisemen, politicians, or Treasury bureaucrats, although it had been suggested by William T. Foster and others. Roosevelt would never really adopt that strategy, either, although inevitable deficits made it look as if he employed deficit spending as a tool. This was not, in 1933, an acceptable strategy; it was obnoxious to Roosevelt personally and incomprehensible to the congressmen he had to deal with.

Monetary inflation had a strong hold on the Democratic party, parts of it, and among agrarians generally. It has some political support, and Roosevelt accepted and engineered some inflation. But this, too, did not strike serious men—in particular the Eastern wings of both major parties—as an acceptable general approach to recovery. Let us have as much of it as will keep the crazies off our backs, going off gold, buying up silver from time to time, keeping interest rates low (which was easy enough), all of which the government did in the 1930s. But the Treasury and Federal Reserve were never sent out by Roosevelt on a militant mission of monetary expansion and inflation.

Could Wilson's New Freedom serve as the administration's intellectual model? Its main economic thrust was toward anti-monopoly and free trade, and it was hard to argue that this sort of thing would bring revived economic activity, except perhaps in the distant future when we were all dead, as Mr. Keynes said. Roosevelt respected his party's debts to these ideas, and borrowed cautiously from that heritage. The early regulation of banks and stock exchanges was a New Freedom sort of tactic, as was the modest reciprocal trade program, as was the attack on large public utility holding companies in 1935 and the angry investigation of monopolies launched in 1938. But these were isolated strokes, reforms with slow and minor economic impact.

No, when it came to adopting a general strategy, fuzzy and shifting as this would always be, the most compelling idea in 1933 was the one recent experience in comparable crisis had appeared to confirm—national planning, as in wartime. In the 1917–18 crisis, when it was clear that the marketplace would not serve the needs of mobilization, the nation turned to planning through various forms of government-industry-labor cooperation. The men of 1933 found the wartime analogy irresistible, despite its inherent implausibility to those of us who now stand above the desperation of 1933. Talk of planning would remind at least some harassed public officials, many failing businessmen, and hungry millions in the labor force of the all-out production efforts of 1917–18. It was an idea whose time—again—had come. This was not Roosevelt's decision, handed down from the Oval Office after he had thought about the country's plight. Support for planning welled up from the bureaucracy, the Congress, and the amorphous swarm of idea-men and volunteers who had checked into Washington hotels in March hoping to be of service. As various administration task forces and ad hoc groups worked on the problems of industrial and agricultural policy especially, or on public works, and as Congress, impatient, began haphazardly to press schemes of its own into legislative form, the idea of planning began to gain strength. By mid-June, at the end of the so-called Hundred Days of early New Deal legislation, much had been done, and there was no neat pattern to it. Budget cutting in March, a big relief expenditure in April, and public works in June, regulation of banking and securities, sending thousands of young city men out to the forests to plant trees, legalization of beer. What did it mean, beyond intense and multifaceted activity? Those who looked to the crucial areas, to industrial and agricultural policy and also to the regional authority set up in the Tennessee Valley, could see embodied in various ways the planning approach.

Yet if planning was an irresistible idea in the crisis of March 1933, *exactly* how did one do it? Like Heaven, everybody talking about planning isn't going there. To the business spokesmen for planning in 1932–33, men such as Swope and Harriman, production facilities swamped demand, and the remedy was *planned* production, at agreed-upon prices. This could not be done either legally or practically in 1932–33, given the anti-trust laws and the tenacity of competitive urges which trade associations and monopolistic arrangements could not control. And so the solution must be to involve the national government in the planning. The government would legalize cartelization, industry by industry, and establish a national planning board of some kind, composed entirely or predominantly of business representatives, to coordinate the plans of each industrial sector. As a further friendly act, the government in Washington might provide business executives with statistical services, projecting accurate forecasts of demand and potential supply and transportation problems. This was the most conservative form the planning idea took, and it had an inherently defensive aspect, allowing industry (large industry) to ride out the economic storm with such labor as it might employ. It envisioned no structural interventions to shift power or advantages in the economy, and thus had no reform thrust at all, unless it was to handicap the small businessmen fatally.

This general conception of planning came in many variations, and those who urged it upon the new Roosevelt administration were frequently willing to compromise here and there when faced with other versions of what planning should be. There was in Washington that spring a liberal conception of planning which was strikingly different. Business planners began with industrial sectors in trouble, and intended by planning a legalized control of production levels and pricing. They were not vitally interested in larger goals or contexts. They usually accepted some national planning board, but had little to say about its mission. The liberal planning impulse began with national goals that went quite beyond adequate profits, and included full employment, rising mass consumption, even public educational standards, health, nutrition. In this view the purpose was not simply the rescue of faltering industrial or economic sectors, but a broad national advance. Planning should not stop with mandatory quotas and price fixing, but involve fiscal and monetary policies, agriculture, transportation and energy policies, investment controls, resource conservation, all major ways that modern government might touch social development. Liberal planners insisted upon a national framework and were much concerned with rational coordination so that the public interest was not compromised in unwatched, unmonitored segments of public policy. Business planners actually preferred planning for single industries (only those in deep economic difficulties), and accepted national coordinating machinery without much enthusiasm.

Reflecting these differing perspectives, which basically arose out of the difference between single-interest and multiple-interest approaches, there was a contrast in the conception of the role of coercion. Business planners stressed cooperation, by which they meant to ensure a dominant role for themselves and a veto on undesirable decisions. After all, they owned the facilities about to be planned. Liberal planners tended to think in these depression days of businesses not as private property but as public utilities, and, while they also stressed cooperation, they meant cooperation between business and labor, agriculture, and consumer, with government both as mediator and special friend of the non-business groups. They assumed that some coercion would probably be necessary, and that governmental authority would be decisive should some group prove to be unhappy with what it was asked to do. Among the liberal Planners, Rexford Tugwell was the most hard-nosed about the prospects for painless mutual adjustment under planning. "Those who talk about this sort of change [planning] are not contemplating sacrifice," he wrote in 1932. "They are expecting gains. But it would certainly be one of the characteristics of any planned economy that the few who fare so well as things are now would be required to give up nearly all the exclusive perquisites they have come to consider theirs of right, and that these should be in some sense socialized."[12] Here was a clear glimpse of the seam along which the administration's planning garment would tear, an intellectual pivot of the whole planning process: some would be required to give up. That was the core of the liberal planning idea, and anathema to the conservative planners. Mere discussion would not bring out its disruptive potential.

In this brief summary of the main outlines of business and liberal planning approaches, one may be disturbed by a certain abstract quality. Hard questions remain unasked, unanswered. The people of 1932–33 were talking about planning in the most ambiguous, shifting, ill-defined terms. John Kenneth Galbraith was right when he wrote that "the early days of the New Deal were distinguished in American history for their foggy semanticism—for meaningless and incomprehensible talk about social planning, guided capitalism, or industrial self-government."[13] The desperation of the moment made many people optimistic about this path to salvation; their critical faculties were muffled in hope, the hard details did not emerge. People rallied to the term "planning," while precise meanings and necessary distinctions passed each other in the night. How could business planners have imagined that they could secure the legal power of government to fix prices and control competition without paying intolerable costs of bureaucratic delay at the least and the intrusion of labor and consumer pressures at the most? How could they dismiss so easily the fears of people like

Hoover that industry-wide planning would stifle the spirit of innovation, both technological and organizational? But business planners tended to aim at planning of limited scope, covering industries they knew well. They instinctively avoided broader social concerns. The liberals whose hopes rode with planning were even less prepared in 1932–33 for the hard realities ahead. How could business be forced to pay for new purchasing power out of its profits and savings, when businessmen owned the facilities, alone mastered the details of production and marketing, and were the best organized interest group in the field? How could the puny government of 1933 mass the expertise to manage a complicated national economy? How could multiple-interest group participation be secured when many interests were not organized? How could the consuming public's interests be forcefully represented? How could bureaucracy be made responsive? How to blend centralization with decentralization? Given the current political system, from county government through Congress, weak parties, low voter turnout and an uninformed electorate, how could liberals be so sure that "the government" would always represent the national interest?

These and other questions could not then be answered. Doubt was the enemy in the spring of 1933, not lack of knowledge. With the arrival of Roosevelt to the Presidency, it was time for bold experimentation, for meeting and solving problems rather than holding back for more analysis.

Only experience with planning in actual practice would sharpen the perception of what was involved, bring an understanding of how many paths there were to planning. That spring, pressed by rising demands for action, Roosevelt and those eager to help him frame comprehensive recovery measures were able to convince themselves that all the advocates of planning could be locked into a room and bring forth planning. This in fact was done. Astonishing misunderstandings and conflicts were the subsequent result. By June 1933, talk had become law, and the New Deal was committed to certain hasty structures of planning. And then the fur would fly.

8

There were fifteen major pieces of legislation thrown together in just over three months in the spring of 1933, and within this program called the New Deal three measures were clearly efforts at planning. They were the regional authority in the Tennessee Valley, TVA, which was something of a special case; a new program for planning of agricultural production, the Agricultural Adjustment Administration, or AAA; and the most important (at the time) experiment, a National Recovery Administration to plan for industrial recovery. It was the NRA which carried the government's chief hopes for economic improvement.

NRA lasted only two years, was ruled unconstitutional and vanished with hardly an institutional trace. But in 1933–34 it was the centerpiece of New Deal policy, the government's chief hope for economic recovery. Basically, the agency attempted to bring a selected number of industries (in the end, more than 500) into a legalized system of planned production. Former competitors would meet with government officials to devise industry codes, specifying production quotas for each competitor, wage scales, unfair practices, even prices. At the least, it was hoped, such cooperation would eliminate overproduction and the resultant downward pressure on prices and wage levels. And some people also argued that the agency would help bring expansion. More conservative sponsors hoped that the end of "destructive competition" would bring optimism, and a renewal of private investment. Liberals reasoned that, if the codes could be so drafted that prices were kept down but wages deliberately increased, industry would, in effect, be forced to come up with the money to revive American purchasing power. Industrialists would not like this at first, but at the higher volume of sales their profits would in due course return. A $3.3 million public works appropriation was passed to assist in the expected upturn of business by stimulating capital goods sales.

To summarize an unbearably complex story (and the complexity of both the American economy and of the effort required to plan it astonished those who had been eager advocates of the attempt), planning for industry did not work out very well. The economy did begin the long climb back to 1929 levels in 1933, so that the 1934 GNP was up to $65 billion and in 1935 reached $72 billion, with unemployment falling from 15 to 10 million in those two years. But this was painfully slow and inadequate improvement, and the most sympathetic analysts of the economic history of the era argue only that NRA probably did not actually impede recovery and may have made some unprovable and slight contribution to turning the economic corner in the summer of 1933. Whatever its small contribution to the small recovery, NRA made few friends among any affected economic group. Large business in general appreciated the chance to end "cut-throat competition" by fixing prices or production targets, but hated dealing with a federal bureaucracy which was not only sometimes slow and obtuse but occasionally suggested unwelcome gains for labor and consumer. Small businessmen found themselves outmaneuvered for shares of the market within the NRA code-making process. Labor expected higher wages, but found prices rising faster. When the Court killed NRA, nearly everyone was pleased.

In retrospect, which is the best place from which to deal with life, it can be seen that the design of NRA was both muddled and faulty. How could it have been expected to bring recovery? It gave a breathing spell from deflation by controlling prices, but where was the engine of expansion? Under NRA there were two possibilities, neither of which was given a fair trial. Some people hoped that the codes would force high wages on employers while holding back prices, thus compelling them to finance an addition to purchasing power. This interesting and improbable idea was aborted when employers achieved predominant power in the code-making process and avoided being caught in such a cost-price squeeze. Another hope was that a $3.3 billion public works appropriation attached as Title II to the original NRA act would somehow (the theory was not well understood) stimulate capital goods spending. But the money was spent slowly, grudgingly, less than $1 billion of it by the end of the first year, so that no significant economic impact resulted.

Thus NRA, without a strong expansionary principle, produced no stunning results. It is rash to attempt to draw useful conclusions about planning from this hectic episode, but let us indulge the urge. There will be unanimous agreement that the American economy was sufficiently complex by 1933 that the effort to manage it consciously, to interfere with prices, wages, and output, ought to have been confined to a few basic industries. There was neither the time, the expertise, nor even the need to attempt to control over 500 industries, including broom handles and wigs. Scholars have argued that the NRA staff—which was showing improved economic skill toward the end—might eventually have achieved some important structural reforms in pricing and marketing as it renegotiated codes, but this would have come slowly. Economist Mordekai Ezekiel, writing in 1939, estimated that it would have taken ten years to develop the trained people and data base to make NRA work. The agency ran out of time in May 1935. A second and related point has to do with control of the planning machinery. Business dominated that machinery, partially because the government overextended itself and partially because of a fuzzy liberal belief (not shared by all liberals, but certainly by FDR and the NRA administrator, Hugh Johnson) that to overrule businessmen was not only unpleasant but would strangle recovery at its source.

The important thing for our purposes is that the experience greatly discredited the very idea of national planning. This was at least intellectually unfortunate, as NRA had been a very, very odd form of planning if it was planning at all. Here we must introduce a typographical convenience. Let us capitalize Plan, Planning, etc., when we refer to national economic and social Planning, and use the lower case when we simply refer to the attempt to plan to achieve selected goals in some subsector of society. Thus the government may be involved in planning in the Tennessee Valley, or in the government printing office, or in the design of new weapons, without being a Planned or Planning society at all. Here I wish to draw attention to the qualities of comprehensiveness and coordination which characterize Planning. There will perhaps be perceived some grey area between the terms, as with most terms. But it will be useful if we may agree that General Motors may plan, and Pittsburgh may plan, and the United States government has planned in many areas, but Planning was not attempted until 1917–18, then again in 1933.

If under NRA the government was involved in Planning, it was a sloppy, poorly coordinated effort that properly ought to have discredited only NRA and not the idea of Planning itself. Indeed, some contemporaries argued that NRA was not Planning, as it brought national control only to most industrial sectors, but left important economic areas outside its surveillance. One such was agriculture. The New Deal devised a planning instrumentality in agriculture, also, but since the manipulation of the two sectors was not related at the top there developed glaring inconsistencies and conflicts between them. Without adequate central coordination, the nation, it might be said, was in 1933 planning in industry and also in agriculture, but not yet Planning at all. We may assess this objection in a bit, when we turn to the problem of the coordination of national policy in the 1930s. But perhaps we ought to know the rudiments of planning on the farm.

New Deal planning in agriculture likewise did not test the principle of Planning. The idea behind AAA was to control production, and, thereby, end both waste and low prices. This was a form of planning, right enough, since it required forecasts of demand and a flexible system of government-imposed production quotas on a national basis. As it turned out, the control methods chosen were inadequate, and production was never controlled. Severe droughts from 1930 through 1939 helped restrain production somewhat, and the war solved the problem of surpluses until 1945. At that point surpluses reappeared, and piled up until new export possibilities opened in the 1960s. The New Deal farm program was reasonably popular, since it combined ineffective controls with benefit payments, and raised farm income. The experiment undoubtedly enhanced the attractiveness of collective action among farmers, but the program was full of contradictions and made little sense as a part of a national economic program. Its contribution to recovery was questionable, and it added to the stream of tenants displaced by acreage reduction programs. The AAA was good for some farmers, and had to be tolerated by consumers who could not match the farmers' political power and awareness of the stakes involved. But it was a one-sector program. The national government was conducting something resembling planning on the farm, but this did not forward the aims or nourish the hopes of those who thought national economic Planning the only solution to depression.

As these two planning experiments produced their disappointing results, the administration recognized their limitations and tried various other approaches to recovery. In the autumn of 1933, it turned to monetary experimentation, manipulating the price of gold in the hope of a commodity price rise. This unorthodox action had little or no effect upon production or prices. In 1933 the administration freed monetary policy from foreign constraints by going off the gold standard, and encouraging low interest rates. But recovery did not follow. Banks held large reserves and offered attractively low rates, but investment did not revive. The administration and most contemporary economists concluded that monetary policy was a poor instrument in a depression, reasoning that "you can pull with a string but you can't push with it." Since Planning had proven disappointing and monetary policy seemed to have insufficient power to achieve the government's economic goals, what was left? The search for a recovery strategy had to continue.

In May 1935, the Court terminated the NRA experiment. Roosevelt was now free to adopt a different political and economic strategy. While he remained personally attracted to the general idea of Planning, he did not call for another grand Planning effort to replace NRA. From 1935 to 1938 the administration's economic program took the form of a series of reform measures to correct structural flaws—more progressive taxes, antitrust activity, some aid to unionization, social insurance, a wage and hours law. Politically, the reform thrust was convincingly successful. But like the trees that Roosevelt loved to plant, economic reforms were very slow in producing change. Recovery continued slowly through 1936 and into 1937. At this time, in the mid-1930s, increasing numbers of administration officials and economists began to turn their minds to the unexplored potentialities of fiscal policy—to taxing and spending, in particular to spending. It is now understood that Franklin Roosevelt always disliked deficit spending and never believed that deliberate deficits (or for that matter, deliberate surpluses) were an adequate or proper tool of economic policy. It is also known that none of his close advisers were disciples of Lord Keynes until the war years. Still, the administration, because of the poor results produced by other recovery strategies, came gradually and apologetically to rely upon compensatory fiscal policy. The government ran deficits every year through the 1930s, not out of choice but because tax yields were low and relief spending combined with two veterans' bonuses and other spending programs widened the gap between expenditure and income. And four years of these deficits, 1933–37, corresponded with gradually increasing economic activity.

But the President gave credit for this gradual revival to a combination of New Deal reforms and a natural cyclical upturn, and in early 1937 the administration cut spending sharply, hoping for a balanced budget. Credit was also tightened, in anticipation of an inflationary surge which mounting bank reserves seemed to suggest. An abrupt recession came in the fall of 1937, raising unemployment by nearly 3 million by spring, 1938, or from 14 per cent back to 19 per cent of the labor force.

After six months of indecision, Roosevelt decided to try an injection of federal spending. It would be financed by a deficit, *faute de mieux;* no new taxes were sought to cover the spending. The economy again turned upward. No one has yet proved that the upturn of mid-1938 was caused by the spending, or the earlier downturn by the effort at a balanced budget. But to many observers, and especially to economists oriented toward government service, this was the clear meaning of events. The

economy could be "managed," the growth of the economy in-
sured, by fiscal policy—in particular, by one aspect of fiscal
policy, federal spending.

The gradual discovery of the potency of fiscal policy combined
with the failure of NRA to push the idea of Planning back into
the crankish corners of discussion from where it had emerged in
1932. Fiscal policy, after all, held certain obvious advantages
over Planning. As a short-term recovery device, fiscal policy was
easier than Planning. In the long run, of course, economic and
social problems would surely force difficult decisions as to whom
to tax and where to spend, but in the short run the government
could simply borrow the money required for a stimulus, and it
made only friends when the spending decisions were announced.
Planning involved the strenuous and continuous effort to
modify and rearrange the economic structure, a thankless enterprise that recruited political enemies with distressing speed.
And, in the 1930s, a part of the appeal of fiscal policy came
from its invulnerability to constitutional challenge. The Supreme Court had ultimately killed the controls attempted under
NRA, and until the "constitutional revolution" of 1937 it did
not seem that controls on wages and hours by the federal government would be legal, either. And even after the Court permitted
government regulation of collective bargaining and wages and
hours, lawyers knew that schemes for Planning still ran risks
of constitutional frustration as the government entered into or
infringed contracts, regulated working conditions, condemned
land, restricted the use of resources, and the like. But there were
few constitutional problems with taxing and spending, and this
gave an added appeal to fiscal policy as the central managerial
strategy. So Roosevelt, after a few words to friends about giving
Planning another try, turned to deficit spending in the spring of
1938. Six months later, having finally secured the regulation of
wages and hours and a constitutionally viable AAA, the administration was fought to a standstill by conservatives, and the New
Deal was essentially over.

Was American society Planned at the end of the New Deal?
No one but an occasional reactionary claimed that it was. Con-

temporaries and later scholars would say that Planning had been tried from 1933 to 1935, had proven something of a fiasco, had been quietly abandoned in word and deed, and other approaches to social and economic management had been pragmatically devised. We shall turn, in a bit, to the nature of the political economy that emerged out of all this. But the planning idea had not been confined to NRA, or agriculture. It left other marks, other short trails hacked into the thicket of American social organization in the 1930s.

9

It seems there is always some truth in the losing argument, even anti-vivisection, anti-woman suffrage, or prohibition. The losing argument in 1933 was the so-called conservative or more properly anti-statist view that the government should not assume additional responsibilities in society merely because the depression was four years old and one worker in four was unemployed. I do not intend to search that opinion for its wisdom, but one must concede the patent validity of one of its insights. The government, fearful anti-statists warned, would not confine itself to merely reflating the economy to the levels of 1929. If it were given the mandate and powers to attempt economic management, it would soon be discovered that "the economy" was actually "the society." Economic activity could not be divorced from other things, and in time the government would have to interest itself in education, science, natural resources on private domain, health, perhaps religion, certainly public opinion, maybe even race relations. The important truth here was obscured by hysteria and overstatement, but the main prophecy was accurate enough. Economic responsibilities led logically to broader social responsibilities.

There was more than logic behind this anxious prophecy. The economy, if by that one narrowly meant the GNP and the availability of jobs, was not the only area where social dislocation was painfully felt in the 1930s. Floods, dust storms, erosion, Mexican immigration, organized crime, growth of farm tenancy, marijuana use, these and other problems were in the news along with unemployment. The nation's sufferings were multiple, and no government with any disposition to act vigorously would be likely to confine itself merely to economic repairs, narrowly defined. The Roosevelt administration was particularly susceptible to a broad construction of its social assignment, because of the strength of two themes in the thought of its activists, from the President on down. One theme was the conservation of natural resources, a special commitment of FDR himself. The other was the idea, which if not prevailing was at least prevalent, that the economy had serious structural flaws which had brought on the depression. In this analysis, the distribution of wealth and income, and the patterns of market power, had become so badly distorted and out of balance as to wreck the economic system. This sense of structural flaws ran deep in New Deal liberalism, along with the mission of restoring balanced relationships through institutional reform and permanent government supervision.

Given these lines of thought, the New Deal would never be entirely satisfied with the goal of simple economic recovery, even if some injection of spending or cheap money might have achieved it. For structural flaws would remain, exploitative and irrational relationships would endure to produce their periodic harvest of injustice and economic instability. The reform mind in the 1930s was quite suffused with this structuralist orientation, and the Planning impulse of course found it entirely congenial. Accordingly, liberal planners sought what a 1934 National Resources Board report called "the strategic points" in a society where social managers must concentrate their efforts.

One of these was the use of land, an area traditionally little governed in America. The sources of our special individualism in this matter are complex, and include the abundance of free land, the evolving Judaeo-Christian attitude toward nature, historic individualism, and other social influences of similar weightiness. The U.S. government took land from the Indians, but it was not supposed to have any interest in the land of free white men. Our national land policy until well into the twentieth century was to give away or sell public lands, and then forget them. Mistreatment of the land was nobody's business until the twentieth century, and then only very haltingly. The conservation movement under Theodore Roosevelt aroused some concern about the loss of scenic beauty and wildlife through private development, and there was also some lesser concern about erosion and floods. Beyond publicity for conservation, and the expansion of public lands through purchase, the pre-World War I conservation movement made little headway. In the 1920s, especially in 1927, floods helped to stir public concern, to raise again the problems which rippled out from the exploitative habits of American agriculture.

Land use decisions in urban America were producing their own social costs in congestion and ugliness, and the zoning movement of the 1920s was bringing a degree of social control that would be widely overestimated. No one proposed a federal role in this area. But in 1931 Hoover's secretary of agriculture Arthur Hyde called the National Conference on Land Utilization in Chicago, and out of this came some general expressions of concern and the National Land Use Planning Committee made up of representatives of federal agencies with interests in land. Roosevelt arrived before this little initiative had produced anything tangible. At once the government became more active, for Roosevelt was a strong conservationist, listed himself in *Who's Who* as a "tree farmer," and was a man whose interest in public issues increased the closer they came to pastoral America.

The first thought was public purchase of either submarginal land that was suffering from exploitative agriculture and was bringing suffering to stubborn rural people, or private timber land which had no protection from disease, clearcutting, and fire. There were major problems with both kinds of private land, as the administration was soon told. The National Resources Board completed a quick study and recommended the purchase of 75 million acres of submarginal land, a figure no one has ever disputed, at least on the low side, as an estimate of land which contemporary agriculture could not operate with profit and

without damage. The New Deal responded in its usual way—
with energy, spreading the program over so many agencies that
it had no central guidelines, and eventually doing less than the
experts suggested. Under Roosevelt the government bought 11.3
million acres at a cost of $47.5 million, and parceled it out for
what he hoped would be (and was) more appropriate uses and
better management to the Bureau of Indian Affairs, the Forest
Service, National Park Service, or the Bureau of Land Management. More than a million acres were transferred to states.

Public purchase was an emergency remedy not only for abused
agricultural land but also for forests. TR's conservation efforts
and those continued in the 1920s had not reversed the drain on
the nation's timber supplies, which was estimated in 1929 as
16.5 billion cubic feet annually. Most of this came from lumbering without reforestation, much came from fire and disease.
Private woodlot owners would not or could not manage their
assets any other way, and by the early 1930s the profession of
foresters and conservationists were thoroughly alarmed, and
ready for radical action. Robert Marshall, in *The People's
Forests* (1933), thought 240 million acres of timberland must be
bought away from the dangers of private use, and he hoped to
get 160 million more through tax delinquency. He spoke for
those who would effectively nationalize the forests. The Roosevelt government did not seem too far behind. A 1932 Senate
resolution established a Forest Service study of the timber problem, and when Secretary Henry A. Wallace submitted the 1,650-
page document in 1933, with Roosevelt's approval, it was boldly
entitled *A National Plan for American Forestry (1933)*. It called
for federal purchase of 134 million acres, state purchase of 90
million (at that time the national government held 88 million,
the states 11 million), and then took the last risky step, proposing federal regulation of cutting on private land. The report
minced no words: "A satisfactory solution of the forest problem
will require the nearest possible approach to national planning."[14] At about the same time the TVA's first chief forester
was urging that it buy more than half the timber acreage of the
valley region, or 7 million acres.

Wallace did not press the issue of regulation, and the New Deal went ahead with its modest purchases which, as we have seen, eventually came to a bit over 11 million additional acres added to public ownership. And by all accounts the care of land under the Forest Service and the National Parks was exemplary. This was not true of the BLM, which managed the 147 million acres in the West that was public range land outside the National Parks and Indian reserves. This was one-half the public land in the West, and, in Wesley Calef's words, "there was practically no administration of it. It was a great commons," leased at negligible cost to ranchers who overgrazed it without restraint.[15] The New Deal produced the Taylor Act of 1934 to tighten supervision of this public domain, bringing a degree of improvement that still disappointed observers. Yet even with low marks for the BLM on public grazing land, the federal government's land management, whether of forests, marshes, or scrub, was vastly better than all but the most enlightened private owners.

But buying 11 million acres of land and turning it to more enlightened management, either non-use or limited use, was not a national land policy adequate to the problem of erosion, flood, and the waste of timber reserves. If most land was to remain private, must not the government reach it with national policy to ensure minimal social goals? There were some stirrings of this option—false starts as it turned out, but interesting ones. The New Deal, reflecting Roosevelt's priorities and perhaps also the malapportionment of American legislatures, was always less interested in cities than in the more healthy Jeffersonian regions outside. Urban areas had much to complain of in private land-use patterns, and the zoning movement had not brought remedy, but there was little that the federal government was asked to do or that it volunteered to do. The public housing program which was commenced on a small scale in 1933 and institutionalized in 1937 might have evolved toward federal ownership, but officials in Washington feared a successful court challenge to their right to acquire land through condemnation and shifted the housing program to local government. Even with federal operation of the housing program there was no disposition to use it for any national goal other than low-cost housing. The Washington government was not pressing for a way to influence urban racial or spatial patterns through purchase of land.

The activist spirit ran higher where rural areas were concerned. The TVA's first chairman, Arthur E. Morgan, wanted the states in the valley to pass laws allowing condemnation and public purchase of farm lands where erosion was found. The Forest Service *National Plan for American Forestry* of 1933, as we saw, urged (but did not spell out) some degree of public control of lumbering. Chief Forester Ferdinand Silcox pushed quietly for this through the 1930s, insisting that private owners had social obligations. Roosevelt had always agreed, and in 1938 he sent Congress a message which confessed that public purchase had not effectively addressed the problems found on private timber land:

> The fact remains that, with some outstanding exceptions, most of the States, communities, and private companies have, on the whole, accomplished little to retard or check the continuing process of using up our forest resources.[16]

He asked Congress to consider again extending federal control to private forest land, and indeed a joint committee was established and reported in 1941. It endorsed stronger efforts to encourage better private fire control and reforestation, but held back from suggesting controls on lumbering. A middle way beckoned, using federal grants to get the states to exert control. A bill was introduced to ban timber products in interstate commerce not covered by a state forestry plan, but it was another early casualty of the war.

So the New Deal edged dangerously close to some kind of national plan for forest land in private ownership, and held back. A similar pattern unfolded with respect to private farm land. The glaring failures of American husbandry under free market conditions were surely the most irrefutable single argument for intervention and social planning in all the arena of social issues of the 1930s. For half a century there had been floods of increasing size and cost as American row farming damaged watersheds, and the great floods of 1927 generated a clamor for national action. Then came the dry cycle of the 1930s, dwindling rainfall in the Great Plains, and a series of dust storms that blew the land-use problem eastward in dark visitations of traumatic intensity between 1932 and 1936. When the storms and floods let up, a flow of poverty-stricken and undernourished humanity out of rural America reminded the country that when the land was mistreated and poor, so were the people. The reformers' hour had come.

But how to encourage, or even require, rational land use? If the question searched for the location of legal power over land use, the answer came clearly out of the history of American federalism: the county. The states had never been heavily involved in land-use regulation, and few lawyers would have suggested that the federal government had a sound constitutional right to enter the field even if it wished to do so. Yet only Washington was ready for action to change national land use habits. Certainly there was no evidence that the counties were. Federal agencies offering subsidies and education could act quickly, and this might be sufficient to the emergency.

The older agencies, however, were not promising. The Department of Agriculture had the most to do with private land, but its programs aimed at profit maximization. New agencies and programs seemed required. Roosevelt rose eagerly to the challenge, sending youths of the Civilian Conservation Corps into the countryside to dike and plant, building dams on the wild Tennessee River and its tributaries, planting the incredible Shelterbelt of trees across parts of the Great Plains. But the central effort to alter American uses of the land came when Roosevelt turned to Hugh Hammond Bennett, "Big Hugh," the apostle of soil conservation whose 1928 book, *Soil Erosion: A National Menace* had told the awful news of the 3 billion tons of soil washed annually out of American fields, of the 730 million tons of topsoil washed yearly down the Mississippi alone. Bennett had been at work since 1933 in a corner of Ickes' Interior Department, and in 1935 Roosevelt set him up as director of a new unit of the Department of Agriculture, the Soil Conservation Service.

Bennett and his secretary, Henry A. Wallace, harbored what must be called radical thoughts. Big Hugh apparently leaned toward a confrontation with the American tradition that individual property owners had an unrestricted right to use their land as they wished. He had praised a 1928 Italian law which, as he understood it, coerced land owners to care for their land and bear the costs of repair. But given an agency of his own, Bennett curbed these ideas, and designed a program in the voluntaristic American spirit, relying upon persuasion, on demonstration, on small subsidies to encourage crop rotation, curvature plowing, soil-holding crops, and other practices quite alien to the profit-taking American farmer. SCS used the carrot, not the stick, with the rural Americans who were responsible for the muddy waters that Bennett spent a lifetime calling to the nation's attention.

Voluntarism instead of regulation was perhaps an inevitable decision, and in any event it did not end the SCS's revolutionary potential. Secretary Wallace imagined the SCS as operating through new units of government, superior to counties. These would be Soil Conservation Districts, covering drainage basins, and set up under state laws to obtain maximum land use authority. There would be 76 of these in the nation. And why not use them to coordinate all of Agriculture's soil-related activities, the crop control and subsidy programs of the AAA, soil erosion, and the educational activities of the Extension Service? The department's activities, at least, would then be planned and concerted.

This was audacious, and also out of the question. County agents and extension authorities, joined by AAA officials, did not want to be coordinated. Wallace retreated and took Bennett with him. In the end, SCS established over 2000 small districts, approximately the size of counties, and quietly conducted its demonstration activities in an attempt to arrest the loss of soil and soil fertility. Farmers' (or developers', for that matter) use of land would not be regulated by the federal government. Federal soil-related programs would not be coordinated. Land was probably better treated in America after the 1930s than before, and the government could claim most of the credit for this. But land use decisions were not planned, and remained the province of metropolitan or county officials who hoped for new subdivisions or industry.

The New Dealers' interest in land use was too strong to be contained by this episode. The writer Sherwood Anderson circulated among the younger New Dealers in the Department of Agriculture and TVA, and exclaimed: "What? You dream of a physical America controlled, plowing of the land controlled—this or that section of America to be permanently in forest—river flow control, floods controlled at the flood source?"[17] Indeed many of them did. Perhaps the states could be led to shoulder their responsibilities to plan the uses of land; the government funded the establishment of 46 state planning agencies and urged them to include land use in their activities. Regionalism seemed the best approach to others, and it was hoped that the TVA would be at least as interested in land use as in the production of electric power (it would not be), and that seven additional "little TVAs" could be established where ecological problems could be approached on a multiple-purpose basis, using the drainage basin as the operating unit (they were not).

Agriculture officials were more practical. The county, after all, was the governmental unit where land use decisions were made. In 1938, planners based in the Department of Agriculture pushed the creation of county land use planning committees, which were to offer advisory coordination to both federal and local projects. Perhaps someday they might assume some of county government's squandered land use planning powers. The Extension Service and county agents, who could not kill the program in 1938, gained control of it and supervised the setting up of 1900 county land use planning committees by 1942. The war ended this blunted experiment. The New Deal had been rebuffed as it reached for land use influence, but for a time the agenda of Planning had been broadened to include another strategic area of social development.

10

Social programs to influence private use of land have always been given less attention than the more direct economic activities in the center of controversy. So have the efforts to influence the distribution of population. Without a conscious government policy in the matter, Americans had been distributing themselves in and around urban centers for as long as anyone living could remember, the net movement from rural to urban places in the 1920s running at about 600,000 a year. Franklin Roosevelt had a stubborn bias in this matter, thinking that life was infinitely healthier and more satisfying outside the great cities. With unemployment highest and most conspicuous in the cities, he had an apparent economic reason to include in the New Deal a set of policies influencing people to reverse the urban flow. A subsistence homestead division was set up in the early relief operation, and it grew eventually into the Resettlement Administration, which hoped to build fifty new towns (it built three "greenbelt" towns) and to move 500,000 families to rural communities (it moved just over 4000). The RA was headed by Rex Tugwell, collectivist and planner, whose presence in Washington in any capacity caused high nerves and loss of sleep among conservative folk, and so the agency had many enemies. Its experimental communities had thin support in any event, but the idea of helping people move back to the farm brought men to their feet on Capitol Hill, and the administration was able to follow the RA with the Farm Security Administration in 1937, which commenced a loan program to establish tenants on farms of their own.

The FSA was an odd combination of the anachronistic and the visionary. It wanted to turn the tide which ran against the family farm, hold men on the land working their small parcels, a social goal that arose out of unexamined romanticism and nostalgia. But the agency recruited the most experimental of the New Dealers, and was involved in setting up cooperative, communal farm projects, birth control clinics for migratory workers, and organizing the rural labor force for collective bargaining. These cross-currents should not distract us from the main purpose behind all these resettlement efforts, which was to exert national influence over internal population migration in the United States. At this they were instructive failures. Resettlement programs were a mere gesture, given their size, and whatever flow of people away from cities they produced was many times canceled by the inadvertent effects of other policies, chiefly the acreage reduction program in agriculture that had the side effect of forcing tenants and farm labor from the land. The first national administration to inaugurate deliberate policies to reverse American migratory trends found that it conducted immeasurably more potent programs with in-advertent effects which reinforced the old trends. Net population flow to the cities in the 1930s dropped to about 250,000 annually from the higher level of the 1920s, but demographers credit all of this to "natural" economic and demographic forces and none of it to government policy. Policy did affect where people decided to settle, but judging from the New Deal experience it would be an imposing task to see to it that conscious policies actually overmatched the unconscious ones working in contrary directions.

11

Planned social intervention in land-use and population distribution had turned out to be more formidable assignments than anticipated. But they were not the end of the New Deal's probing of the strategic points which government must invest with intelligent national policy if it was to Plan for a better future. Much time and effort were spent in trying to gather together the diverse strands of transportation regulation into a national transportation policy. The New Deal concentrated mainly on the railroads, and the ultimately futile search for coherent policy there is nicely told in Earl Latham's *The Politics of Railroad Coordination* (1959). What later generations called "Energy Policy" the New Deal called "power policy," and two Cabinet-level committees were appointed by Roosevelt to search for the elusive unification of governmental activities in this area. That story is told in Philip Funigiello, *Toward a National Power Policy* (1973), and in Thomas McCraw, *TVA and the Power Fight, 1933–1939* (1971). Both are records of eventual defeat, and there is no need to describe their intricate details. Both were battlegrounds where the planning impulse was rebuffed.

The Roosevelt administration was much involved with incomes policies, as well, and toward the end of the 1930s showed some signs of putting the government's interventions on a new level. Taxation, in a vague way, aimed at a more equitable distribution of income, and New Deal tax laws made stronger gestures in that direction than were customary. Then in the spring of 1938, with a recession six months old, Roosevelt lectured successive press conferences on the importance of what he called "a balance of prices"—that it, prices of basic products should not be allowed by the government to go up faster than others, in the interests of stable economic growth. The President seemed on the verge of asking for discretionary price controls. And he thought that executive salaries in industry were invested with the national interest. The president of General Motors, he offered, held "a private office with a public trust," and his salary ought to be public information. This was a strong hint that the government ought to be involved in the compensation of certain business executives, just as the 1938 minimum wage law had involved it with the compensation of labor. These administration stirrings were eventually channeled into the 1938–41 Temporary National Economic Committee investigation of the economy, and no incomes policy ever formally emerged in the 1930s. This is hardly surprising, as it is inflation that drives non-socialist modern governments to Incomes Policy, while all that was quickening Roosevelt's interest in the matter was an economic recession (which he blamed on rising costs in the housing industry) and a personal preference for a more equitable distribution of income.

In all this restless searching for the instruments of social control there was one other important area to which the New Dealers were instinctively drawn which especially strikes the contemporary eye. This was credit policy. Federal credit to stimulate private enterprise was an old practice, going back at least to the farm credit program begun in 1916. And outright subsidies went back much further, to railroad and canal and bridge-building aid in the earliest days of the Republic. The New Deal expanded federal loans and mortgage guarantees to farmers, homeowners, and others. This was undertaken in the usual way, as a rescue operation and set of piecemeal responses to the urgent pleas of interest groups. But in the process the New Deal almost devised a permanent Planning instrument in the form of the Reconstruction Finance Corporation. The agency had actually been set up under Hoover in 1932 to make a few cautious loans to threatened banks and railroads and self-destruct in two years. The New Deal brought its aggressive expansion.

The RFC, under Texas businessman Jesse Jones, made loans to banks and industry, bought bank stock, financed public works, spun off subsidiaries to support commodities markets and buy housing mortgages. Such an institution was a potent instrument of selective economic intervention. If its activities could be meshed with the broad social purposes of the government, the ability to plan social development would be greatly enhanced. Brain truster Adolf Berle wanted the agency to restructure the economy by aiding small business. Harold Ickes pressed it to underwrite his large public works program by buying PWA and municipal bonds. TVA and REA officials turned to RFC for help in financing local electric cooperatives. Roosevelt thought that RFC was just the place for an Export-Import

Bank subsidiary in order to help finance trade with Russia. It could be seen as the nation's development bank, under public control, with many potential uses.

Yet the agency embodied a dangerous form of power. Under political pressure from congressmen, RFC could easily fall into a pattern of bailing out enterprises which either could not meet a market test or any reasonable standard of social usefulness. A congressman can always find reasons to urge that Lockheed or Pan Am be kept flying, and RFC administrators were sure to be tempted to grease an occasional wheel. The White House would have its own interests to pursue, some social, some political. A president who controlled the RFC could reward many friends and screw a long list of enemies.

The experience of the RFC from 1932 to 1953, when Eisenhower abolished it, displays this dual potential. Congress, uncertain which social objectives among many it ought to give to the agency, wrote a statute embodying vague instructions to prevent job loss by saving faltering enterprise. This was an important assignment in 1932, but a limited one if all the possibilities of a development bank are considered. Roosevelt picked the right man in Jesse Jones, who had splendid business instincts and shored up many a shaky bank or corporation. He spent $10.5 billion during the depression, and made a net profit; $23.5 billion more was spent in wartime, expanding defense production and buying scarce materials. From the first, Jones and RFC felt the warm and wooing breath of politicians on the Hill and in the White House. Congressmen were forever wanting favorable consideration for some firm back home. Jones made the necessary minimal compromises, but drove hard bargains. The White House gave more trouble. Jones was sympathetic to suggestions that RFC underwrite public works activities, but he was not cooperative when Roosevelt sent word to him to make loans to friendly newspaper publishers such as David Stern of the Philadelphia *Record* or George Fort Milton of the Chattanooga *News*. There were other frictions with the White House, as well.

How could the RFC be given sufficient independence from

political pressures of dubious or dangerous sort when it must also be a functioning and integrated element in a system of national policies? For this is what the Planning idea would require of a development bank. Integration with national policy would come through making the agency administrator a presidential appointee removable without cause, and seating him with the Cabinet. This was the arrangement. But to build in safeguards against the abuse of the agency's considerable power was a problem that was never really solved. In theory, adequate safeguards would lie in clear statutory standards, congressional oversight, and adequate publicity. One could hope for a measure of restraint from presidents, but this would merely be a hope. Satisfactory checks upon political abuse of the agency were not devised in its twenty-year history. The operating solution was Jesse Jones, who knew how to say no to presidents, senators, and New York bankers. When he left RFC in 1945 it had to be administered by men of more average gifts, and there were charges of corruption, leading to Eisenhower's decision that the risks of this form of state capitalism far outweighed the potential advantages. In 1974 and 1975 the press reported that several business figures and politicians were talking again of the need for an RFC. One hopes they will ponder its history.

12

Franklin Roosevelt's desire for coherence in policy has been largely forgotten by a nation that could not keep track of the alphabetical agencies the New Deal planted on every hand. But talk as he would about the need for a national transportation policy, or power policy, or land-use policy, coherent national policy did not appear. And without it one had fragmented intervention, and this fragmentation was assumed to be a reason why recovery was so slow. Policy coordination had to be arranged at the center of the executive branch, and here Roosevelt's frustrations began. In 1933 Roosevelt was assisted in the White House by a cook, butler, switchboard operators and guards, a handful of secretaries, and two southern newspapermen whom he enlisted as aides. He also could call upon a Navy doctor. There was no Executive Office of the President, no economic or technical staff. Across the street the real government began, the ten departments and scattered agencies of the executive branch. The President had no institutional capacity to see social problems and policy responses as a whole.

Franklin Roosevelt was occupied for his thirteen years as President in a series of resourceful efforts to adapt or invent such an institutional capacity. The Cabinet, as presidents had long since learned, was not that institution. It was a collection—when called together—of ten (in Roosevelt's day) individuals with little in common. Presumably they were loyal to the President. But they had been selected in part because of constituencies they commanded, and these constituencies and the departments they headed were really the chief loyalty of Cabinet officers. They could often be, especially at budget time, the President's natural enemies, as Charles Dawes once said. They saw things persistently from a bureaucratic or narrow interest-group perspective when presidents wished broad programmatic advice and a full discovery of options. Several of them, such as the postmaster or attorney general or secretary of war or navy, had little reason to care about domestic policy. And even if this group were worth something in the way of advice during an hour or two around a table, when they left there was no Cabinet staff for follow-up or advance planning, no flow of paper bringing common perspectives.

Roosevelt knew this from the first. But he could hardly use the so-called Brains Trust to get the help he needed. This covert and shifting assemblage of friends had served well enough during the campaign, but no one would have tolerated such an irregular institution among the regular legal and constitutional centers of power in American national government. The President met with the Executive Council of Cabinet Officers for a few months between July and November 1933, and then was inspired to establish the National Emergency Council. It was composed of only the Cabinet officers who really needed to be involved—Interior, Agriculture, Commerce, Labor (no one knows why FDR left out Treasury)—and four lesser agency heads whose work seemed to have national implications. This novel group had an executive director, and soon extruded a staff, including a central statistical board to standardize governmental statistics as well as serve the council. The NEC also put out a field force of state directors and agents to explain federal programs and sample public opinion. But this was an abberant activity. The main idea was policy coordination, which was to be gained by talk at the Tuesday meetings every two weeks, and by the President's requirement that all departments and agencies clear legislative proposals through NEC's director.

This interesting experiment with a supercabinet did not work out, and the episode illuminated many of the recurring problems in federal public administration. The summary of the NEC experience by Lester Seligman and Elmer Cornwell in their *New Deal Mosaic: Roosevelt Confers with His National Emergency Council, 1933–1936* (1965) would have made instructive reading for Richard Nixon as he faced the same problems in 1969. Roosevelt stopped going to meetings, then department heads sent subordinates, important policy issues were gradually replaced by minor ones, departments ignored the legislative clearance requirement, and by 1936 the NEC was moribund. Some of its weaknesses seem remediable. The staff was too small; the director needed maximum authority in order to do effective battle with refractory department heads, but neither Don Richberg nor Frank Walker were seen as Roosevelt's chief of staff (he did not have one), did not even have offices in the White House. But deeper than these alterable circumstances was the hostility of Cabinet members to the idea of coordination. They would avoid the NEC forum, and go to Roosevelt privately to defend some bureaucratic interest. And he lacked the will, the time, the help, the personal commitment to programmatic rationality required to relentlessly force his department and agency heads to see their activities in a wider setting. Nobody drew a definitive lesson from the NEC story, but it might well have been the extreme difficulty of securing policy review through a body with substantial Cabinet representation. Well, the problem will surface stubbornly again as we go on. For FDR, the NEC had not worked out and he let it atrophy. At best it would have afforded him only one of the aids he needed, policy review, and coordination at the top. But he still needed some consideration of long-range social problems, a staff expertise inside the White House, advance planning on public works especially in the conservation field. So even while the NEC was starting out on the assignment it eventually failed to perform, Roosevelt was cautiously nurturing a national Planning board.

It began down in Secretary Ickes' Public Works Administration in 1933, and was boldly called the National Planning Board. Ickes had told the American Civic Association in 1933 that "we hope that long after the necessity for stimulating industry and creating new buying power by a comprehensive system of public works shall be a thing of the past, national planning will go on as a permanent government institution."[18] He made a vital contribution toward that end by setting up a planning board of three men, the President's uncle Frederick Delano, economist Wesley Mitchell, and political scientist Charles Merriam. All were veterans of the city planning movement, thought of themselves as planners. Ickes asked them to give some order to the planning of public works projects, but soon Roosevelt was encouraging them to conceive of broader planning responsibilities. For ten years, 1933–34, this institution was America's first national Planning board, exploring the requirements and pitfalls of Planning. Its name and composition changed three times, from NPB to National Resources Board (1934) to National Resources Committee (1935) to National Resources Planning Board (1939–43), the name it was best known and remembered by. Through its life the NRPB had a continuity of personnel and basic motivation.

Roosevelt's first concern was to get some coordination of all government public works affecting natural resources. Everything was presently done in pieces—flood control, forestry, recreation, wildlife, soil erosion control, reclamation, and so on, all parceled

out to separate agencies. In early 1934 Congress by joint resolution asked the President for a comprehensive plan for the development of the nation's rivers. Roosevelt was eager to comply.
Such a plan "would put the physical development of the country
on a planned basis for the first time," he said, and "would include . . . flood control, soil erosion, the question of submarginal land, reforestation, agriculture and the use of the crops,
decentralization of industry, and, finally, transportation," and
water power, he added as an afterthought.[19]

How to get such a plan? Perhaps planning began with a
document, an actual plan. Roosevelt asked a Cabinet-level committee to produce one. Overworked department heads sent him
a vapid report which he submitted to Congress in June with
apologies, and asked for more time. Perhaps planning was not
just a plan but a planning agency, a process. Roosevelt drafted
an executive order to take the little planning board out of Interior, bring it to the White House and have it draft the plan
that Congress wanted. Ickes immediately led a Cabinet revolt.
Were public works in the natural resource field to be coordinated by some triad of professors? Roosevelt retreated, and set up
the new National Resources Board (avoiding the word planning)
as a group in which six Cabinet officers outnumbered the three
planners. Six months later this board submitted an interesting
document, *A Plan for Planning* (December 1, 1934). Two things
stand out in the report. First, it had proven manifestly impossible to produce a plan on paper for natural resource development—although several chapters of the report listlessly discussed
irrigation or flood control—and the report urged a permanent
national planning board as the answer to the search for comprehensive development planning. It would be a five-member
board, a "clearinghouse" for all public works in the resource
field, and something of "a general staff," but advisory only,
"standing apart from political and administrative power and
responsibility. . . ."[20] The planners must have hoped for more,
the Cabinet heads must have reluctantly conceded this much.
Roosevelt liked the idea of an institutional solution to the need

he felt for planning of various sorts, in the natural resource field as elsewhere, and he sent the report to Congress with his endorsement.

A second point concerns the reception of the report, and helps to explain its history. For the handful who read it, *A Plan for Planning* presented planning in reasonable and attractive terms:

> Planning . . . does not involve the preparation of a comprehensive blueprint of human activity to be clamped down like a steel frame on the soft flesh of the community, by the U.S. government or any government. . . . Planning contemplates readjustment and revision, as new situations and problems emerge.
>
> Some of those who cry "regimentation" when public planning is mentioned foresee interference with their own practices of private regimentation and exploitation. . . .
>
> It is not necessary or desirable that a central system of planning actually cover all lines of activity or forms of behavior. Such planning overreaches itself. Over-centralized planning must soon begin to plan its own decentralization, for good management is local self-government under a central supervision. Thus wise planning provides for the encouragement of local and personal initiative. . . . Genuine planning really includes planning to preserve and even create noncontrolled free areas of activity.
>
> Planning is not an end, but a means, a means for better use of what we have, a means for emancipation of millions of personalities now fettered, for the enrichment of human life in ways that will follow individual interest or even caprice. We may plan indeed for fuller liberty and are so planning now.[21]

We may plan indeed for fuller liberty! This was the liberal Planning vision, but they were not communicating to doubters. Anti-planners rose up on every hand. It was, after all, the winter of 1934–35, the season of rancor over NRA's extended trial. *A Plan for Planning* raised the awful threat of coordination, and aroused the natives in the Army Corps of Engineers, the Bureau of Reclamation, the Forest Service, the TVA, and elsewhere. Was some board of five professors to decide where dams would be built, swamps drained, trees planted? The bureaucracy hardened against planning, and the hostility was replicated in congressional committees and in the Rivers and Harbors Congress. Of all the areas to pick for a trial of planning, natural resource development was politically the most unpromising. Current arrangements had well-organized defenders. And more general enemies stirred. The *New York Times* saw *A Plan for Planning* and published an editorial condemning "the cult of planning." The *U.S. News* promised that a planning board would bankrupt the nation.

Senator Royal Copeland drafted a bill to set up the five-member national planning board. The unwelcomed bill was sent to the Commerce Committee. Meanwhile the President's support for the existing NRB was strong, and the three planners and their enthusiastic staff continued to probe for the full meaning of the planning assignment. Director Charles W. Eliot thought they ought to get into the field of human resources as well as natural resources, and staff studies broadened in this direction. The Advisory Committee on Science was added in March, perhaps the first step taken in Washington toward what is now called technology assessment. The full board met only seven times in 1935, a mark of the passionate commitment to planning on behalf of the six Cabinet members. But the fifty-person staff published pioneering reports on water pollution, mineral resources, public works, and state planning. Copeland's bill cleared committee but was easily squashed on the floor. In early 1936 a similar bill by Congressman Maury Maverick joined Copeland's legislation, and both had strong administration backing (*presidential* backing; the secretary of war was openly opposed, and others like Henry Wallace at Agriculture were covertly hostile), but could not quite surmount congressional hostility. The Rivers and Harbors lobby held firm for the happy old days of fragmented public works planning. A Planning board was included in the 1937 reorganization proposal, and was deleted when the bill passed in 1939. By this time the rhetoric of anti-planners was well cranked up, and the Planning that was desired in 1933–34 had somehow become socialism. Hugh Johnson, writing in *The Washington Daily News* in August 1937, condemned "the extravagant shell-pink and dreamy visions of the Delanos and Brownlows."[22] It did not help, perhaps, that the board was now ranging outside the natural resources field, and was publishing reports on consumer incomes, demographic trends, and energy policy. When the Reorganization Act passed without the Planning Board, Roosevelt lifted the three planners again from their Cabinet watchdogs, and established them as the NRPB. The last four years were a busy and turbulent time, as the board's studies increased in quantity and quality, as did its enemies. In 1943 the Corps of Engineers had its revenge, mobilizing enough of its congressional friends to murder the upstart in its tenth year.

America's first Planning board had left a puzzling legacy. Probably it never measured up to anyone's definition of a Planning board, even while frightening conservatives with its awful presence in the old Interior Building on the corner of 18th and F streets. Planning public works in the natural resources field implied policy coordination, but this turned out to be a fiercely unpopular idea within the government as well as outside. The board had no statutory authority, limited funds, and almost no political support. All it had was Roosevelt. He provided strong backing and took some lumps because of it, but he had other and higher priorities. Delano was in his seventies, and the other "civilian" members of the board—they were on a part-time basis for years—had no taste for the unending struggles with powerful departmental administrators which the coordinating role required. For this they would need to be in the White House, to be much younger men, to have the President's unwavering support. Department heads defied or ignored them, Roosevelt put them in a committee with the enemy from 1934 to 1939, and the coordinating role slipped away.

What else was Planning, apart from this? It surely involved the analysis of social data, and the pondering of social problems, especially those just over the horizon, a place routine government agencies never look. So the NRPB drifted into a primarily research and brainstorming function. For ten years it produced valuable studies of natural resources, economic trends, housing,

transportation, urban life, nutrition, and other topics of mani-
fest importance. At its demise in 1943 it was working hard on
economic planning for reconversion. It had become a sort of
intellectual spearhead for the administration, educating the
public to areas of social neglect and proposing broad general
solutions—solutions which invariably took the form of government intervention on a continuing and comprehensive basis.

One would have thought this conception of its role would
have ensured the NRPB a certain obscurity. To be sure, nobody
minded inventories of our natural resources, so long as they
were detached from pressure to coordinate government resource
policy. And after mid-decade the board did stand clear of the
administrative thicket, launching its reports while making no
effort to endorse them or to get them translated into legislative
proposals. But the study of emerging social problems irritates
two dangerous types of citizen—the conservative, who does not
like either the social criticism or the constant call for federal
intervention, and the bureaucrat who is the custodian of current
programs. The latter do not mind new missions, but they dislike
suggestions that their work is ineffective or overlaps with some
other bureaucratic assignment and ought to be consolidated.
Presidents now get this brainstorming function from task forces
and presidential commissions. If some rash recommendation is
made on abortion or marijuana, the commission can be disa-
vowed. The NRPB, in focussing primarily upon the analysis of
large and usually long-range social problems and trends, had
still not moved out of the line of fire. It was an agency established by executive order; its reports could not be brushed aside,
they would be followed by others. The impressive study *Security,
Work and Relief Policies* (1942) was likened to the British
Beveridge Report in its call for comprehensive social and health
insurance. It brought the last wavering congressmen to the side
of the Corps of Engineers, and out went the hated thing.

If brainstorming about social problems and their relation to
current and future government policy turned out to be risky
work, it was also serving only one of the President's needs while
excluding others. Policy coordination may have been beyond

reach, if not beyond early imagining, but immediate economic advice was also something the Chief Executive lacked and might have expected from a Planning agency or cluster. The NRPB did almost none of this. Its sights were first on natural resources, and then when they shifted to economic issues it was upon important but somewhat remote subjects such as the structure of industry or consumer buying power. This knowledge was surely useful, but the President needed experts in close touch with the immediate movements of the economy. When the 1937 recession surprised the administration the national Planning board, then the NRC, had no "plans" or detailed recommendations for policy. The same was true in 1940 when the President suddenly wanted advice on the siting of defense facilities. The board had, as Edward Hobbs wrote, "a special orientation toward the distant future," an outlook which "did not correspond to the interests of legislators whose horizons were fixed at two- and six-year terms."[23]

And so the NRPB, like the NRA before it, was construed as demonstrating the unworkability of Planning when in fact it was so poorly designed and hamstrung that a reasonable trial had not occurred. It served a purpose, that of policy brainstorming for future needs, and made a second contribution by gathering data. But it brought the President neither immediate economic plans nor over-all policy coordination or administrative review. "The Board could never decide whether it wanted primarily to be a research, a propaganda, propagandizing, a management, or an advisory agency," says a sympathetic critic.[24] And whatever choice it might have made, there were in the 1930s a host of enemies waiting to crush any threat to their independence.

Roosevelt knew that he had not effectively attacked the incapacitating disorganization of his government and policies, and expected the Republicans to make more of it in the 1936 campaign. They failed to concentrate on the issue. But the programmatic disorder of the New Deal continued to trouble him. To some extent, "loose" lines of authority and the proliferation of agencies with overlapping tasks assisted the President's purposes, but that small virtue was far outweighted by the confusion, cross purposes, and occasional insubordination that even friends of the administration admitted.

In March 1936, FDR appointed the Committee on Administrative Management, headed by Louis Brownlow, with instructions to recommend the consolidation of agencies, the establishment of an economic staff in the White House, and to seek ways to enhance the President's control over refractory career civil servants who were dragging their feet on the New Deal's programs. The committee reported in early 1937 that "the time has come to set our house in order," and recommended the consolidation of all 97 government agencies under 12 cabinet departments; the strengthening of the Presidency by the addition of 6 administrative assistants; a "clearinghouse" planning agency; and other centralizing and streamlining reforms. Their report was "not a request for more power," the committee wrote, "but for the tools of management . . . to bring many little bureaucracies under broad coordinated democratic authority."[25]

In this little-remembered report and its reception there was a crucial pivot in the American governmental experience, and in the evolution of liberalism itself. Brownlow had told an aide that "we can not escape planning" as he readied the report for the President, and one evidence of this conclusion was the recommendation for a permanent NRPB.[26] Roosevelt knew there were some risks in playing upon this note, and in his masterful press conference explaining the proposal in January 1937, he stressed the word "management," not "planning." "The word 'management' is a thoroughly clear American word," he noted, and improved management was all the reorganization aimed at.[27] His low-key approach might have eased the proposal through at an earlier time. In an important sense, what happened subsequently was Roosevelt's fault, for an earlier time had been available. When he first assumed office in 1933 he had the authority, under an act passed late in Hoover's term, to reorganize the government almost without restriction save a right of congressional veto. In the crisis atmosphere of 1933 Congress would surely have denied him nothing in the way of re-shuffled agencies and functions. But he was busy, and distracted. He met with Budget Director Lewis Douglas early in 1933 and tried to decide where to strike while the reorganization iron was hot, but neither man gave the issue much attention. "I had grand intentions," FDR admitted, "but that is as far as we got."[28] The reorganization authority lapsed in 1936.

One year later Roosevelt finally understood that reorganization was the key to governmental effectiveness. He had learned this in a dozen different theaters, but surely most educational had been the struggle for a national power Policy.

Roosevelt had been an advocate of public power for some time before the presidency, and it was no surprise to anyone that the New Deal was soon heavily engaged in the field. TVA produced and sold electricity, the REA helped farmers establish electric co-ops, the Public Utility Holding Company Act of 1935 reformed the structure of private utilities, the Bureau of Reclamation completed the huge Bonneville Dam on the Columbia River and prepared to distribute power in 1937. There were power policies, but no Policy. Roosevelt set up a committee under Harold Ickes in 1933 to prepare a national power policy, but the committee couldn't decide what one would look like and it floundered. With Bonneville power coming on line in 1937 Roosevelt again realized the absence of goals or guidelines for determining what to do with it, and he set up another national power policy committee and gave them two weeks to report. But after one week he deflected them to work on a bill to set up seven "little TVAs," a series of river basin authorities to unify power, water, and land policies. These were confusing maneuvers, and we need no more contact with the details. Of course, no National Power Policy ever emerged, either on a piece of paper, in a government report, or in the preamble to any legislation. "Amid all the debates," concludes historian Philip Funigiello, ". . . a real policy did not emerge—only a series of piecemeal, ad hoc arrangements."[29]

Struggling through all of this had taught both Ickes and Roosevelt a few things, and they hit upon an important insight at about the same time, so far as one can tell. The way to unify policy was to reorganize. To Ickes, this meant a department of conservation, combining all soil, water, and timber activities, all public lands, dams, all of it. Under his direction, preferably. This was a meritorious idea in a general way, but Ickes obscured its promise by allowing it to seem merely empire-building, which it was only in part. The Brownlow Committee did not quite accept his idea, possibly because he had made it unpopular throughout the government, but they did share his instinct for functional reorganization. The twelve Cabinet departments envisioned by Brownlow and Roosevelt do not exhaust the possibilities for functional consolidation, but in placing every government agency and the administrative functions of the "independent" regulatory agencies under them the reorganization proposal took a giant step away from the bureaucratic fragmentation that enfeebled Roosevelt's social programs.

The struggle for power Policy also reminded Roosevelt of the importance of a central agency which he could use for policy coordination. As he worried about what to do with Bonneville power, he was at the same time talking with Senator Norris about the details of a proposal to establish the seven valley authorities, and was wrestling with Congress over flood control legislation. Obviously power, water, soil, trees, all were related, except in Washington, where the President could not get unified treatment of policy options. Thus he welcomed the Brownlow Committee's recommendation of a central Planning agency to prepare for Congress a total set of administration proposals affecting natural resources and the disposition of electric power that was a by-product of flood control. "And then all the work that is being carried on will have some relationship to the work that is being carried on at some other point," he explained in words of hopeful simplicity.[30]

But interested parties were not lulled by Roosevelt's open manner, his assurance of improved management. He proposed his reorganization bill in January 1937, then in February sent down the Court reform proposal, and reorganization was soon caught in a riptide of conservative opposition. A group of reactionaries sprang to the defense of Liberty, and organized the

Committee to Defend Constitutional Government to kill the reorganization. Congressmen talked of tyranny, and other imaginary horribles, and one vigilant member opposed the six administrative assistants on the ground that they would surely be "theoretical, intellectual, professorial nincompoops."[31] These tragically confused patriots would not have been enough, but liberals in general did not understand the reoganization issue, and it had almost no constituency in support. People who ought to have known better became alarmed and rushed to the city gates to repel the Trojan Horse. Walter Lippmann talked of "personal government," Arthur Krock of "dictatorship," and Bernard DeVoto wrote in *Harper's Monthly* that it would "destroy all effective barriers to totalitarianism that exist."[32] As Lindsay Rogers aptly commented in 1938, "the future historian will be puzzled when he exhumes the debate's clichés about dictatorships and totalitarian states."[33]

This hysteria was useful in building opposition to the reorganization bill, but the people who really beat Roosevelt on this one were not worried about dictatorship. They were worried that comfortable relations with existing government agencies would be disrupted when the agency was moved to where its work would be appraised in a broad national context. The American Legion testified that it didn't want the VA in the Department of Welfare, physicians didn't want the Public Health Service moved out of the Treasury, social workers didn't want the Children's Bureau moved from Labor to Human Welfare, railway labor didn't want the ICC moved to Commerce. And the President's own bill was openly opposed by the secretaries of interior, agriculture, labor, the chairman of the NLRB, of the U.S. Tariff Commission, of the FTC, the heads of the GAO, the GPO, the Corps of Engineers, and of the Bureau of Fisheries! FDR complained of misrepresentation and misunderstanding: "Dictatorships do not grow out of strong and successful governments but out of weak and helpless governments," he said in a Fireside Chat in the spring of 1938. This was true, but it did no good. He was forced to weaken the reorganization bill, and it finally passed in 1939 without the Planning Board and the departmental changes. What he got out of it all were the six assistants and the establishment of the Executive Office of the President, a sort of organizational holding company for the little collection of councils and boards and individuals who worked near the White House.

Six assistants and an EOP made no structural alterations in the executive branch of any major importance, although they were helpful additions soon universally approved. But they did not really remedy the weakness of the Presidency. The departmental reorganization and Planning Board were a different matter. With their rejection, the Planning impulse was smothered, and a fragmented, reactive system passed on to subsequent generations as the embodiment of liberal, Rooseveltian government. Without reorganization the disorder of the executive branch remained, and the objection to this is not its untidiness but the structural encouragement it offered to the piecemeal capture of programs and agencies for private purposes. Without the Planning Board there was no central agency to provide any of the services that it might have offered the President— economic advice, policy formulation, policy review, research on social problems. During the argument over departmental reorganization and a Planning Board it was alleged that their passage would bring Planning to America. Whether that is so depends upon one's definition of Planning, and we have decided to let that definition emerge from our history rather than impose it at the start. One can be fairly sure that had Roosevelt been given exactly what he wanted there would still have remained a degree of confusion, contradiction, and error in the government's activities sufficient to warm a conservative's heart. The Brownlow report did not find functional division that easy, and even an optimum allotment of agencies in departments where they belong would surely not end the conflicts that flaw governmental social management. As for the central Planning agency, the NRPB, promoted to permanent status, would not have instantly solved the problems of how one agency can give the President long-range brainstorming, short-range economic advice, policy formulation, policy review, and social reporting.

Years would have been required for Roosevelt and then his successors, and the Planning Board itself, to learn these arts and sciences. Probably other institutions would have to be split off, and some balance of duties found. But if this work could have commenced in 1937, presidents up to and including Gerald Ford would have been spared much time for other things, and the record of social policy since World War II would surely offer less disappointment than we have seen.

13

By 1940 the New Deal era was over. Intentions and hopes no longer mattered, the political economy had taken its post-New Deal shape, and war brought different problems, different opportunities. Through the 1930s Franklin Roosevelt talked much of Planning, and persistently explored the dimensions of planned social management. His administration brought a planning experiment in industry, another in agriculture, another in the Tennessee Valley. It had expanded public influence in the traditional policy areas of fiscal and monetary management, business regulation, conservation; it had entered new policy areas thought fundamental to social control—land-use, population distribution, incomes, energy, public credit. Coming to see planning more as a process than a document, the New Deal had expanded major amounts of energy in pursuit of organizational innovations to provide planning capacities—a national Planning board, executive branch reorganization, technology assessment, regionalization. It had tried to look more to the longer-range future, had accorded a growing respect to expertise, had sought out structural sources of social maladjustment, and proposed reforms.

It had centralized power in the national government, and within that government had shifted power from Court and congress to the presidency, on the assumption, then entirely plausible, that this enhanced The People's capacity to rule. The national government was clearly more responsive to those multitudes excluded from local governance or from corporation boards; the President was the only nationally elected official. In the Fall of 1938 FDR had tried to realign the parties, so that a mass-based liberal political institution might channel popular pressure to legislators and other officials. He directed the curbs, in 1936, upon the power of the most undemocratic section, the South, over the Democratic presidential nomination. His administration tried to organize the unorganized, to spur "grassroots democracy" in new institutions apart from local government.

In these ways the New Deal had charted the agenda of liberal Planning in an inventive and erratic fashion, and run a school of experience which taught mostly lessons of frustration.

We have seen these efforts encounter the American reality, and in varying degrees and ways to founder. The resultant political economy at the end of the 1930s was not Planning, and has been difficult to label. John Chamberlain in *The American Stakes* (1941) called it "the Broker State," a government intervening in an ad hoc and piecemeal fashion on behalf of those groups with sufficient political or economic power to obtain assistance. Not Planned from the center, the system ironically involved a considerable degree of partial planning to control the economic environment of certain groups and sectors. While few interests had rallied to the idea of a fully articulated system of Planning where national and rational perspectives would necessarily come to bear upon every public decision, many groups had welcomed government intervention devised in a different context, opportunistically and in a fragmented bureaucratic setting. As the depression erased profits and intensified competition, why not partial planning, government control of prices and entry in those industries where excess capacity was endemic?

Such partial planning had common characteristics: it involved such structural controls as were necessary to secure profitable pricing and restrictions against new entries into the fields—price controls or quotas, tariff protection, subsidies, or some combination. It was designed to assist one economic sector, and was not bureaucratically meshed into a larger national goal or program.

It was administered by public officials in varying degrees independent of the President, men temperamentally congenial to the regulated industry and closely advised by advisory councils made up of industry representatives. It was also invariably restrictionist. In the midst of scarcity, the government planned curtailment of production; its interventions were producer oriented, not consumer oriented.

One finds this pattern of public intervention extended by the end of the 1930s to most of agriculture; to the coal, oil, and gas industries; to rail, air, and water transportation; to radio; to some forms of retail sales; even to cattle ranching on public lands. The leading producing units in an industry, caught in the shrinking markets of the 1930s where competition was atrophy for all, would reluctantly come around to the need to seek haven in public law. Now governmental powers would be legislated to assist the industry, their administration entrusted to an existing federal agency or, more often, to a new one. The agency would enter upon its duties accompanied by many claims of the triumph of the public interest, perhaps even with zeal. But if regulation was not always in its initial phases completely satisfactory to the regulated interests, the passage of time enhanced the influence of organized groups and reduced the abstract zeal of the regulators. Usually without clear policy guidelines from Congress, the agency would soon adopt a cooperative spirit, consulting with affected groups of private citizens who had economic stake and expertise, often seeking further constituent support by decentralizing some of its decision-making processes. Those who might have expressed different evaluations and goals were screened from the process by bureaucratic walls, or by their own lack of organization or expertise.

Thus the drive for control was stopped well short of comprehensive national control. The framework of fiscal and monetary policy alone was national; government regulation, promotion, subsidies were determined within a smaller compass, limited to a geographic region or an industry or a cluster of related interest groups. Like all systems it satisfied no one entirely, this post-New Deal political economy. But the perceived alternatives, the old (pre-1929) order, or Planning, both promised intolerable uncertainties. Therefore American political, economic, and administrative elites guided the political economy during the tumultuous 1930s toward a middle ground where the context of control was restricted to the perspectives and interests of vitally affected groups. All through the 1930s, Roosevelt's words had pointed toward interrelated social management on a national scale, yet events had marched toward a type of planning which made the job of broad and comprehensive Planning every day more difficult and its realization more unlikely.

By the end of the 1930s the State, which Planners had intended to use to establish sufficient control over the fundamental affairs of the nation, was thoroughly Balkanized, its sovereignty compromised by the invasion along the edges of public policy by private groups with regular and often legalized roles in policymaking. As a result its many programs were not only internally contradictory, but were at odds with the universally desired goal of recovery. Hundreds of groups had secured the haven of public protection from the marketplace, and there they would wait out economic storms, fighting off occasional efforts by the President with his national constituency, to coordinate all governmental intervention. "Government by whirlpools," Ernest Griffith described the government in the late 1930s.[34] Was America planned at all? George B. Galloway of the American Planning Association summarized in 1941:

Much of the so-called planning is scattered, partial, piece-meal, pluralistic, interventionist, uncoordinated, and dispersive. . . . It lacks a clearly defined underlying rationale, a common direction. . . . From the viewpoint of national planning, the New Deal has been like Don Quixote who mounted his horse and rode off in all directions at once.[35]

The point to be underscored here is that something far worse had happened to Planning by 1940 than simply a failure to get itself realized in the most favorable circumstances history had yet provided in the United States. Naturally it is not good for a social theory to be discredited by a premature and flawed trial which does not fairly test its merits, as happened to Planning in the early 1930s. But worse for Planners, the durable Broker State was in place by end of the decade, and while reactionaries thought it closer to Planning than the system Herbert Hoover fought to protect from significant internal evolution, the reverse was true. Planning would be *more* difficult after 1940 than before, for the New Deal era had seen partial planning and broker interventionism built deep into the structure of American public life. Power sectors had been created that would later on resist any nationalizing or rationalizing integration.

Worst of all, liberals—with the exception of just a handful— had decided that liberalism did not lead to Planning after all. The vast majority of them had lost their early faith in Planning, no longer thought hard about it, let it slip out of the progressive heritage. In its place they installed the Broker State with its mix of partial planning and ad hoc interventionism. Conservative attacks upon the post-New Deal Broker State confirmed the liberal assumption that the political economy now embodied all the desirable features that it had lacked in the bad old twenties. If the political economy was so irritating to conservatives, if it could be called The Welfare State, then it was time to defend it rather than join the mood of criticism. Liberal loyalties were tied to the post-New Deal system for forty years, until the 1970s would come to question all the old answers. When the Broker State approach finally ran out of time and began to show its fatal deficiencies as a way of managing social evolution, liberals were disoriented and without programmatic guidance. They had forgotten about Planning.

From Pearl Harbor to the Employment Act, 1941-1946

It might have been thought that America's involvement in global war would alter the nation's political economy more profoundly than the New Deal. Surely the necessity to mobilize an entire society on such a scale would prove sufficient to overwhelm the obstacles that had frustrated Planners and deflected Planning into the half-way house of the Broker State. And the war did bring a vast expansion of social intervention, administrative machinery for the coordination of national military and production efforts, elaborate institutions for data-gathering and forecasting, the dominance of relatively specific national goals. But for reasons we shall explore, wartime controls did not pave the way for peacetime Planning. When the war ended the institutions of control were dismantled, with the Employment Act of 1946—and an invigorated Bureau of the Budget—the only residue. The outcome of the wartime Planning experience was not a new system, but the decisive reinforcement of the post-New Deal, partial-planning Broker State.

2

Pearl Harbor caught the government short in civilian as well as military preparations for war. That little had been done prior to the opening of hostilities to establish mobilization machinery was due partly to the power of isolationist sentiment, which Roosevelt hesitated to inflame further by forthright steps to prepare for conversion to a war economy. But the President's own administrative and political style was part of the problem. Though inclined toward both a stronger and more comprehensive governmental performance, Roosevelt was suspicious of power that he might not be able to control, and would permit no single rival to emerge at the head of a superagency. Throughout the mobilization experience the President hampered the effective centralization of power by administrative traits that had long marked his Presidency. When crises arose, he was inclined to split off a new agency to cope with some problem rather than integrate the solution into existing machinery. He not only tolerated but often deliberately fostered jurisdictional overlap and chaos as a means of retaining ultimate authority in his own hands. These instincts of the Chief Executive combined with his terrible workload and the multiple cultural and political sources of fragmentation with which we have become acquainted in watching the Planning idea through the 1930s to make the wartime mobilization less coherent, less adequately Planned, than efficiency would have dictated.

The first steps toward mobilization were taken in 1939, when Roosevelt established the War Resources Board, after prodding by the armed services. The board must have been named when the President was distracted, for it is hard to understand how he allowed its membership to be so dominated by business. Four industrialists, a banker, an economist and a scientist reported back to the President in late 1939, recommending that he set up a superboard of heavily business cast to command the economy for rearmament. Roosevelt buried the report, and drifted a bit longer on the divided current of public opinion. But the war in Europe took an alarming turn in the spring of 1940, and machinery for at least thinking about a future mobilization could not be delayed. In May the President, displaying his impressive ability to improvise and confuse, set up a seven-member advisory committee under a long-defunct but still authorized Council of National Defense, of World War I days. Now he would not have to go to Congress, could keep the organization for mobilization in low profile during an election year. He was comfortable with the Advisory Committee, which had no chairman and no clear legal powers. It busied itself through the fall, clearing contracts and discussing priorities. The mobilization, small but burgeoning, was not yet planned.

In 1941 the search for central machinery began in earnest. The armed services clamored for supply, defense contracts expanded, and the price system could not much longer handle the scramble for scarce material and manpower resources. The Office of Production Management came into being in January and was given limited powers to manage industrial expansion. But other problems were split off, an old Roosevelt habit. Oil allocation was given to Secretary Ickes, price control to the Office of Price Administration. With untried institutions and harried and confused administrators, defense production lagged, and critics demanded a better performance. Nowhere in Washington was information on all military, civilian and allied requirements collected or made the basis for central decision.

Pearl Harbor brought more decisive habits (while making the mobilization task a thousand times more urgent). The War Production Board emerged in January, with Sears-Roebuck's Donald Nelson as its administrator. WPB was responsible for munitions production, which it tried to coordinate, but much of the economy was outside its influence. Price control rested with OPA, although it required blinders to fail to see that pricing was a vital part of industrial control. And Roosevelt, with Nelson's general acquiescence, continued to split off agencies for special purposes, further weakening the WPB's position as primary center of economic management. Orders were going out from multiple centers, invariably conflicting. When WPB started work it shared its burden with the Board of Economic Warfare, Lend-Lease administration, the Office of Defense Transportation, the RFC, the National War Labor Board, the OPA, all buying arms or regulating their production in some way. Roosevelt appointed "czars" for oil, solid fuels, transportation, food, housing, and rubber, all essentially independent of WPB. Nelson made the best of the situation, working patiently toward cooperation where he could not command. From every quarter came complaints of delay, shortages, confusion.

Yet during the course of 1943 a workable solution to the problem of wartime economic management was patched together. Nelson and his agency had collected too many wounds in the struggle to control the early mobilization, had grown too large and become too deeply immersed in detailed administration. Roosevelt in May of 1943 established the Office of War Mobilization under South Carolina's respected ex-Senator and now Supreme Court Justice James Byrnes, and that agency lasted out the war. Byrnes used a small staff and concentrated on coordination, smoothing out conflicts when they became acute. He was a stronger man than Nelson, had excellent congressional ties, and held Roosevelt's full confidence. Baruch's instinct for one-man control appeared to be confirmed by Byrnes' performance after mid-1943. But personalities were a small part of the gradual improvement from Nelson to Byrnes. The conglomerate of government bureaus and defense industries had somewhat adjusted by 1943 to the novelties of global war. Nelson had been uncertain of his legal authority; but in 1943 Congress passed legislation granting to OWM virtually unlimited powers.

So the job of defense production went forward. A government which bought $10 billion in goods and services in 1940 was buying $95 billion by 1945, almost all of it related to defense. Planes, tanks, ships, guns, first aid kits, boots, an avalanche of military goods went out to submerge the Axis powers. The GNP expanded from $100 billion to $213 billion from 1940 to 1945, and at the peak of efforts 40 per cent of it went into the war. Yet civilian standards of living actually increased over 1939, despite shortages and rationing. Inflation was brought under control by 1943, and amounted only to about 35 per cent over the course of the war. The American productive performance surprised an entire world.

3

And this, indeed, was Planning, at least one form of it. There were relatively explicit economic goals, the target figures of shipping, plane and tank production often set by the President. There was extensive government intervention, touching virtually all prices, most wages and hours, controlling transportation, food and energy supplies. The Selective Service System and War Manpower Commission were a giant manpower agency, not only sending 10 million citizens into war theaters abroad but deciding toward the end of the war whether to keep people in farming or dentistry or electronics, draft them, or allow them to migrate to jobs in defense plants. There were appropriate agencies for all these controls, and a central coordinating bureau at the apex. The essentials of Planning seemed to be there—policy goals, government manipulation of basic social sectors, appropriate institutional machinery for coordination. There was even an interesting experiment in international Planning which may one day attract attention, the Combined Boards where American and British officials met with their administrative counterparts to share information on raw materials and production. All of this over a four-year period, unguided by any tyrannical document labeled The Plan.

But it was a form of Planning that, like NRA, was not to make Planning many friends. Indeed, the defects of the Planning experience in World War II are reminiscent of the NRA episode in basic respects. Again, the government was both too weak and too meddlesome at the same time. Let us take these in order. If managers charged with control of production do not *control,* performance will reflect the inadequate grasp of the interrelated elements of production. And "at no time," concluded a leading study of the wartime mobilization, "were the controls over production fully effective in securing maximum balanced production for war purposes."[1]

This ineffectiveness had many sources, among them the sheer size and complexity of the job and the reluctance of the dollar-a-year businessmen who did so much of the government's work to fasten effective controls upon industries they had so recently left. But probably the most crucial flaw in the government's design for management was the failure to gain control over contracting. Despite some efforts at central clearance and review of military procurement, the armed services and the Lend-Lease administration let contracts based upon their own assessment of military needs. With the contracts out, and their terms negotiated, the WPB or OWM had to manage the scramble for scarce metals, fuels, technical skills, and other resources in short supply. To do this adequately required advance control of contracting, but the military never submitted fully to this imperative. Additionally there should have been coordination between price control and the allocation of scarce resources, but OPA handled the first and OWM the second in relative isolation from each other. The administrative fragmentation of the control of fuel, transportation, food, and manpower contributed to the confusion. A firmer grip on all elements of the productive machinery was required from the beginning, but, as always, Americans hesitated to seek comprehensive social authority. Manpower policy is another good example. Fragmentation was the rule. Over twenty agencies exercised manpower responsibilities, the chief being the Selective Service System. But there was never a general grant of legal authority or policy direction concerning manpower, and the draft system worked in relative isolation from the perspectives of the War Manpower Commission, the Department of Labor, the Office of Education, and the other myriad units of government involvement in human training.

The cost of ineffective central management has not been and cannot be calculated, given the complexity of the mobilization. Had the United States not possessed such impressive physical and cultural assets, as well as geographical isolation from direct military damage, the gap between military needs and defense production would have been wider, and the consequences more serious. But while a major defect of wartime Planning was its hesitancy to establish authoritative and coordinated control of the elements of production, the government gave every appearance of being too meddlesome. Essentially infirm in its grip, the government was experienced by citizens as omnipresent. A forest of agencies grew up, and the snowfall of government paper gorged the mails and vexed businessmen, taxpayers, everyone. Defense production could have been handled without requiring very small business to submit to the regimine of government forms, but the bureaucratic instinct was expansionist. Businessmen had to become familiar with preference ratings, preference orders, and forms of impersonal and inexplicable designation. Form PD-275 required a report on metal consumption and requirements, form PD-26A on plans to ship aluminum. These were perhaps necessary, but why were there four separate control systems operating concurrently in 1942? Order L-36 issued by the WPB prohibited any manufacturer from making men's umbrella frames after November 1942, and order L-104 prohibited the manufacture of metal hairpins in excess of 6-$\frac{1}{2}$ per cent of the poundage produced during 1941 by a given manufacturer—and none of them longer than 2 inches. This degree of bureaucratic control was odious to Americans, and it was surely not necessary that it be so pervasive, so complex, and so shifting. If this was Planning, citizens reasonably concluded, there must be an immediate end of it when hostilities were over.

Perhaps no wartime task of public officials produced more conflict than the search for an incomes policy. A Planned society probably requires an incomes policy, although this is debatable. But during wartime there was no choice. Government spending led to inflationary pressures, Congress consistently passed up the chance to demonstrate its courage by an adequate tax policy, and so some sort of controls on wages became inescapable if inflation were to be kept within tolerable bounds.

No other aspect of wartime economic management produced so many irritations as did the thrashing about for an acceptable incomes policy. Bernard Baruch advised FDR early in the war simply to freeze all pre-war relationships, but Roosevelt wanted more flexibility, and arranged to have it. Incomes of Americans would be controlled through the tax system, OPA price control, and the wages allowed by the War Labor Board. Inflationary pressures in 1942 brought labor disputes and strikes, and the WLB was forced to consider what standard it might use to bring angry unionists and their employers to agreement. The "Little Steel" formula was announced in May, granting a 15 per cent increase to cover the rise in costs which had occurred from Pearl Harbor to May 1942. It was at least a standard, not so good from labor's point of view as a standing commitment to tie wages to an escalator, but one which at least appeared for the moment to recognize the erosion of earlier inflation.

But the formula did not quiet the waters. The WLB granted increases of varying amounts from industry to industry, trying to take into account the different realities which it faced. No one was ever entirely happy with its decision, and most wage negotiations were not reviewed by the WLB in any event. In April 1943, the government issued the "hold the line" order on wages in an effort to halt mounting inflation. But profits were not controlled with equal consistency, and Roosevelt's request for a $25,000 ceiling on wartime earnings by individuals was ignored by Congress. So American workers began to turn increasingly to the strike as a weapon in the struggle for income maintenance, even though labor leaders had promised no strikes when the war began. And it did not calm union tempers that agricultural prices were allowed to float upward to 110 per cent of parity, a gift of a Congress still deeply sympathetic to the small minority who worked the soil.

Against this background there were wage disputes throughout the war, and strikes became a serious problem in 1943 especially. There were four separate coal strikes in 1943 alone, as John L. Lewis' UMW risked what sympathy labor had in public opinion in order to prevent inflation from making workers carry the main burden of the war. Much of Roosevelt's time was taken up with labor disputes, and he was sufficiently irritated to have Lewis' tax returns investigated by the IRS. And labor was not the only loud complainant at the distribution of wartime burdens. When the WLB finally decided what a union should receive, industrialists were obliged to agree, but this was often hard to swallow. Montgomery Ward's Sewell Avery created the most celebrated conflict between corporate management and government when he defied a WLB-ordered settlement of a union dispute and had to be carried by soldiers out of his Chicago office: "To hell with the government," he told the attorney general of the United States. Incomes policy was no fun, and embroiled the government in endless disputes to which there was no satisfactory answer. Four years of this sort of thing heightened the general feeling that conflict of economic groups in the marketplace was preferable to conflict around tables in Washington. With class feelings intense after the 1930s, the government found incomes policy a punishing and thankless task. Shouldering it added enormously to the general unhappiness with Planning during wartime.

4

To what extent were these problems inherent in Planning itself, or to what extent were they situational and remediable? The question is formidably complicated, and no decisive answer is possible. But several scholars have analyzed the episode, and offered thoughts on how the management of wartime economy might have been more effectively handled. War was a time of special pressure where there never seemed to be the time or the margin of social safety to take the long view, to insist upon the best mesh of policies. With more time the bureaucracy of control that had markedly improved its performance from 1942 to 1945 might have been expected to refine its techniques further. For one thing, the problem of adequate data would surely ease with experience. In the early phases of war mobilization there was an almost total absence of adequate data for production planning, and then zealous bureaucrats buried the business community and themselves in a sea of paper reports. The result, in the words of a leading study, was that decisions were made "in an atmosphere of twilight information."[2] But the gathering of data, not merely enough information but the right kind, is a skill that men may hope to master. In 1942 the job was done with great ardor and clumsiness, and unassimilable data swamped and confused those charged with decision. But even the short war period brought some improvement in this area.

Another problem which may well be classified as temporary was the shortage of personnel. As in 1933, the government in December 1941, shouldered the staggering task of national economic control. The civil service ranks, and the pool of university-based social and natural scientists and administrators, willing lawyers with a penchant for public service—these were not adequate to the need. Major use was made of businessmen, for they possessed an invaluable expertise in the complex management of transportation systems, steel mills, mines, chemical plants, finance, purchasing, and all the other areas which an unprepared government had to now master. These men gave invaluable service; but patriotism and energetic commitment to winning the war could not erase the perspectives acquired in business careers, and these were a hindrance to Planning in two main respects.

The businessman in government had a strong initial aversion to public controls, and his influence was invariably thrown on the side of mild and partial controls when market processes must be manipulated. An industry-wide perspective was also predictable. Both mental traits led government agencies to move to nationally integrated controls somewhat later than the situation typically warranted. Yet a further irony lay in the second instinct of such men to include all elements of a given industry within public controls when they were finally convinced of their necessity. Small businesses, scholars are agreed, could often have been excluded entirely from the reporting requirements and other controls of the WPB and OWM, but businessmen in government pressed for industrywide coverage once a painful decision for controls was reached. Thus both early reluctance to exert sufficient coercion, a lack of appreciation for coordination of policy across industry boundaries, and an ultimate preference for extension of controls to all firms in an industry despite their size were natural but pernicious perspectives ingrained in the hard-working new servants of national economic regulation who came from careers in business. Such perspectives would not have been so influential had not the mobilization been as abrupt and massive as it had to be under the circumstances, requiring a virtual forced draft upon executive talent from the private sector.

These thoughts are drawn from the literature analyzing the wartime economic management. Perhaps they are misleading. Economists and students of public administration, who produce what little thorough analysis we have, are after all natural friends of the regulatory state. Perhaps they list administrative improvements which could not then or later be implemented, ignore or minimize the inherent difficulties of Planning. But they do present an impressive consensus that many of the defects in the 1941–45 performance came from situational elements which if properly analyzed promise to make the next experience with Planning much more successful.

In the 1940s it was still possible to believe that war and preparation for war were exceptional occasions for America. The routinization of emergency that we now see as having begun in 1939–41, and which is now one of the central themes of American life, was a development not anticipated by the generation that fought World War II. They did not expect the war to permanently alter their institutions. Yet as soon as it was permissible to consider the opportunity to demobilize it became clear that there would be vigorous argument over just how much of the government's social controls should be dismantled.

5

Friends of the new regulatory state which had been matured in the 1930s feared that the war might seriously weaken the national commitment to "the New Deal," a commitment they had a tendency to underestimate. The perception of the vulnerability of the post-New Deal system was to be proven quite wrong, but it was not without some foundation.

The American tradition was individualistic and Lockean;

suspicion of political power was deeply embedded. The relatively modest expansion of public controls of the New Deal era had come under strong conservative attack in the 1937–40 period, and throughout the war years the opponents of the new liberal state had struggled to minimize the powers of government. Conservatives blocked wage-price controls until late 1942, killed off several reform-oriented social programs such as WPA, CCC, NYA, and even threatened TVA. They terminated the NRPB in 1943, as we know, cutting off its work on energy, land, water, industrial location, the structure of the economy, and postwar reconversion planning. Everywhere in public discussion, especially in the halls of Congress, one could hear the old rhetoric of economic individualism.

Yet in actuality the managed, compensated, or "mixed" economy, as one prefers, was here to stay. Probably it had not been in jeopardy at any time after 1936, and certainly the war cemented into American life the broad interventionist role for government which had emerged fully during the New Deal. A political economy of managed capitalism had enormous momentum, after all, having germinated in the late nineteenth century and built itself layer upon layer, in season and out, rapidly at times (1913–18) and slowly at times (1920–32), but with an irresistible historical logic. And government's evolution toward enhanced social control through bureaucratic means only paralleled, albeit with a considerable lag, the evolution of corporations. There may have been some politicians and businessmen who spoke the old language of self-reliance, a free market economy, and the other nostalgic phrases of the nineteenth century, but the idea of a managed economy took firm political root during the terrible depression of the 1930s. Republican presidential candidates in 1936, 1940, and 1944 affirmed the major economic responsibilities assumed by government under the New Deal, and complained only about administrative details, lack of efficiency, and wounds to the Constitution. There was jeopardy to certain "liberal" programs, but only diehard and fading opposition to the new economic management responsibilities of the national government.

If there had been any doubt of this shift in attitudes about the political economy on the eve of war, it would have been based upon the hostility to Franklin Roosevelt expressed by many leaders of business opinion. Even at that time, however, this animosity was directed toward the President and certain advanced liberal sentiments he was known to hold and encourage. The "positive State" idea was not really debatable. Businessmen themselves were responsible for much of the expansion of governmental power of the 1930s. In any event, the war firmly cemented the government's compensatory role in the minds of a crucial segment of the public. Thousands upon thousands of businessmen and lawyers who still harbored a suspicion of government came to Washington to help staff the war mobilization. As a social class these Americans had been basically conservative and Republican. During the war they learned of the unique exhilaration of public service, and saw the many potential uses of public agencies in rationalizing economic patterns and expanding production and consumption. Wartime Washington, they found, was a capital filled with practical people without noticeably radical inclinations. It was an educational experience for the elites of a capitalist society, and in the end a politically moderating one. The formation of the Committee for Economic Development (CED) in the summer of 1942 symbolized the shift in the business community toward a more positive relation to the liberal State. This organization did not necessarily speak for a majority of businessmen, Karl Schriftgeisser wrote, but they were the "few who had not forgotten, in the stress of wartime, the lessons of the eleven-year depression. . . . They were not frightened by the word *planning*. They did not accept . . . the 1915 dictum of the sociologist, Graham Taylor, when he said that 'the only thing men really plan for is war.' Man could, if he would, plan also for peace—and for prosperity as well."[3]

Another factor working to consolidate the New Deal system was the expanded productive capacity which the war brought into being. Americans at the end of the war were a people whose economic assumptions had been shaped by an eleven-year depression. They tended to believe, whether they were economists or workers or businessmen, that the economic plant was overbuilt, that a structural gap yawned between productive capacity and buying power in America. Wartime spending had closed that gap, yet the war intensified the problem by expanding capacity. How were we to escape another and more disastrous depression when the economy lost the stimulus of government spending? As one of the founders of CED put it: "We were still close to the days of the early 1930s. . . . We determined to put everything we had into an effort to avoid that major calamity . . . [and] we knew the government would have to play its part, probably the major part."[4]

The combination of the depression-borne assumption of a "mature" economy with a structural tendency toward underemployment, and the presence of a greatly enlarged productive capacity, led important segments of the conservative community to accept a system the overwhelming majority had fought in the 1930s. The war years had nurtured alluring visions of sustained growth through government stabilization of aggregate demand. Government spending had reduced unemployment from 10 per cent to 1.2 per cent by 1945, had ended an eleven-year depression. To those who lived through these years, this fact had an almost irresistible power to alter old assumptions.

And so the boundaries of the debate over America's post-war political economy were to lie much farther to the Left than contemporaries anticipated. In the end there was no significant support for a return to the relatively inactive government of the 1920s. The conservative counterattack against the managerial state never materialized. The real issue was not whether government would remain responsible for economic development, and be active in a balancing role; this was conceded. Disagreement focused not upon the fact of governmental economic management, but its forms and goals.

American history presents few occasions when fundamental economic and political arrangements were laid open to wide debate, when major alternatives seemed available and major decisions were made. The years 1945–46 were such a time, reminding one of 1932–33 when so many avenues seemed open on the occasion of the collapse of the economy. The system of wartime controls would necessarily give way to another system, and the alternatives seemed broad. For a time, at least, an economy more closely controlled than that of the 1930s appeared possible, even likely. The word "Planning" returned to American public discussion.

The uncertainties of reconversion to a peacetime economy moved groups toward an interest in economic Planning who would have thought the word synonymous with socialism, and perhaps treason, five years earlier. Planning had not been an acceptable word or concept since about 1935, and even in its 1932–35 heyday had carried a heavy emotional charge. But in 1943 the National Association of Manufacturers named a committee to study national Planning for reconversion, a vice president of General Motors made speeches about national Planning, and the Pabst Brewing Company had 36,000 responses to an essay contest on the correct public policies to ensure post-war full employment. Three of the top six winners in that contest had advocated a central Planning bureau after the war. In February 1944, the CIO's Postwar Planning Committee advocated what it called "advanced planning" under a federal agency to chart the economic future in a context of "overall national action and controls." The AFL advocated a national economic commission to coordinate demobilization and then continue in a coordinating role to ensure economic stability and adequate welfare benefits. And in early 1944 the Chamber of Commerce, the CED, the Kiwanis Clubs, and other organizations reflecting a business point of view joined with the American Farm Bureau Federation at Atlantic City to call for cooperation between government and "free enterprise" to ensure against post-war depression. In the U.S. Senate, Walter George chaired the Special Committee on Postwar Economic Policy and Planning, and Rep. William Colmer chaired a similar committee in the House.

It was apparent, of course, that not everyone used the word "Planning" in the same way. ("Planning," wrote the conservative economist Friedrich Hayek, "a very good word meriting a better fate.") To some, Planning simply meant that the government must withdraw its wartime controls and fiscal stimulus carefully, in timing with a reviving domestic consumer market. In this sense, Planning was a businesslike way to get the government's economic role diminished, not permanently enlarged. A middle position was occupied by the CED, for example. To that organization, Planning meant that businessmen in every community must project their investment for the post-war months, with the government offering economic data, encouragement, and in the last resort a public works program to bridge any gap to full employment. "Look Who's Planning!" wrote Helen Fuller in the liberal *New Republic* when the CED announced its proposals for post-war stability in January 1943.

On the liberal end of the political spectrum, different aspirations milled about. There were some who still thought in the terms of the early 1930s, and called for a genuine collectivist program: explicit national goals in jobs and housing and income maintenance; government-sponsored "planned production" in industry and agriculture, with wages and prices under firm public control; nationalization where necessary, as in public power and some forms of transportation; a central Planning agency. But this expansive vision was held by writers and academics, even socialists, that is, by no one of any practical importance. They talked, but they could not get a hearing where it mattered, in congressional halls or in the Roosevelt or Truman circles.

A milder brand of liberal Planning was stirring in these centers of power. There were liberal political leaders who wanted to go beyond the point where the New Deal had been arrested, and a sound instinct led them to concentrate upon goals. Franklin Roosevelt had been talking about social goals all his political life, and had signed many a bill into law with some declaratory opening remarks aiming at improvements in public standards of life, health, nutrition, and general well-being. But American laws by war's end held only a scattered, amorphous, and vague set of standards for judging public policy. So in January 1944, in his State of the Union address, Roosevelt announced as a war aim the "Economic Bill of Rights"—a right to a job, to an income sufficient to buy adequate food, shelter, and education, to trade without unfair competition. These were merely presidential hopes, not government policy. But they expressed the liberal instinct for more explicit social goals by which to measure policy. It was an instinct shared by other leading liberals. Vice President (1940–44) Henry A. Wallace, in his *Sixty Million Jobs* (1945), set an ambitious employment goal for post-war society. Such goals are the heart of Planning. Not surprisingly, Roosevelt had taken his Economic Bill of Rights from one of the last studies sent to him by the National Resources Planning Board before its demise at the hand of a hostile Congress.

Here we see American liberalism teetering between Planning and the post-New Deal Broker State. These two liberal leaders had only scratched the surface of the matter of national goals, of course. Wallace's full employment goal was narrower than Roosevelt's Economic Bill of Rights, and the latter was excessively vague on the issues of housing and education and did not touch physical and mental health, racial harmony and justice, privacy, environmental protection. Still the two men were advocating relatively explicit social goals where none had ever existed in any real sense. Such goals were the indispensable standards by which public intervention might be measured and public officials held accountable. They would push the political economy from ground where it was evaluated by process—was government reasonably democratic and orderly?—toward evaluation also by substance. If these steps had been taken, and the NRPB or some other national Planning board revived even in its modest role, to that extent the post-New Deal Broker State would have resumed an evolution toward the Planning ideal, an evolution interrupted in the 1930s.

But men who asked for explicit policy goals and a Planning Board of undetermined power were not proposing the final Great Leap to Planning. Many more changes would be required. Most immediately, the executive branch must be reorganized to group agencies by function; presidential policy review capabilities were woefully feeble; the congressional committee organization was archaic; the data-gathering and analysis capabilities in the executive and legislative branches were inadequate; social reporting was primitive and unappreciated; the technology assessment capacity vested in the Office of Scientific Research and Development (OSRD) was new (1941–) and puny and would not survive postwar retrenchment; economic, energy, transportation policies were scattered and had no place to become coherent. How many of these sources of governmental ineptitude could a revived NRPB have rectified? Perhaps Planning might have somehow evolved out of the Broker State arrangements worked out by 1945, if Roosevelt had lived. Rexford Tugwell for one has argued, in his book *Off Course* (1972), that Roosevelt would have resumed the fight for Planning after the war. He would know where government did not have adequate control of social development, and would devise ways to move from ad hoc intervention to comprehensive Planning.

Skeptics will always meet such an argument by pointing out Roosevelt's retreats and vacillations where the essentials of Planning are concerned. The discussion leads nowhere. FDR died of brain hemorrhage in April 1945, and was succeeded by a man without even Roosevelt's fluctuating interest in collectivism. Harry Truman was ready to fight for the New Deal as he understood it, but his conception of that heritage did not run beyond the Keynesian Broker State. He proved in subsequent years to have a genuine desire to expand the welfare benefits of the Broker State which went to the middle and lower classes, but he did not have even Roosevelt's doubts that interest-group bargaining within the existing political system was quite enough.

6

A focus for this swirl of ideas and impulses about the shape of the post-war political economy was provided when Senator James E. Murray and three other liberals introduced the Full Employment Bill in January 1945. The original draft of the bill, in its most important parts, read:

> The Congress hereby declares that . . . all Americans able to

work and seeking work have the right to useful remunerative, regular, and full-time employment. . . .

In order to assist industry, agriculture, labor and State and local governments in achieving continuing full employment, it is the responsibility of the Federal Government to pursue such consistent and openly arrived at economic policies and programs as will stimulate and encourage the highest feasible levels of employment opportunities through private and other non-Federal investment and expenditure; To the extent that continuing full employment cannot otherwise be achieved, it is the further responsibility of the Federal Government to provide such volume of Federal investment and expenditure as may be needed to assure continuing full employment; . . .

To the extent, if any, that such increased non-Federal investment and expenditures . . . are deemed insufficient to provide . . . full employment . . . the president shall transmit a general program for such Federal investment and expenditure . . . as will be sufficient . . . to assure a full employment volume of production.[5]

The bill committed the government, in effect, to spend until full employment was achieved. The President had to submit a national production and employment budget each year to Congress, forecasting the performance of the economy and outlining the policies to be followed to reach full employment. The President would be provided with a council of economic advisors to assist him, and the Congress would establish a joint economic committee to receive the President's report and legislative requests. All of this would in effect have established the sort of "Indicative" Planning that the French were to invent in the 1950s.

Had a depression followed the war there almost certainly would have been a full employment act, giving America a peacetime government with an economic goal of unprecedented specificity. Yet a combination of events and pressures, which few had foreseen, produced a much more limited outcome.

The bill, of course, raised opposition. For one thing, the CED did not speak for the entire business community. There were still many businessmen, perhaps most (and especially those in retail trade and smaller industry) who remained suspicious of a broad managerial role for government. "An occasional depression," said the New York State Chamber of Commerce, "is the price we pay for freedom," a strong statement of the old individualistic philosophy. And then the idea of federal spending seemed full of danger to many in 1945. The government would have to spend *for* something, and this would probably not be facilities which posed no threat to the private order, such as pyramids or burying bottles of banknotes in old coal mines (Keynes' whimsical idea), but perhaps more public power developments like TVA, more philanthropic agencies to assist the poor and disturb class and racial relations. And surely federal spending gave additional power to Leftist intellectuals and bureaucrats who listened to heavenly voices and had never met a payroll. Further, a government that spent had also to tax—the other side of fiscal policy —and no one could be sure that the tax structure might be seriously used to redistribute income.

While these thoughts stirred conservatives against the Full Employment bill, it had support among some businessmen, labor, and most other elements of the old Roosevelt coalition. But that support was eroded by the economic trends of 1945–46, which took the country largely by surprise. Economists had predicted a post-war recession or depression, recalling the slack consumer demand of the 1930s and taking note of the vast plant expansion of the war and the impending arrival of millions of servicemen to crowd the job market. In 1945, *Time* and *Newsweek* magazines predicted 5–7 million unemployed after the war, Senator Harley Kilgore predicted 18 million, and labor leader Sidney Hillman foresaw 10 million out of work.

Instead, a depression-raised generation was astonished to experience an immediate and sustained inflationary boom. Only a few economists had taken account of the huge volume of personal savings dammed up behind wartime rationing and savings bond programs. Quickly the attitude of major groups toward the government changed. In a depression, all needed help and accepted the need for controls and spending. In an inflationary situation, there was money to be made by those who had natural advantages and were ready to move quickly. Beginning in the autumn of 1945, virtually every major group began to demand that the government remove controls on wages and prices and get out of the way. Consumers, who might have stood as a constituency for controls, were powerless as usual. The Truman administration spent a miserable year, from fall 1945 to fall 1946, struggling to maintain some inflation curbs against strikes (United Auto Workers in November 1945, steelworkers in February, United Mine Workers in April, railway brotherhoods in May), receiving criticism from all sides. Against this background the Full Employment bill foundered. A majority in Congress were willing to give the President an economic council and continue the tacit understanding, sealed in the 1930s, that the government had important economic responsibilities. But there was no majority for the firm policy goals of the bill, which would have propelled even a reluctant government into a position of unambiguous responsibility for control over levels of employment and output. On February 20, 1946, Harry S Truman signed the Employment Act of 1946. The word "full" had been dropped from the title, so that the target of policy became a flexible and unthreatening bureaucratic sentence:

> The Congress hereby declares that it is the continuing policy and responsibility of the federal government to use all practicable means consistent with its needs and obligations . . . to coordinate and utilize all its plans, functions and resources for the purpose of creating and maintaining, in a manner calculated to foster and promote free competitive enterprise and the general welfare, conditions under which there will be afforded useful employment, for those able, willing, and seeking to work, and to promote maximum employment, production, and purchasing power.[6]

The President was given a council of economic advisers, Congress established the Joint Committee on the Economic Report. But the National Production and Employment Budget, which was as close as America had ever come to a national economic plan, was eliminated, as was Congress' responsibility to respond to it with appropriate legislation. As Robert Lekachman summarizes:

> Congress had carefully removed the political sting from S.380's tail. A president was asked only to prepare one more report. Congress was directed to do no more than study it. . . . The national budget and the awesome Joint Committee which was to evaluate it were guillotined. Nobody really had to do much more than he was currently doing.[7]

With its weaknesses, the Employment Act was a high-water mark in the growth of public social control. It established a statutory mandate for economic management, along with new machinery for continuous economic surveillance. Taken with the new institutions devised to extend some control over international trade—the Export-Import Bank set up in 1934, the more important International Monetary Fund and American-dominated World Bank established at Bretton Woods in 1944–45—the Employment Act of 1946 provided a sort of culmination for a fourteen-year surge of social control that had commenced with the inauguration of Franklin Roosevelt. Exhausted liberals thought it an admirable capstone. Conservatives reinforced this astigmatism by raising objections to the CEA especially. In fact the Employment Act was a culmination because nothing stronger could be salvaged from the Roosevelt era. But the whole Planning logic of the 1930s remained unfulfilled and, what was worse, misunderstood.

From the Employment Act to the 1960s

When the Employment Act finally cleared Congress and was signed by Harry Truman, the prospects for Planning were not merely bleak, but nonexistent. Roosevelt was dead, and Truman, while he turned out to have standard liberal beliefs on social policy, had nothing of Roosevelt's receptivity to Planning ideas. The economy had not collapsed after the war, and when economic crisis did not materialize businessmen and consumers quickly gained confidence that they could manage without obtrusive government intervention. Then the Cold War settled in, preoccupying the energies and subtly altering the outlook of all those involved in government. Throughout 1945 the new President and his advisers had been ensnarled in an intensifying conflict with the Soviet Union. By January 1946, Truman and his inner circle were deeply alarmed with the lack of progress toward what they thought acceptable post-war arrangements in eastern and central Europe. A month before signing the Employment Act, Truman had tongue-lashed his secretary of state, James Byrnes, for making concessions to the Soviets, and had moved his administration close to a war footing where the Soviets were concerned. On February 9, Joseph Stalin made a rare public speech in which he stressed the incompatibility between communism and capitalism. A month later Winston

Churchill made his "Iron Curtain" speech at Fulton, Missouri. The Cold War was a reality, at least as far as American national leadership was concerned. The Truman government would now give its central attention to alerting the public to its new international perils, and devising strategies to meet it.

In these changed circumstances the Truman administration de-controlled from wartime arrangements, retaining approximately the same authority and range of activities that had rested with the government at the end of the 1930s. Truman was to ask Congress repeatedly for a permanent commission to resist racial discrimination in employment, but this was really the only area of American life in which he proposed more or different intervention than FDR had asked by 1940. The Fair Deal was a continuation of the Broker State arrangements that people somewhat misleadingly called the New Deal, a bit more committed to racial justice, public aid to education and scientific research, entirely uninvolved with Planning ideas.

There have been writers who speculated that Roosevelt, if he had not died, would have resumed in some way the expansion of public intervention in American life. Tugwell's *Off Course* is such a book. Without concluding that there is nothing to be said for this somewhat elusive argument, one cannot fail to be struck by the generally conservative mood of the late 1940s. The American "parties of movement," to use Arno J. Mayer's term for the Left, did not recover the intensity, confidence, and mass potential of the 1930s. The socialists remained weak and politically insignificant, even without Roosevelt to steal their clothes and lure away their leaders to service in his liberal coalition. The tiny communist movement was routed from its ineffective schemings and virtually destroyed by government harassment. But these alternatives had never attracted broad support. In the liberal ranges of opinion one could see more clearly the chastened mood of the Left. Interest groups that had been a part of Roosevelt's coalition were edging toward the center. Organized labor, so militant in the depression, had begun during the war that long evolution back to the narrow unionist perspective that had characterized the Gompers era. By mid-century the communist penetration of the labor movement had been rooted out, and a militant anti-communism reinforced labor's narrowed perspectives. America's farmers had made larger economic gains during the war than any other group, and one heard no more of the angry stirrings of dissent that had come out of the Midwest and South in the inter-war years.

Liberal intellectuals were also moving toward accommodation with existing arrangements. Reading Reinhold Niebuhr, pondering the war and the history of recent totalitarian states, they developed doubts about humanity's basic motives and capacity for wisdom. Max Ascoli, in *The Power of Freedom* (1949), rediscovered the insights of Alexander Hamilton, Edmund Burke, and Tocqueville, developed a new wariness about the plans of bureaucrats. Arthur M. Schlesinger, Jr., warned in *The Vital Center* (1949) against utopian thinking and the concentration of political power. It was a time to appreciate what one had, to be skeptical of grand notions of social improvement. The New Deal–Fair Deal came to be a set of gains to be defended, rather than a mix of gains and aspirations in which unfinished tasks carried the most weight. Liberals wrote as if the distribution of income and wealth had been greatly equalized by New Deal and war, which it had not, and then seemed to lose interest in the issue. The market power of large corporations was even stronger after the war than when Roosevelt set up the TNEC to chart a major anti-monopoly drive. But little was heard of that after the war.

More important than liberal skepticism about the State was a new appreciation of American capitalism, now that it was hedged about with New Deal surveillance. Brain-truster Adolf A. Berle and TVA director David Lilienthal wrote admiringly of the large corporation at mid-century. These were merely two signs of a significant change, in liberal thought, from a primary stress on redistribution to a primary stress on growth. In the late 1940s liberals were finally coming around to the view, so long held by capitalists, that economic growth was a quicker and better road out of poverty than redistribution. No liberal economist put this more forcefully than Leon Keyserling, once an aide to

Senator Robert Wagner and one of Truman's first members of the CEA. Writing in a book entitled *Saving American Capitalism: A Liberal Economic Program* (1948), a collection of essays edited by Seymour Harris, Keyserling urged that the pie not be sliced up differently but, rather, enlarged. Policies to redistribute wealth impeded its formation, and the poor stood to gain more in the end by growth than by confiscation.

Of course, growth would not simply take care of itself. It required an active governmental use of what economist Alvin Hansen in the same book called "cycle policy," alert and timely Keynesian fiscal policies to maintain expansion. But the real source of growth was the private sector, a robust industrial capitalism. Keyserling, Hansen, Berle, Lilienthal, and other post-war liberals were granting important moral ground to those large industrialists and financiers who had been so unappreciated during the interminable depression decade. The new outlook was born in the war, and seemed more appropriate to liberals who now understood clearly that their mission was not to wound American capitalism mortally but to save it through continuous friendly regulation and a guarantee of mass purchasing power. Now both liberals and conservatives could be judged by the same pragmatic standard, the growth rate their policies could produce. As John Kenneth Galbraith wrote in the 1950s: "Everything happens as if Saint Peter, when receiving souls in heaven to send the ones to Paradise and the others to Hell, asked them only one question: 'What have you done on earth to increase the gross national product?' "[1]

This post-war lowering of liberal horizons has been many times remarked. Indeed it has been stressed so single-mindedly that one loses sight of the conflicts that made the political life of the 1940s and 1950s quite strenuous. The end of ideology that Daniel Bell foresaw in the 1950s was about as likely in America as the withering away of the State in Marxist Russia. Parties of movement continued to form up for struggle against existing arrangements. Harry Truman surprised people in September 1945 by going on the offensive, asking Congress for a twenty-one-point program which included more TVAs, a higher minimum wage, improved social security benefits. Senator Paul Douglas spent the late 1940s and the 1950s criticizing the tax system; Senator Estes Kefauver attacked the monopoly power of drug companies and public utilities; Glen Taylor and Hubert Humphrey spoke out against the racism imbedded in American institutions and attitudes. These policy criticisms are not insignificant, ought not to be forgotten. Plenty of heat was generated on these matters. But the boldest demands of national liberal figures pointed only to modest incremental changes. The basic framework of a post-New Deal political economy was assumed, accepted. One need only read the liberal literature of the time to sense its muted style and limited imagination. Some have seen this as post-war realism, the growing up of American liberalism. One either worked for incremental improvements in the post-New Deal system, or became an irrelevant socialist. Americans could choose between the Vital Center, as Schlesinger put it, or unworkable totalitarian extremes. In developing this perception of the practical and ideological possibilities, liberals in the 1940s and 1950s were forgetting that a different system had beckoned in the 1930s, a Planned society.

Events had done to Planning what Khrushchev had said that communism would do to capitalism, had buried it by mid-century. When Lewis Lorwin wrote his *A Time for Planning* in 1945 he was able to fill 266 pages with arguments he thought plausible. They fell upon unreceptive ears. Planning in 1933 was an intriguing new idea; by the late 1940s it had a small but distasteful reputation. One could point to the dismal experience of the NRA, or, with more effect, to the disturbing association of Planning with totalitarian systems of Right and Left, with the U.S.S.R. and Nazi Germany. Perhaps Planning was in the end incompatible with free institutions. The record could be read that way in the mid-1940s, before France, Britain, Sweden, and other Western European democracies had begun their long and diverse experiences with Planning that are today so instructive. And it was read that way in many tracts and books, the most important of them Walter Lippmann's *The Good Society* (1937), which found Planning beyond men's capacities, and Friedrich A.

Hayek's *The Road to Serfdom* (1944), where the objections were moral and political. John Kenneth Galbraith has summarized the poor fortune of the word planning in the following terms:

> Until the end of World War II, or shortly thereafter, planning was a moderately evocative word in the United States. It implied a sensible concern for what might happen in the future and a disposition, by forehanded action, to forestall avoidable misfortune. . . . With the Cold war, however, the word planning acquired ideological overtones. . . . Modern liberalism . . . avoided the term and conservatives made it one of opprobrium. For a public official to be called an economic planner was less serious than to be charged with Communism or imaginative perversion, but it reflected adversely nonetheless.[2]

The experience with totalitarian systems, particularly the Soviet Union, weighed heavily in such opinions. At the same time, American intellectuals had come around to an appreciation of the staggering difficulties involved in managing this vast society. In retrospect, the task faced by aspiring Planners did appear to dwarf contemporary human capacities, as conservatives always insisted. The country was 3000 miles across, held 135 million people who in 1945 produced $213 billion worth of goods and services through a set of interactions which no social scientist understood except in broadest outline. This vast population responded to unmeasured hopes and fears, the availability of credit, the haphazard appearance of new technologies and products, shifting rates of interest, and daily calculations of advantage. The decisions of private citizens were a dark continent of unpredictability, and this was only to a slightly less degree true of public officials. There were 116,000 separate governmental units in America at mid-century, taxing, spending, subsidizing, promoting, and penalizing in a whirl of uncoordinated motions.

In light of such realities, the compromise political economy that emerged helter-skelter out of the 1930s took on a certain appropriateness. John Chamberlain in his *The American Stakes* (1941) saw great merit in the post-New Deal "broker state" which admitted all organized interest groups to a share of power, exercising its light, prudent, consensual managerial role within the confines of what those groups would accept. John Kenneth Galbraith would make a similar defense of the system in *American Capitalism* (1952). To Galbraith, a rational public policy could be arrived at very satisfactorily by the interplay of organized interest groups. If the government found some important group unorganized, such as labor had been in the early 1930s, it could simply assist that group toward organization so that it might join the other bargainers in the marketplace of political power. To set policy by such mechanisms may have been "muddling through," but to post-war liberals it appeared to encourage a vigorous democracy of contending citizens' associations, and was wiser in the end than the five-year plans handed down by remote experts. It was also argued that the post-New Deal political economy reduced the level of conflict by decentralizing and obscuring the sites of power and decision-making, and that the American civil service had an approachable, responsive style quite refreshing by comparison with the commissars or venal incompetents of more centralized regimes both Left and Right.

During a decade and more after the war there was little liberal opposition to the foregoing arguments and the assumptions behind them. There settled in an impressive consensus that the American economy must be managed, and *was* managed quite adequately. The 1948 symposium *Saving American Capitalism* brought together leading liberal thinkers, and their hesitancy about the word "planning" was conspicuous. "The country needs an economic plan," the book began, "or at the very least an economic program for action."[3] The authors concentrated on a Keynesian program, not Planning, with the exception of NRPB veteran Charles Merriam. Seymour Harris' comment was typical: "Monetary and fiscal policy . . . may well suffice in a system of democratic planning and may make advanced planning unnecessary."[4]

This perspective has controlled the future, from 1948 into the 1970s. The dissenting Planners had one last complaint, and then were silent. Rexford Tugwell and Edward Banfield surveyed the prospects for Planning at mid-century and lamented the half-way house America had occupied. The government was busy on many fronts, but "what was most seriously lacking at mid-century was this definition of national goals," as well as a theory of how to set social priorities, and a system of social-interest accounting. "We are a long way still," they were forced to concede, "from the kind of comprehensive planning and action that is required if we are to conserve, develop and use our national resources."[5] Despite many gains for collective controls on social evolution, they found an unplanned society in 1950—a collection of federal agencies moving from year to year and problem to problem without central guidance, a Congress too large and understaffed to seize the initiative, a Presidency with the appearance of great power but in reality half-paralyzed by slack party discipline, congressional delaying procedures, and the multiple divisions of federalism. But their sense of disappointment found no resonance on the American Left. Planning was a road we had not taken, and there was no disposition to look back.

2

If substantial changes in the American system were not to be proposed by the Left after the argument over the Employment Act, what of the Right? Much of the Republican party, the Herbert Hoover wing, had never accepted the New Deal. Such people kept pointing to the losing Willkie and Dewey campaigns in 1940 and 1944, the me-too campaigns, as proof that Republicans should present a sharp alternative—basically repeal the New Deal. This persuasion in the party remained formidable, and the party itself was strengthened in congressional elections in 1942 and again in 1946. Was the New Deal itself in some jeopardy?

Some read that message in the post-war political currents. Old Senator K. D. McKellar led the fight to kill TVA, which he thought socialistic and a hotbed of racial integrationists. TVA survived, eventually, but indulged in no more dreams of changing Appalachian society other than with cheap electricity. Conservatives had more success in attacks upon the WPA, the NRPB, and the FSA; all were removed from the *Government Organization Manual* by 1946. Extend this sort of thing indefinitely, and the country would be back to 1929. Many liberals thought this a possibility.

They misread the signs. Change was not wanted by the great majority. Consolidation was. Groups hostile to the New Deal would have to be satisfied with the little pruning mentioned above, and with the over-rated Taft-Hartley amendment to the labor relations act passed over Truman's veto in 1947. Both parties would learn to live with what irritated individualists called big government, the Welfare State. This was infinitely easier with the jaunty Roosevelt gone. Time gradually brought a certain tolerance of New Deal innovations. Employers who had threatened to leave the country rather than bargain collectively with organized labor found the process more bearable than expected. Wage increases could be passed on to consumers, and union leadership turned out to be reliable in contractual arrangements and mercifully uninterested in influencing corporate decisions outside worker compensation. Social security, which seemed worth a major fight in the mid-1930s, faded into the background without making people lazy, or adding to the tax burden on capital, or even ending economic insecurity for the aged or unemployed. Farm subsidies added a trifle to the cost of government, but at least the farmers were quiet, and were better consumers than before Roosevelt. Budget deficits were less shocking after the war than before, as it became clear that the nation could easily pay the carrying charges not only on the $50 billion deficit that the New Deal ran up, but the $250 billion deficit required to subdue Germany and Japan.

These perspectives were reinforced among businessmen, the natural enemies of the New Deal, by the new businessmen's organization, the Committee for Economic Development. The CED argued that government had an indispensable role to play in economic stabilization, that this might involve occasional deficits and certainly involved regulation, and that this role could be pursued without the class antagonisms and rash social experimentation of the febrile years from 1933 to 1938. Such a government would not be liberal, but conservative in the most obvious sense. The positive State would use fiscal and monetary tools, with sensible regulation, to eliminate or dampen the economic fluctuations that had produced so much suffering and radicalism in the unforgettably recent past.

With the spread of this perspective in American industrial and financial circles, a consensus jelled in the post-war years. It had been incubated by the war, when government and business had worked together with far greater effectiveness and less abrasiveness than either had expected. But its roots actually went back to those far-sighted founders of the National Civic Federation prior to World War I, who had even then urged acceptance by capitalists of the regulatory State. Within the consensus there would of course be room for bitter struggle over the details of regulating, taxing, and spending. But more important under these conflicts was the common ground of agreement which so marks off the 1940s and after from the 1930s and before. With the necessity of a positive State agreed upon across a broad center, with Roosevelt gone and his "boys with their hair ablaze" having bowed out or been pushed out, the nation entered a fifteen-to-twenty-year period of policy continuity. As there was bipartisan agreement on the basic commitment to internationalism in foreign policy, so there was agreement on the positive State at home. As a practical matter, the extremes no longer existed.

This calm reflection is permitted from a distance, but was not clear at all in the turbulent post-war era. People with long memories will object, insisting that the country literally seethed through the forties and fifties with what Mr. Dooley once called "moist and numerous language," with hot debate with hard ideological outlines. This is true enough, and there was at least one occasion when the crazies would appear almost ready to get it together. Strom Thurmond established a third party for Southern racists in 1948, and collected 39 electoral votes. That was the year when the Left also made its most determined break from consensus. Commerce Secretary Henry A. Wallace had departed the Truman Cabinet, criticized the administration's foreign policies, and formed his own third party, the Progressives, out of stray elements of the Left edge of Roosevelt's coalition, socialists, and communists. One hesitates to link the retrograde and racist effort of Thurmond with the Wallace campaign, which expressed so many sound criticisms of Truman policies and American life in general. But in one sense they carry similar meanings. Both claimed a mere 1.1 million votes, and one must take this, along with Norman Thomas' 140,000 (he knew that Wallace was no socialist), as a rough measure of the non-consensual sentiment in that restless year. The total of Truman's and Dewey's votes was 46 million. Almost half the electorate did not bother to vote.

And so the post-New Deal political economy had established an uneasy but basically durable acceptance. It is true that not a year went by in Congress, perhaps not even a month between 1945 and 1960, when some rugged individualist with a third-rate legal education would not rise and call for the abolition of the progressive income tax, termination of farm subsidies, or an end to socialism in the Tennessee Valley. When well placed in committee posts, such representatives had a pernicious influence on the Broker State programs that moderate people were trying earnestly to improve. But their basic desire for an end to government, except for carrying the mails and policing the seas, was futile. Even with the McCarthy movement to give idle hands something to do, the wild men of the Right, the anti-statists, found post-war society truly conservative, much to their disgust. Americans basically wanted no trouble, no change in fundamental institutions. The real enemies of that messy, meddlesome giant, the Broker State, could not get a hearing, were marooned off in Texas or the Midwest, stuck with their radio programs and letters to the editor and thin paperback exposés, unable to elect more than a handful of like-minded individualists to rail in Congress against the United Nations, fluoridated water, and the Welfare State.

3

Harry Truman's virtues have been rediscovered so enthusiastically in the past few years that even Senator Goldwater now lists him as his favorite President, and Gerald Ford displays his bust in the Oval Office. Truman was honest, candid, direct. His profanity was of the good American kind, that is, he used it only when irritated. He did not like Russians, and was "firm" with them. He made decisions when required, and then did not indulge in remorse. There was no excess in him, little pettiness. These and other qualities of the little man from Independence have risen in our esteem as we have observed other presidents after him. The public has long since forgiven him for not having FDR's gifts. (Presumably Senator Goldwater counted that to Truman's credit from the beginning.) At the time when Vice President Truman came so humbly forward to take Roosevelt's place, contemporaries were shocked that he had so little of FDR's air of command, magnetic liberalism, political flair. From the perspective of one interested in Planning, however, what one notices most about Truman is that Roosevelt had been, and he was not.

Truman, one recalls, had come up through a very different America from Roosevelt's. He was raised in a small town, was chiefly self-educated, had no contact with large eastern universities. He had not traveled much, was not familiar with large corporations, large law firms, large cities, complex state governments. Unlike FDR, he had little executive experience before entering the White House, most of it coming in his years as county judge. It is not surprising that while President he never developed an acute awareness of the malorganization of the executive branch. He never expressed anything approaching his predecessor's frustration at the domestic weaknesses of the Presidency itself, even though he faced a stalemated political situation during his entire tenure and FDR did not really reach this barrier until his first six years had passed. Truman was never at ease with experts from outside the political world, especially academics, had found little occasion prior to 1945 to organize their services for his use. He had almost nothing of Roosevelt's appetite for planning staffs to provide data on social developments or a modest bit of warning through forecasting. He did not have FDR's life-long interest in conservation of natural resources, so nourishing to the impulse to see things in their total web of relationships. He hardly had time, with international crisis, to develop that suspicion of hardened bureaucratic arteries that FDR learned in the intense period of domestic experimentation that commenced the moment he took office. Finally, Harry Truman was a friend and product of the Pendergast political machine, and a man whose deepest political instincts were toward regularity. He would not be the initiator, as FDR had occasionally been, of efforts to reform the political system that put him where he was. These individual characteristics combined with the narrowing political boundaries and the Rightward trend of post-war liberalism to make the Truman era a time of little change in the government's managerial structure and functions.

Truman had supported the Full Employment bill, but if he understood the issues at stake he did not fight for them, and was not disappointed with the squashy mandate and minimal policy machinery the Employment Act gave the government. It had passed in February, but by July, Truman had not named his economic advisers. Some liberal pressure developed, and Truman picked the conservative Brookings economist, Edwin G. Nourse, as chairman, with New Dealer Leon Keyserling and a Nebraska dean of business administration, John D. Clark. The President actually did not feel a strong need of economic advice, at least not from economists, and he used CEA very little. This did not trouble Nourse, who was a cautious man who is remembered chiefly for stubbornly defending the view, controverted vigorously by disappointed supporters of the CEA, that the council should be a low-profile agency, never testifying before Congress or lobbying however subtly for its views. In the first weeks of organizing the CEA, some housing bureaucrat suggested that the agency occupy the old offices of the NRPB. Nourse refused to accept those quarters for fear of infection, by association, with the late agency's reputation for radicalism, deficit spending, Planning, and other perversions.

Whatever the sponsors of the CEA had intended it to be—we know that some people dreamed that it might forecast, take the lead in coordination of programs, prepare contingency plans, educate the public, produce analyses of programs, all functions having to do with Planning no matter how defined—it was far less than that under Truman's first chairman. Nourse was not guarded about his own conception of his legislative mandate: "The Employment Act reaffirms and, in fact, makes more explicit and comprehensive than ever before the national policy of adhering to a system of predominantly private enterprise."[6] This was not exactly wrong, but it certainly missed the point liberals were trying to make when they set up the CEA, the economic report, and the Joint Economic Committee—and, almost, the commitment to a goal of full employment. The CEA was to give the President early warning on the inevitable malfunctions of the "free enterprise" economy, if that is what one wishes to call it, and recommend correctives. Nourse had little zeal for the whole idea, and this appears to have suited Truman just fine.

Fortunately for both men, reconversion proceeded without recession, and until 1950 the rate of unemployment never rose above 5.5 per cent. Inflation worried Truman, but it dropped to quite reasonable levels by 1948. If it had not, there are signs that Truman would have waited long and patiently before suggesting an incomes policy. In the first economic report, issued on January 8, 1947, when inflation was uncomfortably high, Truman and the CEA said that only private enterprise could hold the line against rising prices. When the Korean War came, Truman showed a marked disinclination to interfere with free enterprise. The sudden mobilization was sure to produce inflationary pressures and shortages, but Truman asked Congress only for selective controls on credit, although there was considerable Democratic sentiment for wage-price controls. Nourse resigned, and, after some hesitation, Truman appointed the activist Keyserling as chairman. Keyserling was expected to make a big difference, but he didn't. He liked to testify before committees and publicize the fact that he and CEA advised the President, liked to do battle for "the President's program." This was unlike Nourse, and irritated so many Republicans that the future of CEA was in doubt when Eisenhower came to power. But Keyserling's louder advice was rather conventional. He agreed with Truman that the economy was an admirable machine just as it stood, and would sicken under a "strait jacket" of control.

When war spending finally forced controls in 1951, Truman then resisted the idea of entrusting them to a new planning board, as was often suggested. Truman split control authority between an obscure little agency called the National Security Resources Board, under Stuart Symington, and a new Economic Stabilization Agency which eventually grew to the bureaucratic peak of two. These little structures, so half-heartedly added to the government's administrative apparatus, were extinguished in 1953 with no complaints. Truman had invested nothing in them, and in fact he left the CEA in a shaky position, with five economic reports to its credit and Keyserling's aggressive fiscal activism to its political detriment among incoming Eisenhower conservatives. People who had wanted Truman to act upon the most positive interpretation of the Employment Act's muddled mandate were to be disappointed.

4

One major controversy of the Truman years did potentially affect the basic structure of the political economy, and that was that hardy perennial, executive branch reorganization. In the 1930s the subject had come up because Roosevelt found the Presidency as an institution too weak to carry out its expected duties. He was able to improve the situation, but serious flaws remained. Major governmental functions were dispersed throughout numerous agencies and departments, and the executive could not coordinate their activities. This weakness remained after World War II, but somehow escaped public notice. Executive branch organization did in fact come up as a prominent issue, but not because a president appealed for help in carrying out his duties. It came up from a different quarter, and for different reasons.

Congressmen had always thought the executive was too strong. This was their occupational perspective. After a world war had distended the executive branch, it seemed opportune to scrutinize it for waste, for bureaucratic imperialism, for unjustified functions. The Hoover commissions of 1947–49 and 1953–55 arose out of a concern that the executive branch was too large, too strong, and badly organized. Perhaps its power could be cut back? This impulse had the potential for a re-ordering of the political economy, a repeal of the New Deal through administrative reform. As the reorganization controversy of the 1930s did not give Roosevelt the Planning capacities he had wanted, so post-war reorganization efforts did not trim executive power. Both were disappointments to those who initiated them. But their instincts were at least partially correct in both cases. Executive organization was a crucial variable in defining the American system of government. Shift it one way, and the Broker State halfway house would move toward 1929; shift it another, and the movement was toward Planning.

The impetus for reform in the 1940s came from congressional sources. This accounts for the legislative charge of the 1947 reorganization commission, which directed its attention toward the executive branch. Congressional organization was probably the leading scandal in American public administration, but this was ignored in the 1947 resolution setting up what became the first Hoover Commission. Yet the executive branch deserved its own study, however one looked at it. The war had swollen it to unmanageable size and complexity, and even Harry Truman acknowledged that confusion and waste had reached intolerable proportions as the government squirmed back into a peacetime assignment. The National Security Act of 1947 had brought a degree of order to the national security establishment that would seem adequate for more than a decade. But the domestic functions of government cried out for rationalization. Some would say they cried out for abolition. Reorganization had diverse support.

We know of Roosevelt's experience with this non-electric issue. People who are bored by discussions of executive organization ought to know how many times it has been agitated with so little effect. This alone makes the issue intriguing. Theodore Roosevelt had first fretted at the disorder in his own house of expanding bureaucracies, and had appointed the Keep Commission (1905–9) to study what might be done. William Howard Taft had similar feelings about the branch he headed, and set up a committee of his own to remedy its deficiencies. Congress paid little attention to these murmurings. Not until the war, and the Overman Act of 1918, did Congress grant a president the right to regroup the proliferating agencies of the executive branch. But with the end of war came the end of the Overman Act authority. Harding and Coolidge made do with what they had. Establishment of the Budget Bureau in 1921 plugged a major hole. Then came the more alert and far-sighted Hoover, who soon developed a strong desire to reorganize the instrumentalities he inherited. He gained power to propose reorganizations in the Economy Act of 1932, but the eleven orders he issued were nullified by Congress out of deference to the incoming Roosevelt. We have seen how FDR failed to appreciate the extent to which administrative confusion would defeat his purposes, how he let the authority of the 1932 law lapse without using it effectively. And we have seen how little he was able to extract from a non-compliant Congress when he made a leading issue of reorganization in 1937–39.

By Truman's day the government was even larger and more confused in function and organization than in the 1930s. It was also expensive, at least by the standards of the day. A new gesture toward reorganization was inevitable. When it materialized in Congress in 1947, Truman endorsed the idea. This was wise, for he was able then to influence the commission's composition and charge. In the early days of the commission there was talk that its jurisdiction included a mandate to recommend abolition of those governmental programs the commissioners did not like. Truman-appointed commissioners such as Dean Acheson and James Rowe resisted this idea, and the re-election of Truman in November 1948 turned it back entirely. Chairman Herbert Hoover, who had considered with what one must imagine as a distinct pleasure the prospect of deciding whether TVA or social security or mandatory collective bargaining should be dis-recommended, made a statesmanlike decision just after the election returns were in. At a press conference in mid-November he announced the decision to shun substantive issues and concentrate upon efficiency at those tasks the Congress had already voted. The "major functions of government are determinable as needed by the Congress," Hoover declared: "It is not our function to say whether it should exist or not, but . . . to see if we cannot make it work better."[7] With this decision the first Hoover Commission scotched its own potential to repeal the New Deal. It now faced a serious and important assignment.

The commission worked enormously hard for two years and produced a final report in 1949 supported by 2 million words of findings delivered by 23 task forces. One hundred and twenty-four reforms were recommended, and the commission predicted both managerial improvements and savings if their advice were taken. The commission played the "savings" angle rather hard, hoping for a grateful public. But it admitted that at best only 2 per cent of the national budget could be saved by economies, and knew that the chief problem in American government was not waste but executive weakness—in its own words, "division," "diffusion," "weakened management," "inadequate authority." The government had grown four times larger in personnel and twelve times larger in spending since Hoover had taken office in 1929. This would be difficult for a president to administer if it were optimally designed. It was not, as the Brownlow Committee had said only twelve years before. "The President needs help" was at least as true in 1949 as in 1937. Fifty-two separate departments and agencies reported to him, with major functions scattered almost willfully across the organizational map. Conflict and cross-purposes could be found on every hand. Executive authority was inadequate at levels below the President, as well. Cabinet heads often had less staff assistance and reorganizational power than plain common sense required, and this was especially true of the Department of Defense. These problems the Hoover Commission saw, and tried to address.

What solutions would objective intelligence suggest, pondering the problem without tenderness for bureaucratic or political interests? The literature of public administration is full of disagreement over such questions as whether administration can/should be separated from "politics," whether administrators should be detached professionals or committed advocates—but there is broad agreement on the first principle that should guide federal administrative organization. Governmental units should be grouped as nearly as possible by major purpose, so that clear lines of authority and accountability may emerge and cross-purposes be minimized. The Hoover Commission endorsed the "major purpose grouping" idea.

As an experienced BOB official has wisely commented, "adherence to the principle of organizing according to major purpose provides no automatic answers."[8] A government as large as ours will never be tidy, or free of overlapping assignments. One would expect ten separate reorganization commissions to produce ten different reform designs, even if all recognized the principle of organization by major purpose. There was nothing inevitable, for example, about the Brownlow Committee's formula of putting all agencies—including the headless "4th branch" that Congress invented, the independent regulatory commissions—under twelve line departments. What was inevitable as a result of any serious study of executive branch organization was a threat to the bureaucratic status quo. Many eggs have to be broken. The principle of consolidation according to major function is a cannon loose on the cluttered deck of American national government. The only question in 1948, after the Hoover Commission got down to serious work, was how far it would follow the subversive principles of functional organization. When the shouting was over, it had not followed them terribly far.

Many of its twelve members were former bureaucrats; all were cautious, responsible men (no women, not that it would have mattered), not eager to raise a painful controversy. They saw organizational confusion and fragmentation, but the costs were concealed, and were they so high? Something must be yielded to tradition, to ongoing working relationships. And the long days of hard digging into the governmental machinery showed them the federal bureaucrat as a well-meaning and rather competent public servant.

And so the Hoover group trimmed. It had recognized the issue of functional grouping, called it the doctrine of "coherent missions," and actually followed the idea far enough to suggest that the Corps of Engineers lose its dam-building and public works functions to Interior. Certain transportation activities scattered about the government, such as the Maritime Commission or the public roads administration, ought to go over to Commerce, where transportation policy might possibly emerge. Only one new department seemed required, a department of welfare (or social security and education, if one preferred). To build it, one transferred the Bureau of Indian Affairs from Interior, for example, in addition to the obvious social insurance and education activities.

This was nibbling, and here it stopped. If departments are designed for delivery of services, for major functions, how to justify retaining Agriculture for a single day, or Labor or Commerce? These were built upon the constituency principle, placating the three largest interest groups. The commission left them as they were, after shuffling a few agencies around on the functional principle, such as taking the Forest Service from Agriculture and putting it in Interior. Major functions are relatively obvious: Treasury, Attorney General, Postmaster, State, and Defense, none of which were threatened by the functional principle, and after them Human Resources, Natural Resources, Economic Affairs, and Community Development. One might argue about the above functional categories. I have borrowed them from a bold reorganization plan that came twenty years after Hoover's first report. But some such categories as these must absorb the old constituency departments of the Cabinet under a rational reorganization. The Hoover Commission shrank from such a hard duty. Indeed, the commissioners were considerate of existing arrangements across the board. They recommended consolidation of fragments, but somehow left twelve agencies outside departmental boundaries, including TVA, AEC, and the Veterans' Administration. These had simply too much political strength to trifle with. As for the regulatory commissions, Hoover actually told the press that they were not a part of the executive branch at all. Where that left them one could not be sure, apart from their close friendship with certain congressional committees. On the commission's final chart the regulatory agencies were suspended, in C. Herman Pritchett's words, "like Mahomet's coffin," up in a corner.

With the principal flaws of executive organization essentially ignored, the Hoover Commission went on to make over two-hundred recommendations, many of them quite useful. Moribund agencies would be abolished, paperwork reduced, civil service methods improved, and so on. These were perhaps worth the effort of members and staff, and the expenditure of $2 million. Surely it was good for the bureaucracy to be so minutely scrutinized. Looking over the commission report, one concludes that members found the situation desperate, but not serious. Truman accepted many of their recommendations, and forwarded them to Congress. Changes were made. But no important ones. We might check the litmus test for rational reorganization, whether the Army Corps of Engineers had its civil works functions relocated where the President could coordinate them with other activities. This did not happen, a clear sign that little of any fundamental importance had. It should not have surprised Hoover when he was called upon again in the 1950s to address the problem of executive branch organization.

In this entire episode the President had maintained a low profile. He was of course busy through the commission's first months, at least, with an election which might have prematurely retired him. But Truman was about as interested in reorganization as he had been in the issues raised by the full employment bill. Here he simply had none of Roosevelt's perspectives. A long list of matters had a higher priority with him than reform of the government's organization—on the domestic side of the government, at any rate. The organizational flaws on the national security side, it must be said, did not escape his attention. He took a leading and crucial role in armed services unification, and in reorganizing the national security apparatus after the war. But for some reason this sensitivity to organizational weakness did not transfer to the rest of the government, which was to be the Hoover Commission's principal concern. Truman was relieved when Hoover decided to keep reorganization from becoming a conservative purge of New Deal agencies, and after that he let matters take their course. If he had views on executive branch organization, a strategy of any kind, we do not know what it was. In his memoirs Truman mentions the Hoover Commission only once in two fat volumes, recalling the marginal fact that he did not want the RFC moved to the Treasury.

What did reorganization have to do with Planning? To the commission and its friends, absolutely nothing. The goal was "better management," perhaps some savings. Only time would bring out the teleology of "better management," and reveal its inexorable evolution in the Planning direction. Here, as the Dan Smoots of our society have tried so earnestly to tell us, there is involved the matter of creep. Fundamental change sometimes comes in tiny increments, under other names. Reorganization is creeping Planning. Thoroughgoing reorganization of the executive branch would not in itself ensure coherent national policy in basic areas. It would simply make coherent policy intellectually and administratively possible for the first time. Without reorganization, coherent policy was flatly impossible. And national Policy in basic areas of social change is one of the vital elements of the Planning capacity.

5

Harry Truman's reputation has fluctuated considerably in the brief period since 1952. His foreign policies have been described as aggressive or as courageous, his domestic liberalism has been measured against his problems with the verdict ranging widely. Our scrutiny of his Presidency has been somewhat narrowly focussed on his response to the problems of social management in a post-New Deal Broker political economy. Here Truman was a caretaker, with little vision of his own. Not that he failed to go one single step beyond Roosevelt. Liberals were pleased to find Truman far more ready than FDR to expand social intervention in racial relations, to improve national health care and public education. But these were isolated commitments, and ineptly pursued. Truman left behind little record of structural sensitivity, or of long-range perspectives.

One exception to the latter generalization was his appointment in January 1951 of a commission on materials policy. The Paley (after chairman William S. Paley) Commission report came out in five volumes in 1952, and bore the Cold War title, *Resources for Freedom*. Its estimates of commodity and energy needs were in error, as we can see upon arriving at the year it picked for most projections, 1975. But the report was a valuable and unique review of the outlook for key commodities, energy sources, and the likely impact of technology on these. Its criticisms of existing governmental policies were muted but acute, and if they had been adopted much trouble would have been saved later on. The commission was "strongly of the opinion," for example, "that the Nation's energy problem must be viewed in its entirety and not as a loose collection of independent pieces," that "the hydra heads of energy policy must be reined together" into a national policy.[9] It is painful, in retrospect, to recall that Truman did nothing to follow up the commission's lead, and of course Congress was too busy with its blend of routine business and the fight against Communism.

For Truman's part, his short-range, caretaker attitude mirrored the public complacency about domestic institutions. He fully shared the prevailing conviction that the basic direction of American life was correct and touched by the good fates. Foreign policy, in any event, claimed most of Truman's time. His memoirs engage the reader with Greece, Berlin, Korea, China—not with income distribution, nutrition, population, health care, soil erosion. The assignment for political leaders, as he saw it, was to ensure America's international survival and pre-eminence. He never would have counted it grounds for criticism or regret that he handed over to Eisenhower in 1953 a Broker State system little changed from the compromise struck at the end of the 1930s.

6

1952! At last the prospects for governmental change were strong enough to quicken the pulse of conservatives. The Republican Party reclaimed the presidency behind General Eisenhower. Now the government could be driven back from the salients that liberal meddlers had driven deep into private lives. Counterrevolution hung in the air. The Republican platform and the Eisenhower campaign had promised retrenchment of public activity, an unleashing of private choice. But almost nothing of significance changed. This was the central story of the 1950s for those interested in American government.

This outcome was certainly not clear at the beginning. General Eisenhower, although not sure in 1948 which party he belonged to, turned out to be an instinctive Republican. He didn't think the government ought to be doing it, whatever it was, unless there was an awfully good reason. He expressed public doubts about TVA, wondered if it could be sold to some enterprising businessman. He had similar doubts about social security. Conservatives were appointed to Cabinet posts to help the President in the work of retrenchment and reform—Ezra Taft Benson to Agriculture because he did not believe in production controls or a government-supported market, George Humphrey to the Treasury because he didn't believe in deficits. An early announcement assured the country that Korean War economic controls would end, and another promised a 10 per cent cut in the federal budget. Department heads were instructed to come up with their lists of expendable people and programs. "Throughout 1953," wrote Edwin Dale, Jr., "the commonest word in Washington was 'rif' (reduction in force)."[10] While this purifying across-the-board cut was being readied, longer-range strategies were being devised. Eisenhower asked Herbert Hoover to head a second commission to examine the executive branch, in the expectation that this time, with a Republican President and Republican control of both houses, some real changes could be proposed and carried through. And Meyer Kestnbaum chaired a commission on intergovernmental relations to seek out those federal activities that could be graciously and speedily handed over to the states.

The post-New Deal system seemed in major jeopardy. It was not. Frustration, disappointment, compromise became the humiliating daily companions of Eisenhower's "modern Republican" regime. Some 200,000 government personnel were cut from the payroll in that first year, but most of them had been involved in war-related activities that were now at an end. The size of the civilian federal employee force stabilized at about 2.3 million and remained there throughout Eisenhower's tenure, with some tendency to inch upward. The monster bureaucracy of Harry Truman turned out upon examination to be a lean civil service, just barely adequate to its responsibilities.

Ike's people took this as a long drawn out defeat, to which they became reconciled practically but never ideologically. A major setback came when the Kestnbaum Commission reported in June 1955. One could tell at a glance that their search for federal activities which could be turned over to lower levels of government had yielded next to nothing. For their recommendations were nowhere listed in bold relief. The report surveyed major federal programs in masterfully cautious bureaucratic language, occasionally suggesting that if a state came up with appropriations and satisfied federal authorities of its good intentions it might someday be allowed to rent or even buy a program from the Washington government. And at a few places the review backfired and hinted that good management might require nationalization of some state administered activity, such as civil defense or unemployment insurance. Conservatives who had been out of power for twenty years had ignorantly assumed that the structure of federal responsibilities would crumble upon business-like inspection. But when a commission of bi-partisan make-up and staffed by seasoned public administrators and academics made that inspection they found not one single major federal activity that could reasonably be performed elsewhere. As a consequence, wrote an observer, "it would be difficult to find a commission whose report was so vaguely worded and so quickly forgotten."[11]

At least, the Congress and public quickly forgot it. Eisenhower, who had asked for the commission in March 1953, could not bring himself to accept this disappointing outcome. He continued to raise the issue with aides, and in 1957 invited the nation's governors to look over the federal government for programs they might wish to move closer to the people. A committee of governors and top federal officials was formed to conduct a raiding party upon New Deal frivolities, worked for a year, and suggested perhaps vocational education and sewer plant grants. Nothing happened. Eisenhower accepted defeat.

The second Hoover Commission took an entirely different route to the same practical result. Where the Kestnbaum group had not been able to find federal activities to shunt to lower levels of government, the Hoover Commission this time around found the feds doing countless things they had no business doing, and doing them badly. In its 1955 report, which contained 314 recommendations for reform and rested upon 3.3 million words of staff commentary, the commission, in the words of its staff directors,

present (s) a documented picture of a sprawling and voracious bureaucracy, of monumental waste, excesses and extravagances, of red tape, confusion, and disheartening frustrations, of loose management, regulatory irresponsibilities, and colossal largess to special segments of the public. . . .[12]

It hoped to arouse the public with horror stories of waste and inefficiency, telling the taxpayer how much it cost to write a letter from Washington, or the number of different federal forms, or that the Navy used twice as many eggs in a ration as the Army.

Again life was to cheat Hoover. The golden opportunity, if it existed at all, had been in 1953, when Eisenhower was still interested in reform, when ardor for root-and-branch change ran high in the new administration. By 1955 the administration was already tired, somewhat cynical, and a great deal wiser. The Democrats had regained control of Senate and House. And anyway Hoover's report was too long and wordy. Even had it not been, it arrived quite out of phase with favorable political moods. Eisenhower was no longer interested in repealing the New Deal, and armies of Democrats and bureaucrats stood ready to rebuff the General had he tried. Minor recommendations could be put through, and were. But at the end, after Hoover's second great reorganization effort, the executive branch remained much the same as it had been in 1947.

Much more was actually accomplished by a less conspicuous group, the Advisory Committee on Government Organization, a triad of non-ideological liberal Republicans—chairman Nelson Rockefeller and academics Milton Eisenhower and Arthur Flemming. While Hoover's aroused staff searched for horror stories to mass the public against the New Dealish bureaucracy, the Advisory Committee prepared reorganization plans which set up a Council on Foreign Economic Policy, advisory committees on water resources, transportation, and telecommunications, and the Office of Presidential Science Advisor. These were small but enlightened steps affecting primarily the White House, not the departments and agencies. Upon suggestion, Eisenhower took them, even though all added to the bureaucracy.

The change in the administration's mood from early 1953 to 1955 was striking. At first they had been determined, even jaunty reformers, "modern" Republicans at last in charge of a government which for twenty years had been misused by liberals. Reality curdled virtually all of their hopes, and after the 1954 elections it was apparent that the best that could be expected was a sane tight-fisted management of the existing system.

Most disappointing had been the experience with the federal

budget, the $79 billion that the government took from citizens and spent in largely foolish ways in Harry Truman's last year. Eisenhower had tried to cut by 10 per cent at once, and expected the end of the Korean War to make this figure not only achievable, but perhaps only a first step. A reasonable goal might have been to reach Truman's last peacetime figure, $44 billion (1950) and then hold it there while population growth actually further shrank the degree of federal participation in American life. Harsh realities intruded at once. Eisenhower's Cabinet heads found little in their own departments to eliminate, although they cast a critical eye upon their neighbor's budget. They had been out of office for twenty years, and had not realized how little of the budget any administration could control. More than 60 per cent of it went for defense, which the admirals and generals warned them not to reduce with the Russians and Chinese ready to take over the world should America appear to weaken. And much of the rest was obligated spending for social security, unemployment insurance, or veterans' benefits, which no one could touch.

For the rest, militant lobbies and groups—and Democrats —stood ready to repel the idea of retrenchment. At a Cabinet meeting on May 22, 1953, after working for hours to find some palatable budget cuts to send down to the Hill, Eisenhower was to say: "My God, when you think of the pressure and the pressure groups . . . the bills for the farmers . . . and the veterans . . . my God."[13] They cut the budget some, and sweated it down to $73 billion by 1955, when it started irresistibly up again until it stood at $92 billion when Ike left office. He was not pleased with the results in this area, and more doctrinaire conservatives were outraged. Senator Robert Taft, when he saw the figures for the 1954 budget emerging in 1953, told the President: "The one primary thing we promised the American people . . . was reduction of expenditures. Now you're taking us down the same road Truman traveled. You haven't moved an inch from the Truman program."[14] Not only would federal spending remain much higher than conservatives thought proper, so would the debt. Ike endured five deficits in his eight years, the 1959 deficit of $12 billion being the largest in peacetime history.

Of course the Republicans were able to make some difference, now that they had their own President. One could find examples of their presence in Washington during those years, such as the termination of the old Reconstruction Finance Corporation (1932–53) that Roosevelt had used to spend money, tighter budgets for the Bureau of Indian Affairs, and so on. But it was endlessly astonishing how often Eisenhower would find himself doing things that Roosevelt and Truman had done. A recession came in 1954, complaints rose from all sides that the government should do something, and there seemed no politically reasonable course but to turn to Keynes. The administration eased credit and increased spending, accepting its New Dealish responsibilities for economic management. The economy recovered.

Then in 1957 a quick slump came in the autumn, and again the government turned to expansionist policies, modestly applied but unmistakable. It was galling to nurse the economy back from serious employment in this way, but it was impossible simply to sit there, Hoover-like, and ask people to retain their faith in free enterprise. The voters had a way of punishing the party that declined to address public problems with a reasonable show of ingenuity. In his eight years Eisenhower learned that farmers did not want to face the free market, Tennessee Valley consumers of electricity did not prefer free enterprise to socialism, and no group currently subsidized welcomed a return to the jungles of competition. During that distressing eight years the first Republican President since Hoover signed a major public housing law, the first civil rights laws since Reconstruction, sponsored a program of federal aid to education, inaugurated an expensive new public works program in highways, and increased social security benefits three times. At the end of the decade Americans had a national government very much like the one Truman headed while Eisenhower was still president of Columbia, a large and complex government with a wide array of social responsibilities. It intervened everywhere, to promote welfare, prepare for warfare, regulate and subsidize enterprise, promote science and education. It was expected to solve social problems. But it was not expected to Plan.

Eisenhower would not have been surprised to find historians concluding that his presidency did not move the country noticeably toward Planning, or away from it. He and his party had certain vague but important social goals—peace, prosperity, stay in office to keep the Democrats from resuming their ruinous ways. Planning was not an issue, not a word that either party used. It was something the Russians did. Only a few scholars knew that several capitalist countries were experimenting with the thing, most notably France and Japan. To ask some contemporary what bearing the Eisenhower years had upon Planning would have been to call upon mental categories not activated since the 1930s. The difference between intervention and Planning was not understood, not even contemplated. The federal government was large and powerful. The 1930s were far in the past, and few people talked of the absence of specific national goals, of the extreme weakness of central institutions for policy formulation or coordination or review, of the almost total lack of long-range forecasting, of the primitive condition of social reporting, of the proliferation of policies but absence of national Policy for energy or transportation or land use or population distribution and size.

When the Planning capacity is thus summarized it may appear remarkable that Eisenhower did not notice and address these weaknesses, even if it meant claiming that his guiding principles were those of modern Republicanism and had nothing to do with the heritage of Roosevelt. He was, after all, a man who had spent his mature years in large organizations—the army, Columbia University, NATO. He was the organizer of victory, the man who managed the cross-channel invasion, an administrator rather than a tactician. One might well have expected from him more sensitivity to organizational confusion, to the institutional powerlessness that surrounded him after 1952. Certainly the corporation executives he brought into high posts knew how to plan the affairs of large, complex systems, and might have encouraged a revolt against governmental weakness. In fact, while Eisenhower made little record one way or another on either approaching or retreating from a theoretical Planning capacity, what little record his government made is worth our attention.

Eisenhower displayed an unusual tolerance of the absence of policy-coordinating institutions available to the Presidency, considering his background. What body could he turn to for a review of what the government was doing to meet major social problems or for anticipation of new problems? The Cabinet. But presidents before him had found this institution ill-suited to a coordinating assignment. The secretaries' main loyalty was to constituencies and existing bureaucracies, not to the Chief Executive or his program, if he had one. The Cabinet had no staff. It met when called, and faced itself across a huge table with no common flow of paper having passed between its members. If decisions were arrived at, there was no staff to follow them up.

Eisenhower should have known that this body could not help him formulate policy, that its deepest instincts were to limit his options. But he assumed they would be statesmen, not bureaucrats, wise men with endless time to devote to larger questions outside their little specialties. He gave the Cabinet a secretary, and met with it doggedly every week or so, at least at first. But it was a large group; its members preferred going to Ike privately instead of engaging in broad debate; they had no briefing papers to read, and, if they had, would not have read them. Increasingly their meetings took up trivial issues and avoided important ones, and "the Cabinet officials," concludes one historian, "too often conducted themselves like contentious heads of rival departments rather than like statesmen who were members of a corporate body."[15] Ike scheduled their meetings less frequently, but never faced the problem squarely, never worked out an alternative.

He certainly could not use the CEA, for it was merely three economists. In fact, Eisenhower came to office doubting that he needed that group at all. He and his friends did not like the idea of a board of professors, did not like the Keyserling style, the New Dealish aroma. Ike might well have abolished it, but

Sherman Adams and adviser Gabriel Hauge knew more about American government than the general, and dissuaded him. And Ike liked Arthur Burns, an intellectual and economist in whom he was astonished to discover sterling qualities. He appointed Burns head of the CEA, and let it continue preparing the annual economic report. But he hardly spent his afternoons there, assigning the agency wide-ranging tasks of policy review and coordination. He added White House aides, kept trying to make the Cabinet work, and served his eight years without making or suggesting an institutional change to meet the needs of his office.

This is a surprising lassitude in the face of clear institutional deficiency, surprising not only because Eisenhower was supposed to be a skilled administrator, but also because he proved so adroit in bringing his national security machinery closer to an adequate planning capacity. The National Security Council had been established in 1947, a little subcabinet with a staff to give the President policy review and coordination. Truman had been wary of it, concerned that it might somehow usurp presidential authority. He attended few of its meetings until the Korean War broke, and explained only that he did not want to stifle discussion with the presidential presence. His real feelings remain clouded. Eisenhower seized at once upon the NSC and, scholars agree, brought it to peak effectiveness during his administrations. It met each week, and took up major policy issues, both pressing ones and contingency plans. The NSC under Ike divided itself into a planning board to prepare papers on all major policy issues, and an operations board to implement decisions. "Eisenhower's belief in continuous policy planning," wrote one of NSC's staff directors, Robert Cutler, "was based on his long experience in war planning. . . . More important than what is planned is that the planners become accustomed to working and thinking together on hard problems; enabling them—when put to the ultimate test—to arrive more surely at a reasonable planning or policy."[16] The NSC staff grew to 65 under Ike, from between 20 and 30 under Truman, and the council itself was a respected institution with a reputation for taking up only the biggest questions. A foreign service officer from those years, Smith

Simpson, told Patrick Anderson: "A way had finally been devised of assuring a careful enough study of every country of the world to uncover problems and needs before they became crises and to evolve basic, long-range policies. The federal establishment began to look and plan ahead in unison."[17]

None of this happened on the domestic side. There Eisenhower tolerated administrative arrangements which President Roosevelt had found crippling and Truman had occasionally recognized as less than optimal. Perhaps the fundamental reason was that Eisenhower really did not care about domestic issues, shared the feeling of most contemporaries that America's internal affairs were nicely taking care of themselves. Only to foreign affairs did he bring his best energies and organizational talents. Rebuffed by the failure of the Hoover and Kestnbaum commissions to produce workable ideas or mobilize public opinion leading to a smaller government, unable to cut the budget substantially or avoid deficits, the Eisenhower administration gave up on reform and administered the received system as it had found it. The President had no adequate institutional capacity for forecasting, or for policy coordination or review; but he devised no remedies. The executive budget was prepared only one year ahead, and was reviewed by Congress in the most casual way; Eisenhower never questioned these traditions, nor suggested longer-range projections or expenditure. He did not complain that fragmented social policies were so contradictory that they did not add up to national Policy. He remained, so far as one can tell, entirely satisfied with the social data gathered by the government, and with its analysis.

The only important exception to this summary would be Eisenhower's appointment in 1957 of a special assistant for science and technology, and also a science advisory committee. This was farsighted, but was unfortunately a rare contribution in those years to the government's capacities to anticipate and influence social change. Eisenhower's state papers endorsed many virtues, but never talked, as had FDR's addresses and messages so repetitiously, of the interdependence of all parts of society, and of man and nature. He did not teach homely little lessons, as Roosevelt had tried to do, of the necessity for organic approaches, system-wide thinking.

Were there no stirrings at all of the Planning impulse in the 1950s? If not, one would be astonished; for the idea of planning was making considerable headway in corporations and other large institutions in the private sector. That is another story, and an important one. But the national government through the 1950s remained strangely isolated from these currents of thought. It continued to run its business on a routine from-crisis-to-crisis basis, surprised by every social development, short on information, its deliberate social policies of dubious effectiveness and its many unconscious policies shaping the society in unintended ways. Occasionally some fragment of the Planning idea would break through. The Housing Act of 1954 contained a Title (VII) that set up an urban planning assistance program, providing matching grants for the preparation of plans which would be required for urban renewal assistance. Somebody knew that planning was needed as America grew, but of course only at the city level, where it long since had been accepted. Through the 1950s these "701" grants flowed out to stimulate a rudimentary planning machinery in American cities, even though the federal authorities did not know what sort of plans to reject, had little sense of purpose about the whole program. Still, it was a straw in the wind. And while local governments used 701 money chiefly to hire consultants to dazzle the feds and secure their grants, or hired temporary planning people without giving them civil service benefits or hope of permanence, the local planning capability nourished briefly by the NRPB in the 1930s was revived by the 1954 Housing Act. Much later, this step would be followed by others.

This little program, along with the appointment of a science adviser, would be about all the Eisenhower administration could carry to the seat of judgment, if the Archangel asks national leaders what they have done about Planning, or even planning. In 1959 Eisenhower did apparently become disturbed that the nation did not know where it wanted to go, and appointed the National Goals Commission, whose 1960 report clarified nothing. A crippled system limped into the 1960s, cushioned by material abundance, screened from criticism by a mentality of international siege. Effective decisions about the American future remained in the hands of land developers, industrialists, bankers, inventors, and tycoons, each in pursuit of maximum private advantage. But the people trusted in their government, the powerful, awesome giant, the post-New Deal Broker State.

The Democrats, 1961-1969

"We didn't know how bad things really were," said John Kennedy a few weeks after assuming office. It is not surprising that he was surprised. In the campaign he had been the critic of things as they were, but the Democrats' alarm had not gone very deep. They were the dissatisfied party, but over what now appear to be marginal issues. America, they urged, should be more clearly first. Its GNP should be expanding more quickly; full employment should have a higher priority in government policy than inflation control. The missile gap should be closed. Mostly we needed a new president, a new party in power. And more energy, more ideas, more *joie de vivre* in Washington.

These themes in the Democratic campaign sounded dangerously reformist to some people, but apart from style the Democratic presidential candidate was not offering a very sharp alternative to the Republican. One re-reads the famous four television debates with surprise at the narrow substantive differences. Nixon judged the public mood to be a bit closer to dead center, although as a sort of incumbent he had little choice. He raised even fewer doubts than Kennedy about America's guiding values, its political economy, its basic direction. And in the end he received just a shade under 50 per cent of the votes.

The 1960s were to catch both men, and nearly everyone around them, off guard. William O'Neill, in publishing his history of the 1960s, entitled it *Coming Apart*. It was an apt title. Not even the Kennedy circle, keyed to the discovery of errors and mistakes in the way things were being done, had sensed how bad things really were, or were likely to get. Many social problems were both intensifying and converging. The country was on the threshhold of a long-deferred confrontation with its racial history. It was coming to the end of a heedless spree of waste and consumption, and would soon have to live with deep anxiety about the way resources were used in American society. A rigid set of attitudes and policies toward international life would lead to grievous mistakes in foreign affairs. Ahead lay urban riot, campus disturbance, alienation.

None of these troubles were suspected by the bright company that John Kennedy brought to the city on the Potomac early in 1961. They came with an aggressive confidence in their leader, themselves, and the country—usually in that order. Roughly three years later the leader was assassinated, and the era of liberal political dominance entered a second phase. Yet in that short three years the Kennedy people, and those who watched from the outside, began to catch a glimpse of problems they had not charged against the Republicans, and had not bargained on.

Kennedy's international efforts are well remembered. Some, like the Cuban missile episode and the test ban treaty, are usually judged a success. Others, like the invasion of Cuba, were clearly wrongheaded and clumsy. But always, we recall of those days, there were the pressures of international crisis— Cuba, Laos, Berlin, Vietnam. These "challenges," as presidential rhetoric identifies them, placed domestic events and developments somewhat in eclipse. But within the borders of the country, Kennedy's troubles began just as promptly, and were if anything more intractable. They were merely less dangerous.

Despite the aggressiveness of his 1960 campaign, Kennedy did not seem to know exactly what domestic issues he should address, in what order of priority, with what solutions. "Getting

America moving again" implied expanding the economy, a goal of universal popularity. Beyond expansion, where other economic problems might lie in hiding, Kennedy had not given much thought. He was enmeshed in foreign crises very early on, and in 1961 did not come up with much in the way of a domestic program. As a sort of reflex of liberal Democrats, the administration asked for an increase in social security payments and the minimum wage. Aid to education and a medical insurance program for the aged were trustworthy Democratic proposals, and Kennedy supported them. These were four familiar ideas; nonetheless, Congress accepted only the first two, after much niggling. Kennedy spent much effort on a reciprocal trade bill, a familiar issue given far too much concentration. Neither the country nor Kennedy's modest program were moving very much. Unemployment started down from the 8 per cent it had reached in Eisenhower's last winter, but there was considerable excess capacity and a continuing balance of payments drain. The administration attached itself to the promising idea of special subsidies for depressed areas, which Senator Paul Douglas had been pushing since 1954. The Manpower Retraining Act of 1961 committed less than $400 million. Yet here they were breaking important new ground, as time would show.

By 1963 Kennedy had finally given domestic questions sufficient attention to have developed a sense of urgency about current trends, as well as one or two rather new ideas. That was the year he set his advisers to work on a poverty program, he pressed the novel fiscal policy requiring a tax cut along with tax reform, and was trying to catch up with the civil rights movement which was bringing a new and unexpected crisis of its own. Congressional opposition, encouraged by a large degree of public apathy, blocked Kennedy at every major turn. By fall 1963, he had entirely given up on tax reform, and worried about the tax cut and the civil rights program. We recall that he went to Dallas a thoroughly stalmated president, thinking ahead now to the 1964 election which might in some serendipitous way produce a breakthrough.

Why was this attractive young man having such enormous

difficulty shaping a domestic program? With the clear vision of retrospect we know that much of his inability to produce a domestic record of which he could be proud lay in the substance of his own leadership. He was a truculent cold warrior at heart, never doubting that his own relationship to world communism was the most important issue facing humanity. He naturally gave more attention to foreign than domestic affairs, not only because they seemed always more pressing, but because he actually enjoyed that side of his office much more. In international relations he could act; at home, he could try to persuade, and be bled and humiliated by a pack of quarreling politicians on the Hill whose lives were keyed to defending established local interests from change. This concentration upon foreign affairs required a rhetoric of crisis, and diverted attention and resources from going to internal problems. To a significant extent this happened because Kennedy was Kennedy. Another person might have played the hand a bit differently. One is led to some tolerance of his record in this regard by a number of reflections, however. In a nuclear age these foreign problems are never edged from top priority. And the remarkable zest Kennedy felt when he played Chief Executive on a world stage compared to the drudgery of domestic issues was hardly peculiar to him. Every president in the post-war era had led the public to see waging the Cold War as the country's major business, had shared Kennedy's preference for international over national questions. And this taste ran down the line, through virtually every aide and politician and newspaper reporter and historian. Kennedy had difficulty with his domestic leadership in part because he gave it his second-best efforts. But in this he was comfortably in the mode established in about 1946, or even in 1939.

3

But to stress Kennedy's personal shortcomings is to court the same mistake that Kennedy himself made. He and his friends thought the country's problem was that it had the wrong man as President from the wrong party. They were successful in changing that. The problems continued. In pondering the snail's pace of reform we must remind ourselves of Kennedy's razor-thin margin in 1960, and the implaccable resistance of a rural-elderly dominated Congress that had stalemated presidents since 1938. This was the reasoning of the Kennedy loyalists themselves. And they concluded that the cure lay in a big victory in the 1964 election, giving the President an irresistible mandate and a more liberal Congress. Perhaps the 1963 *Baker v. Carr* Supreme Court decision, providing for more equal apportionment of congressional districts, would in time help move the legislature toward more enlightened membership. But the main thing the country needed was a Kennedy landslide in 1964.

Then 1964 produced a liberal landslide, and the apparent end of stalemate. In a few pages we shall see how much and how little came of this. Lyndon Johnson would sign many laws, but social problems would prove astonishingly stubborn. As a result of the entire experience of two liberal presidents during the 1960s a critical introspection would develop, a deepening appreciation of the structural problems that made the country hard to govern no matter who was President or how many laws he passed. The Kennedy era was the starting point. In that short time the President, his associates, and sympathetic outsiders began to awaken to the unplanned, short-term, short-sighted, and generally inept characteristics of both federal policy and administration. Arthur M. Schlesinger, Jr., in his study *The Age of Roosevelt,* makes an important distinction between the structural theme that was dominant in early New Deal liberalism and the shift to Keynesian manipulation toward the end. Schlesinger finds the former at least potentially more radical, as it portended alterations in the relative power and income of groups. After 1937–38, liberalism was increasingly content with fiscal approaches to growth, less interested in pursuing structural questions. This is an important insight. Under Kennedy the structural sensitivity began to revive, as alert people whose favorite president was experiencing enormous difficulties with his domestic role became increasingly aware of structural flaws both in the economy and in government, and groped around for remedies.

A good example was the announcement of wage-price guideposts in 1962. The CEA had been circling warily around this issue since before 1952. Wages and prices, in conventional opinion, were set by the interplay of market forces and were outside the government's responsibilities, except in wartime situations like 1942–45 and 1950–53 when the government imposed controls. But economists in and out of government recognized the existence of monopoly power by big corporations and big unions, and knew there were sectors of the economy where wages and prices were pegged higher than market forces would have permitted. This was one likely source of the inflationary pressures in a time of excess capacity that worried Eisenhower throughout the 1950s. In many an annual economic report in that decade the CEA fretted about this structural source of economic malperformance, but could not bring itself to propose federal intervention. For one thing, what standard would the government use to correct price and wage decisions if it were to do so? This was a thicket the Eisenhower government would not enter, and Truman had always been wary of it. Eisenhower's CEA contented itself with issuing bureaucratic exhortations toward "responsible conduct" by business and labor. The President made occasional remarks to the same end, and similar effect. Every businessman and labor leader thought that this was good advice for his neighbors to take.

In the 1962 economic report, the Walter Heller-chaired CEA made a formal statement of guideposts that should govern price and wage decisions. The standard to be used was productivity increase; where productivity warranted, wages could be raised without inflationary effect. Prices should go up only when costs, other than labor costs, forced them up. All of this came in a very technical discussion. The issue was difficult intellectually as well as politically. The CEA knew, of course, that the President had no authority to do anything with the guideposts but print them. But Kennedy had absorbed the idea that certain prices and wages had such economic impact that the public interest was involved. He used the productivity-guidepost idea to jawbone his way into the steel price controversy in mid-1962. When this dispute was over one could see a bit more clearly. The President had demonstrated that the moral and political resources of his office were sufficient to impose a form of price controls if he chose to take a determined stand. But the political costs of his doing so without statutory authority or a fully informed public opinion appeared to be high. He may have been officially a liberal, but John Kennedy did not want the sort of enmity from the business community which the steel intervention had brought. The 1963 economic report carried another cautious discussion of the guidepost idea. But there the matter of an incomes policy rested when Kennedy died. It was an ambiguous place to leave the issue, but the place where it was left was farther down the road to an explicit national incomes policy than in that cold January inaugural week in 1961.

Movement toward an incomes policy came in response to stubborn evidence that the discipline of the marketplace was simply not operating in important sectors of the economy, and that the resultant inflationary pressures might have to be contained by some sort of government action. Kennedy did no more than put that issue on the national agenda; it is still with us, insoluble as ever. In his short tenure Kennedy ran upon even more vexing structural problems in the organization of the national government itself. Congressional reform, it might be said, was none of his business, and in any event the urgency of that issue was not acknowledged by a majority of congressmen until later in the decade. Kennedy did support the enlargement of the House Rules Committee, and in a bruising battle that minor reform was grudgingly made. But in the executive branch that he nominally led he found problems he had not anticipated.

Enlightenment on the government's organizational flaws came early. The President-elect asked old New Dealer James M. Landis to prepare a report on the regulatory commissions prior to inauguration. Landis, chairman of the SEC in the 1930s and of the CAB in the 1940s, was discouraged by what he found.

"Twenty years and a fresh look at federal administrative justice have not been entirely enchanting," he wrote in his December report. Time has not realized the "hopes so bravely held some two decades ago by those who believed that the administrative agency . . . held within it the seeds for the wise and efficient solution of many new problems posed by a growingly complex society."[1] Landis discovered what students of the regulatory agencies had long known, that those institutions had an irresistible tendency to adopt attitudes congenial to the regulated industries, while the public interest got lost in restrictive practices legalized by government. He recommended to Kennedy some internal reforms bearing upon the commissions, and touched the central problem of policy confusion when he suggested an office for oversight of the regulatory agencies in the executive office, to assume the "oversight" functions which Congress had never adequately provided. Landis explicitly called for the coordination of scattered regulation through the formulation of national energy, transportation, and communications policies.

Kennedy apparently agreed with the analysis, but had to tread warily. The regulatory agencies were an anomolous set of institutions, "nonconstitutional newcomers to the governmental complex," in Rex Tugwell's words, the "creatures of baffled legislatures."[2] They were described as "independent" of the other branches, an odd constitutional position at best. Presidents nominated their members (could not always name their chairman), but Congress approved budgets and had oversight committees to which regulatory issues might be taken if they became a scandal. Were the agencies even in the executive branch? Both constitutionally and practically this seems compelling, but many congressmen stubbornly insisted that the commissions enjoyed a special relationship to that body and should not accept presidential direction. Kennedy knew that he could not move on this question without loud objections, and that there was no clientele for reform. He decided against Landis' centralization proposal, and thereafter whatever changes he asked would not address the basic problem. Still he sent down five reorganization plans in 1961 affecting the SEC, FCC, CAB, FTC, and NLRB in minor ways. Their procedures were to be altered to allow more delegation of adjudicatory matters from commissioners to staff, and to expedite commission business. Kennedy left the ICC entirely alone, although it was acknowledged as the most cumbersome (eleven members), leaderless (it had no permanent chairman), and short-sighted of all the regulatory agencies, as well as one of the most important in its economic impact. He respected the hornets that would arise in a swarm from the railroads and trucking interests if the commission they knew so well were to become in any way more consumer-minded, or meshed in with larger national concerns.

The President's caution was well grounded. Many commissioners on the agencies he proposed to modernize in small ways came out in public opposition to his plans. In the end the situation remained as Landis had found it in 1960, the nation without a coherent transportation, energy, or communications policy. The best the Kennedy reform instinct could produce was a monthly voluntary and almost clandestine meeting of "the Tightrope Club," where Newton Minow of the FCC, Najeeb Halaby of the FAA, and other stray commissioners met to discuss "some coordination, particularly among transportation agencies, and . . . to compare experiences."[3] This was just a hair more than nothing in the effort to bring some rationality to regulatory policy.

The larger issue which is by now so familiar—the organization of the executive branch—was one which Kennedy had insufficient time to confront. Lyndon Johnson would appoint a committee to recommend on it, and Richard Nixon would finally face it in 1970 with a radical proposal that at least caught up with the Brownlow Report of 1937, and probably went beyond it. Yet there is evidence that Kennedy before his death had developed not only a deep but an increasingly educated concern about the structure of the administrative side of government. According to the textbook, the President was supposed to secure control over the far-flung agencies beneath him through two institutions. The Bureau of the Budget gave him, the theory held, prior review of budget and program requests. The Cabinet gave him a place where horizontal coordination could be achieved. Kennedy's experience very soon proved the weakness of these institutions, especially the Cabinet. He did not like Cabinet meetings, and regarded them, as his Postmaster General J. Edward Day wrote, as "a waste of time."[4] He found Cabinet officers incurable one-sector advocates, men who could not and would not see the whole, the presidential perspective on things. He came to this conclusion quickly, after a perfunctory early effort at making the Cabinet system work. At his first meeting with the Cabinet each member got a thirteen-page summary of President-Cabinet relations, stressing the goal of policy coordination. But this and subsequent meetings must have disappointed the President, for they became less frequent and shorter. Day recalls that Kennedy called twenty-six Cabinet meetings, one every five weeks on the average. One lasted ten minutes, many half an hour. Only twice was every Cabinet member allowed to speak. Richard Fenno lists three potential functions of Cabinet meetings—as a policy sounding board for the President, as a place where coordination can be achieved, and as a gathering to kindle administration esprit. Fenno found that Kennedy's Cabinet fulfilled only the last.[5]

Some of this is directly attributable to Kennedy's personal temperament. Day thought him impatient in large meetings, an impression many others have confirmed. He was reputedly unhappy with extended discussion, and irritated when men spoke out strongly against what he wanted to do. This characterization is probably accurate. It applies to all presidents in recent memory, but does not go far enough. Eisenhower was known for the tight ship he ran, for a formal staff system and a well-structured decision-making process. Eisenhower's reputation for orderliness was a trifle exaggerated, but there was substance in it and Kennedy's people all came into office feeling that part of the problem of substance was a problem of style. The Republicans were too uptight, too rigid; their respect for organization inhibited innovation and creativity. If the new administration was to be anything, it would be more free-wheeling, more open, than the old. This attitude radiated down from Kennedy himself. He liked to keep channels open and fluid, and had an innate suspicion of structured committee activity. He had never been an administrator, and this gave him the advantages of a suspicion of structure and the vulnerabilities of an ignorance of it. Where the Cabinet was concerned, he seems basically to have given up. But what would replace that institution and bring program coordination?

His working answer appears to have been the BOB, and a vigorous and enlarged set of White House aides. Yet we have excellent testimony from one of those aides that Kennedy's mind was reaching out for bolder solutions. It was characteristic of the New Frontier to find young men, relatively new to their positions, searching for new techniques to move the old machinery. Arthur Schlesinger, Jr., tells us in *A Thousand Days* that Kennedy admired the governments of Western Europe which could "face technical problems without ideological preconceptions" and could "coordinate the elements of a national economy and bring about growth and prosperity," as he put it in his remarkable speech on the economy delivered at Yale in June 1962.[6] He asked Walter Heller to report to him on European planning methods, and through Heller and other sources he learned of the so-called "indicative" planning of the French, where governmental economic goals were urged upon key industries, without the tight centralized control common in Eastern Europe. Schlesinger recalls that Kennedy found all this "a perfectly rational way to run a modern economy," that he was "predisposed . . . intellectually toward the idea of combining decentralized decision-making with national economic targets."[7] Certainly he and many others were not satisfied with the usual Keynesian fiscal tools, and knew the guideposts to be only of educational value in their present form. McNamara more than anyone else encouraged Kennedy in his instinct that the entire system could be managed much better than it was, so long as it was managed as a system. It is Schlesinger's belief that Kennedy in time would have gone beyond the guideposts to an incomes policy operated through appropriate new institutions, and that this would have been only a "part of a rational economic plan—and, if other things were equal, it was in this direction, I believe, that Kennedy's economic thought, with its pragmatic and managerial instincts, would have moved."[8]

An interesting and entirely plausible surmise. But the business community did not like the Yale speech, and Kennedy, whose desire to remain on good terms with the business community has been much underestimated, decided that the time was not right for any more public speculation on new ventures in governmental social management, let alone any concrete steps in that direction. We will never know when he might have taken a next step, nor what it might have been.

Kennedy's interest in European planning, however strong it was, is the leading sign of his administration's awakening to structural flaws which frustrated even aggressive new leadership. What seemed to draw him to the examination of European planning was the growing difficulty of managing the American economy merely with fiscal and monetary tools and the vague goals of the Employment Act. Had he lived, Kennedy might well have found his interest in planning kindled by another sort of problem—the problem of "the permanent government," as Schlesinger nicely puts it. This was the standing bureaucracy of the executive branch, which had developed a continuity of interest and conservatism of outlook which made it a natural enemy of the "presidential government." The latter were those people from Cambridge and New York, from law offices and universities and corporations who had answered the glamorous summons of a new President. This "presidential government" did not have the normal outlook of the civil service. It was almost if not entirely liberal Democratic in its faith; it was fiercely partisan to the President, and to his goals. After solving the problem of finding a house in Washington, the presidential government at once collided with the permanent government.

The latter, as Schlesinger puts it, exuded "the feeling that presidents could come and presidents could go but it went on forever."[9] It wanted to go on doing things as it had been doing them, and suspected the President—rightly—of bearing the seeds of disturbance. For Kennedy, the effort to control the bureaucracy became

> a central theme of his administration, and, in some respects, a central frustration. The presidential government, coming to Washington aglow with new ideas and a euphoric sense that it could not go wrong, promptly collided with the feudal barons of the permanent government, entrenched in their domains and fortified by their sense of proprietorship; and the permanent government, confronted by this invasion, began almost to function . . . as a resistance movement. . . .[10]

If the CIA and the foreign policy establishment in general had first jolted Kennedy with the magnitude of the problem of controlling the bureaucracy, he was to have corroborating experiences with the domestic agencies.

One remedy was to appoint his own men whenever he was politically free to do so. Another was to encourage the idea that the President was actually watching everything, through informal and unannounced phone calls and visits and memos to junior people. Perhaps in eight years this would have some effect. And, like Roosevelt, he would create entirely new agencies, such as the Peace Corps, when he suspected that established institutions could not summon the imagination or energy required for some novel assignment. To improve the executive's ability to appraise programs with scientific content and complex technological impact, he established in 1962 the Office of Science and Technology and put it under the direction of the science adviser that Eisenhower had brought into the White House in 1957. Above all, he could work long days, and expect his presidential government to do the same. Perhaps he could move the government in his direction simply by sheer effort. His assassination prevents us from concluding that these solutions would not have matched the problem. In the end, FDR had been forced to propose drastic reorganization. Kennedy did not come to this, but his time was cruelly short. His open frustration with the problem, however, permeated the presidential government, and carried over into the Johnson and even to the

Nixon administrations with gathering momentum. Both his successors would build upon his frustrations, and both would take up the reorganization solution. They would also continue Kennedy's pragmatic and gradualist response to the problem, the steady enlargement of the White House staff. A common goal, irrespective of party, was to pull a maximum amount of decision-making power into the hands of the President's men from the cautious, unimaginative civil servants in the bureaucratic empire that stretched out to the East and West along Pennsylvania Avenue, spilled across the river into Virginia, and spread north into Maryland.

This seemed the obvious thing to do at the time. The President spoke for the people. Almost alone in the government, it sometimes seemed, he proposed national solutions for pressing problems. Congressmen and bureaucrats were narrow-gauge, tied to special interests. The White House staff, inspired by this truth, grew larger as presidents searched for the instruments of control. Fourteen years later Richard Nixon would be driven from the Presidency for abuses of presidential power laid not only to himself but to presidential aides whose zeal—leaving aside their judgment, or their ethics—was not unlike that which burned so brightly on the New Frontier, or in the Great Society. It was 1962, not 1972, when a White House aide told Thomas Cronin that "everybody believes in democracy until he gets to the White House and then you begin to believe in dictatorship, because it's so hard to get things done."[11] One source of Watergate was the structural weakness of the executive branch in modern America. Kennedy probed the problem in illuminating ways, but had not the time to formulate a solution more satisfactory than a large and spirited White House staff, a partial solution which was to become a problem of its own.

4

In the five years after Kennedy's death, with Lyndon Johnson in the White House, the stirrings of the planning impulse were to continue, and to intensify. More than under Kennedy, there was expansion of public control into areas formerly left to market forces, and some motion toward the reform of the structure of government. Contemporaries saw no basic pattern in this, certainly not an evolution toward national Planning. They saw a surge of social policy under Johnson, a sort of rounding out of the New Deal–Fair Deal–New Frontier. Indeed one heard in criticism of Johnson's administration that it was "merely the old New Deal" trotted out again, the application of tired theories three decades and more out of touch with modern realities.

This criticism must have rankled Johnson considerably, for he was both devoted to New Deal principles as he understood them, and nonetheless sure that he had made important personal contributions to the history of American liberalism. But the criticism is in error for quite another reason. The old New Deal was richer than people recall. To Johnson's critics, spending a lot of money on people who are failing to meet the tests of life on their own was the New Deal way. Spending the money, of course, meant Big Government, assuming itself responsible for all sorts of utopias. And it is true that the main thrust of the Great Society was throwing money, and federal bureaucracies, at problems. But this was only one of the New Deal's techniques. As we know, there was a strong structural sensitivity in 1930s liberalism, and in the Planning side of the New Deal we find an eagerness to institute long-range planned social interventions through a restructured public policy apparatus. These commitments laid out quite an agenda that was never adequately addressed. Lyndon Johnson's social policies did bear a strong resemblance to the Keynesian, late- and post-New Deal liberalism with its reliance upon growth produced by fiscal policy, and its supplementary subsidies for groups with special difficulties that expansion did not adequately reach. Yet there was also much evidence of the revival of lines of thought which run back to the Planning idea—appreciation of the interrelatedness of social life, the need for broader social policy, the need to make periodic structural changes in the distribution of both economic and political power, the need for more social data and better ways of analyzing it.

The beginnings were conventional enough in substance, if not in style. First there was the Kennedy-liberal program that everybody knew. This began with the need for economic expansion, which Democrats decided could be achieved best through a tax cut. Then there was the anti-poverty program, its tactics and strategies yet to be fully devised, and the requirement for a legislative solution to racial troubles. Kennedy had made these the main elements of his domestic program—after growth—and it is hard now to understand why he had such difficulty with congressmen on these issues. The tax cut was the most conservative form that expansionary fiscal policy could take, especially since the accompanying tax reforms had been dropped by Kennedy when he detected serious signs of resistance. Doing something about the poor was hardly new in American policy, even if a lot of them were black people. A civil rights act built around a public accommodations provision was a significant expansion of federal intervention, but the underlying principle was nothing new. Yet it took the trauma of Kennedy's assassination to shake loose the jam. In 1964, President Johnson signed all three ideas into law with others we shall in a moment take up. Harry Hopkins had said in 1935 to his staff, "Boys, this is our hour!" Thirty years later came another of those rare moments when liberal social legislation broke through the dams that always contained it. Before the moment passed, social policy had moved several steps closer to Planning, although in a hesitant, irregular way which still left miles of distance between the old interest-group broker political economy and the Planning ideal.

5

Senator Everett Dirksen in 1964 gave an obscure Victor Hugo quotation a new currency when he explained his unexpected support for the 1964 Civil Rights Act by saying "stronger than all the armies is an idea whose time has come." Certainly it was true that in the 1960s the time had come for legal equality between the races. Nobody made this sort of remark about manpower policy, but judging by the public policy record at the national level it, too, was an issue that time had now made inescapable. Indeed a strong case could be made that manpower policy was the main interest of the Great Society. What is manpower policy? It is policy designed primarily to affect people in their occupational capacities, guiding or shaping the labor force toward the optimal fit with occupational markets. Without policy, the market is in control here, forcing people as individuals to decide how to train themselves, where to seek or accept employment. It has to do with government measures to alter—to improve—the supply side of the labor market.

Measures of this kind are far from new. Long before the concept received a name and a recognized existence, the government had been involved in whatever it was. The Freedman's Bureau in Reconstruction days was manpower legislation, providing schooling and other aid to ex-slaves to assist them toward life as independent agricultural capitalists. Laws limiting Chinese immigration, then all immigration, have important manpower effects; vocational aid to education was manpower policy, as was the railroad retirement pension, both accomplished prior to World War I. New Deal public service employment, social security retirement provisions, establishment of the U.S. Employment Service, federal child labor legislation, all were manpower policies. But there was no concept to unify them. The subject was dispersed—legislatively, administratively, intellectually. Systematic consideration of government manpower policies as an influence on the allocation of human resources did not take place anywhere. Pieces of the thing were scattered about. During both wars there was of course a vast and inescapable manipulation of manpower, ending with the termination of hostilities. The nation's closest brush with A Manpower Policy came in 1944–45, with the active consideration of national service legislation. The debate over a full employment bill a year later was a second serious encounter with a national policy in this area. From 1946 to the 1960s there was a lull in manpower-related innovations at the federal level, the major exceptions being the G.I. bill, the peacetime draft enacted in 1950, and federal aid to education voted in 1958 after the Sputnik scare. All of these were undertaken for different reasons, having nothing consciously to do with improving the fit of the labor force to the existing and anticipated needs of the economy.

In its fragmentation, manpower policy resembled water policy, transportation policy, energy policy, or any other area of federal activity one might name. A number of developments pushed the irrationality and ineptitude of manpower policies to the front in the 1960s, however, while the other major policy areas remained more adequately screened from scrutiny. Chief among these developments was a persistent upward trend in unemployment figures. After climbing irregularly through the 1950s, joblessness reached 8.1 per cent in the winter of 1961. Economic growth was not accommodating the growth of the labor force. This figure would probably have forced even a Republican administration to some sort of action. Since Kennedy was a Democrat, unemployment was acknowledged as a major domestic problem as the new president considered what he ought to do for his country.

Another catalyst to policy reconsideration was the demographic bulge produced by the post-war baby boom. As the New Frontier came to Washington, the babies, now teenagers, began to hit the high schools and also the job market. This just at a time when technology was suspected of automating an undetermined number of jobs out of existence every day, and by common agreement was requiring occupational readjustment at a rising tempo. An 8 per cent unemployment rate would have been bad enough if it had been uniform in impact. But as Kennedy learned while campaigning in West Virginia, some parts of the country were especially pained by joblessness. Certain groups were also considerably worse off than others, as the administration discovered when it studied juvenile delinquency or warily observed the rising tide of black agitation.

144 · Toward a Planned Society

There were two general strategies circulating in the Kennedy government to meet the unemployment problem. In one view, unemployment reflected inadequate consumer demand and would respond to expansionary fiscal policy. This was the Keynesian perspective, and as we know the Democrats went down (or up) that road in 1963–64. The stimulus of a tax cut (1964) and later a war in Vietnam nudged the economy into an expansion which reduced unemployment to 5 per cent by 1965, to 4–5 per cent in 1966. Deficits were traditional Democratic strategy, although the tax cut technique required some re-education of backward congressmen.

But it was not an entirely satisfactory response. The inflationary potential of such a policy course was underestimated. And expansionary fiscal policy made only a slight dent on the unemployment rates among the *lumpenproletariat* of rural migrants and high-school dropouts, or on the stranded ex-working class in Appalachia or New England textile towns. For reasons of race or age or education, millions of people found no acceptable employment opportunities in an economy becoming yearly more characterized by technological innovation. A premium was placed upon being educated, mobile, white, male, confident, and motivated; for individuals without those qualities there was a high risk of social uselessness, and for the society at large the result was a growing misallocation of human resources. The market, one must concede, is often a harsh master. Human beings were not responding to the market's signals with the required alacrity and wisdom. Job markets, economists would say, were not even as efficient as product markets. Depressed industries, regions, social classes took no real succor from general expansion, and seemed to need structural, not macroeconomic remedies.

The Democrats were not without ideas as these structural problems became acute. Senator Paul Douglas throughout the 1950s had advocated public works spending to build infrastructure in so-called depressed areas, and bills to this effect were vetoed by Eisenhower in 1958 and 1959. His vetoes stopped the legislation, but not the migration out of rural areas that ran to 10 million people through the 1950s, a migration that was both a cause and an effect of rural economic decline. But if Ike was not ready for depressed-area aid, the Senate was. Eugene McCarthy chaired a special subcommittee on unemployment which held hearings in 1959 and made an impressive case for federal programs to attract industry to depressed areas, retrain unemployed workers, and launch a public works program in conservation like the New Deal's CCC. With this momentum it was relatively easy to enact the Area Redevelopment Act in 1961, and this time it was signed.

Judging from the results, Eisenhower needn't have gone to such pains. The federal budget was not distorted by area redevelopment. It was a puny program measured against the need. ARA was funded at less than $400 million, and was spread out over many parts of the country for maximum political effect. A general development strategy was lacking, and when this began to be remedied after 1965 when the program was renamed the Economic Development Administration, the scale remained inadequate to the task.

In any event, the impact of area redevelopment programs upon structural unemployment were less than had been hoped. But the Democrats were not satisfied with one good idea given inadequate implementation. The pattern would be repeated. It seemed a good idea to put the government into the retraining business in a more substantial way. Why not assign to public agencies the helpful task of matching the labor force to the labor market more efficiently? This idea was embodied in the 1962 Manpower Development and Training Act, and in the 1963 vocational education amendments. When the war on poverty became possible in 1964 there was a dazzling profusion of retraining programs. The liberals outdid themselves in bureaucratic proliferation. During Lyndon Johnson's time the unemployed citizen might find him/herself retooled for greater earnings ("opportunities") in the On-the-Job Training program, in the Job Corps, the Neighborhood Youth Corps, in Work Experience and Training, in Operation Mainstream, in New Careers, in Special Impact, in the newly enriched vocational education programs of the states. Retraining money flowed everywhere, from the Labor Department, the Commerce Department, HEW, the OEO, every state and many cities, from corporations on government contracts, even from the DOD. One firm had 70 different federally funded programs in operation at one time. By 1970, $1.4 billion had been spent under the MDTA, 1.4 million people had enrolled, and 987,000 had completed training. Compared to the past, it was a fury of activity. High school students, ex-prisoners, unemployed laborers found things to do, and job counsellors never had it so good.

Evaluation of these policies is extraordinarily difficult. I stress "policies." The fragmentation of these efforts is striking, even to those who are hardened students of American government. A Senate committee concluded in 1965:

> Employment and manpower policy in the U.S., insofar as it exists, has been formulated on a piecemeal basis as special problems reached crisis proportions. . . . The manpower revolution . . . demands a more comprehensive and better integrated policy. . . .[2]

Too many agencies and separate programs were in operation using untested techniques for the really successful efforts to stand out from the spurious. Not only was manpower activity spread out through the federal departments, it was even more dispersed by the touching commitment to decentralization. The administration and Congress somehow came to the decision to push most retraining out of federal hands onto local governments and private enterprise. This is a questionable strategy for this particular national problem. When nine of every ten dollars spent on retraining is actually spent by a businessman or a local public official, national accountability and assessment become virtually out of reach.

Bureaucratic fragmentation was in a way a symptom of a deeper problem. The Great Society explosion of manpower policies did not become Policy chiefly because of the lack of a fundamental strategy. There seems no better way to phrase the matter than to say that political considerations guided the efforts at area redevelopment and retraining; a different rationale was and is needed. The Economic Development Administration, inheritor of the ARA initiative, put its money where the people were poorest—out of humanitarianism, doubtless, but also because congressmen from those areas were the squeakiest wheels. And in the entire retraining effort, from the old (1933-   ) U.S. Employment Service through all the Great Society's corps and programs, the welfare motive was inevitably dominant. The era of urban riots gave manpower retraining activities a special urgency, but also brought a divergent purpose from the goal that a team of economists might have designed. Retraining was an indispensable adjunct to riot control. One student of manpower policy estimates that of the 2.2 million people enrolled in retraining activities by 1972, only 18 per cent of them had been involved in serious retraining. The rest was after-school, summer or part-time busy work to keep them off the streets.[13] E. Wight Bakke has brilliantly argued, in *The Mission of Manpower Policy* (1969), that the welfare motive must give way to a broad national purpose before manpower policies will have a viable and effective rationale. For one thing, this would imply a degree of physical relocation that has so far been absent in federal programs. "There are indeed many miles left to travel," as one scholar observed, from the current fragmented, welfare-oriented set of national manpower programs to a unified manpower Policy adequate to the ever-shifting needs of the modern American economy.[14]

Another shortcoming was simply the matter of scale. Garth Mangum estimates that 250,000 people were involved in all manpower programs in an average year during the 1960s; this was out of a labor force of 75 million. Not enough was spent on retraining relative to the size of the labor force. Yet students of the issue argue that, even had the area redevelopment and retraining efforts been given major funding—say, on the scale of the moon shot, if we may be utopian, or of the resources put into agricultural subsidies—structural unemployment would not be entirely eradicated. Many people suggested that the federal government make itself the employer of last resort, and the

National Commission on Technology, Automation and Economic Progress irritated Johnson when it endorsed this idea in its 1966 report.

When the Johnson era was over some would conclude that the manpower efforts of the Great Society had been, to use the 1930s word, another federal boondoggle. Manpower policies had got themselves dangerously entangled with welfare policies. Both seemed to divert tax dollars to black people, and shiftless white people, who never seemed to have a job before or after they had been touched by the federal wand. These attitudes would become so widespread after 1969 that manpower policy was no longer a fun issue for social reformers, liberal politicians, or bureaucrats with a slight taste for new things. Had it mattered at all? The amount of federal money spent to educate people for jobs had risen ten times over the 1961–69 period, and the total stood at $9 billion. Yet one survey found that two-thirds of slum residents had never heard of government manpower programs, or the war on poverty. Could a social intervention so superficial survive? "There is no federal manpower policy in the dictionary sense," wrote Mangum in 1969, "a policy that is a definite course of action selected from among alternatives, and in light of given conditions, to guide and determine present and future decisions."[15]

There may have been no Policy, nor any tangible success which the Great Society could show for its investment in human resources sufficient to offset the declining political support for this form of federal social policy. Yet even if the manpower issue receded somewhat on the governmental agenda, it was permanently with us. Given the rate of technological change, structural unemployment seemed planted in the economy. And once having assumed the responsibility for investments in human capital required both by economic efficiency and humanitarian considerations, the government would not find it easy to shift it away to the market again. As a leading student of the matter was to summarize at the end of the 1960s:

One achievement is undoubted. Manpower considerations have

historically been dependent variables in most public policy decisions. They have now been elevated to independent status.[16]

6

Population policy was a late comer to the national agenda, having to wait its turn behind assignments in economic management or manpower policy which were less controversial—even though less important. Population size as well as distribution are at the heart of the problem of social management by modern governments, yet this was the last major source of social change to be addressed openly and frankly.

Until the 1960s the government did not recognize population as an area for policy judgments. The government was officially leaving that issue to private enterprise, as it were. Any knowledgeable politician or bureaucrat, however, could have named a number of policies affecting population size—deductions for dependents in the revenue laws, the Comstock Law of 1873 banning the mailing and importation of contraceptives, military family allowances, the structure of the welfare system, among others. These and other policies not only affected population, they were uniformly pro-natalist, as was the culture. The government was far from neutral on population. But the issue was successfully ignored except on rare occasions such as the time when Margaret Sanger challenged postal regulations and had to be prosecuted, with much unwanted publicity. But such incidents did not expose a pro-natalist policy to discussion. The 4 million Americans of 1790 became 151 million by the mid-twentieth century. In all this time no president had ever spent any words on population policy. The direction of events was satisfactory to virtually everyone.

Population trends would eventually disturb this happy conspiracy of silence. Not trends at home, but the fecundity of peoples in the underdeveloped world, combined with falling death rates from health care modernization. From 1945 to 1972 the human population of the globe expanded by half again, most of this growth in the underdeveloped countries. There was no immediate reason for Americans to notice this, and most did not. But the responsible officials in the national security apparatus who were charged with promoting economic development as a defense against communism could not forever ignore the issue.

They ignored it for quite some time, actually, from the beginnings of the era of economic aid as an adjunct to American anti-communism, all the way to the year 1958. When people in public positions first dared to speak of population growth as a proper subject of discussion it was only after a long period of involuntary education and irritation visited on them by private citizens. The population issue was as hard to force onto the national political agenda as had been alcohol control, or woman suffrage, or slavery. When we think of those responsible for pushing the population question into public arenas, we think naturally of the long struggle of Margaret Sanger and the eventual organizational expression of the birth control movement, the Planned Parenthood Federation (1942–   ). But as is often the case the immediate breakthrough to the official establishment came not directly from some tactic of the so-called extremists, but when men of solid business credentials used the paths especially open to them to nudge public officials onto controversial terrain. The crucial people here were Hugh Moore, president of the Dixie Cup Corp., a relentless educator for the cause of population control, and John D. Rockefeller, III, who established the Population Council in 1952.

In 1958 their opening came. Eisenhower, pressed by members of the Senate Foreign Relations Committee, appointed the President's Committee to study the U.S. Military Assistance Program with New York investment broker William H. Draper as chairman. Ike assumed that the committee would focus upon economic and military aid, although Draper, who was not at first particularly interested in population questions, recalls that the President tossed off a remark about the need to look into that issue along with others. As soon as Draper was appointed, Moore and Rockefeller went to work. Before long Draper was himself converted to birth control, and he nagged a reluctant commission (one secretary refused to type reports with the word "contraceptive" in them) to include in their final report the recommendation that family planning assistance be extended to all cooperating governments engaged in the struggle for non-communist economic development. The Draper Committee also called for expanded U.S. research into human fertility. This of course meant research into better birth control measures. In 1958, the advanced world was using jellies, condoms, and the rhythm method; the underdeveloped world mainly relied upon starvation and disease to limit family size.

The Draper Report was the major entry of birth control upon the American national agenda. Its few hesitant sentences on the subject could not be exorcised. Eisenhower, asked about the reference to birth control at a press conference, tried with considerable firmness to push the issue back into the shadows:

> I cannot imagine anything more emphatically a subject that is not a proper political or governmental activity or function or responsibility. . . . This government will not, as long as I am here, have a positive political doctrine in its program that has to do with the problem of birth control. That's not our business.[17]

Presumably the President was both expressing sincere personal conviction, and acting to minimize the politically adverse consequences of the Draper Committee's unfortunate indiscretion. And the Catholic bishops did condemn the raising of the issue, saying that "promotion of artificial birth control is a morally, humanly . . . politically disastrous approach to the population problem."[18] The American Public Health Association and the World Council of Churches, on the other hand, hailed such advanced thinking. Perhaps Eisenhower misjudged the political risks of the small step the Draper group proposed. Actually, Eisenhower was personally worried about population increase. But his brand of conservatism told him that the greater danger in 1959 came not from the failure to act upon a difficult and pressing social problem, but from arousing the passions of the natives—the American natives, especially the presumably powerful and united Catholic community—at a time when a national election was upcoming with its divisive potential.

Given the President's statement, that seemed the end of the issue for the moment. The election of 1960 found both candidates most happy to keep birth control out of politics. But since the population explosion was a fact, this position was only a rearguard action. The national government's responsibilities for social management at home and orderly economic progress abroad implied population control. Neither ideological opposition nor political caution could forever keep the matter down. President John Kennedy, a Catholic himself, answered occasional press queries on birth control with the usual disclaimers of federal responsibility. Yet inside his State Department, where the Draper Report had a special significance, there were men like George McGhee, Robert Barnett, and Richard Gardner who could not be prevented from circulating memos urging that the government go public with its population concerns. This sort of internal agitation began to wear down resistance, to demythologize the issue. Outside official circles the situation was fast changing. In 1963, liberal Catholics were emboldened by Dr. John Rock's *The Time Has Come,* where they found support for the use of oral contraceptives. In the same year the National Academy of Science released *The Growth of World Population,* a report that had a broad impact. Sales of oral and IUD contraceptives continued to climb, reflecting public acceptance of birth control.

The changed climate was sharply etched when former vice president Richard Nixon made a statement in 1963 urging that the population issue not be "swept under the rug," and asked for a "critical reappraisal" of the government's position on population measures in the foreign aid program. Then General Eisenhower, whose boldness on the issue, as Phyllis Piotrow remarked, increased with the decline of his ability to do anything about it, wrote in the September 1963 *Saturday Evening Post:*

> When I was president I opposed the use of federal funds to provide birth-control information to countries we were aiding because

I felt this would violate the deepest religious convictions of large groups of taxpayers. As I now look back, it may be that I was carrying that conviction too far. I still believe that as a national policy we should not make birth-control programs a condition to our foreign aid, but we should tell receiving nations how population growth threatens them and what can be done about it.[19]

Before Eisenhower's reversal, Kennedy had decided to change his own front. On June 5, 1963, the President publicly acknowledged that population increases—the reference was clearly to those abroad—were of serious concern, and research on human reproduction was "very useful, and should be continued." His statement and Eisenhower's had about the same effect. Nothing happened. No research budget was expanded, and certainly no birth control information was sent to the fecund dark-skinned women of Pakistan or Peru. But these statements were nonetheless crucial. The top political figures were testing the public water, and lesser figures, including bureaucrats, were watching the response. In 1964, ex-presidents Truman and Eisenhower, both of whom had opposed discussion of population policy, agreed to let their names be used as honorary co-chairmen of Planned Parenthood. On capitol hill Senator Fulbright successfully amended a foreign aid bill in late 1963 to authorize research and technical assistance on population control. In the spring of 1964, AID actually began to send communications and instructions to its field force on how birth control might be approached. So far, no politician, no bureaucrat had been banished into private life for population activities. The alleged ferocity of Catholic Middle America had not materialized, although the bishops of the American Church had made critical statements as government policy began to show signs of a shift. Birth control activists sensed a breakthrough.

Still the caution of presidents and bureaucrats was towering. Lyndon Johnson refused to grant an audience to General Draper or John D. Rockefeller, III, in 1964, for he knew they wanted to talk in urgent tones about the government and birth control. Johnson was going to prove very stubborn, but not firmly obstructionist. Dean Rusk, who had eased his own early opposition, persuaded Johnson to add this sentence to his January 4, 1965, State of the Union Address:

> I will seek new ways to use our knowledge to help deal with the explosion in world population.[20]

It was a welcome sentence to population activists, but there was still no movement within the inert executive branch. AID population efforts were minimal, and research efforts remained small. It fell to Congress, that body so justly despised for its inability and unwillingness to face emerging social problems early and squarely, to take the lead in population policy when the executive branch rested on its newly enlightened rhetorical position. To be accurate, it was not Congress who took the lead but one senator, Ernest Gruening of population-thin Alaska; a brave handful of senators and representatives soon followed him.

Gruening had been in favor of birth control since 1909 when as a student he had witnessed the poverty and overcrowding of south Boston. As a newspaperman he had tried to get his editors to cover Margaret Sanger, and from a position in the Department of Interior in the 1930s he worked, with as little success as on previous occasions, to have American maternal and child health programs in Puerto Rico include family planning. Gruening in 1963 was seventy-six years old, and one would assume he was nearing the end of an admirable liberal career. Yet two major efforts lay just ahead—his opposition to the Vietnam intervention, and perhaps more important in the long run, the series of hearings he held on population policy between 1965 and 1968.

In 1963, Gruening and Senator Joseph Clark, another liberal Democrat, introduced a resolution to authorize NIH research on human fertility and to establish a presidential commission on population. They received no support. For the administration to move in these directions the public must apparently be proven to be thoroughly docile on the subject. A manned trial balloon would have to be ridden by others. So Gruening, as chairman of the Subcommittee on Foreign Aid Expenditure of the Senate Government Operations Committee, began hearings in 1965 on his S. 1676, a bill to reorganize HEW for more effective attention to domestic population issues.

He opened the hearings with a letter from former-president Eisenhower, which included the words:

> If we now ignore the plight of those unborn generations which, because of our unreadiness to take corrective action in controlling population growth, will be denied any expectation beyond abject poverty and suffering, then history will rightly condemn us.[21]

After Eisenhower, Gruening was able to recruit thirteen congressmen, three Cabinet officers, and a dozen prominent Catholics to stand up and be counted in favor of expanded governmental family planning research and services—at home. Gruening had shifted the issue. From the Draper Report to 1965 the scene of the population struggle was within the administration, specifically within the State Department and AID. And the question was framed in terms of governmental involvement in family planning *abroad*. Gruening brought the issue into public view, and he brought it home. He and his carefully selected, sympathetic witnesses asked why the American poor should not have the freedom of choice that the wealthy had—to "plan" their families, to have or not to have children. The moral climate of the Great Society made this virtually an unanswerable question. Population control picked up support from Senators Fulbright, Clark, Tydings, Packwood, Cranston, and Mundt, and from Congressmen Todd, Taft, Udall, Scheuer, and Bush. On balance, the issue attracted liberal Democrats, but the interest of Taft, Bush, and Mundt revealed the inherently unideological nature of the issue.

At this stage, in fact, it seemed that population control pitted bureaucrats against more reasonable, enlightened people. The liberal Secretary of HEW, John Gardner, testified defensively before the Gruening subcommittee in 1966 that HEW didn't need or want more legislative authority in fertility research or family planning. He resisted Gruening's proposal to create an assistant secretaryship for population issues. Eventually Gruening's persistence, and the facts of world population growth, began to thaw the icy reserve of administration officials. Lyndon Johnson in 1965 made four separate public references to the population crisis, and by 1967 Gruening could cite for the record forty-one presidential comments in the same vein. Still AID and HEW were cautious. A report on population research in HEW by Oscar Harkavy in 1967 was sharply critical of the agency for foot-dragging. Congress appropriated funds for family planning research in the 1967 amendments to the Social Security Act, and increased the funding in 1968. HEW was slow to react. Senator Tydings' comment in 1969 reflected the frustration of many on the Hill: "The opportunities created legislatively in 1967 have been largely squandered by HEW."[22] Congress pressed for reorganization of family planning research and services, and began to earmark funds to limit bureaucratic discretion.

All of this represented ten years of intense struggle to get politicians and bureaucrats to face the facts of population growth abroad and at home, and to openly explore alternatives to the pronatalism of population policy reaching far back into the past. While population control activists made these Herculean efforts to get the population problem nudged inch by inch up toward the bottom of the national agenda, the world's population each year in the 1960s grew by 60–70 million. Huge exertions produced tiny little gains to cheer the crusaders: a presidential comment that population growth was a real problem; the news that AID was sending more jeeps around Turkey with family planning displays; the establishment in 1962 of a family planning clinic in Washington, D.C.; the gradual expansion of such publicly supported clinics to most of the states. In 1968, when Johnson left office, the American birth rate was dropping, as it had been since a peak in 1947. But everyone agreed that the cause was economic and cultural modernization, along with the improvement in birth control technology. Dr. Rock had done far more for family planning than any government, and the pill, unlike the other major technological breakthroughs of the post-World War II era, was produced without public funds. The government could claim no important role in reducing the American birth rate. Only 773,000 patients were served by all private- and public-supported birth control clinics in 1968, and 60 per cent of American counties still had no program or clinic at all. Activists knew that the decline of birth rates in America would not avert disaster in the long run, and that birth rates were still explosively high in the non-industrialized world. Yet as little as government had done, public policy increasingly seemed the only road where hope could travel. The resources and influence of private voluntary organizations were swamped by the task.

After ten years of inching forward, a break came in 1968. Two inches were gained that year instead of one. Lyndon Johnson was a liberal, which might be stated as meaning that he assumed deep inside that the government ought to be doing more about social problems rather than less. After 1965, he was increasingly preoccupied with Vietnam, where he was doing more rather than less to manipulate social change. He seems, from the little evidence we have, to have been genuinely sympathetic to population control. In his memoirs, written as they all are when the balance between caution and boldness has permanently shifted, Johnson told of his conversion to population control on a visit to Pakistan when he was vice president. He recounted with some pride the expansion of federal spending for population control from $6 million to $115 million, and could recall at least one occasion when he forced AID to make its activities more effective.[23] And he certainly made all the forty-one comments that Gruening liked to cite. In 1968, yielding at last to pressure that he may to some extent have welcomed, Johnson established the President's Committee on Population and Family Planning, co-chaired by John D. Rockefeller, III, and Wilbur Cohen of HEW.

By this time the population control movement was broad and deep, and almost any committee a president might have named, unless chaired by the Pope, would have come up with recommendations for more government activism. Johnson's committee

—birth control activists had preferred the more elaborate study and publicity that a commission implied—reported before the year was out, in *Population and Family Planning: The Transition from Concern to Action*. It reviewed the alarming figures on world population growth, recommended that the research budgets of HEW and OEO be increased to $150 million, that family planning services be extended to every American woman unable to afford them, and suggested the establishment of a presidential commission to give the problem further study. For reasons that are not clear, Johnson did not meet with his committee for a formal presentation of the report, and it was issued without fanfare in January 1969.

Perhaps the President had cooled on the issue, or had done as much as he cared to. His 1970 budget showed a cut in funds for family planning activities. Yet Johnson's population control effort had been vitally important in the gains made since 1963. Richard Nixon would inherit the momentum of these years, and would surprise most people by moving with rather than against the current. The population control movement in the 1960s had pushed the issue from the far periphery to an important, permanent position on the national agenda.

It is interesting that the search for an acceptable euphemism for population control led to the term "family planning." These words made the goal quite palatable to the cautious. The phrase beckoned those who warmed to the idea of Americans planning their families, and made room for super-enthusiasts who hoped some people would plan not to have families at all. Many in the birth control movement hoped that planning of procreation done by couples would curb population growth in time. But increasingly the demographic data made clear that planning by individuals was neither planning nor control for the society as a whole. What was social policy to be in this area? National goals, if they were ever articulated, might conceivably be quite minimal. As Oscar Harkavy pointed out in 1969, the United States did not really have any population policy at that late date, but President Johnson in 1966 had talked of access to birth control information and technology for all women, however disadvantaged. That would be one conceivable goal for policy, not a very brave one, but perhaps the best that could be immediately established. Beyond this one could conceive of circumstances that would extend policy to encompass the size, even the composition of the population, and its spatial distribution. National control over the size and composition of the population was definitely an idea whose time had not come. The public was not ready for such talk, even though immigration laws had already been passed to control the proportion and absolute numbers of Chinese (1882–), Japanese (1906–), and all other national groups (1921–) allowed to enter the United States.

But one step was possible, in the late 1960s, beyond the goal of extending fertility control technology to all couples who wished it. Out of the population policy debates of the 1960s there arose naturally and irresistibly a concern for population distribution, and the realization that national policy on growth patterns was even more irrational and in need of coherence than national policy on family size. This led to the movement for a national growth policy (hereafter, NGP), the closest approximation of a drive for national Planning since the Planning movement of the early 1930s.

7

Where would Americans live between Portland and San Diego, Key West and Seattle? This, surely, was none of the government's business. Individuals decided where they would live, exercising unencumbered that sweet American right, freedom of choice. They piled into their wagons or their Fords, circled up or parked where individual choice determined. In places that people seemed to like, the nation would grow. Places they disfavored would stagnate, or actually lose population, the ultimate humiliation. Until well into the twentieth century this was thought to be the breaks of the game, and South Dakota or

Kentucky, Florida or California could not blame or thank the distant government in Washington.

This assumption may have deflected some pressure from the federal government, even though it was erroneous. Throughout the nineteenth century the government was involved in influencing where people would reside—digging canals, giving land grants to railroads, fighting Indians, building forts. These influences were of course nowhere near as strong as those exerted by the "natural" forces of the marketplace, but the tradition of interference was real. The only common feature in government policy affecting population movements was that it was ad hoc and without any unifying strategy at all, beyond a general expansion westward.

Not until the 1930s was this situation challenged in an important way.* The depression filled the cities with unemployed and presumably volatile masses, and strong sentiment developed for the government to devise policies to move these people back to the farm. This represented an important shift. Formerly, policies affecting population distribution were designed to help people go where they wanted to go anyway. Now the idea was to move them—with incentives, of course, not by any un-American compulsion—where they apparently did not want to live according to their own choices. This was social policy with a manipulative cast. Like much social policy—like much of the New Deal, indeed—these efforts were marginal, and did not approach the goals which had been intended. The Resettlement Administration (1934–36) and the Farm Security Administration (1937–46) utilized various programs to move farmers from worn-out land to more promising areas, and to attract people away from congested urban places by establishing experimental rural communities where agriculture could be combined with light industry. New towns were also planned. It was an exciting set of experiments in the decentralization of industry, in deliberately

* Henry George's Single Tax movement, which was of some political significance in the 1880s and 1890s but waned thereafter, directly challenged the growth implications of traditional property taxation. But as this was a local matter, the focus of Single Taxers' effort was local government.

shifting the rural population away from un-economic areas to new communities. But the scale of it all was puny. Only about 5000 families were resettled by RA and only three new towns were completed before Congress squeezed off the funds and ended the programs. The marketplace remained solidly in control of people's settlement decisions, combined with custom, and fear, and ignorance, and love of home. Government policy failed in its first explicit effort—apart from the manpower and industrial mobilization of World War I—to influence consciously where Americans would live and work.

Then came another war, four years in which social policy was suddenly quite potent in influencing patterns of settlement. At its end, so most people thought, population distribution was de-controlled along with prices and wages. Both New Deal utopian communities and wartime boom towns built by government contracts and training camps were at an end by 1945. People were free again to settle where they wished, answering to the signals of the market, or, like the stubborn sharecroppers and mountain people who loved the old home grounds, to ignore those signals and tough it out. But of course the government did not go back to its pre-depression passivity in the area of human settlement. Its public works projects, its military installations, its aid to road building and airways, all influenced where the country would "grow" after 1945. And as a result of the New Deal, some influence in these matters was exerted by unemployment insurance and "welfare" payments, which by deliberate policy were allowed to vary from state to state, by the public housing program, by agricultural policy—one could go on. But these influences, admittedly, remained minor in the total set of factors converging on citizens' locational decisions. Probably at mid-century the movies were a more potent influence, depicting the glories of the far west or the glitter of New York. With federal growth policies minor and without the slightest rationality, the nation entered the Cold War.

And of course the country grew without plan in the post-World War II era, as it always had. Little by little the federal government's acquiescence in unplanned national growth, shaken off in the 1930s and war years and then restored, began to erode again. The pains of growing erratically in the 1950s first roused officials in the field of urban housing. The urban renewal program begun under the Housing Act of 1949 proved unexpectedly disruptive of urban residential patterns. As some pointed out, it was a Negro Removal Act, displacing lower-class (chiefly black) populations to make room for freeways or office space. One response was Title VII of the Housing Act of 1954, which set up matching grants to stimulate local planning agencies. It was an idea which even conservative Senator Taft found reasonable. Planning was apparently needed in urban development; the feds, who were a minor but visible part of the dynamics of urban change, would try to get local government to do its traditional planning job more effectively. From Washington came the urging, Let's you and him plan your urban growth.

This idea proved so compelling that it was adopted in other areas. In 1961 Congress required area-wide planning as a condition for housing grants; in 1962 it required "a continuous comprehensive transportation planning process carried on cooperatively by state and local communities" before highway grants would be made; in 1964 came down the requirement for "comprehensive planned development of the entire urban area" for grants in urban mass transportation; in 1965 a housing and urban development act demanded planning in connection with water and sewer grants; in 1966 the Demonstration Cities and Metropolitan Development Act specified that all applications for federal funds to build airports, hospitals, libraries, and water projects be submitted first to an area-wide planning agency for review. These citations do not exhaust the examples. By 1973, some $230 million had been spent on development planning under the 1954 Housing Act "701" program alone. It was an astonishing surge in planning activity, all caused by federal appropriations made in the hope that growth could be controlled by local governments and jurisdictions. The New Deal had tried the same route to growth control, through local planning, when the NRPB stimulated planning agencies in every state. But their tiny grants and technical aid had implanted nothing like the flourishing apparatus of local planning groups and agencies built by federal policy from 1954 to the end of the 1960s.

If the word "planning" meant anything, surely the federally inspired revolution in local planning would bring an acceptable degree of control, preventing major blemishes of congestion, over-burdened public services, and other costs of unplanned growth. This was the intention. The most immediate tangible result of a planning boom was, of course, a lot of new government jobs. Planners were hired by local governments which had never employed them, fifty-five planning consultant firms sprang up by one count taken in 1972, and the number of graduate schools in urban and regional planning jumped from twelve in 1954 to forty-two in 1972. Louis Loewenstein and Dorn McGrath made these estimates in 1973, and added that the numerical strength of the urban planning profession had been boosted by the twenty years of tangible federal encouragement from 249 to 6200 members.[24] This book would run to several times its length if we turned aside to trace the fascinating story of the failure of local planning to bring reasonable social control of growth. Failure is perhaps too harsh a word. But the whole effort looked inadequate to any urban resident of the 1960s, having survived rising rates of crime; falling tax yields in the center city; spiralling governmental budgets in which the most uncontrollable item was often welfare payments; the intensification of racial segregation and conflict; and riots, beginning in 1964 in Harlem, and raging each summer until a crescendo in 1968 forced out the tanks and national guard to defend the very capital.

These disorders were often laid primarily to race. This was the official conclusion of the presidential commission set up to investigate the riots, and no constructive approach to urban problems can be made without acknowledging the cogency of this view. But a broader perspective also broke through. Federal urban programs in all their dazzling variety, plus local planning staffs and boards, had not added up to a coherent, effective strategy. The social costs of metropolitanization were painfully high, and no public authority had perceived them, mitigated them with acceptable success. Lacking an urban growth policy, the national government had made the problem worse with one hand while failing to make it better with the other. And grants for city, metropolitan and regional planning did not bring planning, just more planners.

Who would call for a national urban growth policy? One might well guess Robert Weaver, or Mayor Daley, or perhaps Adam Clayton Powell. Ironically, the call came from Lyndon Johnson's secretary of agriculture, Orville Freeman, from the open spaces of Minnesota. Few were as well placed as Freeman to hear the complaints of rural America. For example, the concern that one-half of America's counties were losing population in the 1960s. This migration to urban areas was not good for business in small towns, it diminished the influence of the family farm, it filled the cities with poorly adjusted people. Freeman persuaded five other Cabinet officers to host a conference in December 1967 called "National Growth and Its Distribution: A Symposium on Communities of Tomorrow." As Freeman explained for his co-sponsors: "We had to agree that the country had never really addressed itself to the question" of whether federal policies should depopulate rural areas and expand the metropolis—and this was the net effect of federal policy that touched population distribution. The conference aired a set of interlocking complaints. Federal development policies were charged with fragmentation and cross-purposes; rural and urban America were considered separate policy areas, although they were indissolubly linked; the current thrust of national population growth and settlement carried with it unexpected and intolerable social costs that seemed avoidable. "We need a national urban policy," said the Mayor of Minneapolis; "We need a national migration policy," said a HUD official. And there in an auditorium of the Department of State, with six Cabinet secretaries within hearing, Phil Hauser of the University of Chicago said:

The time has come to extend the concept of planning, in a respectable aura from local, to metropolitan, regional and even

national planning. This should be regarded as a respectable concept in 20th century American civilization. And planning means
nothing more than rational decision-making to achieve the desired
goals.[25]

Freeman had apparently wished just such ideas to be expressed,
as foreign as they were to the usual business of the Department
of Agriculture, or to Great Society circles in general. He had
said in an earlier speech in January 1967: "An unplanned policy
of exporting rural problems to the city has drawn urban
America into the rural crisis. . . . We lack any accepted national goal in rural-urban balance."[26]

This would be a persistent theme from Freeman's conference
forward, the absence of a national growth policy. It would crop
up irresistibly on Capitol Hill, in the White House, in scholarly
journals. Four months after the State Department conference
these notes were struck again, as the Advisory Commission on
Intergovernmental Relations published its report, *Urban and
Rural America: Policies for Future Growth* (1968). The report
was cautiously and respectfully critical of the absence of over-all
policy affective urban growth. How this policy might be formulated and what it might look like were matters the commission
avoided, but it did speculate that industrial location might
properly be influenced by federal incentives (not disincentives).
The report also ran up for a trial the idea that local land-use
patterns might be matters affected by the national interest. In
this same year, 1968, both party conventions mentioned growth
policy in their platforms, and the National Governors' Conference went on record in support of the idea, as did a Republican
task force headed by Rep. George Bush.

Still the national growth policy idea found no powerful sponsor in the time remaining to the Johnson regime. The President
was exhausted and irritable, his dying government not a hospi-
table place for dreams of yet another federal mission in social
control. The prevailing view of the Great Society, among voters
and analysts from the universities, was that it had in fact taken on
too much. The early calls for an urban growth policy did not

ignite an immediate response. The National Commission on
Urban Problems chaired by Senator Paul Douglas issued a report in 1969 called *Building the American City*. It listed the
cities' problems, but failed to close with the incoherence of
federal policy. Students of the issue might well have feared that
the talk of urban or national growth policy had been stillborn.
Time would prove them wrong. The 1960s had prepared many
minds for the idea of national growth policy. Some liberals who
picked up the idea, like Senator Fred Harris of Oklahoma who
called for NGP in a May 1968 speech, were on their way off the
national stage. Others, like Hubert Humphrey and Vance
Hartke would encourage their staffs to nourish the idea on Capital Hill. And one liberal, Daniel P. Moynihan, would carry the
NGP idea directly into the White House in 1969.

8

John Kennedy and his vice president from Texas had not run in
1960 as men who would take this country toward Planning. Nor
did the country appear to want any such thing. But had this been
one of their contributions? Right-wing enthusiasts, alert to subversion during the Kennedy-Johnson years, have alleged a creep
toward socialism under these—and earlier—liberals. The issue
may be looked at another way, although it rarely is. Anti-
Planners might make an interesting case that the 1961–69 years
were a time of creeping Planning. Not only were more government agencies doing all the old New Dealish things, but there
had been significant federal invasion of the manpower field and
the area of population control. There was also talk of a national
urban growth policy, and whatever that was, it sounded suspi-
ciously like an override of local rights in land-use decisions.
Weren't our lives daily more controlled from Washington; and
wasn't that Planning?

The remedy for these fears would have been to consult a real
Planner, if one could be found in a country so devoted to muddling through in the pragmatic ways of the post-New Deal broker

state. Rexford Tugwell, for example, could easily have reassured a frightened anti-Planner that the evolution toward Planning under the two liberal presidents of the 1960s had been minor indeed. If extended to their logical conclusions, the probes in the areas of population policy and national growth policy did lead in the end to effective national control of population size and distribution. These were indispensable in any Planned social order; they were also only theoretical extensions of muddled beginnings. Judging by the tempo of change in the political economy from 1961 to 1969, anti-Planners and their distant grandchildren were safe in the exercise of their individual rights. Population growth in the United States was not under the control of federal officials, whose family planning activities were miniscule and who could not even adequately police our borders against illegal immigration. There were no mechanisms for national or even urban growth policy, no consensus that it was legitimate to discuss the idea. If these were the foundations of Planning, they were puny enough when Johnson left for the Pedernales.

Certainly the government busied itself with macroeconomic manipulations of varying degrees of effectiveness, was deeply involved in transportation, energy, communications, natural resource use, education, public health, research, even the arts. None of these areas endured less government involvement in 1969 than in 1961, many of them saw more. But in no area was there anything like the coordination of effort, forecasting, explicit goals, and social reporting required to justify the word "Planning." Anti-Planners could take heart. The government was big and busy, but was not in control. It was as bumbling as ever, as ineffective at restraining individuals from monopolizing commerce, or stripmining, or selling heroin or robbing banks or having big families than it had ever been. The old broker state with its familiar melange of agencies so sensitive to interest groups was still comfortably in place.

With a bit of effort one may imagine a discussion along the foregoing lines between white-haired Rexford Tugwell in his Santa Barbara office and some worried individualist from Texas, sent by his Birch Society chapter to inquire about the prospects for further collectivism. One cannot imagine either of them convinced. The individualist knows in his bones that collectivist tendencies never seem to tend back the other way. And Tugwell or any other thoughtful observer of American society would know that the trends we have been following ride upon deep social currents that must run stronger with every decade. The planning ethos penetrates everywhere in contemporary America where large institutions are found. The managerial temperament with its instinct for order, predictability, rationalization, systemic thinking, these are well nourished in modern America. On an ever broader front they work against the loose, haphazard, personalized, traditional ways of a civilization shaped by the frontier. Each generation seems to appreciate security more than adventure and daring; interdependence gains against independence; collective habits against individualistic ones; routine against caprice. There have been setbacks for rationality and social control, many chastening blunders. Popular stump-speakers still warn that men cannot understand the world or control the future, and their evidence is ample and persuasive. Still the managerial impulse flourishes, and meddling expands with the technological capacity to meddle. The Planners of the 1930s would have been envious of the data-gathering and data-processing and analytical technology of the 1960s and 1970s. There was no Planning in America in the 1960s, but there was more planning than ever. This social evolution is obvious, and disquiets the old-fashioned individualist, who sees in the expansion of planning, whether in corporations or universities or hospital administration or urban government, the portent of Planning.

Here again we have brushed the edge of another book entirely, one exploring the interface between planning and cultural modernization. We must concentrate upon the political economy, where there is complexity enough. If deep tides ran toward social control and at least planning, could the liberal presidencies of the 1960s have produced so little advance toward more effective social management? In fact, the stirrings of the Planning idea were more vigorous than we have yet sketched. Expansions of social intervention to touch population size and distribution, and to shape the labor force to the labor market, these are at least some of the components of Planning, but much more would be required. The government's organizational capacity to pursue this broader agenda of goals is as crucial to Planning as the goals themselves. And here, too, there were important experiments and innovations in the liberal era. These were not undertaken to prepare for Planning. They made sense as incremental steps toward more effective government. But had Planning been the distant objective, these steps would be requisites. I refer here to the PPBS experiment launched by McNamara and Johnson, the social reporting movement, and Johnson's late interest in executive branch reorganization.

Visitors to the White House receive a powerful impression of order, competence, and authority. Alert policemen patrol every bush and sidewalk, Marine guards open doors, the visitor to the West Wing encounters attractive, poised people in spacious offices, muted telephone rings, an air of controlled, purposeful activity without a trace of frenzy. The closer to the Oval Office, the more pronounced the air of authority and control. It is all profoundly misleading. The White House is in complete control of its visitors, but of almost nothing else. Every president in recent years has recognized the institutional weakness of this "most powerful office on earth," particularly in domestic affairs. Even Eisenhower learned this, though he had little in the domestic area that he wanted to do. The Presidency has been strengthened by stages, in ways formal and informal, and every reform to give the Chief Executive enhanced managerial capacities has been outrun by the increasing size of the governmental enterprise and the complexity of its tasks. From the White House perspective, the problem has not been how to control the country, but how to control the bureaucracy. Managing the country seems forever delayed by the unsuccessful efforts to deal with the latter. As one senior White House aide told Thomas Cronin: "The White House stands precariously atop . . . a bottom-heavy administrative system, consisting of departments and agencies equipped with research, clientele and historical baggage that continually threatens to outthink and outrun the tenuous political management capabilities of the White House."[27]

As we have seen in earlier pages, presidents have turned for remedy to three main tactics: reorganization to group agencies along functional lines for improved accountability; more White House staff; and the BOB program review for control of agency and department activities. Lyndon Johnson discovered a fourth, PPBS. All of these were actively explored in the 1960s.

For years it had been recognized that the budget, not just the document but the process, was the president's primary means of controlling the executive branch. The primitive view of first BOB director Charles Dawes, that "BOB . . . is concerned with no question of policy, save that of economy and efficiency," had not lasted through the 1930s.[28] Roosevelt instituted BOB clearance of agency requests for legislation in an effort to bend the bureaucracies to the President's program. This review grew in acceptability and in smoothness during the 1940s and 1950s, but it had many shortcomings as a policy instrument. The President's room to maneuver was tightly limited by the yearly requests for appropriations which the agencies sent up the line. It was the orderly anarchy of incrementalism, each year's budget being compiled from the bits and pieces of agency requests emerging from below and looking just like last year's appropriation with a slightly larger price tag at the end. The President found himself locked in. Shifting resources in a major way was enormously difficult. All the BOB could do for him was to trim the total and try to catch glaring inconsistencies. "Negative and piecemeal review of individual programs flowing up from agencies to the Chief Executive," in the words of a recent study, "cannot produce an integrated governmental program at the time it is required."[29]

Those who entertain the hope that the BOB may one day provide the President with the long-range policy planning that he required to break free of incrementalism, could cite little signs such as BOB director David Bell's 1961 request that all departments and agencies send in a summer preview with five-year projections of program goals. But such hopes were proved faint in the 1960s. The agency had all it could do with trimming department requests. And in any event monetary policy, taxation, credit policy, and debt management were outside BOB reach, since it reviewed expenditure only. The budgetary process on the congressional side was, of course, chaos itself, and by contrast budget-making in the executive branch appeared marvelously rational. The contrast helped to obscure the failure of BOB review to fill the President's need for instruments of policy control.

The Department of Defense in the 1960s was a good example of a bureaucracy out of control of its top management, including the President; it was also the site of an important remedial idea. Historically, the secretary of DOD was unable to control the military chiefs, and the center of his weakness was the budgetary process. Instead of being an integrating policy instrument, the DOD budget was a bookkeeping device for dividing funds between the three services. The Rockefeller report of 1958 pointed out in a critical tone that DOD budget categories were purchase categories, not functional ones. The secretary did not start with national security objectives, devise strategy alternatives, establish force requirements, and then allocate resources to basic functions. Instead he worked year by year from service requests, which contained much duplication of effort. Yet every year the Air Force seemed to get its 47 per cent of the defense budget, the Navy its 29 per cent, the Army its 24 per cent. After the funds were allocated there was no performance measurement, so that next year's budget was not likely to be altered by some demonstrable failure.

These arrangements made the secretary a mere referee at budget time, a role that Ford Motor Company's Robert McNamara found intolerable when he came to DOD as secretary in the first Kennedy Cabinet. Charles Hitch of Rand Corporation, drawing upon the progress that had been made in systems analysis and operations research, gave McNamara a budgetary system that for the first time promised to centralize power effectively in the secretary, and to break the annual lockstep of appropriation requests that were impossible to challenge. The Planning-Programming-Budgeting-System (PPBS) is admirably complicated, possibly to justify the time expended in devising it by high-powered help like Charles Hitch. But its essentials are straight-forward enough, and one can grasp them easily upon reading Alain Enthoven and Wayne Smith's lucid study, *How Much Is Enough?* (1971). PPBS starts with the whole, not with parts; it forces explicit statements of assumptions; it begins with strategic goals, sets up alternative plans for their realization, quantifies costs and benefits. It works to expand executive choice rather than limit it, as traditional budgeting had done. For the traditional procedure with its unexamined assumptions, lack of performance rating, and short-term outlook, PPBS aims to substitute explicitness, objectivity, adequate data on all options, and a self-correcting tendency. Programs must be justified by hard data, in light of alternate ways of achieving goals, and of costs direct and indirect. The main purpose of PPBS is to flush choices out in the open, to bring top management some escape from incrementalism.

McNamara's success in controlling the military services through PPBS and the "whiz kids" on his planning staff is a controversial and complex subject, and one we can avoid. The important thing is that LBJ saw at once that PPBS promised to strengthen central authority against bureaucratic empires, and on August 25, 1965, he surprised all Cabinet members and agency heads with the announcement that PPBS would be put into effect throughout the government. The BOB was expected to devise and implement the system, which Johnson claimed would enable the President to identify national goals with precision, choose among alternate methods, assess costs and benefits for from two to five years ahead, measure performance, and reallocate resources in light of results. He did not say what must have been obvious, that none of them were being satisfactorily achieved under the current system. At the breakfast Cabinet meeting when he announced the adoption of PPBS, Johnson predicted that it would allow policymakers to "establish the relative payoffs, say, of building a dam in Florida, or improving . . . schools, or eradicating syphilis."[30] "In a fundamental sense," wrote Charles Jacob, "this was an attempt to approach comprehensive planning."[31]

Johnson apparently meant business with PPBS. At first the BOB wanted to institute the complicated system in four or five departments, but in accord with Johnson's usual expansive style they were soon pushing PPBS on the twenty-one largest departments and agencies. LBJ sent around a memo in 1966 repeating his order, and insisting that all agencies "question objectives, evaluate progress, seek alternatives, and make the hard choices."[32] He spoke on the subject again in the budget message of January 1967: "Our most comprehensive effort to improve the effectiveness of government programs," he claimed, "is taking place through the planning-programming-budgeting system."[33] In the meantime, BOB tried to teach the system to skeptical department heads and their staffs. BOB guidelines, issued on July 18, 1967, required a flow of intriguing paper: PMs (program memoranda), SSs (special studies), and PFPs (program and financial plans). Behind all the nomenclature was a serious attempt to develop a stream of reliable information so that managers could determine if measurable objectives were being achieved, and at what costs. Since government programs did not have to face the market test, they would now face the healthy discipline of PPBS.

The old phrase "a noble experiment" comes to mind in connection with the McNamara-Johnson attempt to bring such systematic budgetary analysis to American government. Objections arose like a cloud of bees. PPB pressed every objective toward quantification, but many benefits and even some costs cannot be quantified. The PPB analysis required a range of data which the government did not begin to have in most areas. Like everything else about the federal government, its data-gathering operations were scattered into so many independent bureaucratic nests that the total effort was most inadequate. Twenty-one federal agencies had significant statistical programs, at a cost of $125 million annually. Johnson's budget director convened a panel of experts in 1966 to report on federal data storage and access, and it stirred up a controversy by recommending a national data center. Reasonable people were concerned about the possibility of invasion of privacy implicit in a national data bank, and unreasonable people worried about 1984. Nothing came of this idea, and the condition of confusion in federal statistics which had produced it was one of the factors that confounded the PPBS experiment.

Because PPBS potentially threatened existing programs and strengthened the hand of higher as against lower management, it was resisted by those who preferred bureaucratic security to the delights of programmatic flexibility and choice. Edwin Harper of BOB undertook a study of PPBS's progress in 1968, and found little real compliance. Agencies lacked personnel trained in systems analysis, and were either indifferent or hostile to the system itself. Where the agency head gave the system support, as in HEW, OEO, and USDA, there was at least some tangible effort to examine basic assumptions. But in Commerce, Justice, Department of Transportation, NASA, Post Office, and HUD, Harper found outright defiance of the letter and spirit of PPBS. He discovered little real impact in Interior, Labor, and the Treasury. In sum the 1968 survey found policy analysis "not performed much differently than it was before the advent of PPB."[34] BOB retreated in late 1968 from requiring the full apparatus of PMs, SSs, and PFPs, and the future of PPB was clouded when McNamara left for the World Bank and Johnson went home to Texas.

It had been a brief war against creeping incrementalism, in William Gorham's phrase, and Johnson's success with it appeared to about match his success in Vietnam. Cynics gathered to bury PPBS with the judgment that it had been preposterous, and they took an odd pleasure in the faltering performance of rational intelligence in its encounter with Washington reality. Aaron Wildavsky, in a biting essay entitled "Rescuing Policy Analysis from PPBS," insisted that the system had produced only an avalanche of paper at high cost, that not a single successful implementation could be documented, and that "it requires ability to perform cognitive operations that are beyond present human (or mechanical) capacities."[35]

Without question the PPBS experience had been another humbling episode in the history of the planning impulse. The new system did not eliminate cross-purposes in federal programs, at least not in three-and-a-half years, did not provide top executives with simple measures by which to weed out unsuccessful activities. The bureaucracy, in that period, survived quite intact and unchanged; the federal budget for 1969 looked little different than it had in 1966, apart from size. Yet those who thought the matter closed by the inability of PPBS to work a revolution or win over all hearts were mistaken. The death of PPBS was highly exaggerated in several ways. The system, despite acknowledged shortcomings, had its defenders. In a Joint Economic Committee symposium on PPBS in 1969, Jack Carlson of BOB argued that PPBS had raised the level of policy analysis and clarified objectives throughout the federal bureaucracy. Its total impact, he thought, had been entirely to the good. Some 49 programs could be listed where the amount and allocation of resources had been affected by PPBS, presumably for the better. Other observers fell somewhere between this cautious optimism and Wildavsky's corrosive doubts. Robert Haveman, a well-informed analyst on the Joint Economic Committee staff, reflected the difficulty of conclusively evaluating the Johnson administration's chief evaluation tool when he wrote:

> Advocates of the PPB system argue that the progress that the system has already made has been substantial. . . . However, even the most enthusiastic admit that, for a number of reasons, substantial progress . . . has yet to be made.[36]

Arguments and evaluation to the side, PPBS had sufficient momentum to carry over into the Nixon era. Some 825 professionals were at work doing PPB in 21 agencies in early 1969 when the new administration arrived, at an estimated cost of $40 million. And the system had begun to spread to state and local governments. Perhaps PPBS was too complicated and pretentious, was not the answer to the problem of short-sighted incrementalism and uncontrollable budgets. Perhaps the Nixon administration, skeptical of Democratic governmental inventions that cost money, would kill PPBS. But something like it would surely rise again in the corridors of national government, unless one assumed that somehow the government would remain the only large institution in America where resources were unlimited and top executives had no interest at all in bringing to bear upon the ancient incremental habits of national public expenditure the budgetary innovations arising out of corporations and schools of public and business administration in the last generation. As Alice Rivlin of HEW wrote:

> I view PPBS as a commonsense approach to decision making. The terminology may well change—and probably should—but I fail to see how a Secretary of Health, Education and Welfare . . . can get along without planning ahead, evaluating the effectiveness of programs, analyzing alternatives carefully, and making decisions in an orderly way in the light of maximum information. It does not matter what he chooses to call it, but he badly needs the basic tools of PPBS.[37]

9

We do not normally think of the Johnson presidency as a fertile source of more orderly and rational administrative behavior. That government spawned programs and agencies promiscuously, and left to its successor an administrative and legislative tangle that made Kennedy's Washington seem a place of Greek simplicity. Johnson, as one top White House aide told Thomas Cronin, "was really a legislator; he was never very involved in administration or even keenly aware of administrative implications."[38] Yet so immense were the problems of managing modern government that Johnson was forced to become something of a reformer of the administrative structure and capabilities of the executive branch in general and the Presidency in particular. The PPBS experiment was a major stride toward control of the bureaucracy, and one whose lessons have yet to be fully drawn out. This was not the end of Johnson's attack upon the problem. He took up the reorganization issue as had every President in an unbroken succession back to Hoover. Some observers credit him with major achievements. They have in mind the creation of the Department of Transportation and the Department of Housing and Urban Development. A close look reveals how few problems the creation of these new departments solved. Major transportation policies remained outside DOT control; the same was true of the responsibilities of HUD. And their missions overlapped, to compound the untidiness. Johnson knew this, and hoped the secretaries would get together and coordinate.

Here we have the familiar LBJ pattern repeated. There was great activity, but a weak or non-existent over-all strategy. In addition to DOT and HUD, Johnson made a curious proposal to join Commerce and Labor in one department (1967). In this he was garbling a sensible staff proposal to establish a department of economic development, blending the two constituency-oriented departments into a mission-oriented unit. The way Johnson brought it out, the idea merely startled reporters. This, of course, was a separate achievement to him. But the lack of guiding principles in his reorganization efforts must have come home to someone in the White House, if not the President, for in 1966 Johnson appointed the Task Force on Government Organization, with Ben W. Heineman as chairman.

Its June 1967 report (which Johnson would not release) struck themes which are by now familiar. Roosevelt and Brownlow would have found much in it to approve. "Federal social programs," the report found, "remain badly coordinated, in Washington and in the field. . . . The President lacks institutional staff and machinery . . . to anticipate . . . to control and pull together . . . to plan ahead . . . to review." This could have been drawn from the 1937 report, could even have been inserted into it without incongruity. The Task Force found that the President and his Cabinet officers "preside over agencies which they never own and only rarely command." Their aims are frustrated by bureau chiefs, the career civil service, Congress, interest groups.

And in language uncannily like that of 1937: "The President needs brainpower loyal to him, in touch with his broad perspective and particular needs, yet free from day to day operations with time to think and to plan."[39]

After these discoveries the Heineman group's recommendations were to some extent predictable. They took up some of the unfinished tasks of the Planning movement of the 1930s. There should be set up an institutional point where policy could be formulated—an office for program development, in the White House. And another institutional place where policy could be coordinated—an office of program coordination. In a sense it was the old NRPB, but split into halves. For rationalization of the government's incredibly fragmented operations outside Washington, they suggested a field force in ten regions to resolve inter-agency disputes and monitor social programs. This revived another idea from the 1930s, when NEC had put a field force into each state.

Either the Heineman group was rushed, or it picked up presidential signals warning it not to become too engaged with the subject. It did not take the obvious step, after its description of organizational problems, and propose a sweeping department and agency reorganization by function, although an unclouded mind would have moved in that direction.

Johnson received the report in the tense summer of 1967, facing eight months of political punishment that would lead to his stunning decision of March 1968 not to seek a second term. It is not clear that he would have pushed the Heineman suggestions vigorously in any event, as his interest in organizational questions was episodic. Given the exceptional circumstances of the end of his Presidency, nothing came out of it, at least not directly. But reorganization was certainly in the air when the next President moved in. In July 1968, a bipartisan bill to set up a new commission on reorganization passed the Senate. Six months later, Richard Nixon would send business executive Roy Ash in search of the ever elusive goal of providing the President with the tools of modern management.

10

Now we may see at how many places the Planning instinct was at work in the 1960s, probing the weaknesses of a reactive political economy, reaching for the levers of adequate social control. Two liberal presidents spent most of their time either with the heady maneuvers of diplomacy and war, or in piling up more government programs upon the defective structure they inherited. Yet certain initiatives emerged that pointed toward a new system, some with the assist of presidential leadership, some without. The government edged toward venturing an explicit population Policy, and when it came it would be anti-natalist, unlike the hidden policies of years past. There was talk of the need for urban growth Policy, even national growth Policy, to replace the tatterdemalion and hidden policies which were unacknowledged. Johnson frightened the bureaucracy with PPBS, and was apparently attracted to reorganization. Some connection may be seen in all of these activities, each a different aspect of the instinct to locate the sources of the ineptitude of social policy in the American post-New Deal system, and to remedy it.

One expression of this instinct was the criticism of the lack of adequate social data. Economic information the government had in abundance. Major improvements were needed in this area, for public authorities both collected too much economic data and not always the right kind. Students of federal economic statistics know how many changes are required before decision-makers will have reliable and current information when they need it. People who were shocked in 1974 to learn that the government had to rely upon the oil companies to tell them of the condition of national petroleum supplies had not studied the government's statistical operations. But at least the gathering of economic data was well established, taken seriously, and improving. In the 1960s the much greater inadequacy of non-economic information came to the attention of some public officials and scholars, and their responses were constructive.

Early in the Kennedy administration, Wilbur Cohen in HEW began to publish monthy *Indicators* and annual *Trends,* compilations of social statistics designed to complement the economic data generated and published for years by the Treasury, Commerce, Agriculture, Labor, and other departments, and in the President's annual *Economic Report* since 1947. These HEW documents raised no general excitement, but they were a heartening sign to the group of scholars interested in social reporting. Sensing an opportunity, they pressed the Johnson administration to do more. In January 1966, the National Commission on Technology, Automation and Economic Progress reported, and urged a national system of social accounts to help measure the side-effects of growth. And just a year earlier a highly placed aide to both Kennedy and Johnson, Richard Goodwin, had signalled the administration's interest in more sophisticated ways of measuring and directing governmental activity when he said: "The Great Society is concerned not with how much, but how good—not with the quantity of our goods but the quality of our lives."[40]

In March 1966, Johnson directed the secretary of HEW to "develop the necessary social statistics and indicators to supplement those prepared by the Bureau of Labor Statistics and the Council of Economic Advisors."[41] John Gardner turned to the universities, where social indicators and accounting had many friends, and appointed a panel chaired by Columbia's Daniel Bell and Alice Rivlin of Brookings and HEW, with members like Raymond Bauer of Harvard and Bertram Gross of Wayne State University who had long pressed for social accounting. An especially important member, as it turned out, was Daniel P. Moynihan of Harvard and the Department of Labor. They produced a pioneering 101-page document, *Toward a Social Report,* which Secretary Wilbur Cohen forwarded to Johnson in the very month that Richard Nixon came to office, January 1969. It contained exploratory chapters reporting on the national condition in the areas of health and illness, social mobility, physical environment, income and poverty, public order and safety, learning, science and art, participation, and alienation.

Social reporting was now a sizable movement, hoping to move on into the next administration. The idea of social reporting had much to recommend it. The government, after all, had been collecting social statistics for years. Everybody knew of the FBI crime statistics, which were (erroneously) thought to tell us a great deal. Social statistics were as old as Herbert Spencer. But they had always been the stepchildren of the federal government's data gathering efforts. Only once had the government's ignorance of non-economic trends been addressed in a major way, and that was in the historic study completed by the Hoover-appointed Committee on Social Trends, and published as *Recent Social Trends in the United States* (1933, 2 vols.). The study was a brilliant but isolated effort.

At the end of the Johnson era the government knew a lot about the production of goods and services, chiefly because of the machinery set up under the 1946 Employment Act. The national income and product accounts were known to be annually rising; people should therefore have been happy. They were not happy; some even rioted. Apparently the nation was not doing so well in areas not measured by the usual economic indicators. We knew the size of the GNP, but could not distinguish between the purchase of a gun or a viola; we knew how many people were alive, but could not measure their physical vigor or mental health; we had no reliable measures of the purity of the nation's air; we could not record or analyze unreported crimes against personal security, could not reliably estimate the condition of the arts. Government programs could be measured by inputs, by dollars spent or social workers deployed or trees planted; but outputs in terms of satisfactions to the public were an uncharted area, and second-order effects routinely escaped search or detection.

The advocates of better social data knew the difficulties involved in measuring the non-economic aspects of life, but were encouraged by the great advances made in the gathering and analysis of economic data since the primitive skills of the early 1930s. What seemed needed was an annual social report, a training ground for social scientists like the Economic Report had been for economists. No individual agency, such as HEW, could be expected to produce statistics which would be used, among other things, to evaluate its own programs. In 1967 Senator Walter F. Mondale, a liberal, took the logical step and introduced a bill to establish the Council of Social Advisors, require of it an annual social report, and establish the Joint Committee on the Social Report to receive it in Congress. Mondale was picking up the debate of 1946 where it had left off, reaching for one of the goals that planners of that era had failed by such a wide margin to achieve.

Hearings on Mondale's bill in late 1968–early 1969 found the social scientists of the nation enthusiastic for a chance to serve the country as had the economists. But friends of a social report could see problems ahead. The structures set up by the 1946 act had nurtured loyalists who now suspected their rival. Senator William Proxmire, chairman of the Joint Economic Committee, testified at subsequent hearings on Mondale's bill that a separate report and joint committee were unnecessary, that the current CEA could readily broaden its charge. More formidable doubts were raised in the ensuing discussion. Conservatives did not like the questioning of growth which seemed to be the hidden purpose of those who wanted "second order effects" and "the quality of life" measured and then exposed to a restless world. They also knew in their bones that any new agency for gathering social data would be a hotbed of liberal-radicals, "a center of unrest and dissatisfaction under the guise of research," as Melvin Levin summarized these fears.[42]

These reservations were politically important, if intellectually unimpressive. There were also the quite reasonable reservations of social scientists and statisticians about the actual design of a system to gather and analyze data which was so inherently elusive and subjective. And would the government gather social statistics like it counted bodies of "their" Vietnamese, with flagrant bias and intent to manipulate the public? As Albert Biderman wrote early in the discussion of social indicators, the liberals had a sensible suspicion that they would become "social vindicators" and the conservatives an equally sensible suspicion that they would instead be "social indictors." These were doubts that deserved respect, considering the nature of governments. Any administration would be powerfully tempted to stifle unfavorable information.

Still, on balance, many liberals were drawn to the idea. Economic data tended to encourage complacency, especially by failing to report the damage to the environment, to the poor, to those daily who endured overcrowding and noise and social contempt without a means of being heard in protest. Perhaps a social report could adequately reflect these qualities of American life along with rising physical output, and thereby increase pressure for changed lifestyles, racial attitudes, and social priorities. But the new President in 1969 was a conservative, head of a party that showed a resolute lack of interest in such changes. The future of social reporting looked at least momentarily unpromising. Yet the situation was not entirely so. Daniel Moynihan, social scientist and member of the panel that wrote *Toward a Social Report,* moved into the Nixon White House along with the delivery of the report in January.

11

In the preoccupation with war, riot, race, and the other tumult of the 1960s, no one seems to have perceived the gathering momentum of planning impulses in our national political life. We will recall that Roosevelt, in that earlier flourishing time for planning and Planning, devoted some time and energy—not enough, as it turned out—to the democratization of the political system. This was worth doing for its own sake, but was particularly urgent in view of the power which the New Deal had conferred upon the national government. Did the liberal governments of the 1960s also combine this instinct for political reform with the accelerated impulse toward social control? The pattern of the 1930s appeared again. The Kennedy and Johnson administrations, while pressing toward population policy, growth policy, manpower policy, incomes policy, social accounting, budgetary, and executive branch modernization, edged also toward political reforms designed to make the national government more responsive to majorities. Kennedy expended precious political capital in the House Rules Committee reform effort, and narrowly won an enlargement of this ancient barrier to majority rule. The struggle was more intense than he had apparently expected, and it seems to have cooled his enthusiasm for congressional reform. These people did not appreciate a president's interference in their internal affairs, however scandalous they were. Kennedy turned to the Democratic party, and campaigned in November 1962 for liberals in Democratic primaries, much as FDR had done in 1938. He intervened in six races, was successful in two. That was about FDR's success, twenty-four years earlier. David Broder, a close observer of national politics, argues in his book *The Party's Over* (1971), that Kennedy was headed toward an effort to realign the parties. He had endorsed the report of his commission on campaign costs, which recommended tax credits for small campaign contributions. He sent a bill authorizing this reform to the Hill. He favored greater centralization of his party's fund raising and distribution, a change that would permit the disciplining of legislators who broke party ranks too frequently. He favored reapportionment of delegates to the presidential nominating convention so as to shift power from party bosses to voters. All of these reforms worked in the same direction, toward a politics of movement, a clearing away of obstructions to majority will.

In this direction lay more ideologically coherent parties, a national party structure with greater authority to discipline elected officials, a reduction in the political advantages of lobbyists, old men, Southerners. Roosevelt, Kennedy, and Johnson were all cordially disliked in the South after their administrations were fully understood, a good sign that they had allied themselves with majoritarian political reforms. And of course the liberal presidents of the 1960s resumed the pressure for a stronger Presidency, expanding the White House staff, manipulating public opinion to bring pressure constantly to bear upon congressmen and bureaucrats, authorizing a more aggressive use of intelli-

gence agencies in the struggle to best their political opponents.
These were all natural objectives for liberal presidents who had
lived through a generation of stalemate while social problems
they thought government could ameliorate were compounding
themselves.

Political reform and the strengthening of the Presidency
would surely have been continued after Kennedy if the vice
presidential nomination had gone to any one of a number of
possible liberals—Stevenson, Paul Douglas, Humphrey. Because
that position went to Lyndon Johnson, majoritarian political
reform lost the little momentum that John Kennedy had given
it. The existing political arrangements had worked awfully well
for Lyndon Johnson, and he had little intellectual or visceral
interest in laboring to change them. And of course the stalemate broke up in 1964, and Johnson was too busy ramming social
legislation through a suddenly receptive Congress to work also
for reforms in campaign financing, nominating procedures, congressional committees, party structure. The stalemate returned
in 1966, since it had only been breached by the unique circumstances of the Kennedy assassination and the Goldwater debacle.
But by 1966 Johnson was quite preoccupied with his war. He
threw out in his 1966 State of the Union address the odd and
surprising proposal that representatives be elected for a four-
year term, coterminous with that of the President. It is still not
clear how interested he was in the idea, or what impact it would
have had. Johnson seemed to believe the effect would be to give
congressmen more time for policy and less for politics, and that
it would strengthen the President's ability to carry his program.
It had a European sound to it, and some political scientists
thought it might result in more decisive, less checkmated government—for better or worse. Johnson did not push the idea, which
required a constitutional amendment.

There were many stirrings of political reform in that liberal
era, but they were typically not launched or supported by Johnson. In 1965 the Democratic House caucus stripped two Southern congressmen of senority for supporting Goldwater; in 1966,
the DNC made an unprecedented effort for the freshman

liberals of 1964. The need to realign the parties, nationalize the party system, introduce some policy discipline in the congressional delegations, all of this was beginning to be felt very widely in the political community, at least among those who were eager to mobilize national political power against social problems and privilege. But Lyndon Johnson did not focus the gathering pressure for such reforms, did not give it that vital ideological definition. He was a good educator on race, and on poverty. On these issues he made a contribution to sharpening the social vision of the liberal Left, the entire nation. But he simply had no real reservations about the systems through which his life had found fulfillment. In a revealing comment about his political philosophy, Johnson once said:

> I am a free man, an American, a U.S. Senator and a Democrat, in that order. I am also a liberal, a conservative, a Texan, a taxpayer, a rancher, a businessman, a consumer, a parent, a voter, and not as young as I used to be nor as old as I expect to be—and I am all these things in no fixed order.[43]

This was a political statement aimed at Texans, but it pretty well represents his life-long tendency, from which he ventured only on the race issue. He would not intensify social conflict by clarifying the structural sources of privilege or of disadvantage, would not encourage thoughts or emotions which involved redistribution of economic or political power. He spoke often of justice, but it seemed to mean charity. He was a representative product of the post-war era, a Broker State liberal who believed in economic growth and equal access to the feast of American life. In this sense he was perfectly justified in claiming to be an heir of Rooseveltian liberalism; all of this had been a part of the liberalism of the 1930s. The other aspect of that tradition, the Planning impulse with its instinct for structural reforms and the redistribution of social advantages found little resonance in his career. Kennedy's Presidency was too brief to reveal how much differently he saw the world from the way Johnson saw it. And so the years 1961–69 produced significant and often feverish activity, but little real redirection. The liberal Left, increasingly frustrated with the existing political economy, drifted unevenly and unconsciously toward Planning. But it did not perceive this, or debate it. Conservatives fought rearguard battles wherever they could, and remained under the false impression that the election of a conservative President would reverse the tendencies toward public intervention and an imperial presidency.

Richard Nixon, 1969-1974

The year 1968 was a febrile time for Americans, with unsettlement at the center and apocalypse at the edge. The political system at the end of the year brought Richard Nixon, the old nemesis of liberalism, to the Presidency. The consequences for the faltering, much-criticized political economy promised to be substantial. The President-elect was associated with the middle-to-Right zone of his party's opinion, with his sympathies running more Right than middle. He and those attracted to his candidacy had a long-standing grudge against the government they were about to control. It had been doing too much since the 1930s. Nixon had held this view for years, and the national experience under the party that so narrowly defeated him in 1960 confirmed his instincts. For eight years after 1960 the country had been fed on promises to end poverty, regain world leadership, command space, eliminate ancient racial attitudes, correct the malfunctions of the capitalist system by government regulation. Instead, there was riot, protest, and discord, much of it a reaction against the Vietnamese intervention, but much of it also produced by gaps everywhere between liberal promise and social reality. Disenchantment reached sufficient intensity to make Richard Nixon the nation's leading presidential candidate in 1968 and George Wallace its third.

With Nixon's election, conservatives had reason to anticipate an early retrenchment in federal activities at home—in particular, less federal economic regulation and an end to Great Society programs that coddled those who had failed in life.

This was a common analysis toward the end of 1968. It ignored much that cut the other way. For one thing, Richard Nixon was by nature an activist. He assumed he ought to be doing something strenuous and backed by high purpose. Until 1968 this predisposition had been satisfied merely by running for ever higher office, but once in the Presidency it might require other outlets. And apart from Nixon's personal inclinations, American society was caught in a set of social problems that showed every sign of worsening in the 1970s. More demands would be made upon the national government, not fewer, regardless of what man or party claimed the Presidency. Then there was the memory of John Kennedy, which every study of Nixon (perhaps especially Gary Wills' *Nixon Agonistes*) discloses as a shaping influence. There are reports that Nixon envied Kennedy his lofty rhetoric and his image of accomplishment. Nixon's speeches often carried phrases reminiscent of the Kennedy-Sorensen style, usually a touch on the awkward side, and of course always haunted by a secondhand quality. Wills tells us that Woodrow Wilson was one of the presidents Nixon most admired. This was another man of lofty phrase and a definable social program. They were straws in the wind, blowing toward a complex mix of activism and the curtailment of governmental power.

And there were institutional reasons to expect the next president after Lyndon Johnson to gather power rather than dismantle it. We need only go back to John Kennedy. He found the Permanent Government waiting for him in Eisenhower's Washington. A central theme of his presidency had been the effort to control it. We are familiar by now with this problem. Nixon too was greeted by the Permanent Government, a politically neutral, temperamentally evasive, cautious bureaucracy, sprawling beyond his sight and comprehension, anchored to organized constituencies and congressional committees and their elderly chairmen. And Nixon suspected the Permanent Government also of being largely Eastern-Jewish-liberal, a mass of resisting material which was 90 per cent bureaucratic inertia and 10 per cent (or more) leaning to the Left. This condition would require of him, as it had of FDR and all the others in that office, the centralization of power into the circle of the White House.

Given this mosaic of pressures and motivations, the Nixon administration could not be what Republican loyalists clearly hoped. From the very first there would be contradictory policy patterns. We will remember that Nixon diminished the role of OEO, and according to the U.S. Civil Rights Commission managed to send some invisible signal to all federal agencies that the efforts to integrate blacks into white society were now to be perfunctory. These currents were early remarked as fulfilling the expectations of retrenched federal power. On the other hand, the President sent down to Congress in 1969 a welfare reform measure so surprising in its benefits to the poor that both liberals and conservatives never managed to clarify their battle lines. Nixon was not at once repealing the Great Society, let alone the New Deal. In fact, he seemed to think that the federal government had domestic responsibilities it had not yet shouldered. This surprising tendency came to the surface in connection with the population issue, inherited from the presidencies of Johnson, Kennedy, and Eisenhower.

By the time Nixon came to the White House the "population problem" was no longer a cause only for cranks. Alarm at the growth patterns of global population had penetrated deeply into the ranks of those elites who ran America's universities, foundations, international corporations, federal government. During the 1960s, while liberal administrations tiptoed an inch or two forward toward an explicit policy on human numbers, the world population grew at an annual rate of about 75 million, and the U.S. population even at its slowing rate of growth reached 195 million at the end of the decade. Environmentally sensitive people had come round to the belief that this expansion should now be opposed. There were not many of these people in the Nixon cadres, but his administration was not without its own suspicion of unlimited population growth. The John D. Rockefeller, III, type of Republican worried about global starvation and unrest, and there were conservative citizens associated with Nixon's success who reflected that much of the increase in population represented black babies who would go on welfare, commit crimes in the street, and do other things so characteristic of people whom the world did not really seem to need.

Johnson's population committee had sketched a goal for federal policy—family planning services for all women who lacked the resources to secure it for themselves. Nixon might perhaps have left the matter there. The birth control lobby was not to be feared; the Catholic lobby surely was. But Daniel Moynihan, a liberal (and a Catholic) who had thought deeply about the best and the worst in Kennedy-Johnson liberalism, pressed the President to go out in front on the issue. This Nixon did in a July 1969 presidential message on population, the first in history. He asked Congress to create the commission that Johnson's group suggested, and asked that it be assigned to develop population projections and to estimate the impact of an anticipated 100 million increase in the U.S. population by the year 2000. In the interim the President called for more research "on birth control methods" (he actually used those edgy words), and for an expansion of federal family planning activities. It might be said that Nixon's message established a national population Policy, in fact, when it said: "We should establish as a national goal the provision of adequate family planning services within the next five years for all those who want them but cannot afford them."[1] This was a major step away from the unspoken pronatalist policy which had been the operating stance of the government since the beginnings of the Republic. And it was of course a step toward national public control of a basic source of social change.

Later on, when the commission reported, Nixon would stand on the other, the anti-government-intervention foot. Let us come to that, and the circumstances that produced it, in due course.

Fluctuations in Nixon policy were of course relatively frequent, owing to the conflicting pressures inside the administration, the requirements of the swirling political universe, and the President's philosophic flexibility (shall we call it). Nothing in Nixon's first year so exemplified the administration's active-passive style than the message on the New Federalism. The New Federalism itself was at least doctrinally a recognizable offspring of traditional Republican conservatism. Liberalism, especially the Lyndon Johnson brand, had considerably altered the practice and structure of federalism. National objectives had been thrust upon reluctant state/local governments with the sweet enticement of money, at a rate that enlarged the size of local governments but noticeably reduced their independence. Republicans thought this one of the Great Society's most pernicious achievements. Nixon promised to reverse the flow of power through revenue-sharing with few strings attached.

This was to be a central theme in his administration, talked about a great deal, occasionally acted upon. The net effect of this thrust has yet to be fully appraised—although it is quite clear that less came of it than was promised. *Plus ça change.* But in September 1969, when Nixon announced the New Federalism, it was rightly regarded as the real beginning of the long-expected Nixon campaign to shrink the influence of the Washington-based government which he headed. When he repudiated the "overly centralized, over-bureaucratized" governmental structure built up since the 1930s, when he labeled the New Federalism as a venture "in which power, funds and authority are channeled increasingly to those governments closest to the people," he rang familiar notes which had been heard in the long wars of opposition since the New Deal.

This, finally, was what Republicanism was all about. Yet as he gave away federal power with some sentences in the New Federalism message, Nixon gathered authority with others. There was the rhetoric of Wilson-Kennedy liberalism, of great things promised: "We stand on the threshold of a time when the impossible becomes possible—a time when we can choose goals that, a generation ago, would have seemed as unreachable as the moon, and reach them." And "we in America can afford to dream—but we have to put drive behind those dreams. . . . These reforms represent a New Federalism; a new humanism; a new realism. . . . They represent not an end, but a beginning." Perhaps the President had not pondered how promises made by the nation's chief executive, if not carried out by the mayors and governors to whom he now sent bags of money, would devolve back upon himself. Or perhaps he was prepared to do more from Washington than busy himself with supplying the sinews of social intervention to lesser politicians with parochial perspectives. In the speech there were the clear notes of the planner. The President asserted the national need "to command our own future by commanding the forces of change," and offered a curious pledge to make "the first five years of a child's life . . . a period of special and specific federal concern. . . . We have made it our business to fill that void." There was also, there in the early autumn of 1969, reference to "a coordinated system of forward planning of needs and resources" in the White House.[2]

Thus the New Federalism message gave notice that the Nixon administration was feeling contradictory impulses; it would devolve power, it would also assume and centralize it.

There was more in 1969 to keep Nixon-watchers off balance. How was one to square the conservative past and constituency of the man with the Family Assistance Plan, or the population message of that summer? Eventually there would grow up the view that whenever the administration departed from the negative course of cutting back or ending some social intervention designed years before by liberals, whenever it had "positive" new ideas for government at the federal level, this had to be laid to the influence of Daniel Patrick Moynihan.

For some reason Nixon had been attracted to the articulate, energetic Irishman from Harvard. Some thought it was because it pleased him to have retained a bit of the Kennedy era with its flair. Some thought he kept Moynihan around as a sort of protection against Ted Kennedy, whom he feared as Lyndon had feared Bobby. Whatever the reason, Moynihan was there in the White House with the short-haired ad men from the West Coast. And while the loyalists Nixon brought with him were finding their bearings inside the sprawling government, Moynihan the veteran, the liberal conservative, was putting together programs. The FAP was his idea, sold to a president essentially without any ideas of his own on the welfare problem. And Nixon was glad to take the initiative to keep the liberals off balance, especially with a program suggested years before by conservative economist Milton Friedman. FAP promised a clean sweep of the old welfare system, and its cost was bearable to a conservative president when he reflected that the money was now to be sent to the poor, not to nosy social welfare experts trained at big eastern universities and comfortable on their $20,000 a year. In that same year Moynihan managed the President's July population message. He was undeniably the most creative mind in the White House in those early months, and he was hatching initiatives in another area of far more significance than FAP or a population commission. One year after the inauguration he had the words "national growth policy" in Nixon's public mouth.

2

The growth policy debate, as we know, was opened when Orville Freeman began to question the role of federal policy in what he saw as a distressing decline of rural America in the 1960s. As Freeman had quickly discovered, rural growth problems were the other end of urban growth problems, and there the unintended policy consequences were if anything more painful. For the cities, decades of rapid growth had brought overcrowding, housing shortages, noise, crime. Translated into the perspective of many whites who knew how to find their way to the voting booths, urban growth since the early 1940s had meant a stream of black people dismounting from Greyhound buses and trains just in from the South, spreading the ghetto outward toward the city limits, sending whites scattering before them into the suburbs. Anyone familiar with the history of urbanization in America knows that our cities have periodically —and since the late nineteenth century, almost incessantly—staggered under waves of rural and foreign immigrants. Their histories are a long story of crisis management, the effort to house and transport masses of humans, carry away their wastes, bury their dead, jail their violent members, accommodate their racial and ethnic hostilities. Yet the urban problems of the 1960s seemed more acute than earlier. Cities were recognized as a leading social problem. Much thought was devoted to the subject, and in this way the urban disquiet became a stepping stone toward Planning. For wherever thoughtful people looked at the urban crisis, they kept finding the federal government as an unwitting agent of the disorder.

The trail of federal involvement led back to the New Deal. Thirty years of agricultural policy had abetted a highly capitalized farm economy, and contributed to the flow of 40 million people who chose urban over rural living between 1940 and 1970. While federal farm policy helped fill the cities with white and black people with agricultural skills, federal highway programs compounded urban economic problems by helping affluent whites move their bedrooms and their tax base to the suburbs, and encouraged the cities' worst enemy, the auto. Federal regulatory policy enervated the rail system, federal tax and mortgage insurance policy encouraged single-family suburban residences and exploitative ownership of apartment houses. Federal housing policy shored up segregation. Everywhere one cared to look in law and administration, federal policies reinforced demographic and economic tendencies that were crippling our large and middle-sized cities. Of course, people might well have done just what they were doing even without the impetus of federal policy—i.e., leave Grundy County with the family, rent an apartment in Detroit, buy a six-hole Buick, and start figuring a move to a "better" neighborhood in the suburbs. But toward the end of the 1960s a few alert people began to question whether federal policy had to continue to reinforce trends which brought such painful consequences.

The Johnson administration addressed urban problems more aggressively than its predecessors, producing what one official called "a blizzard of federal cash."[3] This left the issue of policy confusion untouched. Johnson's HUD Secretary Robert Weaver was to say in 1967, at Freeman's conference on growth, that "the increasing concentration of population in our great metropolitan centers is a phenomenon being experienced in all of the nations of the world. Whatever our feelings may be about this trend, there is no evidence available that it is reversible."[4] This statement expressed some ignorance of European growth policies (which we will examine in due course). It probably also reflected a black man's wariness of the racial antagonisms that might be moving beneath the surface of the growth policy issue. In any event, the acquiescence he advocated would not long be dominant. The Great Society binge of legislation was substantially over by 1966, and in the last two years of Johnson's Presidency the problem of "program indigestion" began to bother the people who had bitten off so much. Freeman's conference was one such occasion, as was the 1968 report of the Advisory Committee on Intergovernmental Relations: "There has been no overall policy regarding the location of urban growth," the committee said, and the government should devise "a comprehensive, long-term policy for urban growth" to prevent congestion and diseconomies.[5] The report encouraged the growing dissatisfaction.

It might be thought that the Nixon administration would take Weaver's view rather than that of the commission. Were they not conservatives, skeptical of the wisdom and potency of federal intervention to channel social change? Certainly that presumption was deep in the entrails of the Nixon people. But other factors made the administration surprisingly receptive to the suggestions lingering in the Washington air when they arrived that something ought to be done about this growth issue. In Nixon's natural constituency, rural depopulation and black domination of the cities were almost another side of the law and order issue. Such matters most emphatically belonged on the desk of government. And many different meanings could after all be attached to the phrase, "We need an urban growth policy." To men like Vice President Agnew, who came up the successful trail of life through a string of real estate adventures, the need for an urban growth policy suggested federal intervention to finance the building of new towns and cities out in the tragically undeveloped countryside. In that light, one is not surprised to find Agnew writing an introduction endorsing the 1969 report of the ad hoc National Committee on Urban Growth Policy (a group of mayors and others interested in urban affairs), which recommended federal support for the construction by private developers of 100 new towns and 100 new cities by the year 2000. This was an urban growth policy to bring excitement to many parts of the Nixon circle.

There was yet another way to understand the phrase Urban Growth Policy. Pat Moynihan had concluded that social policy must take a systems approach. Since all parts of urban society were interrelated, the basic error of the Great Society had been the proliferation of 400 separate programs affecting metropolitan areas, without a coordinating strategy or perspective. "Everything relates to everything," he listed as one of the "master propositions" of policymaking.[6] This being so, federal policy toward the cities—both the direct policies such as model cities or public housing, and the indirect policies such as the highway program—must be meshed into *Policy*. This orderly instinct appealed to Nixon, and his first Executive Order, issued on January 23, 1969, established the Urban Affairs Council under Moynihan with the mission to "devise a national urban policy." "What we have never had is a policy," said the President, probably in Moynihan's words, "coherent, consistent, positive as to what the national government would hope to see happen; what it will encourage, what it will discourage."[7] The administration had without any hesitation decided to pick up the stray threads of interest in growth policy in the last days of the Johnson administration and bring them into a design.

What happened in the next five years on this subject is still too close for us to sort out with finality the sources of policy change, the cause and effect in the broadening growth policy discussion. At this distance we may see that several strings were vibrating when the issue of urban growth policy surfaced. One string was procedural; the other substantive. Judging from Nixon's message establishing the UAC and from Moynihan's interesting and somewhat confusing published comment,[8] what was intended was *an* urban policy to reduce the intolerable cacophony of the 435 separate programs inherited from what Moynihan liked to call Johnson's "Great Barbecue." This would require a policy coordinating mechanism above the competing departments; hence the UAC. Such a marked procedural improvement might reduce glaring inconsistencies and contradictions, might institutionalize a reasonable unity of governmental purpose. If this procedural string were plucked some octaves higher, it sang of the need for Policy; for a *national* growth policy relating rural to urban development, and all in between. The logic of things soon led Nixon to this, as we shall see.

Men who would link "separate" areas into a national whole are dangerously infected with the virus of Planning. But there is no Planning without goals. Whether talking of rural (Freeman, 1967), urban (*Urban and Rural America* [1968], Nixon, January 23, 1969), or *national* growth policy (Nixon, State of the Union Address, 1970), the subject was *growth* policy. To mesh urban policies into Policy, for example, was a procedural and conceptual matter which would not necessarily in itself answer to the problem of "unbalanced" growth. And all the flap was after all about "unbalanced" or painful growth, not growth itself, which of course all Americans admired. The *substance* implicit in the phrase national growth policy was population distribution—and redistribution. Played in a low key, as with Agnew and the notion of new towns, this became an inoffensive and thoroughly un-radical proposal to build more houses for Americans in the tried and true manner, hiring capitalists on government contract. Agnew certainly meant nothing reminiscent of Tugwell's experimental communities of the 1930s, built by the government on force account, publicly owned, and infested with all sorts of collectivist ideas. Played

several octaves higher, NGP meant the deliberate public control of population distribution. It implied development in selected rural areas, and disincentives to discourage settlement in
selected urban areas. Hard decisions lay along this path, and
cautious politicians could easily imagine the howls that would
come from communities where NGP decreed that growth be discouraged, or the terrific lobbying pressure from communities
desiring to be on the government's "growth encouraged" list.
The conflict would be greater than that over major defense contracts; indeed, would subsume it. Every instinct in the seasoned
legislator worked to keep such policy impacts and decisions sub-
merged, fragmented, lest interest groups become more mobilized
and excited than they were already.

Thus the issue Nixon picked up from the tag end of the
liberal era had implications which might not have been fully
perceived in the White House in 1969. Urban growth policy
led irresistibly toward national growth policy, and any kind
of growth policy implied a more explicit grappling with the
issue of where people were to live than had ever been dared.
Moynihan liked to point out that the country already *had* a national growth policy; it was the Highway Act of 1956. Of course
it had others. Every time a fighter contract was awarded, or a
part for a rocket, or a change in the import quota for sugar, that
was a growth policy. But such decisions were taken apart from
any larger context where they might attract undue attention
and controversy. An explicit NGP held dynamite for the administration that must fashion and defend it. It threatened all
the comfortable arrangements by which the Congress and executive agencies made decisions on housing, public works, defense
contracts, transportation, welfare, education. Suggestions for
change would rouse sleeping enemies.

In a demonstration of remarkable bravery, the Nixon
administration pressed ahead on the issue. Moynihan again supplied ideas and impetus. He was convinced that the main business of the Nixon administration should be to lead the way from
the scattered and multitudinous social programs of the liberal

era toward consolidated policies conceived and applied in systemic terms. "We are moving from program to policy-oriented government," he wrote in 1970, and "the idea of policy arises from the recognition that the social system is just that, a system. . . . In a system, everything relates to everything. If one part is changed, all other parts are affected. It thus becomes necessary to think of the total effect, not just the partial one."[9]

A self-evident truth, but one honored in the breach in Washington. How was the new administration to observe it? Moynihan's first idea had been the UAC, to coordinate all urban policies. His second was to provide a place where social data could be gathered and analyzed, policy choices illluminated, progress toward goals measured. Another hard-pressed public official had rediscovered the merits of the dead NRPB.

A conversation or two with a receptive Richard Nixon, and Moynihan had midwived the National Goals Research Staff, which the President announced in July 1969. It was installed in the White House basement with a fuzzy mandate. Moynihan later explained that the NGRS would undertake social reporting, and in a general way try to "learn how" to look at the system as a whole. Director Leonard Garment understood his assignment more modestly. The group would not set goals for the American nation, and would certainly not be involved in "planning," but would analyze alternatives and stimulate debate. Nixon's own statement upon establishing the NGRS—a statement that Moynihan perhaps wrote—directed it to engage in forecasting, in monitoring social indicators, in measuring alternative courses of government action, in integrating and summarizing the findings of social research. Nixon ordered a report by July 4, 1970, and "annually thereafter, setting forth some of the key choices open to us, and examining the consequences of those choices."[10]

All this was very expansive, and in practice would turn out to be a bit muddled. Roosevelt would have found all of it congenial, as the NGRS's suggested functions had to do with enlarging the government's ability to plan in a number of ways. Even LBJ might have appreciated the founding of the NGRS, as the agency's assignment had Johnsonian qualities of being grandiose, multiple, and poorly focussed. At the very least, four quite different planning functions were expected of one brand new White House unit with no statutory authority: forecasting, social reporting, clarification of goals, analysis of policy choices. Moynihan was right; nobody knew how to do Planning. He had convinced Nixon to plunge in.

On July 4, 1970, the NGRS produced what proved its first and last report, *Toward Balanced Growth*. It was not free of the usual insipidity of government reports on controversial themes, presenting a meandering discussion of subjects such as Technology Assessment and consumerism and offering projections in the areas of health, education, trade, and so on. Progress toward goals was not closely measured, social reporting was not rigorously done, policy alternatives were not seriously addressed, and judging from the intellectual life of the nation in subsequent months, not much discussion was stimulated. Members of the staff admitted, later and privately, to confusion as to their exact mission. "There never was any clear notion of what we were to do. Was it social indicators? Was it long-range forecasting? Was it national planning? We were struggling to define our identity when time ran out."[11] The "Germans" upstairs, Haldeman and Ehrlichman, were apparently becoming uneasy about what might come out of the nest of social analysts in the basement. The NGRS never prepared another report.

But *Toward Balanced Growth*, as its title indicates, took the growth policy issue seriously, and ventured an important step. It put the administration on record as a sponsor of NGP. The report considered that "trends toward megalopolis in some areas and under-population in others are reversible," and strongly hinted, insofar as a suffocating bureaucratic caution allowed strong hints to come through, that "a coordinated national strategy" should be devised to achieve that reversal. Weaver stood contradicted.

The fact is that while the federal government has no cohesive population policy, it is continually developing policies that have secondary consequences for the migration and distribution of our population:

. . . FHA and VA mortgage insurance, the interstate highway system, federal and state tax policies, state and local land use programs, all contributed to the massive suburbanization of the last 25 years.

. . . Defense contract awards have accelerated the population boom in Southern California and along the Gulf Coast.

. . . Agricultural research and support programs have accelerated depletion of the rural population.

These policies make individually positive contributions to society, but their collective impact may not be desirable from the standpoint of distribution of population and economic opportunity.[12]

These words came from an official group in the very bowels of the White House, on Independence Day 1970. The timing was intended to be dramatic, but the appearance of a document with this thrust was no real surprise by the summer of 1970. For Nixon had given the green light six months earlier. In his State of the Union Address of January 1970, he said:

For the past thirty years our population has been growing and shifting. The result is exemplified in vast areas of rural America emptying out of people and of promise—a third of our counties lost population in the sixties.

The violent and decayed central cities of our great metropolitan complexes are the most conspicuous area of failure in American life today.

I propose that before these problems become insoluble, the nation develop a national growth policy.*

In the future, government decisions as to where to build highways, locate airports, acquire land, or sell land should be made with the clear objective of aiding a balanced growth for America.

If we seize our growth as a challenge, we can make the 1970's an historic period when by conscious choice we transformed our land into what we want it to become.[13]

It is difficult to tell how much more thought Nixon gave to growth policy after that speech. Moynihan himself became too busy with the struggle over FAP to bring forth the requested urban growth policy, although he was able to publish an article in the autumn of 1969 in which ten likely components were listed. There are some signs that the White House intended to go farther than speeches and hortatory reports. John Roy Price, Moynihan's replacement as the executive secretary of the UAC, told a symposium in 1971 that a Cabinet committee had been set up in 1969 to study "whether or not there should be a national population distribution policy."[14] He at least had penetrated beneath the euphemisms. But he did not say what the committee had concluded. Some months after the NGRS's *Toward Balanced Growth,* Congress took the initiative on the issue and required the establishment of an identifiable unit in the White House to prepare a report on urban growth. The administration was not alone in its interest in growth policy. Some observers suspected that, with Moynihan leaving the government in late 1970, Nixon had done all that he intended to do. For whatever reasons, the next big event in the NGP debate waited until 1972.

But in pondering the matter and deciding in 1969 to speak a few words for urban growth policy and in 1970 a few more for NGP, Nixon had apparently realized the urgent need of reforms in the government's policy-making machinery. He could easily call for growth policy, or population or transportation or energy or communications or TV late-movie policy. But as President he lacked the structural capacity to take a comprehensive view of problems and alternative solutions. The President still needed help.

* One must not make too much of a mere sentence in a presidential address. Nixon, in the same speech in which he called for an NGP, also said: "What this Nation needs is an example from its elected leaders in providing the spiritual and moral leadership which no programs for material progress can satisfy." He never gave us an NGP, either.

3

This is not an easy thought for Americans, may even have surprised ex-vice president Nixon. He had been elected to The Most Powerful Office on Earth. He knew the initial euphoria at the trappings of office—the helicopters and gunboats at instant command, Shangri-las in the Catoctins and more lordly retreats west and south, jewels for the wife, state dinners with every culinary delight, ice without holes in it from his specially purchased machine, twenty-one-gun salutes, deference in every cranny. We know that Nixon hugely enjoyed this paraphernalia, indeed put the White House police into fancy suits with a distinctly Prussian Imperial resonance. The imperial Presidency exists, and Nixon's taste for it was well nourished, by all accounts. But Nixon in his workday role soon had other impressions. Even after eight years as vice president, he must have been appalled at the frustrations enshrouding his power.

He found the Permanent Government busy at work when he arrived, burdened with the mountain of assignments left by the Great Society and other less prolific eras. To make any mark on history at all the new President would have to direct that huge bureaucratic machine toward Nixonian ends. A crowd of limitations lengthened the odds against him. He and his circle were sure that the bureaucracy was heavily liberal and Democratic, and, as Special Counsel Harry Dent told Allen Drury in 1971, "this means a Republican administration always has to paddle upstream."[15] There may have been some truth in this, especially in the middle levels of the civil service. The remedy for this problem lay in time, persistence, and leadership. They worried too much about it, and it added to the siege mentality and combative stance that led to later mistakes. But that is another story. Perhaps Nixon might not have taken all of this so personally if he had recognized the element of continuity in the executive's troubles. Given his inner makeup, he did not force himself to study Arthur Schlesinger, Jr.'s, *A Thousand Days*, and probably paid no attention when liberal John Gardner, upon resigning as secretary of HEW in 1968, said: "I believe that the federal government cannot go on much longer with its present organization of agencies on the domestic side of government. . . . For the past twenty years the problems of overlap and conflict of mission have grown steadily worse."[16]

Nixon recognized other and more important limits upon his power. In the simplest sense, too much was going on, too many agencies reported to the President. One might rejoin that most of them were grouped under the Cabinet departments; the President on paper controlled most of the executive branch through those twelve men, his Cabinet. Nixon soon realized that this instrument was useless. At first he seems to have carried over Eisenhower's assumption that the Cabinet ought to have meetings where something important happened. He appointed John Whitaker "Cabinet secretary," but Whitaker found little to do as Nixon let the Cabinet settle into its accustomed torpor. If the President contemplated some programmatic redirection, department heads could be counted upon to narrow his options to those which enhanced existing departmental responsibilities. Nixon was bored with Cabinet meetings, especially so with certain members who liked to talk too long.* Whitaker soon found himself spending a good deal of time arranging White House tours for Cabinet wives.[17]

If not the Cabinet, then why not have the Bureau of the Budget take on policy planning and coordination? Roosevelt, denied a vigorous planning board, had pressed the BOB into service to attempt to bring departments and agencies into alignment with the President's program. But the BOB, although a sizable agency with respected expertise, could not be the institutional answer Nixon sought. The agency's coordinating abili-

---

* Some members made a speech at each meeting, John Ehrlichman related to me, and "finally had to be told politely to shut up." FDR was always impatient with the congenital narrowness of view of the American congressman, and placed his own department heads not much ahead of the congressmen in ability to take a national perspective. Ehrlichman made it clear that Nixon felt the same way. (Interview with John Ehrlichman, December 17, 1974.)

ties, working through legislative and budgetary review, were of some value, but major new departures seemed forever unlikely to come from BOB. And of course major areas, such as monetary or regulatory policies, were outside its purview. It was free of constituency claims and quite loyal to the President, but over the years had become so accustomed to cutting and paring and managerial review that it had no real time or capacity for innovation in policy. It was almost as mired in incrementalism as any line department.

These were old problems, new only to Nixon. Part of FDR's answer was to enlarge (after the 1939 reorganization law permitted it) his White House staff, and successive presidents had done the same. The White House staff totalled 37 people in 1939, reached 53 by 1945, 283 by 1953, 250 by 1968. Nixon's expansion of the White House staff to 510 people by 1973 indicates the intensity of his own desire to have a presidential policy formulation and review capacity independent of the permanent government.[18]

Yet numbers alone were not the answer. The remedy, Nixon decided, lay in organization. First he tried Cabinet subgroups— the UAC, a Cabinet committee on economic policy, an environmental council. Nixon fretted under the unsteady flow of paper and ideas. A model lay ready to hand, and soon he noticed it— the National Security Council, established long ago, in 1947. It provided the President with a policy cluster of the agencies interested in defense matters, along with a staff of about 70. The disarray on the domestic side seemed to beg similar handling. Nixon pressed John Ehrlichman, the bright Seattle lawyer whose instinct for order was at least as strong as Nixon's, to devise a domestic counterpart to the NSC, and it was settled upon in early fall of 1969. Ehrlichman's ideas meshed with the thinking of a committee on government organization that had been meeting since April under Litton Industries executive Roy Ash. The result was the Domestic Council, proposed in Reorganization Plan #2 of March 1970.

Reorganization Plan #2 formalized the transfer of policy activities to the White House that had begun with FDR's six assistants in 1939, leaving BOB, after a thirty-year battle to perform both missions, with administrative functions only. As Nixon said in the proposal, "what we do" would now be clearly separated from "how we do it," the former lodged in the DC, the latter in the BOB under its new name, Office of Management and Budget (OMB). OMB would stress the evaluation of agency performance, suggest improvements in managerial practice, develop information systems and training programs for public officials. It would continue to pursue program budgeting, not through the cumbersome PPB system, which the administration dropped in 1971, but through a new procedure imported by Roy Ash from corporate experience. This was Management by Objectives (MBO), in which all agencies annually listed their objectives and the President selected those to be given top priority. All of this was important work, but there was no way to disguise the fact that that budget office had now irretrievably lost its informal invitation to help the President make policy.

That function now rested with the new Domestic Council, made up of the President, Vice President, all domestic Cabinet Secretaries, and a small number of other officials such as the chairman of CEA. Nixon's accompanying message identified the DC as the culmination of a search for policy machinery that reached back to FDR's 1937 reorganization bill and included the Hoover and Heineman commissions. The council would be more than merely a slightly reduced Cabinet. As Roy Ash explained to a House committee in April and May, it would have a staff like the NSC, and thus provide an "institutional memory." It would operate through task forces assigned to work on matters the President thought urgent—busing, the environment, health, crime, energy, welfare. Ehrlichman, the council's first executive director, was especially pleased with this arrangement. Task forces could include second-level officials who would work hard where Cabinet officers would not; they could mobilize to attack a problem, report, and disband; plenary council meetings would be rare, most of the work being done by flexible subgroups which would presumably never develop bureaucratic inertia. The council as a whole was assigned five specific policy functions:

clarification of goals, development of alternatives, formulation of policy, coordination of policy, and review of policy. Here was the dream of Franklin Roosevelt, a place where things could be seen whole. Not even the NRPB had aspired to assume all the functions of Planning; the council's charter contained them all.

Congress did not greet this strikingly coherent proposal with the joy it would have produced in a convention of professors of public administration, although it allowed the plan to go into effect. For congressmen were less interested in managerial principles than in protecting their own influence over the executive branch. A member of the House Committee on Government Operations asked Ash if the establishment of the DC did not increase the President's independence of Congress, since the new DC director, as a presidential assistant, would not routinely testify before standing committees of Congress as had the heads of BOB and CEA. Ash's answer did not relieve the gentleman's concern. He explained that "we do not believe this is centralizing the governmental process. . . . Quite the contrary." The President, Ash said, intended to delegate more power, but to delegate power an executive must first achieve central managerial control.[19] It was hard to argue with the large, balding, no-nonsense figure of the former president of Litton Industries, chairman of a committee charged to bring the best of modern corporation management methods to the backward corridors of American national government. Congress let the plan go through, with misgivings. Nixon, Ash, and Ehrlichman had devised a proposal so rational to replace a system so inept that the opposition could find no toehold. Unlike Hoover in his reorganization efforts, the DC-OMB plan came with no promise of budgetary savings; only efficiency was promised. This being in so much shorter supply than money, the plan swept through. Soon Ehrlichman was recruiting a staff that would reach about seventy people, presumably a highly expert group, heavy with systems analysts, economists, statisticians, management specialists. Caspar Weinberger told Charles Jacob that the council set to work at once, holding six plenary sessions in 1971 and eigh-

teen in 1972, and having a decisive impact upon the administration's programs in health, welfare, energy, and revenue
sharing.[20] "Then there's national growth," added a council staff
member in an interview with John Kessel; "People aren't saying, 'What's the greatest problem in the country? National
Growth.' But that's the sort of thing that he [Nixon] wants
something done about regardless of what the public wants."[21]

If these early reports are true, they record an auspicious start
for an institution designed to give the President managerial
capabilities that had been sought since the 1930s. Whether the
DC would actually provide a full Planning capacity or not, the
study of goals/alternatives/policy formulation/policy coordina-
tion/policy review promised in the March 12 message, was a
matter for time and the Nixon people to decide.

4

Nixon and Ash then turned to the rest of the unfinished business from Roosevelt's encounter with administrative reform, and
proposed a reorganization plan of their own. The Ash Committee, a sort of institutionalized presence of modern corporation management within the new government, had been
appointed in early 1969. In this Nixon was just a step ahead of
the liberals. Senators Ribicoff (1968) and Muskie (1969) had
both put in bills to establish a new Hoover-type commission. At
its peak workload the committee employed 47 staff, and it sent
13 reports to Nixon from August 1969 to November 1970. Based
on their work, Nixon in the 1971 State of the Union Address
promised an early message on reorganization. The message came
on March 25, 1971, and it is hard to disagree with Congressman
Chet Holifield that it was "the most far-reaching reorganization of the executive branch that has ever been proposed by a
president of the United States."[22]

Nixon's message rang notes familiar to the handful of people
who knew the tradition implied by the names Brownlow,

Hoover, Rockefeller, Heineman. The President had found the executive branch "a series of fragmented fiefdoms" where "the capacity to do things . . . is exceedingly fragmented and broadly scattered throughout the federal establishment."[23] For example, there were nine departments and twenty agencies involved in education, seven departments and eight agencies in health. This meant not only duplication of effort but diffusion of responsibility, defeating all hope of clear lines of accountability.

The President's answer was reorganization around basic goals. Nixon proposed to abolish seven existing Cabinet departments, and to substitute for them four new ones: the Department of Natural Resources (made up of parts of Interior, the Forest Service, Soil Conservation, the planning and civil functions of the Corps of Engineers, the civil power responsibilities of the AEC, etc.); the Department of Community Development (made up of parts of Commerce, Agriculture, Transportation, and HUD, the Appalachian Regional Commission, the REA, some of OEO, etc.); the Department of Human Resources (most of HEW and OEO, the Women's Bureau from Labor, etc.); and the Department of Economic Affairs (most of Agriculture, Labor, Commerce, and Transportation).

An impressive parade of bipartisan support came forward to urge congressional acceptance. Ben Heineman, who had headed the reorganization study committee for Lyndon Johnson, told a House committee that he found "a great similarity" between the Nixon plan and his committee's views. Johnson's Budget director Charles Schultze was a witness in support of the reorganization, as was Joseph Califano of Johnson's White House staff, who spoke of the "cacophonic confusion" of agencies competing for the President's attention and congressional appropriations. The parade of Democrats included Robert Weaver, Johnson's HUD secretary, John Gardner of HEW, and John Connally, then a Democrat and Nixon's secretary of the Treasury, who told the House committee: "Believe me, the crying need in this government is to consolidate on a functional basis." Support also came from the American Institute of Architects, from an

IBM executive, and a representative of the Chamber of Commerce of the United States. Reorganization, apparently, was neither a partisan nor an ideological issue.[24]

Roosevelt had found that reorganization was, however, an issue among his own official family of bureaucrats, and he had not been able to get the support of several of them, including the secretary of war. Nixon presented a united administration. Even Cabinet heads whose departments would be dismembered and replaced came down manfully to recommend their own bureaucratic assassination. George Romney of HUD, for example, worried not about HUD but about the Domestic Council, which was bogged down in putting out fires of inter-departmental conflict in the unreorganized system of 1971. In the absence of reorganization, he argued, the DC was "constantly being distracted from matters of high policy by the need to focus on administrative details of . . . conflicting programs administered by scattered bureaucratic units." The new Department of Community Development, which Romney came specifically to endorse, would provide a framework within which most disputes were resolved by the secretary, leaving the DC "to take its intended place alongside the NSC as a presidential instrumentality specializing in policy coordination . . . free from operating chores."[25]

Every consideration seemed to reflect credit upon the new reorganization plan, every scrutiny of the existing system bared glaring defects. But Nixon learned again what Congress had taught FDR, that a cogent reorganization by function, supported by thoughtful students of public administration and most high-level bureaucrats, was not welcome on Capital Hill. Long-standing arrangements between congressional committees and constituency-oriented agencies were threatened by any reorganization, particularly by one so sweeping. The typical congressman's lack of enthusiasm was matched by organized interest groups who had worked their way to close relationships with their old buddies in the Bureau of Mines, or the Bureau of Land Management, or the Farmers Home Administration—examples of the many agencies that would be rudely uprooted from comfortable surroundings and thrust into new environments where their merits would perhaps not be appreciated.

The Nixon-Ash theory was that departments ought to be organized for delivery of services. The old organization, while not based on any clear theory, was best justified as an expression of the lobbying or representation concept. Every major group ought to have its department—farmers, labor, business, even oilmen (who enjoyed the helpful support of the Department of the Interior). These groups were not charmed by the proposal for change. Nixon encountered especially stiff opposition from farm groups, and in November 1971 he caved in and exempted the Department of Agriculture from the reorganization. On a revised organization chart he stuck Agriculture up on a little shelf of its own, segregated from the others for some undisclosed peculiarity. Since no rational argument could possibly be made for exempting Agriculture from the new architecture, it was suspected that Nixon might be driven to other compromises. As Congressman Erlenborn asked a triumphant Agriculture secretary Earl Butz when he came to the Hill in January 1972 to report the President's concession, if Agriculture were saved from being broken up just so that angry farmers could retain their very own department, how were businessmen and labor to be reconciled to losing theirs?[26] Nixon admitted that he had yielded on Agriculture to gain support in Congress for the rest of the reorganization. Thus he led neither a gallant fight nor a successful tactical retreat. The concession confused the issue and encouraged other groups to resist. Reorganization did not move through Congress, and Nixon went into the 1972 campaign without it.

But he and Ash had spread considerable light. The reorganization plan clarified the irrationality of current organization, and educated those interested in such matters by offering a model for organization around delivery of services rather than traditional interest-group representation. An irritated Nixon in March 1972 told Congress that "the sand is running in the glass, and the hour is growing late, for enactment of a critically needed reform."[27] Perhaps never had Richard Nixon said anything more likely to be judged profoundly true by all students of American government, perhaps even by future generations who are likely to remember him mostly for activities of less unerring wisdom.

5

We have sketched the highlights of the Nixon administration's commitment to strengthening the government's capacity for social management. These events must fall into the category of unexpected. Just as it was not anticipated that the most conservative president inaugurated in twelve years would end his first term having increased the federal deficit by $100 billion, so it was at least as unexpected that this lifetime enemy of federal power would create within the executive branch an institution for policy planning, would send to Congress the most radical reorganization plan in our history, would call for a national growth policy, would appoint a commission on population growth, and suggest a national population policy. Yet he had done all these things in the first term. If there had been anyone in Washington deviant enough to have the word "Planning" in his working vocabulary, these steps would have been identified as steps toward Planning. This startling idea will require more attention. But the focus so far has been too limited. Others were moving in that same direction at a pace that at least matched that of the executive.

The origins of a major expansion of national control over social development, the Environmental Policy Act of 1969, were in Congress. The Act had many sponsors, pre-eminent among them the liberal senators Jackson and Muskie and Congressman John Dingell. The act made it public policy to maintain and restore the environment, and set up institutions—a council (CEQ) and annual report—modeled on the 1946 Employment Act. This apparently went beyond what Nixon thought necessary. He had established the Cabinet-level Environmental Quality Council in May 1969. Congressional environmental forces decided, probably correctly, that this was a cosmetic move and that Cabinet officers do not solve large problems outside their normal jurisdictions. So they legislated a sort of twin to the CEA, the CEQ. One can think of no legislation which is more squarely based upon the planning idea than the NEPA. It required, as Arnold Reitze put it, that government agencies think before they act, that costs be estimated in advance, secondary effects calculated, and alternatives considered.

Nixon signed this law without public complaint. Still, the administration was generally expected to drag its feet on environmental protection, since it was a traditional commitment of what passed for conservatism in the United States to resist public regulation of the use of private property, to assist private exploitation of resources rather than curb it. Richard Nixon, like his impetuous secretary of the Interior Walter Hickel, surprised environmentalists. He took the offensive, insisted that his administration was leading the public crusade to stop environmental abuse. All of Nixon's annual environmental messages, the reports of his Environmental Protection Agency (established in December 1970 to consolidate the government's anti-pollution programs) and the CEQ, these annually aligned the administration with the cause of environmental control, and presented a long list of legislation which a laggard Congress had not passed. His environmental message of February 15, 1973, for example, reaffirmed an active federal role in the matter, called for national drinking-water standards, requested the opening of the Highway Trust fund for mass transit purposes, supported a national land-use policy act, asked for laws to force the states to regulate the siting of key facilities, requested a powerplant siting law which would establish a "long-range planning process," suggested a federal tax to discourage development of coastal wetlands, criticized the weakness of federal management of public lands, and asked that it be made a federal offense to take the life of an animal of an endangered species. And he reminded Congress that they failed to act on 19 crucial laws to bring these and other controls to the private use of resources.

This was Richard Nixon? Perhaps there was less affront to traditional conservatism here than meets the eye. A definitive treatment of the administration's environmental protection record has not been written, but it may be pointed out that presidential messages are what we say, not what we do. John Mitchell warned Nixon-watchers about that. On the Santa Barbara oil spill, on the cross-Florida canal, on other occasions such as these the administration revealed distaste for interference with economic "progress." And since the country and Congress (to a lesser extent) seethed with what conservative people called environmental extremists—since several of the states and localities had begun to enact very strict controls—it may have been seen the path of enlightened conservatism to steal the fanatic's clothes, enacting moderate national controls before the mob stampeded for stricter local and/or national regulation. Nixon's budget requests for pollution control tend to bear out such speculations. The Clean Air Act was authorized at $375 million for FY 1972, but Nixon asked for $167 million, less than the loan guarantee to Lockheed Aircraft. Authorization by Congress for solid-waste programs for FY 1972 were $152 million, but the President asked only for $19.3 million, which is only one-sixth of the sum he asked for military assistance for Greece. And he requested twice as much for military aid to Turkey than for acquisition of National Park lands.[28]

Lacking a definitive judgment, it seems clear that Nixon's environmental record was exceptionally positive and substantial compared to his predecessors; compared to state and congressional inclinations, it seems that he was frequently a restraining influence. Yet if he was driven toward environmental control faster than was his natural inclination, he certainly participated resourcefully and as a self-proclaimed activist in the epochal turning point of the late 1960s-early 1970s when the national government first gained the legal and institutional capability to limit environmental damage.

In 1970 came three more gifts of enlarged authority conferred upon the government by Congress. The Economic Stabilization Act of 1970 thrust upon a reluctant executive the authority to impose wage and price controls. Control authority was voted by Congress for a variety of reasons, most of them shabby. While a few liberals believed that time for a strong incomes policy had arrived, others noticed that public support for wage/price controls had reached 50 per cent, highest since the Korean War, and if the buck were passed to the President he would bear the blame for not using them or for using them poorly. In any event Congress would appear to have done its duty to stem inflation.

Wage/price controls were one of those rare gifts of power that Richard Nixon did not want. A lifetime in conservative circles had convinced him that controls were bad for capitalism, and his own ten months in the OPA during World War II had left distasteful memories of the bureaucratic empire that controls required. He came into office on a crest of inflation generated by policy decisions—military, fiscal, and monetary—of his predecessor. It was at once clear that he did not contemplate any of the structural approaches to inflation control, such as an incomes policy or anti-trust activity, but would rely upon traditional fiscal and monetary restraint.

Nixon never really found the political courage to hold to that course. Ike thought he would be a one-term president due to a stiff recession brought on by appropriately tough anti-inflation policies. But Nixon thought he had lost the 1960 election largely because 8 per cent of the work force was unemployed, and he would not cut the federal budget sharply enough to produce a recession of inflation-stopping size—however large that might have been. He was especially tender with the defense budget, yet disappointed conservative advisers in not cutting sharply into Johnson's social budget. And so inflation accelerated through 1969, and the administration's hesitant and blurred policies came under attack from all sides. In late 1969 economic adviser Arthur Burns had very reluctantly concluded that a gentle jawboning on price and wage increases was now necessary. It was an incomes policy, but just a tiny, voluntaristic edge of one. Burns was joined by the secretary of the Treasury and others, but Nixon held out until the summer of 1970, when he announced to an unexcited world that the CEA would issue periodic "inflation alerts" to spotlight inflationary price and wage increases.

This amusing step raised economic uncertainty even further; inflation went on despite considerable unemployment. November elections produced a rebuff for the Republicans. Nixon's economic policies, or "game plan" as he preposterously called it in the beginning, were a political and economic failure, unless one had unusually lenient standards. The President's 1972 re-election was threatened. This menace broke through the President's philosophical convictions—when this happened with FDR, it was usually regarded by liberals as laudable pragmatism—and produced the surprising decision of August 1971. Richard Nixon, under the authority thrust upon him by a Democratic Congress, invoked a 90-day price and wage freeze, set up a Cost of Living Council to devise a set of "temporary" controls, set a 10 per cent tariff on certain imports, and suspended gold payments in order to float (devaluate) the dollar. Nixon called this "the most comprehensive new economic plan to be undertaken in this nation in four decades"—since the new economic plans of FDR, presumably.[29] Controls had last been employed during the Korean War; these would last until the spring of 1974. They would, it was hoped, contain the inflationary pressures which the administration intended to release through monetary and fiscal ease in order to produce sufficiently full employment by 1972 to bring voters to the polls in the right frame of mind.

Nixon actually had considerable business support for controls in the summer of 1971—including the CED. This helped overrule his lifetime convictions, and of course he also consulted his political instincts. Economists and others have faulted the decision in retrospect, having forgotten that economic advice in those trying days (and after) had been ineffective and contradictory, that some reliable people favored controls under the circumstances, that the public and Congress seemed to want them, and that for a president to want to be re-elected over his untrustworthy opponents is entirely a part of our system. In any event Nixon, in addition to all that he had previously done by 1971 to toughen and extend the government's influence over American society, had now added an incomes policy. Uneasiness over controls was widespread, in fact was perhaps strongest in the administration itself. C. Jackson Grayson, chosen by Nixon to head the Price Commission, was to write:

> Have we taken the big stride toward the perfectly planned economy? I hope not.

Yet farther on in his memoir of the 1971–73 period of controls, Grayson gloomily concluded:

> I am personally convinced that our economic system is steadily shifting away from private enterprise and a free market, and toward central direction and public control.[30]

6

Environmental legislation and controls, unlike the steps earlier mentioned, originated in Congress. Another unasked grant of executive authority was the requirement, written into the Housing and Urban Development Act of 1970 as Title VII, to submit a biennial report on urban growth. Congressmen saw this as forcing the administration to take the next step in growth policy after the tentative sentences that peeked through Nixon's 1970 State of the Union Address. There were signs in the 1970 Act that Congress had made a feeble effort to define an NGP before turning the problem over to Nixon. The preamble listed eight elements that would certainly be a part of an NGP when one was finally born. Beyond this list mere congressmen were not at that time able to go. The ball was hit deep into the administration's court with the requirement for a report on urban growth. For his part, Nixon opposed Title VII, preferring not to be locked into a reporting cycle every two years when he would be expected to show steady progress toward this thing Moynihan had pushed under his tent. The administration wanted more room to maneuver in dealing with a matter about which it was internally divided, uncertain, and apprehensive.

A third new policy area was opened up by congressional liberals in 1970—land-use planning. With the broadening discussion of growth policy it was only a matter of time until the nation's land-use practices would come under critical appraisal. National attention to land-use surprised and irritated the local officials and developers who were involved in the process in the 10,000 units of local government where decisions were made in the late 1960s. Like family size, it was one of the last areas of private activity where the national government had not meddled. Admittedly, one-third of the nation's acreage was in the public domain, and was managed by agencies like the Forest Service or the Department of the Interior. Neither the government's right to manage this land nor the manner of doing it had been seriously questioned since the dust storms of the 1930s. Few people recalled that it had ever been an issue. On the rest, private land, the government had no say. FDR had suggested with some diffidence that lumbering practices on private land ought to be a matter of some reasonable federal regulation, but he was rebuffed. The average American was exceptionally irritable when property rights were threatened, and no national politician from Roosevelt into the 1960s returned to his suggestion. Developers of land were well organized and dangerous antagonists. Critics of the existing decentralized system were not an important lobby. Who would propose federal involvement in this turbulent area, with the government so busy defending the free world and keeping the economy out of trouble?

The first brave soul to tread on these fiery coals was Senator Henry Jackson. But if he had not been born, others would have stepped forward. Awareness of land-use crisis was no individual's creation, rather an opportunity. Jackson produced the first legislative focus for the issue when he submitted the National Land Use Policy and Planning Assistance Act in January 1970. One cannot be sure what brought him so tenaciously to this risky issue. His major interests prior to 1970 had been national security. Perhaps no uncanny instincts were required to perceive this rather exposed problem. Jackson was intelligent; he was from Washington State, where growth issues were increasingly sensitive politically as a recreation-oriented public pondered urban encroachments; he had a strong national orientation, nurtured during years of involvement in defense questions and from pondering his own presidential ambitions; he was orderly by nature, and was therefore easily aroused by the chaotic land-use system his country relied upon as it entered the final thirty years of the twentieth century. Other Senators might easily have been brought to this issue along similar paths. But Jackson's reputation as a serious, responsible moderate with no ties to the woolly edge of the Democratic party meant that he would be taken seriously if he said the country had a problem requiring federal action.

And the arguments for action were virtually unassailable. Population growth put enormous pressure on supplies of open land. America from 1970 to 2000 would convert 28,000 square miles of land from rural to urban use, would strip-mine and build power lines and freeways, power plants, and housing, adding in thirty years as much of man-made America as it had since 1789. Yet the process of deciding where and how all this would take place was, as Jackson put it in 1973, "chaotic, ad hoc, short-term, crisis-by-crisis, case-by-case."[31] Profit guided the plans of developers, minimal expense guided the plans of the municipal officials, political considerations guided the awarding of government contracts. Everywhere the organized interests pressing for short-term profit overwhelmed the capacity of decision-making agencies to consider competing claims, to take broader perspectives.

What was required for the future, Jackson thought, was to raise the level of land-use decision-making. Local jurisdictions endowed with land-use authority were easily dominated by organized interests, and their decisions were often economically or environmentally irrational in a larger context. Jackson wanted a broader context, but he was not eager to be cast as a communist or visionary. He settled upon the state as the appropriate unit for land-use planning, a decision which was politically inescapable. Larger regions existed in economic and environmental reality but not as political entities, and no practical man would propose elevating these decisions to the national level. Jackson accommodated to the federal system as he found it. His bill proposed the extension of the federal grants of about $100 million a year to entice states to establish land-use planning covering four types of development—areas of critical environmental concern; areas contemplated for key facilities such as energy sites or highways; areas of regional benefit (by which he meant obnoxious uses of land which neighboring areas might want placed elsewhere, uses such as sanitary landfills or sewage treatment plants or low-income housing); and areas where large-scale commercial or residential developments were proposed. Other land-use decisions, having to do with small parcels, single dwellings, or commercial enterprise, would remain the joyous responsibility of local authority, as of old.

Jackson intended his bill to seem a moderate and reasonable approach to a pressing problem, but he cannot have been surprised to encounter people who thought otherwise. At first the opposition came from those who wanted reform but hoped to go about it differently. The initial resistance came from Congressman Wayne Aspinall, who proposed to lump federal lands in the same bill, affecting private lands. This unnecessary complication managed to muddy the water until 1972, when Aspinall was defeated in a primary. With this diversion out of the way and the Nixon administration supporting land-use legislation in a bill similar to Jackson's, the interested parties got down to serious conflict. Jackson wanted to confine the bill largely to *process,* firmly leading the states toward their planning duties but leaving the substance of planning in the law minimal or nonexistent. This might diminish the outcries about federal dictation that one heard as a sort of reflex from the guardians of the Constitution. Jackson thought the feds must dictate that there be a national network of state land-using planning systems, but not what their goals and standards should be. This was not quite possible, although Jackson approached it as closely as he could. Some minimal national standards had to be tucked away in the bill, or recalcitrant states would make a mockery of land-use reformers' hopes for actual planning in place of what we already had. This aspect of things Jackson downplayed. The bill would "require the states to exercise states' rights," the senator said, to underline the conservatism of his approach.[32]

With federal land-use legislation a serious possibility one might have expected a stand-up war between growth and no-growth armies. Jackson's bill passed the Senate in 1973, a relatively quick passage from hopper to successful floor vote, because that war did not take place. From 1970 to 1973, while successive hearings in Senate and House gradually channeled the contending interests, neither the development-oriented nor the slow-growth oriented (nor the no-growth oriented) could decide whether their goals would best be achieved by lodging regulatory power at the federal, state, or local level. Senator Muskie reflected the traditional liberal instinct when he urged more specific federal standards to ensure adequate nation-wide environmental protection. But many environmentalists felt safer with state governments in states such as Maine, Vermont, Delaware, Colorado, California, Florida, and Hawaii where local environmental and slow-growth sentiment had already begun to effect what observers had called a "quiet revolution in land-use management." They feared that the Department of the Interior might force energy installations on reluctant states more often than the other way around. Subsequent events had proven this fear not unfounded. In any event, Muskie's effort to strengthen federal standards was beaten. He then attacked the Jackson bill for lack of adequate sanctions, and this sort of pressure eventually forced Jackson to add "crossover" penalties by which states not devising adequate land-use planning procedures would lose a graduated percentage of federal funds for other projects.

This issue, the strength of federal sanctions, had produced for the first time a relatively clear division between the real estate-construction industry lobby and the environmentalists. Another came when Jackson decided to put the federal administration of the law (one couldn't openly call it "enforcement," since the whole issue of federal standards had been muted) in the Department of the Interior. Muskie and other environmentalists knew that Interior was a conservative agency with strong emotional and political ties with oilmen, land-developers, ranchers, and other undesirable citizens. They thus preferred to lodge enforcement in the new, relatively consumer-oriented EPA. On this Jackson prevailed in the Senate, and the Udall-managed bill in the House retained similar administrative provisions.

One might have thought that some legislators would make trouble for Jackson by suggesting that land-use legislation be enacted only as a part of a larger NGP. This made logical sense, but political sense suggested a sloppier path of advance. Incrementalism was the habit in Congress, and there was no important support for delaying land-use action until a structure for NGP was in place. One took what one could get, piecemeal. The NGP forces scored a minor victory by passing the Coastal Zone Management Act in 1972, but more was at present impossible. When Jackson's bill or some other land-use legislation passed, it would take its place among the gathering parts of an NGP, and coherence would have to be arranged later.

Jackson had a lot to say in support of his bill, and most of his arguments faced to the Right. No new controls were being proposed, he stressed; the federal government was not invading the last sacred area, land use. The National Land Use Planning Act was "the nation's best and probably last chance to preserve and to invigorate state and local land-use decision making and to insure that basic property rights are not infringed by faceless Washington bureaucrats. . . ."[33] It was effective camouflage of a piece of legislation which marked a radical expansion of social claims upon individual behavior. As with virtually every such measure, it could not have gotten very far if conservative interests of substantial size had not decided that it was this law today or a more threatening one tomorrow. Jackson's bill was endorsed by the *Wall Street Journal, Business Week,* and other business organs and groups. It had the support of the National Governors' Conference, the AFL-CIO, and the American Institute of Architects. Enlightened conservatism had rarely been mobilized so promptly. These groups were not put off with Jackson's thought that land-use decisions ought to be changed from "selfish, short-term and private" to "long-term and public," even though these words implied collectivism of uncharted dimensions.[34]

Where was the administration in all of this? It was on the side of those proposing reform, change, better planning. Nixon supported Jackson's bill from the first, although the administration submitted a slightly different draft (with strong cross-over sanctions). In each environmental message, 1971–73, a national land-use planning law was listed by the President as "must" legislation. Rogers C. B. Morton, secretary of the Interior, said in Los Angeles in 1972: "If we fail in our generation to inaugurate a national land use policy, we will let the next generation down. . . . This country cannot grow like Topsy. There has to be a sense of order."[35] In some respects, the Nixon government was more eager for national intervention in land-use than Jackson was. The administration submitted power siting and deep-water port legislation which Jackson thought radical, as it provided for federal pre-emption. Through 1973 the administration remained committed to national leadership in land-use planning, although it left to Congress the daily struggle to produce a majority for this controversial expansion of public authority.

7

The year 1972 was an occasion of considerable importance in the history of American Planning. I am reluctant to call attention to this, as it tends to confirm a vice of historians and other people, that they think presidential elections are Very Important Events when they often are not. But to the Nixon loyalists the election of 1972 was a transcendental occasion, and its approach brought a powerful re-direction to the administration's activities. In 1969, 1970, and into 1971 it had taken the lead in institutional reforms designed to augment and centralize the government's capacities for social management. The President established the Domestic Council to achieve horizontal integration of policy and study both long and short-range problems; he proposed a sweeping reorganization of the executive branch; he established the National Goals Research Staff to work on both goals and social reporting; he appointed the first population commission; he called for a national growth policy; he supported a national land-use law; he extended controls to wages and prices.

All this had taken place in a society churning with anxiety over the direction of things under current arrangements. The country fairly sprouted with spontaneous local efforts to control social change through public intervention. The states of Hawaii and Oregon, for example, the city of Petaluma, were in their own spheres bolder pioneers than the federal government along the paths of public control of social development. Many citizens, recognizing the limits of local authority, were putting sustained pressure upon the national government to energize itself. Especially sensitive to the gathering social disorder were environmentalists, natural and social scientists, city planners, architects, engineers, mayors, even some governors.

In Washington the executive and the Congress both responded to this public mood and to the emerging realities of finite resources squeezed by population growth. The response of both branches was slow, halting, and inadequate. But one was surprised to see the dog walking on its hind legs at all. The national government's record revealed an ingrained sluggishness; still, the steps taken from 1969–71 toward adequate social management of our national development compared well with any two years of that creative managerial era, the New Deal. In this burst of activity the executive had been more interventionist, more activist, than the legislative branch.

This changed in 1972, and the initiative shifted to congressional liberals. Moynihan had left for Harvard late in 1970, and while this premise would be much too simple, it did appear that the ardor for national growth and population policies went in his suitcases. The 1972 growth report was published in February as the law required, and the administration showed a respectable degree of courage and logic by calling it *Report on National Growth*—urban growth was seen as too limited a concept. But the report disappointed those who hoped the executive might move the growth policy discussion forward. On looking more closely at growth policy the administration had found it both conceptually more diffuse and politically more unsettling to elements of its constituency than had been foreseen. "I think they are beautiful words," said Undersecretary of the Interior John Whitaker of the growth policy issue in 1973, "and when you try to get down to what they mean it is an extremely difficult problem, the center of that problem being who decides who is going to grow. . . ."[36] *Report on National Growth, 1972,* offered demographic data, deplored disparities between rural and urban growth patterns, and appreciatively reviewed the administration's efforts to meet the problem. But it struck ideological notes discordant in the NGP discussion by insisting that it was vain to hope for a single policy to correct the situation, that "our planning for national growth must rather seek to help individual Americans develop their unique potential and achieve their personal goals,"[37] and that the main responsibility for growth policy rested upon the shoulders of local governments and individuals. The administration that had called for NGP two years before now took several shuffling steps to the rear.

Congressional and public supporters of NGP were greatly irritated. Rep. Thomas Ashley, one of the prime movers behind Title VII, arranged for hearings on the report in June. All the witnesses were hostile:

Arthur A. Davis of the Conservation Foundation: [the report] "does not address the issues adequately."

Alan Rabinowitz of the American Institute of Planners: it "left a great deal to be desired" and "fails to be reponsive to the Congressional mandate."

Archibald Rogers of the American Institute of Architects: [the report is] "unacceptable" and "calls for a 'no policy' policy." ". . . too little, too late and too subordinated to the shackles of its 19th and 18th century value system."

R.P. Burton and Harvey Garn of the Urban Institute: "inadequate both in concept and vision."

Bernard Weissbourd of Metropolitan Structures: "a sorry reflection upon the United States of America and its national leadership at this time" and "an apparent confession of intellectual bankruptcy.[38]

Many objections were raised. Those who wanted American perpetual growth assumptions challenged did not like the report's assumption that growth was inevitable. Could it be an accident that *Population and the American Future,* product of a governmental commission and published one month later, had received not one single reference? Most fundamental, the report stressed the difficulties of devising an NGP when, as one witness said, "we already have one, fragmented, disparate, conflicting, and inadequate as it is.[39] This fundamental truth had lay behind the growth policy movement from the start, but the authors of the report apparently preferred the invisible hands of undeclared policies to a Policy that would give its inevitable enemies something to focus upon. The mayor of San Jose, Norman Mineta, described with undisguised irritation how federal mortgage insurance, tax, and highway policies had helped lure 25,000 people a year to San Jose through the 1960s and forced their spatial arrangement in sprawling, racially segregated suburbs. He did not enjoy reading in the Report that growth patterns should be left to local governments and individuals. But this was June, and sour grapes. The administration had made its decision, and published in response to the 1970 congressional mandate what the *New York Times* was to label "a mausoleum of words."

Some observers thought that the administration drew back principally because an explicit NGP would inevitably mean some effort to disperse blacks from center cities to suburbs. A Republican President would have difficulty explaining this line of activity to his constituency, especially in an election year. NGP advocates did not sympathize with the Executive's unwillingness, whatever his party or philosophy, to gratuitously clarify the impact of policies with such fundamental but scattered influence upon where people would settle, who their neighbors would be, and where builders would be allowed to make their contribution to America. And few were generous enough to concede that the vacuity of the report, apparently written in haste by John Ehrlichman after earlier drafts pieced together by the bureaucracy proved unmanageable, owed much to the inherent complexity of the issue. By now the administration probably wished it had never heard of growth policy. But Title VII of the 1970 housing act locked them into a remorseless reporting cycle. There was no way to kill the monster; one could only keep it quiet, and underfed. In May 1972, the *Wall Street Journal* disclosed that Ehrlichman had sent a memo to all Cabinet officers with a long series of questions on growth policy. Apparently he intended to be better prepared next time—just two short years away.

The issue was gradually appropriated by liberals, who found it more congenial. In May 1972, Senator Humphrey, then a strong contender for the Democratic presidential nomination, announced his intention to draft legislation committing the nation to an NGP and establish institutions to produce it. He spoke at the Commonwealth Club in San Francisco, and did not perhaps appreciate the appropriateness of the site he chose to join the Planning movement. Here Roosevelt had expressed his strongest endorsement of Planning in 1932, in the same month just thirty years before. Humphrey had some company. Senator Vance Hartke submitted in 1972 what he hoped would be the National Growth Policy Planning Act of 1973, and the American Institute of Architects called for an NGP in its report, *America at the Growing Edge* (1972). And if anyone read the Democratic platform for the 1972 race, they would have found in it a pledge for a national urban growth policy "instead of today's inadvertent, chaotic and haphazard one that doesn't work."[40]

Such ideas might conceivably have led to the establishment of NGP at a stroke, as the 1946 Employment Act had finally codified all the economic management traditions of the 1930s. Incrementalism, as we have noted, was more likely. In October 1972, Congress passed PL 92-583, the Coastal Zone Management Act, recognizing the special importance of coastal waters and adjacent shorelands, and encouraging states to develop adequate land- and water-use "management programs." This presumably meant planning. The content of these "management programs" was loosely defined, and for some reason the administrator was the secretary of commerce. The law was little understood, even by its authors. It held no sanctions if states did not care to join, and was therefore not paid much attention in the press. Nixon included no funds for its implementation in the 1974 budget, without explaining whether he did so out of distaste for this piecemeal approach to a serious subject—NGP—or because he was souring on the whole enterprise. The law was an odd event. Some 50 per cent of the American people lived within the coastal zone as there defined, and most of the national energy production took place within its borders. NGP was apparently being constructed by parts, and well ahead of public consensus or understanding.

In any event the momentum of the multifaceted movement toward Planning had shifted away from the executive branch and now appeared on Capitol Hill. Congress stirred with novel ideas. Congressman Emilio Daddario led an inquiry into the government's research and development arrangements, and did not like what he found. The government was spending $17.4 billion on R&D in 1974, more than three-quarters of it in Defense and space, the rest scattered about in places like NSF, NIH, Agriculture, the Food and Drug Administration, and so on. All this brainy activity was remarkably dispersed, and next to impossible to evaluate or shift in new directions—from military to civilian purposes, for example. Coordination could hardly come from Eisenhower's science adviser, but it was hoped in 1962 that Kennedy's OST might serve as a focal point for appraisal and control. This arrangement satisfied both presidents and scientists while federal R&D funds were climbing through the 1960s, but scientific opposition to the Vietnam war and to projects like the SST and ABM caused both sides to question existing arrangements. Daddario, Ted Kennedy, and others in Congress groped for new formulas, convinced that science policy required centralization. One result of their labors was the Office of Technology Assessment of 1972, set up to provide what was called "an early warning system" to help Congress monitor "second order" and other indirect effects of technological innovation.

This was helpful, but did not correct the situation in the executive branch. There, in the words of Harvey Brooks of Harvard and the National Academy of Sciences, the status quo was quite unsatisfactory:

> The American system with its emphasis on pluralism, decentralization and competition among sectors for R and D funds, performed pretty well until the mid-1960s. However, we've moved into an era where resources for R and D are limited, thus necessitating more careful planning and coordination at or near the highest government decision making level. . . . In addition, a new and more difficult task of interweaving science policy with national social, economic and political policies would seem to call for a unified, coherent strategy.[41]

Words of a planner. And in the front part of the Nixon era, they might well have been followed by an appropriate presidential response. If OST was not strong enough at budget time, strengthen its ties with OMB, as one strategy, or—as Lee DuBridge, Nixon's science adviser urged—establish a council of science advisers. But the administration, in 1972, had their minds on politics, not Policy. The White House staff had not liked OST advice because it wasn't "packaged in a way they found helpful," and in more clarifying words, "kept coming with answers that . . . didn't fit the political realities."[42] That is, OST, and to a greater extent the President's Science Advisory Committee, had too openly opposed the SST and ABM and space shuttle, administration-backed measures. In January 1973, the announcement came. Nixon would abolish the whole OST-PSAC apparatus, and the NSF would now give the President scientific advice when he wanted it. Scientists almost unanimously condemned the move, as "downgrading" scientific advice. Congressmen noted that the Defense Department's R&D activities received no scrutiny from a White House body with scientific expertise. Apparently, Congress had taken a step toward better technology assessment and the executive one step away, within three months of each other. It was a sign of the times.

We now know, in dispiriting detail, that beginning in 1971 the Nixon administration was concentrating upon the November election with remarkable single-mindedness. The White House was absorbed in the effort to control the media and the nominating processes of the Democratic party. It had no time to resume the reforms of 1969–71 designed to improve control of domestic policy formulation and administration. What time was left from re-election activities would go to the higher claim of foreign policy. The trips to China and Russia came in 1972, and more of the endless negotiations and military adventures associated with the war in southeast Asia. About the only step taken by the administration in 1972 toward improved social management was the broadening of the scope of OMB circular A-95, a little noticed document that was responsible for some improvement in the confusion of grant programs by requiring state regional planning organizations to review federal aid in order to reduce overlapping applications.

The population commission reported in March, and held some surprises. "There is hardly any social problem confronting this nation," it said, "whose solution would be easier if our population were larger. . . . We have concluded that no substantial benefits would result from continued growth of the nation's population."[43] This conclusion came in a report written with more clarity and candor than many had expected from an official commission on such a sensitive subject. It offered some sixty-two recommendations, including an end to discrimination based on sex, the liberalization of abortion laws, that the government "develop a set of national population guidelines" and set up the Office of Population Growth and Distribution. Another vote for NGP. All these worked toward the same end, that "the nation welcome and plan for a stabilized population."[44]

Readers of Nixon's population message of 1969 might have expected that the report would have his endorsement. Instead he politely thanked the commission members, and in a few days chose two of the recommendations, on liberalized abortion laws and the availability of birth control information to minors, for specific repudiation. Nothing was said in support of the report's general thrust, nor of the administration's plans to "welcome and plan for a stabilized population." Several people felt disappointed in Nixon's response, even betrayed. The President "cast a rather wet blanket over the potential interest of quite a few Federal agencies," said Robert Parke, the deputy director of the commission.[45] The administration had dropped the population issue. Moynihan, of course, was no longer around to urge a more positive response, but the President's negative public attitude owed to more than this. It was an election year, and he was trading a critical position on part of the commission report for Catholic votes in November.[46] It is painful to recall this bargain after counting the avalanche of votes that put Nixon back in the White House. The administration that in 1969 could claim to have taken the longest strides toward control of the major destabilizing force in modern history had in 1972 set itself against further discussion of the issue. Eisenhower's reminder that "history will rightly condemn us" had been forgotten. "At times," wrote Moynihan three years after leaving Washington, "the White House of 1971 and 1972 reminded me of Bourbons and Hapsburgs in the 1820s in Europe going around taking down gas lights and abolishing smallpox vaccination programs."[47]

8

At least one of the reforms necessary to improve social management which had been stalled in 1972 had lost momentum because Congress, not the administration, had decided against it. This was reorganization of the executive branch, a reform apparently much closer to Nixon's heart than population control or NGP. Not even the campaign pushed the subject from his mind, and in a meeting at Camp David on September 20, 1972, the President and Ehrlichman decided to go ahead without congressional approval. Nixon, like other presidents before him, wanted his chief advisers to command functional areas. Reorganization would have given him a Cabinet with that design. This the Congress had been too backward to approve. So he and Ehrlichman drew up a complicated new system that could go into effect without congressional assent. They must have been unusually tired and distracted. Five presidential assistants would form an inner circle, channeling information and analysis from the areas of White House operations (Haldeman), Executive Management (Ash), Domestic Affairs (Ehrlichman), Economic Affairs (Shultz), Foreign Affairs (Kissinger). Of the four new proposed Cabinet departments in the Nixon-Ash reorganization, only one, Economic Affairs, had hit the inner ring. Beneath this ring, Nixon put three counsellors, actually current Cabinet officers on special detail: Human Resources (Weinberger), Natural Resources (Butz), Community Development (Lynn). They would report through the Domestic Affairs Assistant.

Only seasoned White House watchers followed this easily. It did seem clear enough that the old constituency-oriented departments had been downgraded a notch to make room for an intervening layer of functional coordinators—"counsellors." Cabinet officers must now sit down from them at State dinners, unless one of them happened also to be a counsellor. Above both Cabinet secretaries and counsellors was a tight ring of five assistants. These complex changes were announced in January

1973, along with a reduction in Domestic Council staff and other shufflings. Observers did not know quite what to make of it. It was obviously another presidential effort to get control of the Permanent Government, and while Nixon's organizational clarity had blurred, his tenacity on the issue was still perfectly clear.

The new arrangement lasted less than six months, when it was dismantled (May 1973) in the intensifying crisis over Watergate. Nixon never got his reorganization, but of all the changes he sought to enhance the government's managerial and potentially Planning capabilities, reorganization of White House staff and executive branch was his most sustained interest. It is difficult to say how much of what he did and wished to do will make a lasting mark. The reorganization plan itself, and the Ash reports, are full of insight and fresh ideas, and may have more ahead of them than dust collection in a library. The Domestic Council was retained by Gerald Ford, and appears as permanent as the NSC.

But the DC disappointed its backers more than is openly admitted. Its chief value has been as a base for inter-agency Task Forces which have produced some innovative policy thinking in a government very short of new ideas. But it has shortcomings as a place for policy coordination. Its members are after all department heads who do not take on a national ("presidential") perspective simply by driving over to the White House from the Department of Agriculture. The DC is quite large, and Nixon, according to the report of a White House aide, disliked the meetings and scheduled them with decreasing frequency.[48] Here again, the distorting influence of the election was felt. In 1972, by many reports, the DC staff worked mostly on political speeches, position papers to refute and confound Democrats, and smothering fires within the administration that might politically embarrass the President. This was the staff that was supposed to provide the President with an "institutional memory" which the Cabinet could not possess. This must have been evolving to some extent, since the staff reached about seventy persons and they dutifully kept files. But much of their remem-

bering seems to have had to do with the transgressions and vulnerabilities of "the enemy." Instead of the experts and specialists
in domestic problems one would have expected to find in the
DC, John Donovan found more political generalists, political
associates with whom Ehrlichman and Nixon were comfortable.
He identified three of Ehrlichman's seven deputies as former
advance men for Nixon.[49] Nixon's choice as the director of the
DC after left was Kenneth Cole, a candid, engaging man of extremely conservative views, who comes close to believing that the
government can do nothing well. "The only thing we learned,"
he said of his DC experience, "is that no one here is smart
enough to manage an economy as big and complex as this one."[50]
Could Nixon (or Ford; Cole served until February 1975) have
expected the DC to flourish as a coordinating and policy planning agency when directed by a man who thought Nixon's most
significant domestic achievement had been ending the draft?

Some of these problems of the DC were structural, some were
inevitable in every pre-election period, some derived from the
special characteristics of Nixon and his men. Sorting them out
will take some time and access to the primary sources. In any
event the DC did not become the Planning Board that its
founding executive order had sketched in 1970. Nixon actually
preferred to get coordination of domestic policy through one
man, as he had designed it on the foreign policy side where
Henry Kissinger overawed potential opposition. He first tried
Arthur Burns, then John Ehrlichman, whose performance in
1970 and 1971 as domestic coordinator may rank higher someday than most people think. Eventually, political concerns related to the election, then to Watergate, reduced Ehrlichman's
ability to coordinate a government resistant to coordination.
The DC was given over to Kenneth Cole, and with Ehrlichman
gone in April 1974, domestic coordination went to Melvin
Laird, whose thoughts for some time had been on fleets, bomb-
ers, and bases. Then came William Rush, as Nixon continued to
assign one White House aide the job of domestic coordination.
The Kissinger example, and his own preference for rooms with a
very few people in them, led the President to place impossible

demands upon selected individuals. The institutional base for policy coordination, the DC, was very much in limbo in 1973 and 1974. Optimists might have assumed that it, or one of those listed presidential supercoordinators, was managing to eliminate the gross inconsistencies of American domestic policies which had been so glaringly exposed in the studies of the 1960s. The energy crisis would dash those assumptions, and reveal how short of adequate Planning the Nixon government had stopped when in 1972 it took the fatal low road to political success.

9

From the election to the jolting end of the Nixon presidency in August 1974, the pattern of congressional initiative and administration drift continued to characterize the landscape of policy issues which involved the capacity to plan. In the spring of 1973 the Senate hoppers held two Planning bills, relatively parallel efforts by Senators Hartke and Humphrey. These proposals did not stun the capital, no hearings were scheduled, there was no media rush to probe their implications. But their appearance was a remarkable event. Senator Humphrey was not thought to be an exciting figure in American national life after the 1968 defeat. He was said to talk too much and not to say new things. He had made the mistake of being Lyndon Johnson's vice president and defending the war; he had not written a best-selling book. These considerations inclined informed liberal opinion (conservatives agreed for different reasons) to have a strong lack of interest in Humphrey's last years in the Senate. This will one day be recognized as a serious error. Humphrey's own view is more accurate. He has stated that the most important single legislative proposal he has ever been associated with is the Balanced National Growth and Development Act which he promised in May 1972 and drafted in early 1973. In 1975, the altered bill had picked up bi-partisan support and was candidly titled the Balanced Growth and Economic Planning bill. (See Chap. VI, p. 278.) The long shunned word was out in the open. If it were enacted, America would have a framework for Planning more comprehensive and promising than anything Franklin Roosevelt administered or even proposed.

At a stroke, liberalism had converted back to Planning. Humphrey proposed a sophisticated law that would deploy all the functions of social Planning in an entirely new structure. Perhaps he was braced for denunciation as a socialist, a Planner, a radical. Surely this would have been so in the 1930s, the 1940s, the 1950s. In making a daring proposal, and finding that it was not thought to be very interesting, he had opened some intriguing possibilities. The political culture no longer equated Planning with revolution or socialism. It received the word "Planning" from a leading national politician with a thoughtful silence. Indeed, there were indications that the calm that stalled Humphrey's proposal for Planning might gradually be replaced by a gentle wind behind it. Senator Hartke submitted his own S1286 in March 1973, the National Growth Policy Planning Act. Hartke was burned nowhere in effigy for being a Planner.

The two senators were not alone in raising the standard of Planning. A seminar of scholars and public officials at the Woodrow Wilson International Center in Washington in May 1973 concluded:

> . . . Problems with long-term implications and broad dimensions cannot continue to be dealt with on a day-to-day, ad hoc, piecemeal basis. It is fair to say that, despite the plethora of "planning staffs" scattered throughout the federal structure, . . . no arrangements for systematic, integrated, long-range planning exist within the U.S. government—nor, except in times of great crisis, have they ever existed.[51]

The seminar then suggested an office of strategic policy assessments, which they would have preferred to call candidly a Planning board but "there is a long-standing and probably justifiable popular suspicion attached to national planning."[52]

Here and there in Washington the need for Planning was breaking through into public discussion. Yet if no one appeared to be horrified, it was also true that no congressional committee until 1975 proposed hearings on this emerging novelty. Before long, close examination of these ideas would be essential. Even knowledgeable people who talked to or around the idea of Planning did not appreciate the choices to be made even after the need for Planning was accepted. Humphrey's Planning board was not made up of Cabinet officials, like the Domestic Council, and there must be discussion of the shortcomings of this arrangement as well as its virtues. What regional, state, and local structures were required to facilitate grassroots participation, sensitivity to local variation and needs, prompt social reporting? Could Planning work without executive branch reorganization, a structure and method for social accounting? Other questions swarmed around the issue. Above all, were there essential differences between Planning as it might be designed by a conservative government like Nixon's, or as it might evolve from the liberal tradition reaching back to FDR? In 1973, these issues only stirred beneath the surface. The evolution toward Planning still went on piecemeal, without a larger intellectual framework.

10

One salient of this evolution was land-use planning, which reached a threshold in the spring of 1974. The Jackson bill had passed the Senate in June 1973 by a lopsided vote of 64–21. A national land-use planning bill! Ghosts stirred with astonishment in the old Interior Department offices once used by the NRPB. Were the defenders of property rights so easily routed? The Senate vote seemed to revive them. Opposition in the House built during the autumn, and the House Rules Committee kept the companion Udall bill from the floor until June 1974. Udall finally managed a vote on a bill stripped of sanctions to reduce the opposition, but no concession stilled the bells of patriotism in the defense of a man's right to treat his property as he wished. In floor debate, Congressman Broyhill of Virginia said that the bill "had frightening implications for the future of this Nation," for "zoning and land-use decisions would no longer be made by familiar local individuals who have an understanding of the needs of the community" but by distant bureaucrats. Another vigilant defender of current arrangements wondered "how long will this short-sighted and dangerous march of power to Washington continue?"[53] The Chamber of Commerce thought the bill held too many federal standards, would perniciously interfere with local autonomy. The National Association of Home Builders decided that the bill, despite Jackson's and Udall's disclaimers, was a Trojan Horse for the no-growth fanatics.

The language of federal dictatorship was hard for land-use supporters to meet. The bill was easily misunderstood and misrepresented by interest groups with a stake in unrestricted development. It was a national land-use law, but it placed heavy responsibility on the states. From one angle, it looked like a conservative substitute for the radical national control that would probably be coming along in a very few years. One Republican congressman thought it was a model of the New Federalism, and couldn't fathom the intensity of the opposition. Another pointed out that, since it gave land-use power to the states, "this legislation cannot, even by the wildest stretch of the most suspicious imagination be seen as expanding any federal power."[54] But there were many suspicious imaginations focused on the muted issue of federal review of state plans, and on the possibility that the sanctions in the Senate bill might prevail in conference. The bill's supporters manfully repeated the facts that had moved the law this far, facts easily forgotten in the comfortable chambers where legislators deliberated. Representative Anderson noted that during each week of congressional debate on the bill, 27,000 households were formed in America, requiring housing covering an area equal to that of the city of Kalamazoo. Hoping to alarm his colleagues, Representative Udall offered the data that every twenty-four hours 10,000 acres of open land went under the asphalt of freeways and subdivisions, located, like energy facilities and industrial plants, without study of regional/national costs or benefits. The House voted 211–204 against the bill.

Henry Jackson was furious, and placed the blame upon Nixon. The President had supported Jackson's intentions from the beginning. In three environmental messages in a row, in the second State of the Union Address in 1973, the administration endorsed a strong national land-use planning bill. Then early in 1974, as talk of impeachment underscored Nixon's need for conservative support, he decided to abandon the effort. The administration switched to a weak substitute designed by Arizona representative Sam Steiger to defeat every aim of national land-use planning, and this switch provided the margin of defeat. Again the need to keep Nixon in the White House had put an end to the Nixon administration's early interest in strengthened national controls over social development.

11

Now the administration bore little resemblance to its earlier self. It conserved its energies by taking negative positions on population and land-use, drifted on growth policy, paid no more formal attention to national goals. Its achievement in reorganization was in place—a domestic council, a doubled White House staff, a new OMB. There was less progress toward a Planning capability than one would have expected of a two-term president when the activism of the administration emerged in 1969–70. The task of re-election had largely accounted for the stall in the policy thrust we have outlined; after re-election, Watergate engulfed a White House which piled error upon error until it had committed an unbelievable suicide. In the last months in office, certainly during 1974 and most of 1973, the Nixon administration put a brave face on a crippled condition. The White House had its attention riveted upon its legal and political perils. The still enormous tasks of rationalizing domestic policy were unaddressed. Every agency was dispirited and rudderless, especially the crucial arms of the President, OMB,

CEA, and the new energy administration. "It's no longer a government," commented Congressman Henry Reuss in May 1974, "it's a bunch of roving feudal bands." Routine business was conducted, but there were inadequate moral and intellectual resources to cope with emerging problems. The growth report required in February 1974 did not appear. It had not appeared when Nixon left the capital for retirement.

The disarray of 1974 owed almost entirely to the constitutional crisis over the apparent crimes and excesses of the President's re-election committee, his closest White House aides, and himself. Impeachment pre-empted other public business. History would show that the Nixon administration, even though losing momentum in 1972, had made important progress in equipping the federal government for the job of social management it had been performing so poorly since the 1930s. Important progress, but how much measured against the mounting challenges to American stability? In simpler times, surely enough to earn much praise. But the dimensions of our national crisis in the 1970s set harsh standards for those who had accepted power and promised to lead. The government's continuing ineptitude after five years of Nixonian leadership was painfully exposed when the energy crisis came in the winter of 1972–73.

The "energy crisis" may seem a large enough problem to stand on its own, but it was only the most severe manifestation of material shortages that became endemic in the early 1970s. It was oil in the winter of 1972 (and forever thereafter), but timber shortages had appeared a couple of years earlier, and the supplies of various raw materials were suddenly discovered to be inadequate given current demand. Petroleum shortages of course led the list of vexations in a nation so married to the automobile, unlimited hot water, electric gadgets, and jet travel. Oil, it turned out, was behind everything Americans enjoyed. The painful shortages of late 1972 raised questions about where the government had been as the crisis was building.

The administration's record on materials policy, of which energy policy is the most critical subset, would prove hard to defend. Congress had required the appointment of the National Commission on Materials Policy in the Resource Recovery Act of 1970. Nixon duly appointed an industry-dominated seven-man commission. It spent $2 million, and its report in June 1973 was not comforting. It concluded that market forces should continue to allocate our material resources; that environmental costs ought to be reflected in market prices; that recovery ought to be spurred; that a national land-use policy was desirable; that perhaps the big car ought to be taxed and mass transit encouraged. These were cautious appraisals, avoiding the alarm that was actually justified. Yet certain policy reforms came irrepressibly into their conclusions. The administration was not interested, apparently, in materials policy, nor in an early 1972 preliminary finding of a task force of the commission that petroleum shortages were imminent. (The petroleum shortage had also been foreseen in other parts of the government, for example in a June 1972 report in the Office of Emergency Preparedness; information of this sort did not rocket up to the President.) "There was no great interest shown at the White House," admitted Materials Policy Commission chairman Lynton Caldwell, "with respect to the commission or its mission."[55]

The White House torpor in this area was real enough. But what president had been interested in materials policy? Harry Truman had appointed the only other commission of that name, and little had become of its report. Nixon, like his predecessors and virtually every congressman, did not set aside a few minutes a week to worry about materials policy, or energy policy either. The Ash committee's studies of regulatory agency performance had not focused upon the failures of energy policy coordination, as numerous as they were. Nixon's reorganization plans included a department of natural resources, a useful unification of agencies which was not presented in terms of energy policy rationalization. Americans did not think about energy. Richard Nixon was a typical citizen in this regard. He opposed a Senate study of the energy field which Senators Jennings Randolph and Henry Jackson pushed in 1971, and the reports of his CEQ treated energy policy in a cursory way even after Congress in 1971 required its separate treatment. His energy message of 1971 was drafted by a Domestic Council task force which then became inactive. Apparently drafting the message had been the goal, not a major realignment of policy. As the first presidential message on energy the occasion was historic. The substance of the message was remarkably unimaginative. The urgency on energy problems felt in other parts of the government and among interested experts had not apparently risen to the Domestic Council level. If one wished to propose a course of action least disruptive of established business interests and consumer patterns, this was the message one would draft. Conservation was given only a ceremonial mention. The rest of the twelve-page message had to do with expanding production of energy supplies, with oil, coal, and nuclear sources taken most seriously and solar energy granted only a small corner of the energy future. At the end the President displayed his (or his message writers') acute sensitivity to organizational disorder by deploring the fragmentation of federal energy policy, and proposing that the hoped-for Department of Natural Resources have all energy research and development activities consolidated within it. This was in June. Seven months later, in February 1972, Nixon appointed one Charles DiBona his first energy adviser. Of course nothing differently happened thereafter. In the usual pattern, American government waited for the problem to deserve higher priority by becoming unmanageable.

It did so in the winter of 1972–73, as the Arab oil embargo and a shortage of refining capacity produced long lines at service stations, snowbound homes without heating oil, rising prices and tempers. In April the President produced another energy message, this one longer and more substantial. Now the administration was concentrating upon the issue. Its grasp of the details of energy sources, utilization, and federal policy was stronger. But the basic approach was the same. Inviting and coaxing private enterprise to produce more energy was the administration's main solution; bringing about altered life styles to reduce energy dependence by that necessary margin was not. Nixon proposed that the government de-regulate most natural gas prices at the wellhead, increase shelf oil drilling, build the Alaskan pipeline, and extend the benefits of the investment tax credit for oil exploration. It also seemed time to ease air pollution requirements so that coal use could be expanded. This program did not envision any changes in American life of any significance. Gas and oil might cost more, coal less. The emergency did not appear to the administration to require what some saw as the desperately needed reorientation of American culture away from Detroit products and wasteful consumption of energy toward modes of life more forgivable by our ancestors.

Nixon might have proposed heavy taxation of large autos, or a crash program of mass transit, or gasoline rationing. He skirted regulation or coercion, the use of the tax system to alter consumer habits, and relied upon raising prices. "Energy conservation is a national necessity," he said, "but I believe that it can be undertaken most effectively on a voluntary basis."[56] Of course the government had its role to play in energy conservation. The President put in his message a sentence about the need for a national conservation ethic, and established something called the Office of Energy Conservation in the Department of the Interior, of all places. And he ordered the Department of Commerce to develop a voluntary system of energy efficiency labels for home appliances. Richard Nixon would survive the energy crisis, at least, without proposing any measures which threatened the profits of corporations involved in energy, or which threatened the southern California culture of Cadillacs, jet planes, and warm swimming pools. But Nixon still cast something of a planner's eye upon problems, or at least his Domestic Council did. When it came to governmental organization, the Nixon White House harbored reformers. This second energy message complained again of defective organization: "The current fragmented organization of energy-related activities in the executive branch of the government must be overhauled," which meant—he must have been tired of saying this—a department of energy and natural resources (perhaps the realigned title would move an incredibly torpid Congress).[57]

Congress, led by Senators Metcalf, Jackson, and others, was

actually well along in its own study of energy policy. And whatever Congress did about the DENR, Nixon's White House organization for energy policy was weak, and he could change this without legislation. This he did in June 1973, appointing Governor John A. Love of Colorado to head the new Office of Energy Policy which merged other units too obscure to require listing. Again on this occasion Nixon asked for a DENR, repeated that conservation must remain a voluntary obligation of citizens, and suggested that air-conditioning thermostats be turned up by 4°.

The new energy office lasted six months, and ended under circumstances that are not entirely clear. On December 4, 1973, Nixon sent Love back to Colorado, set up the Federal Energy Office under Treasury official William Simon, and proposed that Congress establish a federal energy administration with broad powers to coordinate policy, and an energy research and development administration to centralize R&D activities now scattered from AEC to Interior. There are indications that Love had pressed too hard for mandatory fuel allocations as the second energy crisis winter approached. For his part, Love testified that the President really had other things on his mind, still, than energy policy. "It has been difficult to try to do anything meaningful and even to get the attention of the president," he said upon resigning.[58] In any event, the bureaucratic shuffle of energy agencies finally produced the FEA and rested there (no DENR), after congressional liberals had disappointed the President by narrowing the agency's requested powers, specifying its accountability to Congress, and requiring public access to oil and coal company data subpoenaed by the government. In eleven months national energy policy had been scrutinized, its planlessness and lack of focus admitted even among moderates. The FEA now drew together some of the scattered powers affecting energy. That Congress intended this to bring planning to national energy policy was clear. In the act establishing the FEA it required the director to submit a comprehensive energy plan in 120 days.

While the trend was clear enough, the distance moved was not very great. Senator Jackson had correctly summarized the

situation in December 1972 when he said that the Nation not
only lacked an energy Policy, but had "no single forum or decision-making body in which alternative means for meeting our
energy needs can be weighed against the nation's economic, environmental, and security objectives."[59] Not long afterward a
staff study of energy organization was produced by Jackson's
Senate Interior and Insular Affairs Committee. It reinforced the
conclusion that little or nothing had been done by mid-1973 to
improve policy-making organization. "Policy is presently administered by a diffuse and ill-defined assembly of agencies," the
study found, a condition of energy policy which had escaped
the notice of every reorganization commission from Ash back
through Hoover to Brownlow.[60] Forty-six agencies administered
programs with specific impacts upon the energy system, eighteen
more exerted important influences although this was not in their
charge. Fragmentation was one problem, energy-industry domination another. Advisory committees allowed energy industries
a powerful voice in setting policy, and the very data the government used came chiefly from industry.

This report slipped quietly out in 1973. A year later, in April
1974, the GAO released a study of commodity shortages that
made somewhat more impact. And the report was critical, even
if every conclusion was familiar. It found the commodity decision-making process "essentially ad hoc and crisis-oriented,"
with the invariably multiple agencies involved without coordinating mechanisms, without adequate data. Naturally the government had not anticipated the shortages in meat, lumber,
zinc, soybeans, steel, wool, and fertilizer that mushroomed in
the 1970s. Export controls were placed on various commodities,
in a process the GAO found "complex but chaotic." "There is
no comprehensive computerized material or mineral inventory
system in the federal government, and there are no plans to
implement one." To problems of agency fragmentation and inadequate data were added wrong assumptions, or at least complacency: "The possibility of scarcity as a possible enduring
feature of the international economy has not fully penetrated
the government." In a word, we had been surprised by energy

and oil and other commodity shortages because there was no Planning:

> In contrast to decisions responsive to immediate needs, a long-term policy planning system would attempt to project possible futures and to modify basic economic and political forces in directions compatible with the nation's long-term objectives. Such a system would require a coherent set of national priorities which would lend direction and substance to the policy planning system.[61]

This was the voice of Planning, emerging from a respected place in the Washington bureaucracy. Facts had forced cautious men a long way from old moorings. The Nixon administration, after risking an out-front position on Planning capacities in its first two years, found itself by 1974 criticized for running an unplanned government, not by radicals and professors, but by senators and bureaucrats and who were themselves a part of the planless system.

12

What are we to make of Nixon's five years? Every month brought surprises, until this presidential era came to the most astonishing of all conclusions. Which president has left more to be pondered than Nixon, who deposited in five years and a half such an avalanche of words, reorganizations, reform proposals, contradictory initiatives of every kind, juxtapositions of liberal and conservative thrusts, a trip to China, tape recordings of every spoken word in the Oval Office, impeachable offenses? The interpretation of all this will long be a national quandary.

Did his administration have a central purpose and pattern? If it did, was it one the President chose, or were other men, impersonal forces the architects? There is evidence that the Nixon loyalists at the White House and in the executive agencies came to Washington and worked there with a clear purpose.

One finds this conviction in virtually every interview. In talking with Novak and Evans, with Dan Rather, with Allen Drury, with Thomas Cronin, and others who interviewed well-placed Republicans, the Nixon people defined their mission in common terms: to make the government smaller and less involved in social manipulation (except for the area of "law and order"), to liberate capitalists, to end the liberal practice of promising too much, to invigorate the market, to decentralize power, to bring a major change in governing philosophy. "The New Deal is dead," summarized John Roy Price, who enlisted with Nixon before the 1968 nomination.[62] Or as the new attorney general is supposed to have said in 1969: "This country is going so far to the right that you won't recognize it."[63] Or as a White House aide told Dan Rather after Nixon's re-election: "During the first term, we stopped their revolution. Now we can move forward with our own."[64]

This may have been the guiding vision of aides, speech writers, party workers. But it was not translated into substantial reality. Admittedly there were some shallow tracks left by the so-called conservative philosophy. Nixon delivered a passionate New Federalism message, then proposed revenue sharing, claiming that it would send power flowing back to "the people," or at least to levels of government presumably "closer" to the people than the one in Washington. In many speeches he fanned the enthusiasm of citizens who wanted less national government, more free enterprise. He appointed many quite reactionary, free-market men; we remember Haynsworth and Carswell and Rehnquist, and George Shultz, Caspar Weinberger, Alan Greenspan. Nixon searched for new ways to articulate the administration's conservatism, encouraging writer William Safire to write in December 1969 a *New Federalist Paper #1* (which Safire signed "Publius," to raise the tone of the occasion) for internal circulation. The paper groped for a name for Nixonian conservatism, failed to ignite enthusiasm for "national localism." But everybody seemed to be comforted by the reaffirmation of conservative principles.

Much more than this was hard to claim in the service of these principles when Nixon was done. He proposed a new American Revolution (not very conservative phraseology). The heart of this was to be a backflow of "power" from Washington, where too much of it had collected under liberals, to "the people." How do we judge his success at this? The job is forbiddingly complex, and there has been too little time for adequate reflection and analysis. But some preliminary signs may be read. Let us sit down with that earnest social document, the federal budget. May one discern the term in office of a conservative president in the years 1969–75?

If a conservative president presided over any of these years of budget-making, taxing, and spending, his mark is modestly inscribed. Consulting the admirable Brookings studies of the federal budget for 1974 and 1975, we find instructive trends. From 1960, when federal spending was 18.6 per cent of the GNP it increased to 20.6 per cent during the liberal decade, and actually inched up to 20.8 per cent by 1975. Not much flow of power back to the people, if the right to spend one's own money without any governmental interference is power. Indeed, the figures in one sense seem to reflect the accession of a liberal president sometime about 1970, for defense spending which was 53.7 per cent of the budget in 1960 was down to 44.6 per cent by 1970 then dropped sharply to 31.6 per cent by 1975. On the domestic side, cash income maintenance went up more sharply in half the 1970s than in the entire 1960s, and Nixon's tenure saw grants for social programs slightly increase over Lyndon Johnson's substantial beginnings.

This is on the spending side. On the taxing side, Nixon had surprisingly little interest in the structure of federal taxation, at least no interest in changing it to advance certain broad social goals. He was only interested in the tax structure as a taxpayer, eager to find all the deductions he could. Possibly his attitude in this reflected a lawyer's understanding that American taxation did not actually burden the upper classes more than those beneath them, myths of progressive taxation to the contrary notwithstanding. Nixon signed the Tax Reform Act of 1969 but never had a clear position on it, and neither the tax changes of 1969 and 1971 nor the administration's reform proposals of April 1973 brought much change to the revenue system. The payroll tax associated with social security continued to climb under Nixon, as it had under predecessors, and as this was a regressive tax he cooperated fully with congressional preferences here. Under Nixon, personal and especially business taxes were trimmed as payroll taxes climbed, and deliberate loopholes, which economists now wisely label "tax expenditures," were multiplied. The authors of the Brookings monograph on the 1974 budget conclude that "a heavy share of the federal tax burden falls on the poor and the near-poor and that share is increasing."[65] None of this was a departure from the liberal tax programs of the 1960s, which were shockingly illiberal.

It may be said that Nixon made little impression upon the federal budget and tax system (let us assume that the tax system basically satisfied him) because he could not control a Democratic Congress. But how hard did he work at the job of shrinking the government's fiscal dimensions? The record shows a great deal of practical realism and moderation until the very end, when perhaps a militant anti-statist peeked out. From the beginning, Nixon compromised with budgetary reality. The budget was after all not simply an expensive list of boondoggles. It was first of all a tool of fiscal policy, and cutting liberal programs might well bring on a most destabilizing depression. Through 1972 Richard Nixon fashioned the budget in a practical rather than an ideological spirit. He must have wished to check the rising domestic spending of his predecessors, but recession beckoned that way, as well as the focused anger of former beneficiaries. He had his men ponder a long-range answer, and bide their time until the November 1972 hurdle could be put safely behind.

Then in 1973 the President began finally to act the militant conservative—where the budget was concerned. The 1974 budget, submitted in January 1973, represented the sharpest break of his presidency. Now he would cut federal spending by a noticeable amount, and almost entirely on the domestic side. Inflation was a major problem, and a spending cut was infinitely more palatable than a tax increase. Some $2 billion was cut from the defense budget, but more than $10 billion from the domestic side. This $10 billion was accumulated not merely by trimming expenditures on space, transportation, parks, and the like, where no national policy issue was involved in the reduction, but reflected a $6 billion shift away from social grant programs from Great Society days—in health, education, manpower training, housing, environmental control. Here Nixon intended not simply to cut spending, something Eisenhower and George Humphrey had tried to do. He wanted that power to flow back to somebody outside Washington, and revenue sharing, enacted in 1972, was the vehicle. General revenue sharing was to continue at the programmed rate of about $6 billion a year to state and local governments, with no strings attached. Special revenue sharing, proposed to an unresponsive Congress in 1971, was put forward in a revised form in 1973. For fiscal 1974 Nixon asked the consolidation of most categorical grants into four special revenue-sharing block grants* to be spent by lower-tier governments.

The President claimed a lot for this proposed budget, which more clearly reflected his conservative leanings than any of its predecessors. His message read:

> The 1974 budget proposes a leaner federal bureaucracy, increased reliance on state and local governments . . . and greater freedom for the American people to make for themselves fundamental choices about what is best for them. . . . Two years ago, I spoke of the need for a New American Revolution to return power to people and put the individual *self* back in the idea of *self*-government. The 1974 budget moves us firmly toward that goal.[66]

Brave words. (Over at the *National Review,* they must have wondered why they had not been spoken in 1969). The principle strategy for achieving this end, Nixon's economic counsellors

---

* In manpower training, urban and community development, elementary and secondary education, and law enforcement assistance.

frankly told the Congress at hearings on the budget in 1973 and 1974, was to cut back on ineffective grant programs by omitting them from new budgets and impounding voted funds, while adding revenue sharing to provide lower governments with resources to be used as they wished. This would keep total federal domestic spending about the same, in theory.

Questions have been raised among ardent fiscal conservatives about Nixon's personal sense of urgency about all this. The record shows much delay, and much caution. To the Nixon circle, the key to the eventual outcome (which was disappointing) was the Democratic Congress. Unquestionably the Congress did not agree that its social objectives could and would be better achieved by cancelling its own legislative record going back to the early 1960s and then mailing money down to governors, mayors, and county supervisors. Congress changed the 1974 budget in important ways. Special revenue sharing was largely rebuffed, general revenue sharing kept small. The President, caught in an internal crisis that sapped his strength from a hundred cuts, was not a strong antagonist. Occasionally resolute, he would impound or veto social spending. But frequently some political calculations known only to himself would lead Nixon to go along with Congress toward an active national role, such as in the enlargement of the food stamp program, Medicare and Medicaid, increases in social security benefits, on more aid to the humanities, arts, and education. In February 1974 he had another chance to show what he would prefer in an ideal world, when he sent down the 1975 budget. It was not quite so militant as the year before, but clearly a Republican conservative had fashioned it. Military spending was up $7 billion with projections for increases through the decade. Some $19 billion more was added for social security and other income maintenance programs. A $3–4 billion dab was added to environmental and mass transit spending. Social grant programs were again squeezed, for in holding such spending to roughly 1974 levels Nixon was letting inflation cut the budget in those areas for him. Congress, of course, changed this somewhat, but Nixon had made a small mark. From 1972–75, spending on education, community development, and manpower training was held while inflation eroded their relative position in the budget. That was the largest scalp he had taken. The budget data for 1960–75 show little other signs of a militant conservative. Shockingly, the 1975 budget revealed that spending on income maintenance ran higher than on defense for the first time in American history.

In shaping federal budgets, Nixon must be conceded constraints of towering proportions. Congress was in Democratic hands, and never liked him. But Nixon had conservative critics who do not think he seized the opportunities available. For a man who advised that we lower our voices, he made unusually grandiose claims for his major idea, revenue sharing. It cannot bear the ideological weight he placed upon it. Revenue sharing was not, in fact, a conservative idea. It was proposed by a Task Force appointed by Lyndon Johnson in 1964, and its possibilities were ideologically varied. General revenue sharing might well have made the nation's tax system more progressive by substituting federal taxes for state and local ones. With certain standards, it could redistribute income from rich states to poor ones. Or it could be designed to let local governments drop their progressive taxes and hold to regressive ones. Everything depended on formulas and standards in the enabling legislation.

The bipartisan revenue sharing law of 1972 was muddled. It is not clear just what it allowed and encouraged local governments to do with their tax and spending plans. In any event, general revenue sharing provided only 5 per cent of state-local governmental funds, and would have little impact either way in any direction. It may have been new, but it was not a revolution. As for special revenue sharing, which was to replace Lyndon's profusion of categorical grants, this tactic did not put much power in flow to the provinces, either. Grants only constituted 9 per cent of the federal budget in any case. Nixon consolidated some of those into special revenue sharing, which was a sane move in any administrator's book. But there were some federal strings even in special revenue sharing. Some power flowed to lower governments. The effect was not cosmic.

The federal budget is of course not the only place to look for the currents of power. Nixon caught little public attention with his budgetary efforts, since they were cautious, circumscribed, hard to measure at the end. But many people noticed how he arranged for certain kinds of power to flow up to Washington —specifically, to the White House. The White House staff nearly doubled in size under Nixon, and the President through his staff secured extraordinary influence over parts of the federal bureaucracy that had formerly been relatively independent—the Bureau of Internal Revenue, the CIA, the FCC, even the Bureau of Labor Statistics, to name only a few institutions feeling hot presidential breath in the 1970s. This sort of thing was not what conservative doctrine had proposed. The New American Revolution moved power around in ways that did not fit with the script.

Apart from his impact or lack of it on the locus of power, Nixon kept his admirers and detractors off balance in other ways. He chided Congress for failing to pass his environmental legislation. He proposed a more expensive welfare plan than any yet heard of, with a guaranteed annual income from the government. He supported an expansion of the liberals' food stamp program. He went to Red China. Great Society programs lived on into the 1970s, Nixon only whittling away at them gradually. The agency at the heart of the War on Poverty, OEO, for example, lasted until 1974. John Mitchell is said to have advised: "Don't watch what we say, watch what we do." Watching what they did, one finds that it was not always what they said they would do.

For this there are surely many explanations. Some are embedded in the structure of American politics. All presidents have promised change in the government's size and functions, and have fallen short of announced goals. The budget is very difficult to alter, almost impossible in the short run; the bureaucracy has its own goals, and tenaciously and resourcefully resists any change but the expansion of whatever it had been doing; Congress resists reforms of any kind, Left or Right, and Nixon faced large Democratic majorities which protected Great Society programs. Constituencies for existing programs are alert, constituencies for imagined new things are dispersed. Nixon said, "That is the watchword of this administration: reform"; but like FDR, Eisenhower, and Kennedy, all of whom promised wonderful new departures, he didn't get much from the system, in part because it is designed to resist reform.[67]

This explains something of the shortfall of conservative expectations, but it does not go far enough. The activism of 1969 —the year in which Nixon asked for FAP, proposed a population commission, launched reorganization, decided to keep Model Cities and OEO and other Johnsonian programs—was traceable in some important degree to Moynihan's influence. He is said to have convinced Nixon to follow the Disraeli model, taking the liberal program away from the liberals and managing it in a Tory way. Neither man has denied the influence of Moynihan's ideas, but still the nub of things is Nixon, not the extraordinarily persuasive Harvard professor.

Nixon's mind is not easily penetrated. He leaned toward traditional conservative ideology, but the evidence strongly suggests that he had no convictions. It was always said of FDR that he was a pragmatist unhampered by doctrinaire views, and much argument has been conducted around the extent to which he actually had underlying social purposes beyond the possession of power. Whatever the extent of the social purpose at the center of Roosevelt's pragmatic nature, Nixon pretty clearly had less. Men close to him such as Richard Whalen, George Romney, and Wally Hickel have publicly concluded that there isn't any inner Nixon. "I don't know what the president believes in," Romney once said, "maybe he doesn't believe in anything."[68] And a senior White House aide told Allen Drury: "If Nixon has an over-all policy, I wasn't able to find it when I was working over there."[69]

Romney, Whalen, Hickel, and other Republicans who left the administration with varying degrees of disillusionment are convinced that the exceptional philosophical vacuum within Richard Nixon was a fatal flaw. John Ehrlichman admitted that Nixon had no philosophy, but did what was feasible and tactically shrewd. And he thought this right and proper for a chief executive in a turbulent, changing era. Richard J. Whalen, a writer in the 1968 campaign, heard Nixon himself say: "Flexibility is the first principle of politics."[70] I will not venture into this thicket, which to some extent is produced by loose use of terms like "pragmatism." More important for present purposes is to recognize the opening which Nixon's exceptionally opportunistic outlook gave to the Planning idea.

For in the end he presided over a more rapid evolution toward Planning than any other president since FDR. Perhaps Nixon himself would be surprised to see these actions summarized: encouragement to national growth policy, encouragement to population policy including appointment of a population commission, establishment of a national goals research staff with suggestions that it become a base for social reporting, a proposed radical reorganization of executive agencies by function, establishment of the Domestic Council for integrated policy consideration, support for national land-use policy, and a dozen lesser actions to encourage forecasting and long-range projections. These are the building blocks of the planning mode, and if pursued far enough must lead to comprehensive national Planning.

Nixon would have been shocked at this extrapolation of certain elements of his presidency. After all, he was the man who said: "God knows, you turn the social planners loose and it is sorry," and similar sentiments.[71] His interest was in international politics. He had even written an article published in the journal, *Foreign Affairs*. Domestic affairs bored him, unless they were directly related to his own political future. He told Haldeman in late 1969 to get the Domestic Council going so that he could at last devote all his time to foreign affairs, where a Democratic Congress could not frustrate him.

After the 1972 election he confided to Theodore H. White: "I've always thought this country could run itself domestically, without a president. All you need is a competent Cabinet to run the country at home. You need a president for foreign policy."[72] Before the tapes were released, we would have said that this obviously intelligent man by his own admission reserved his deep thoughts for international issues. Actually, considering what the tapes reveal, it seems better to say that he cared only about international issues, but didn't really think deeply about them, either. Perhaps he thought deeply about the theatrics of being president, about how to stage a dramatic international move. Certainly he was good at this. But we know that most of the details of international life bored him just as did all the details of domestic life that did not have to do with voting. Haldeman asked him in June 1972 whether he had received a report that the British had floated the pound:

NIXON: "No, I don't think so."
HALDEMAN: "They did."
NIXON: "That's devaluation?"
HALDEMAN: "Yeah. Flanigan's got a report on it here."
NIXON: "I don't care about it. Nothing we can do about it."
HALDEMAN: "You want a rundown?"
NIXON: "No, I don't. . . . It's too complicated for me to get into."

When Haldeman went on to report Arthur Burns's concern about the speculative pressure on the lira, Nixon replied: "Well, I don't give a (expletive deleted) about the lira."[73]

These characteristics of Nixon's mind were not unusual. Many politicians with higher ambitions do not give themselves the time to develop genuine convictions on the forbiddingly complex issues vexing this society, are not really interested intellectually, only politically, to ride the turmoil upward. Strong convictions are inherently dysfunctional in politics. Historians mostly argue, pointing to the Hoover-Roosevelt episode, that a degree of opportunism is absolutely required in national leadership to prevent doctrinaire attachment to beliefs that have been made obsolete by change. However this may be, Nixon, to a far greater degree than those pragmatic opportunists Lyndon Johnson, John Kennedy, or even Eisenhower, was a man without a durable set of prescriptions for domestic America, and without serious intellectual interest in it. Liberals in 1969 feared that he would implement the simple, anti-government views of suburban Republican conservatism to which he had always paid tribute. Since he did lean toward those views, and attracted like-minded men from Pasadena and Seattle and Chicago and elsewhere, Nixon did make many speeches with a distinctly Hooverian ring that went over well among the businessmen of Peoria. But little of the architecture of his administration reflected a conservative crusade.

For he found when he reached the White House, especially in the early days, that bright people he respected were not advising him to let the marketplace reclaim its benign power over the American future. He respected the brilliant Moynihan, Nixon's trophy from the New Frontier, and Moynihan steered him toward a form of conservatism that the man from Whittier and Duke Law School had never encountered. This was an activist, interventionist conservatism, which understood that only enlightened social management by national government could anticipate and deflect the threats to social stability and national security posed by concatenating technological change. It required Planning. This was not just Moynihan's view, or it would not have carried much weight. Nixon got these views, as Johnson had before him, whenever he consulted the senior bureaucracy in Washington or experts from the universities and think tanks.

He also got planning advice when he consulted the nation's business elite. There were exceptions, of course. But this was not the 1930s, when rugged individualists like Tom Girdler or Sewall Avery or Henry Ford, self-made men who came up through the production end of the business, fought a holy war against social regulation. A different perspective had grown up among the larger capitalists. After a generation of cold war and forty years of the regulatory state, they had come to appreciate the stabilizing effect of a government-business cooperation. They preferred Johnson to Goldwater, when that choice was suddenly proposed. Large-horizoned businessmen realized what only a handful had appreciated in the 1930s, that the enjoyment of life in America by people who had hustled and succeeded was in fact more threatened by uncontrolled social change than it had ever been by the haphazard meddling of the liberals. More important, the modern business elites were trained managers, steeped in the managerial ethos as it had evolved to cope with large enterprises. They used the language of systems analysis, preferred to make decisions surrounded by cost-benefit studies, insisted on adequate data and projections, worked toward the orderly meshing of institutional components to balance centralized authority with the incentives of decentralization.

The Democrats discovered this sort of businessman when Robert McNamara came to the Defense Department. In Nixon's official family, two of the most forceful and influential men of this sort were Litton Industries' Roy Ash, head of the reorganization study group and director of OMB and Treasury Secretary John Connally. Some old-fashioned "conservatism" might be found in the talk of such men, meaning by that a preference for less regulated markets. But the modern executive, and the lawyers and economists and statisticians and engineers who served with them, had by the late 1960s thoroughly absorbed the planning ethos. If the government were inevitably to be involved in some necessary activity, they would naturally recommend that its dispersed and contradictory doings be centralized and rationalized, that its scattered agencies be controlled by proper review, that goals be defined, costs and benefits weighed along alternative lines, thought be given to emerging problems, constant feedback be institutionalized. Any president would have received such ideas in the 1970s. They had been dimly heard as far back as Theodore Roosevelt, then with mounting pressure, forcing the evolution of the ramshackle system of government management toward Planning in the ways we have surveyed. When Richard Nixon had this sort of advice, from Pat Moynihan and Ash, from Romney, from his civil service, from businessmen and lawyers serving on commissions, from John Ehrlichman who had practiced zoning law in Seattle and long been a member of the American Institute of Planners, he let them shape his unshaped domestic strategies. The Planning impulse found a receptive president, himself a man with a strong sense of order, a desire to take the offensive and be a reformer, and a shrewd appreciation of the political advantages of having a "positive" as well as a "negative" thrust in his presidential performance. "He attacked planning," James Reston had presciently said of Nixon as early as 1962, "but planned everything."[74] So planning flourished, and Planning stirred, in Washington while Nixon was president. One is reminded of a comment of Walter Lippmann, writing in 1935: "Does not . . . history . . . teach us that radical transitions in a nation's life are best carried through by conservative men?"[75]

As we know, this remarkable evolution was arrested during 1971–72, then to considerable extent reversed. Nixon had advanced toward Planning on several fronts because he had an open mind, and was receiving Planning advice without anybody using that word, at least obtrusively. And the actions being recommended did fit with his general inclination toward order, toward centralized, effective power in his own hands. Then when Haldeman and Ehrlichman had replaced people like Moynihan and Burns, and when a close Republican look could be taken at Nixonian-sponsored ideas like growth policy, population policy, land-use policy, and social reporting to monitor progress toward explicit national goals, the administration drew back. All that remained of the early broad advance toward effective social management were those reforms that strengthened the President's grip upon the bureaucracy—reorganization, which he could not pry out of Congress, and the Domestic Council-OMB-White House staff innovations which we have observed. Impeachment fears had something to do with the abruptness and thoroughness of this retreat, as Nixon began to work toward a clearer traditional Republican image so as to rally his natural supporters. The entire cycle had taken but half a decade, and in the turmoil of the era it was not easy to perceive. Orange County perspectives had easily given way in 1969–70 to sophisticated planning perspectives from New York-Cambridge academic and corporation sources. But the roots had been shallow. He was still Richard Nixon, and whatever he did was tentative.

Would it all be washed away in Watergate? Some might argue that there was little to wash away. There cannot have been much in the way of a Planning apparatus or spirit, for the commodity and energy crises were neither anticipated nor adequately managed when they arrived. Whatever Nixon had done to bring a Planning capability, the government he headed was to all appearances still the same reactive, short-term, crisis-management system it had always been. Conservative economist Pierre Rinfret put it: "We accuse this administration of totally miscalculating the need for advance economic planning before it got into office and for being totally unprepared once it did."[76] And Jeb Stuart Magruder spoke from closer to the center, of the general atmosphere of decision-making: "At the White House we had often talked about long-range planning, but we rarely did it—we were almost entirely crisis-oriented."[77]

Apart from these observations of the administration's unplanning mode of operation, one calls the roll at the end of the Nixon era and finds almost none of the contemplated parts of a Planning apparatus in their places. Despite presidential talk, there was no reorganized executive branch, no national land-use planning, no national population Policy, no national growth Policy. Manpower policies remained fragmented, had even been substantially remanded to the states and cities. Incomes Policy had been given a trial that set it back considerably. Energy policies were in confusion, but at least the need for coherence and rationality there had been recognized. Only at the very center, at the White House, had the government's decision-making capability been markedly rationalized, with the establishment of the still-to-be-proven Domestic Council. Small progress had been made in social accounting, most notably the publication in 1973 by OMB of a document called *Social Indicators* which was much more sophisticated than the 1969 *Toward a Social Report*. But no one claimed that the United States had anything close to a system of social reporting, or a demonstrated desire to match its economic with its social self-knowledge. On the Hill, where the President of course had only an indirect influence, just the first steps had been taken toward a technology assessment capacity, and reform of antediluvian budgetary procedures was months away.

This summary, factually true enough, misses the significance of what had happened, and it must be amplified. Certainly re-election passions, and Watergate, had halted and then to some considerable extent reversed the thrust toward Planning which had been felt from the Nixon White House. But time will lead us to see the 1971–74 period only as a moratorium (it may well extend through 1976, a matter for the next chapter). The extent to which the Nixon era educated the civil service, other federal politicians, and the influential public in the themes of Planning as a path out of contemporary crisis is probably unmeasurable. Steps were taken, institutionally as well as intellectually, which would not be retracted. Nixon's own contribution to this national development, as these pages reveal, is difficult to assess with precision. He was the elected head of America's conservative party, and in the end he failed to give what passed for conservative ideas a vigorous and effective realization in the 1970s. But these ideas for the most part were a narrow set of class prejudices not viable either politically or socially. Another Nixon—it sometimes seemed—saw much farther, and made a try at the Disraeli role, attempting to lead the powerful, suspicious, defensive American conservative elites and their working class following toward a new and yet still conservative social philosophy. This was a vision of social stability through international conciliation abroad and orderly Planning at home.

Of the international side of this we shall not speak, except to say that the performance, while wobbly, was widely acclaimed a success. As a domestic leader of enlightened conservatism Nixon also ventured out, and here he fell far short, ruined in the turbulence of re-election politics, Watergate, and personal irresolution. But in the process Nixon made a contribution which remains an important part of our political landscape. When he writes his memoirs the ex-president is not likely to claim the contribution I sketch here. Yet whether consciously or not he managed to rough in the outlines of a conservative form of Planning, and presided over an educational era which legitimated for American conservatives the idea that Planning is preferable to the inept and inflationary broker political economy with which we even now attempt to navigate the last third of

the twentieth century. The era of Planning was still over the
horizon when Nixon returned to San Clemente, but the discussion of Planning—what kind, directed toward which social ends
—could now begin in the United States.

Crossroads

Discussion *could* begin, at least, with the impeachment crisis resolved. But when that transfixing figure at the center of our political life limped aboard Air Force One for the last time in August 1974 and one turned to consider his successor, it appeared that the discussion would be postponed. Richard Nixon's most negative single contribution to the search for a different political economy, adequate to the needs of America's future, was his decision to appoint Gerald Ford as vice president. Nixon, surely, had been looking for other qualities when he settled upon Ford—the ability to be confirmed; sound Republicanism; perhaps the need for someone of candor and a bit of Truman-esque honesty. Ford supplied these well enough.

But he possessed none of the qualities that would have fitted him to participate creatively in the evolution toward Planning. He came from a long, mediocre, and apparently dulling congressional career and typified what John Ehrlichman with telling inflection referred to in an interview as "the congressional mentality." Nixon had always carried an activist streak; Ford found his sudden leadership role unnatural as well as unexpected. He had not spent eight years in the executive branch plotting initiatives, but twenty-five years in the House preparing resistance. When the Presidency fastened upon him Ford had no established habit of handling a large staff. He could turn to a much smaller and less tested band of cronies; no Pat Moynihan, with the social scientists' systems approach, no Roy Ash with the reorganizing instinct of modern management. Ford was a slower study than Nixon, not quite sure—along with everyone else— how it had all happened. He would need time to sort things out. He inherited monumental economic snarls, the worst since 1937. If re-election planning and then Watergate had greatly diminished Nixon's momentum toward Planning, the swearing in of Ford in August 1974 seemed to stop it entirely.

An early indication of the direction of Ford's presidency came when he formed a "transition team" in August 1974 to advise him on White House organization. He could hardly have set these gentlemen to work much earlier, at the risk of appearing too eager, but it was regrettable that difficult organizational questions that had preoccupied skilled administrators from Brownlow through Hoover to Ash were dealt with in two weeks. Perhaps longer reflection would not have changed the team's recommendations. Their August 21 report, which is not published but was widely summarized in the press, reveals the mature outlook of four ex-congressmen.* It is probably the only study of executive organization that appears to have been conceived not from the presidential perspective but in the very lair of his congressional-Cabinet opponents. By all accounts Ford had given the team no specific charge, but what he should have said to them was:

Study the organization of the White House office and personal staff—we don't have time now to look at the entire executive branch—and try to locate the institutional sources of the Watergate errors, if there are any. Suggest appropriate changes. Be sure

* Rogers Morton was then secretary of the Interior, Donald Rumsfeld was ambassador to NATO following duty as head of OEO and the Cost of Living Council, William Scranton was ex-governor of Pennsylvania, John O. Marsh a lawyer from Ford's vice-presidential staff; but all were ex-congressmen, and Morton was a Nixon Cabinet officer who had known the rough hands of a White House staff bent upon controlling little empires like the Department of the Interior.

to distinguish between Nixon's organizational mistakes and his organizational improvements, for there must have been some of these. He was there five years, and was always interested in organization.

This, of course, would have been too much to expect. August was the hothouse month when the Presidency of Richard Nixon toppled from impeachment tremors, putting the country in a totally unprecedented constitutional crisis, and Gerald Ford in no mean crisis of his own. The roots of Watergate must be pulled up over there at the Nixon White House. The country required it, as did Ford's credibility at the start.

And so the transition team went on the offensive. The Presidency must be more "open," access to the President less restricted. The German Guard at the door must be replaced with a bit more traffic. This was to be accomplished, Rogers Morton told the press, by reducing the power of the chief of staff so that he "coordinates but does not control" the work of other officials, whatever that meant.[1] Presumably it meant that Haldeman and Haig ought to be replaced by Hartman and Rumsfeld, who were friendlier men. Beyond this, the team recommended— and Ford adopted—an organizational chart showing nine aides with a line of access to the President, the chief of staff and eight White House counsellors. Of course, if Ford wished to shut himself up with Rumsfeld the chart would do no good, but the team had done what it could to exorcise the Palace Guard. They also urged a 10 per cent cutback of the entire White House staff. Doubtless they knew it had doubled under Nixon, and decided that 10 per cent of the total had somehow been unnecessary. Probably the plumbers.

Then the reforming hand of the congressional-Cabinet mentality reached out to dismantle some Nixonian arrangements that deserved more appreciation. Since the late 1930s the Budget Bureau had been the President's indispensable and only instrument of departmental control, gradually curbing departmental independence somewhat through budgetary review. Under Nixon the reorganized OMB had placed its own men deep into many departments and agencies to attempt to bend their activities in directions congenial with the President's program. The transition team urged that OMB be sharply curbed, so as to "put more power back into the departments and agencies."[2] In an interview with the press Governor Scranton repeated the advice that power be allowed to flow out of the White House and back to the federal agencies, a sort of District of Columbia New Federalism. He also advanced the idea that the vice president be assigned the duty of handling regular contacts with the Cabinet and also formulate domestic policy. Even Gerald Ford must have wondered if his old friends from the House had quite made the transition themselves.

But perhaps he did not. By all reports Ford "welcomed" the report, and began to implement it. Six months later, in February, journalist John Herbers reported:

> The way in which the executive branch operates has changed drastically. Mr. Ford appears to have gone 180° from the highly concentrated, tightly controlled system that existed at the height of President Nixon's power, to the more traditional one of dispersed authority under which Cabinet members are permitted to identify with and speak for their constituencies.[3]

Herbers found the Domestic Council concentrating upon "long-range" issues, its work not likely to have impact until the fall of 1976—in time for the campaign. Routine policy decisions had drifted back to the informal negotiation between White House aides and Cabinet officers that Nixon (and his predecessors) had found deficient. According to John Osborne, who had closely watched the Nixon White House, the Domestic Council "hasn't met since December 1971 and has never amounted to much."[4] Only in the matter of White House staff, according to these journalistic accounts, had Ford held to Nixon's habits. His transition committee had commended a 10 per cent cut in personnel, but Herbers found the staff after six months of Ford's administration to be the same size as Nixon's.

Ford, apparently, was misreading the Watergate episode and

failing to comprehend the situation of the modern Presidency. White House crimes had obscured the full meaning of Nixon's struggle with the bureaucracy. Perhaps even ex-congressman Ford will awaken to the error and attempt to reclaim the power he has deeded back to the chieftains of organized special interests and bureaucratic inertia. The transitional report was retrograde, perpetuating the crippling disabilities of the Presidency, but Ford so far has followed it. As the new President and his advisers grow into the presidential perspective, as one assumes they will, much time will be lost for the consolidation and improvement of Nixon's better insights into the problem of executive branch organization.

The transition, in any event, was short. Nixon flew to San Clemente without even all his personal effects, and Ford came at once up against the economic crisis that had been building for months, even years. Nixon not only left Ford the problem of stagflation, in the awful word coined for the astonishing new behavior of the economy, but a set of advisers. The advisers did not come chiefly from Nixon's interventionist period, 1969–72, when he had been a Keynesian and a wage/price controller and liked having Pat Moynihan around. They came from his final months, when he was gathering his conservative constituency for the final battle. Nixon put Alan Greenspan, the True Believer of laissez-faire capitalism and admirer of Ayn Rand, in charge of the CEA, and had moved a man of similar ardor for the free market and less government, William Simon, to the Treasury. The structure for making economic policy was the Domestic Council, at least on paper, and coordination and final advice came from Counsellor William Rush, a former law professor.

With this structure and crew the new administration plunged into its economic problems, first holding the remarkable "economic summit" with professors, businessmen, and labor leaders in September and October, then getting down to the formulation of Ford's program. When the records are opened, Ford's handling of economic issues will have close scholarly attention. We are interested here in his emerging relationship to the themes of planning and Planning—how he dealt with the issues of coherence and systemic approaches, long-range perspectives, forecasting, social reporting, social control of basic sources of change. Some general impressions stand out in his brief record.

An early step was the establishment, in September, of a new Economic Policy Board, combining "all of the Federal Government economic effort, domestic and international."[5] The chairman was Secretary Simon, and the composition of the board included eight Cabinet officers and appropriate others. This action appeared to show a far-sighted understanding of the need for policy coordinating machinery. Actually it showed confusion, and must have produced it inside the White House. For the membership of the EPB was almost exactly the same as the Nixon Domestic Council. Did Ford understand that the Domestic Council stood ready for such assignments as coordination of economic policy, or did he intend to confine it to other matters, such as, say, crime or medical care? It was too early to tell, but the White House now had two policy coordination boards of Cabinet officers of roughly the same composition, and both would probably not survive the months ahead.

Apart from organizational questions, the substance of Ford's economic policy, even as it shifted from inflation-fighting in October to recession-fighting in January, suggested that Ford did not share in the mounting dissatisfaction with the post-New Deal political economy. Faced with his various options, Ford at virtually every point chose the path that minimized structural change. In October he declared his decision to fight inflation with a 5 per cent surtax and recession with a higher investment tax credit. In selecting these mild fiscal measures, he was rejecting tax reform to alter the distribution of income, substantial cuts in the federal budget, or an incomes policy. On the latter he acted to ease the pressure for controls, asking Congress for a council on wage and price stability to "monitor" inflation and work for voluntary rollbacks. A bit of the jawbone, so as not to end too abruptly a practice that had by 1974 become routine in Washington.

Many economists had urged the President to attack monopoly

pricing. In his October 8 economic speech he said: "I am determined to return to the vigorous enforcement of antitrust laws," and suggested that fines be increased.[6] Apparently he was not *very* determined. An anti-trust drive to significantly reduce administered pricing would require rethinking of the anti-trust laws and their administration. Some economists proposed this, but they had not apparently communicated to Ford the inability of the existing laws, even with higher fines, to achieve this purpose. Another structural source of inflation, of downwardly rigid prices and impaired productivity, is the huge jerrybuilt system of federal regulation. Ford called for a national commission on regulatory reform, a promising idea, recalling FDR's appeal for the Temporary National Economic Committee of 1938–41. Congress did not leap at the idea, and Ford's own sense of priorities allowed him to wait six months before making his next move. In the spring he talked again on the subject, promising to support some deregulation of banks and railroads. He called a meeting of the chairmen of ten regulatory commissions in July, but they disagreed with his suggestion that major reforms were needed. At the end of a year in office, Ford's attack upon structural flaws in the political economy, especially those leading to inflation, had proven gentle, episodic, verbal, and without tangible effect.

These were Ford's October decisions, and he held to them through the last quarter of 1974, as the GNP dropped off at an annual rate of 9.1 per cent, the second worst showing since the Great Depression.

The same pattern appeared in Ford's response to energy shortages. His instincts ran toward caution; when lines of policy were chosen, they usually tended to be those making least change in national habits and power arrangements from among the options open to him. The situation obviously required some combination of increased production and reduced consumption of energy. The least disturbing strategy was to encourage production by private companies. (The Project Independence report out of the FEA contained the idea that the government itself explore the continental shelf for oil, and Senator Adlai

Stevenson pushed legislation to put the government into exploration and production, but not retail sales. Ford ignored these
suggestions.) This could be done by deregulating natural gas,
by higher quota or and/or tariff walls against foreign oil, by
softening the pending strip-mining controls hovering over the
coal industry. Ford endorsed all of them. High domestic prices
would spur Exxon and Mobil and the others to drill more holes
in the ground, coal companies to dig deeper and wider.

But everything relates to everything. Letting the market price
of energy rise would be stimulating to the capitalists who decided how much energy to produce, yet if too severe it would
unsettle other parts of the economic structure. It fed inflation.
It hurt the automobile industry, near which Ford had grown
up. It gave warm regions advantages over cold ones. So price
increases must be modest—perhaps 10–15 cents per gallon of
gasoline, Ford decided in January. He hoped this would entice
the producers to greater effort, without hurting auto sales more
or adding noticeably to inflation. So far the strategy had been
to encourage production through beckoning profits. This was
conservative enough. But most observers thought it did not do
enough to encourage conservation. For this, Ford should let gas
prices double. This he could not do, considering inflation, and
Detroit, and New England, and jet air travel. Perhaps conservation could be nurtured through patriotic appeals. Through the
autumn the President relied upon WIN buttons, asked citizens
to walk more and turn the thermostat down. The quite respectable Ford Foundation came out with a study that recommended rationing, curbs on low-mileage autos, and other
interferences with American freedoms. Others were critical of
the administration's feeble conservation efforts—such as one
John Sawhill, Federal Energy Administration head. Ford fired
Sawhill for advocating a more vigorous conservation program.
The President was very negative on rationing.

The experts even now debate these issues. My point in so
briefly reviewing them is to underscore the tendency of the Ford
administration to seek out the policy mix that minimized governmental interference with established customs, profit levels,

industries. In January the President announced a new set of energy and economic plans—if we may call them that—and the economic decisions were in line with the established pattern. Faced with a recession that looked very much like a depression, the President turned Keynesian, but in the most reactionary way. His fiscal 1976 budget requested defense spending of $104.7 billion, up $15.7 billion from 1974. Elsewhere there was retrenchment. One heard that a new welfare reform plan hatched in HEW was remanded to the shelves because of its expense. The budget was in deficit, perhaps as much as $50 billion. This was resourceful conservatism; it looked toward revived profits, lowered social tension, a bigger defense establishment and smaller "social" programs. And merely at the cost of a bit of borrowing.

But Ford worried about the borrowing, and about the growth of the transfer payments part of the budget, which he mistakenly called "income redistribution programs." Just before the January budget message, OMB director Roy Ash told the press that the administration saw this as a drift toward socialism, and would fight it. Budget time was torture for conservatives. But Ford made the best of it he could. Apart from the budget, he endorsed a tax cut, the most conservative way to achieve a fiscal stimulus unless one pumps money into a military/space program or a war, or drops treasury notes from a plane over Beverly Hills. At least, that is true if the tax cut does not make the revenue structure more progressive. Ford's proposals, on balance, would not. They were allegedly graduated to modestly favor lower-income families, a gain that would be wiped out by the increase in gas prices, which had a regressive effect. And the proposed rebates on last year's taxes were larger the higher a taxpayer's income, to a maximum rebate of $1000. These details are perhaps tedious, especially since they were only Ford's proposals, which have been getting nowhere in Congress. But they do indicate a relatively consistent approach to economic and energy policy, that of the market-leaning conservator of the post-New Deal political economy.

The rest of Ford's presidency may conceivably give the lie

to these early judgments. A number of circumstances apart from Ford's philosophy and style make this unlikely. Even if he had the sort of visceral and intellectual dissatisfaction with the crisis-oriented and disjoined governing apparatus that Nixon and his circle possessed, there would be limits to reform. Ford's re-election is closer than the usual four years, and there is good evidence that he is thinking much about it. Re-election, we know from the past, reduces presidential interest in structural changes that will have only a long-range payoff. Another enemy of structural reform is the relentless daily pressure Ford now faces from economic and energy problems more severe than America has known since World War II. Probably our problems are the most difficult the nation has ever confronted, for both the domestic and world economies are more interconnected now and there are complicated trade-offs everywhere that had to be guessed at. And always for Ford there were foreign policy crises to intrude, Middle Eastern wars to fend off, Southeast Asia to be lost with honor, the Central Intelligence Agency to be circumspectly defended. And always there was the Democrat-controlled Congress, seething with presidential hopefuls, irritated at "strong" Presidents, united it seemed when the President proposed something but totally unable to propose coherent alternatives. Circumstances encouraged short-run crisis management using the tools available, and the husbanding of political capital for immediate emergencies.

The only important factor at work toward reform would seem to be Vice President Rockefeller. His background was impressive schooling in modern administration; he had learned the instincts of a planner. Rockefeller had chaired a committee to study executive branch organization in the 1950s. He was known to be sympathetic to population control. He was governor of New York for four terms. He had set up the Critical Choices Commission in New York in the early 1970s to ponder the nation's future. Fate had spared him any immersion in the congressional perspective. And he would apparently be an influence within the administration. Ford many times promised to give his Vice President a leading domestic role, announced that he would normally chair the Domestic Council, and named a Rockefeller man as director of the council to replace Kenneth Cole. This was James Cannon, who by late spring was reported to have taken vigorous hold on the Domestic Council (now shrunk to about 30 people), giving it a bilateral structure to allow for consideration of both short and long-range policy issues. It remained to be seen how quickly Rockefeller would see the need for a planning capacity, how much action he could propose without threatening the President.

While Ford concentrated upon immediate economic issues, and for relief upon Arabs and Russians and Cambodians, the important Planning-related issues of the Nixon years quietly slipped from White House concerns. National land-use legislation, reorganization of the executive branch, national growth policy, national population policy, national goals, and social reporting, all lost their places on the presidential agenda and went up for grabs to congressmen or extra-mural crusaders. Domestic Council director Kenneth Cole, who was to leave in February, had not forgotten about land-use legislation, but when he raised it on the Hill among Republicans being briefed on ideas being considered for the State of the Union address: "Bam! I got landed on."[7] He was told the White House ought to concentrate upon energy and the economy. Obviously it took the advice. Udall and Jackson reintroduced their land-use bills in 1975, but the administration was divided and as of May had taken no clear position. Interior Secretary Morton, moving over to Commerce, publicly criticized the White House for its apparent decision to oppose land-use legislation as being too expensive. In the area of population control the administration slipped backward. The 1976 budget cut 20 per cent from HEW's family planning funds. At the end of Ford's first year in office, one could read the weekly compilation of presidential documents and find no mention of population at all.

The growth policy issue was somewhat more difficult to dodge. A second biennial report was required by law in 1974, and it was finally released in December, ten months late. The first report, we will recall, was scalded with criticism when it came out in February of 1972. The second was no improvement. Virtually everything about it was to disappoint the congressional and public forces who handed the administration the problem of growth policy in 1970. They had wanted "an identifiable unit" of the Domestic Council to prepare these reports and carry on the search for a NGP. But the administration had twice rushed together a report with a task force that disbanded, the second time with a group called the Committee on Community Development of the Domestic Council, suggesting an unusually narrow view of the subject. The report frankly acknowledged the central problem, that the country was growing by inadvertence, paying high social costs for the results; that the federal government influenced the outcome in countless ways that it did not intend or understand. It respected Moynihan's spirit: "We live in a world where . . . everything is related to everything else."[8] The government needed to understand its unintentional impact upon growth, to clarify its own goals, gain a forecasting capability, improve its social measurements, coordinate its policies.

After these beginnings the 1974 report was as retiring as its predecessor. Admitting the need "to assess the intertwined consequences of these [federal] programs,"[9] it spent only nine pages in a superficial discussion of the impact of federal grants, public works, tax policies (one paragraph!), environmental regulation, defense contracting. But its heart was not in this inquiry. To mesh all this into one rational Policy was too formidable, would take many years. The report had other points to make. It paid strong tribute to the primary role of private enterprise; it insisted that growth was inevitable and desirable; it devoted twenty-six pages (the report was 97 pages long) to state and regional activities in control of growth, and insisted that "the States are uniquely suited to managing growth and development processes because of the constitutional powers they enjoy and their relation to local governments."[10] This awful job of directing growth, it seemed to hint, should really be done at other governmental levels. Witnesses at the 1972 hearings on the growth report of that year had expressed disappointment at not

finding in it suggested mechanisms for turning policies to Policy.
The 1974 report made the same default, except to recommend a
rudimentary "decisionmaker's checklist" which occupied a page.
This might help all federal officials to review the multiple effects
of growth-related programs.

Plainly the Republicans did not want to create a national
growth policy. They would put out these reports, would strew
them with interesting statistics, would circle round the problem in honest prose, would speak despairingly of the imposing
difficulties inherent in the issue. Perhaps they were right. Many
mayors, congressmen, architects, and others did not think so.
There already *was* a NGP, inadvertent but powerful. Couldn't
it be changed? The 1974 report, like its predecessor, essentially
reported that it could not, not now. The 1972 report, at least, had
listed a number of Nixon's enacted and un-enacted proposals at
the end, as evidence of a sort of commitment to the problem.
Ford's report hoped vaguely for better coordination and social
monitoring, invited the Congress and the states to do better, and
let it go. Many critics thought the government was doing absolutely nothing on NGP. I suspect this is wrong in an important if intangible way. Certainly the Domestic Council had
not seized upon the NGP issue, taken the lead. But it had assigned some top talent to the report—James Lynn of HUD,
Herbert Stein, recently of CEA, Russell Peterson of CEQ, rank-
ing people in many departments. John Ehrlichman once conceded that the NGP idea was useful "as an intellectual construct,
up there on the wall, against which to refer" as one works on
some part of the problem.[11] The preparation of the 1974 report
at the very least must have spread the organic perspective more
broadly among bureaucrats whose daily activities nurtured the
old segmented approaches.

Ford's administration is just one year old as this book goes
to press. At least where the White House is concerned, the
frost of the late Nixon years continued to lay upon the Planning issues that had been explored so vigorously at the beginning. America stood on the eve of the bicentennial with her

future still determined by forces that the people had no collective ability to control.

2

The unsympathetic cast of mind of President Ford and the people helping him set policy and select issues for public education could not stifle the Planning impulse. The discussion of Planning could be conducted without the President. It began in February 1975. At hearings of the Joint Economic Committee, Henry Ford II submitted the opinion that the nation should consider Planning. In that month the *New York Times* said the same thing in a lead editorial, and Leonard Woodcock of the UAW convened a group of economists and others who called themselves "The Initiative Committee for National Economic Planning." Their purpose was to "open a public debate on planning and strip from it the notion that it would be un-American."[12] Speaking for the group, Robert V. Roosa, an undersecretary of the Treasury under Kennedy and Johnson, said: "The time has come to develop a truly homegrown American form of national economic planning," and insisted that democracy depended upon Planning rather than being threatened by it.[13] One member of that group, Nobel economist Wassily Leontief, asked in 1974 if it isn't "high time to revive President Franklin Roosevelt's National Resources Planning Board?",[14] and Alfred Heller urged that the NRPB be re-established in an article in *Cry California* in the autumn of the same year. That article found its way into the *Congressional Record*. If one dips into the literature of the environmental movement, written by natural and social scientists who have pondered the human future, the Planning idea sprouts like spring grass. As one example, Lynton Caldwell, professor at Indiana University and member of Nixon's materials policy commission:

There is truly one only course open to modern industrial man that offers a real prospect of solving his ecological problems. . . . An "edited" culture and a guided economy based on ecologically valid principles. . . . Regardless of . . . misgivings regarding social planning, the predicament of modern man forces him into it.[15]

Even the economics profession, heartland of market loyalty, nurtures a growing number of Planners—Leontief, Gunnar Myrdal, Galbraith, others. *New York Times* writer Soma Golden, surveying the views of business and academic economists at the end of 1974, finds them suspecting that 1975 "could usher in a fundamental transformation of the American economy towards increased government planning and controls."[16]

The ferment about Planning has not gone unnoticed among alert people who would prefer it to stop. C. Jackson Grayson, chairman of the Price Commission from 1971 to 1973, went out of his way in his recent memoir of that episode to warn against a looming possibility:

> With feelings running high about inflation, shortages, credit crunches and depressed capital markets, the time will be ripe for a push to create "national planning." This would be going in the wrong direction.[17]

More recently, President Ford and Roy Ash claim to perceive a strong trend toward "socialism," which may be their confused shorthand for Planning. If so, their intimations were accurate. On May 21, 1975, Senators Humphrey and Jacob Javits introduced the Balanced Growth and Economic Planning bill,* and

---

* The bill would establish in the executive branch a three-person economic Planning board with broad responsibilities including forecasting, goal clarification, policy coordination, and the submission of a "rolling" six-year Plan; a council on economic planning, made up of department heads and other Cabinet-level officials; a division of economic information to coordinate federal statistics; a division of economic planning in the Congressional Budget Office; review of the National Economic Plan by the Joint Economic Committee; its adoption by concurrent resolution of Congress.

The six-year Plan would not be binding upon the private sector, and in this respect resembled Indicative Planning on the French model. But it would be binding upon the government.

two weeks later a conference on planning was sponsored by several senators and representatives in an office building named after the vigilant anti-planner, now deceased, Senator Everett Dirksen. The issue had come boldly to the front. America had worked its way finally back to the point it had reached in the late 1930s when the discussion over Planning had ended in the Broker State solution. And now it would decide the question again, forty years later.

3

Would history perhaps repeat itself? Conceivably the nation would debate Planning again, in the rough way that it decides these things, and conclude again against Planning. Herbert Stein, Nixon's last chairman of the CEA, is one who thinks so. The latest surge of interest in Planning is no more than the top of a predictable cycle, by which Planning is ardently discussed every fifteen years, and then (happily) the subject is dropped.[18] Stein's assessment, one supposes, rests upon certain familiar judgments. The public, it is frequently said without any real evidence in support, is hostile to Planning. It is not the American way. Apart from the public, whose attitudes are difficult to appraise, the argument against Planning has been made with compelling persuasiveness by a long line of thinkers in a tradition that still flourishes. The classics in the literature of anti-Planning are well-thumbed. When the Planning idea first swaggered across Europe there appeared the grand rebuttals, still worth re-reading—Walter Lippmann's *The Good Society* (1937), Henry Wriston's *Challenge to Freedom* (1943), Friedrich von Hayek's *The Road to Serfdom* (1944). These were written before the capitalist democracies began to Plan, and were therefore somewhat limited in their application. They took up the fight against Marxist Planning, but the American audience needed little inoculation against that virus. Then the British and French began to dabble in Planning, and those interested in a skeptical appraisal could consult John Jewkes' *The New Ordeal by Planning* (1968) or Stephen S. Cohen's *Modern Capitalist Planning: The French Model* (1969). Ex-Planners, like ex-Communists, wrote especially convincing books of apostasy, such as James Meade's *Planning and the Price Mechanism* (1949), or Edward Banfield's *The Unheavenly City* (1968). The journal *The Public Interest* in recent years has published notable essays by the skeptics of the planning and Planning impulse, by conservative liberal writers like Aaron Wildavsky, James Q. Wilson, and Irving Kristol. They speak to the general reader, and remind us that humans are ignorant and impulsive, governments are inept, politicians are merely specialists in expediency, societies are too complex for the human brain and skills to manage, and the future is endlessly heavy with surprise. They turn to history as a lode of confirming experience for the skeptic of the pretensions of social management.

Professional fields such as public administration, welfare economics, even philosophy have their own anti-Planning literature, requiring a greater degree of dedication to appreciate. There is for example Yale's Charles Lindblom, perhaps the most prolific and dedicated skeptic of what he calls the "synoptic" or comprehensive approach to social management. In a series of articles and in his book *The Intelligence of Democracy: Decision-Making Through Mutual Adjustment* (1965), Lindblom argues that decision-makers cannot and do not know enough to approach the synoptic ideal, and that mutual adjustment, interest-group bargaining, and incrementalism are best suited to human capacities. It was Lindblom who urged that "muddling through" not be a term of light scorn but be recognized as the wisest approach to human governance. The Planning idea is undercut in other professional literature, even less accessible to the curious layman. There is for example economist Kenneth Arrow's argument (1951) that no objective standard exists by which to arrive at priorities among social values. And philosophers and political scientists know of the body of writing which holds that there is no definable entity that one may call "the Public Interest."

These are weighty arguments. The general perspective they

represent proved too strong for the American Planning movement when it surged to life under FDR. There is much evidence that they do not have their earlier strength, relative to the Planning idea. No one has yet tallied the score in the literary struggle between Planners and anti-Planners, just to speak of one way to guess at the future. Until a decade ago, a rough count might have suggested a stand-off between the critics of Planning, noted above, and the classic Planning appeals written by Mannheim, Tugwell, Wooton, Finer, Lorwin, Landauer, Devons, Myrdal, and others. Using the most impressionistic methods, one must now be convinced that the balance has shifted. Planning journals spring to life, and flourish. Articles on planning force their way into the periodical indexes in growing numbers. If we judge by what is put in print, Planning has resumed the intellectual momentum of the 1930s. Its advocates are a varied cast. For example, economist Gerhard Colm and student of public administration Luther Gulick:

> We . . . conclude that the time has come. The time is ripe . . . for a further step toward concerted planning.[19]

or economist John Kenneth Galbraith:

> The creation of . . . planning machinery . . . is the next major task in economic design.[20]

or the urbanist and public official Robert C. Wood:

> Planning [once] was equated with Plato's philosopher king, and in some circles even with socialism. That mythological image is behind us. The planner is being pushed, willing or not, to the front line of the struggle to guide the catastrophic forces shaping the American city.[21]

or the head of the AFL-CIO George Meany:

> We need long-range economic planning and priorities to minimize unforeseen major developments and reduce the degree to which

American society has stumbled and fumbled along in the past few years.[22]

or the ex-Secretary of the Interior under Richard Nixon, Walter J. Hickel:

There has been an enormous and thoughtless lack of planning in the development of the United States.[23]

One could multiply such statements into a significant avalanche. Planning, of course, will not come because many writers call for it, even if they were calling for the same thing when they used the word. Writers are reflecting other sources of the surge toward a more rationally controlled human community.

Who can fail to notice the thrust of contemporary history toward control and away from randomness? The planning mode is being explored in every large institution. Cities have been planning longer than any other American collectivity, although for various reasons they have been planning more ineffectively than the institutions to follow. Corporations have explored the habits of planning since the early part of this century, but with special effect since World War II. In the late 1940s, McGraw-Hill found in a survey of large corporations that only 20 per cent of them could provide summaries of their investment plans for four years into the future; by the early 1960s, 90 per cent were able to supply such plans. Neil Chamberlain's summary is concise: "Comprehensive corporate planning and budgeting, which had just been picking up steam in the period prior to World War II, spread with a rush in the years after, so that most business in medium to large-size corporations became personally involved in . . . planning programs in their own companies."[24] Neil Jacoby adds: "The scope of corporate planning has become more systematic and competent as business executives have come to see the complex interconnections between the performance of the enterprise and the multifaceted and changing environment for business."[25] John Kenneth Galbraith finds planning so pervasive in the affairs of the largest 1000 corporations which produce half the private-sector goods and services that he designates this "the planning system." The other 12 million American business firms may and do plan a bit, but they have not planned sufficiently to control their environments and therefore remain exposed in the market system.[26] For the purposes of his argument, he may well underestimate the strength of the planning idea among medium-sized firms. An example came recently in the mail: "Growing in good years and bad in the most competitive banking state in the nation," reads the 1974 Annual Report of the American National Bank of Bakersfield, California, "could not take place without comprehensive planning. . . . Planning is a dynamic process at American and . . . assures that policies are made and executed by design and not by events."[27]

Such examples could be infinitely multiplied today, not only in the business world but in all contemporary institutions of size and complexity. The military services have been planning for many years, and since World War II have been planning in a recognizably modern and orderly way. Notice the internal administrative life of other large institutions nearby—city governments, corporations, foundations, health care complexes, research institutions, professional athletic organizations. Which of them has not evolved toward routinized attempts to anticipate and forecast, set long-range as well as short-range goals, cost out its alternatives, monitor the environment in which it lives, review performance, realign policy? Turning to the University of California, one finds it currently engaged in revision of the state Master Plan for higher education, and for the first time requesting plans of each campus. "The time has come," states a recent administrator at Berkeley, "for the university community to reassess its commitments and to engage in long-range strategic planning. . . ."[28] And a former university vice president: "People will listen to us, if we have a plan. . . ."[29]

Other tracks of planning are plain to see in the years that have passed since FDR. Planning departments proliferate in municipalities. Universities multiply schools and institutes engaged in planning studies; the membership of the American

Institute of Planners grows steadily; the journals devoted to planning double and triple in number and circulation. The word "planning" is strewn across the flow of paper in corporate boardrooms, scholarly conferences, presidential messages, public agencies. Forty years ago FDR set up one planning board in Washington; the government harbored no other planning agency, except in the War Department where planning for war went forward under the famous Rainbow Plans. Yet in 1974 when Congressman Jerry Litton requested of all federal agencies a report on the nature and extent of long-range planning at the federal level, the response filled 74 pages. Every department and agency proudly claimed to be involved in long-range planning of some sort, of five years or longer, except the CEA![30] So much for the fears that the CEA would slip socialism into the inner councils. Litton found the Forest Service involved in projections up to 100 years, the Bureau of Reclamation making seven-year plans for weather modification, the National Park Service drawing up Master Plans for park lands, the Department of Transportation with an office of planning and program review, the Treasury with an office of planning and evaluation, the Justice Department run by a management by objectives (MBO) plan, and so on. Whatever else is going on in these bureaucratic corners, they are a breeding ground for the ideas of interdependence, anticipation, control. In the 1930s a congressman from Missouri like Litton would probably have wanted this information in order to launch a search-and-destroy investigation to root out communist planners in the New Deal bureaucracy. But Litton only wanted to assure himself that there was enough planning, and of the right kind.

A glimpse of state planning activities reveals a similar evolution. In 1932, only two states had any planning agency at all. The NRPB offered federal grants to nourish the planning capacity, and by the end of the decade 46 states had set up some sort of planning instrumentality. Virtually all of these vanished during or just after the war, most to become development boards to attract new industry. The lost ground was only painfully regained. The 701 grants from 1954 on, then the planning-grant features of Great Society legislation gradually rebuilt state planning institutions. No one, of course, claims that these are as yet very potent or confident of their mission. But the environmental movement continues to force states to interfere with private development. In 1973, 21 states had goals commissions, 6 had population commissions with 10 others passing stabilization resolutions, 4 enacting land-use laws, and others controlling coastal zones.[31] Fred Bosselman and David Callies seemed right to refer to this as a "quiet revolution" in state control of growth.

Clearly the planning habit has worked its way deep into contemporary guidance systems, private and public. And how could it have been otherwise? In Roosevelt's day the men of power in politics had been born in the late nineteenth century, raised on farms and small towns, pored over the classical curriculum in a liberal college, studied law in a small office, co-mingled with farmers, clergymen, small businessmen. They knew no science, had rarely been responsible for large and complex institutions, were not attuned to the gathering and analysis of social data, and were unreflectively optimistic about the natural unfolding of the American future. Men of power in the business world had somewhat more exposure to modernized large institutions than the average national politician, but many were still the Henry Ford–Tom Girdler–Sewell Avery type, self-made entrepreneurs who were builders and buccaneers rather than trained managers. Such people naturally felt massive hostility to every social encroachment upon private decisions. The planning mode had produced too few cadres, made slight inroads upon traditional American habits. Veblen in the 1920s had hoped that engineers would turn soon to social engineering. The process was slower than he had imagined.

Today these circumstances have been transformed. The cultural basis of American individualism has been eroding for more than a century, but with remarkable rapidity in the last generation. The rural/small town political elite has yielded much power not only to people of more varied skin colors and sexes than has been the American pattern, but to more cosmopolitan people, shaped by urban life, large institutions, travel, the habits of social science. In the business world, men who manage huge enterprise, whose own careers are caught up in a search for expanded control and predictability, cannot have quite their grandfathers' or even their fathers' horror at the idea of a managed society. Some of them, indeed, come to the idea with zest and a sense of personal calling. Robert McNamara, speaking in 1967, said:

> Some critics today keep worrying that our democratic free societies are becoming over-managed. The real truth is precisely the opposite. As paradoxical as it may sound, the real threat to democracy comes from under-management not from over-management.
>
> To create the necessary organization for a precise formulation of the different options which underlie our decisions is an exalting adventure.[32]

Business executives have not long been guided by such a social outlook; but the tide runs that way. Perhaps more influential is the so-called "new class" of professional, scientific, and technical workers in corporations, foundations, government, universities. Many authors have described their ascent to social influence, attempted to forecast their values and historic mission. James Burnham, in *The Managerial Revolution* (1940), thought that he detected a totalitarian future in the growing ranks of the managerial class. David Bazelon, in *Power in America: The Politics of the New Class* (1967), doubted that this new cadre had the vision for social transformation, as he observed their taste for suburban living. John Kenneth Galbraith, in *The New Industrial State* (1967), held out the hope that the "technostructure," as he labeled that segment of society that had emerged between top management and labor, would ally with the lower classes and lead a drive to public-interest Planning. Whatever the political impact of the technostructure or whatever one calls it, these Americans are raised in the planning ethos, and exert pressure within all large institutions toward planning.

4

One major barrier to the idea of Planning for the United States that has fallen almost unnoticed is both the reality and reputation of Planning abroad. In the 1930s when FDR gently urged measures of Planning upon a resistant political environment one of the major weapons of the opposition was the apparent symbiosis between planning and totalitarianism. Russia was the world's first Planned society, fascist Germany and Italy employed tight State controls that some called Planning. Intelligent people came to assume that Planning meant socialism—perhaps National Socialism, perhaps communist socialism, perhaps British or Swedish socialism, but socialism, and was thus irrelevant in the United States, or abhorrent, or both. The strong commitment to Planning in socialist literature confirmed their intimate connection. Democratic Planners in the United States were strongly on the defensive for want of acceptable models of capitalist or mixed-economy Planning that were both economically and politically attractive. Marquis Childs' 1936 book *Sweden: The Middle Way* succeeded in offered American liberals a European model for a mixed economy that combined a bit of nationalization, a vigorous free enterprise sector, plus strong cooperative and labor movements. But Childs' Sweden looked like an advanced New Deal come to fruition, and it was not suggested that the Swedes were Planning.

Until France established a planning commission to draft the Monnet plan for post-war reconstruction in 1946, Planning was a phenomenon strictly of the command economies of communist Eastern Europe. This remained a comfortable assumption for some time. The French plan was ignored, and the British labor government after the war paid even less attention to its Economic Planning Board (1948–). Planning confirmed the suspicions of Americans by refusing to take when grafted upon market-oriented political democracies. Both France and Britain experienced sluggish economic recovery from the war, perhaps because their dalliance with Planning had somehow wounded the venturesome capitalist spirit.

Gradually this was to change. Though few people noticed it during years preoccupied with cold war confrontations, the European (and Japanese) experience with Planning steadily became more complex and interesting than at mid-century. Market economies began to plan with apparent success, and command economies in the Soviet bloc began to discover the virtues of the market. An economic convergence matched the political convergence of Marxist and non-Marxist societies that has been noted many times, and in the process Planning had to be reevaluated as an instrument of variable forms which was conceivably ideologically neutral.

The mutation of command-socialist systems of Planning began with Yugoslavia, the first communist country to return important economic sectors to the market since the Russian NEP period from 1921 to 1928. During the 1950s the Yugoslavs, while on a politically independent path charted by Tito, returned most of agriculture to private enterprise, and instituted reforms to decentralize decision-making power to local industries, even firms. When this experimentation with combinations of centralized control and decentralization or market influence was not checked, there soon appeared other hybrids in the communist Planning world. By the 1960s Michael Kaser and Janusz Zielinski in their *Planning in East Europe* (1970) identified four types of socialist Planning: (1) the Soviet "command economy," which by 1970 only Albania utilized!; (2) a looser sort of command economy, now used by Poland, the USSR, East Germany, and Rumania, in which targets are fewer, rewards are paid to managers, and plant profits are calculated in order to establish superior performance; (3) the guided market system used in Hungary, and in Czechoslovakia before the 1968 intervention; (4) the Yugoslav system, which, although loosely planned for over-all goals, is market oriented with assets vested in workers' collectives at the plant level. These the authors call the bureaucratic, technocratic, managerial, and syndicalist forms of Eastern European Planning.[33] Shockingly enough, variety flourishes in

Marxist Planning, and the market has become a useful tool of Planners. As Charles Lindblom said in 1965: "The most significant *administrative* advance that has come to attention in many a year is the market mechanism."[34] Or as Kaser and Zielinski quote a Planning reformer from Eastern Europe: "Without government planning no purposive development can be achieved and without market relations no rational allocations can be realized."[35] It has become difficult to regard Planning as a road to dictatorial socialism when it has led so many command Marxist economies toward Western forms. In Eastern Europe, Planning has apparently been a Trojan Horse for free enterprise!

During the same period that Marxist Planned economies evolved away from the original Stalinist model, Western European democracies gradually extended the ventures into Planning initiated so tentatively after the war. France was by far the most interesting model for Americans. There a planning board had been compiling plans since 1946, but for some time it was the sort of process that brings to mind American city planning, in that nobody had to pay much attention to it. Sometime in the 1950s the idea and practice of Planning began to gain real authority in France. The General Planning Commission (Commissariat Général au Plan) has now formulated a series of four-year plans, then a five-year plan to reach 1970, and France now works with its sixth plan.

The French way, as the terminology goes, is "indicative" rather than "imperative" Planning. The planning is exhortatory, deriving its power from persuasion rather than coercion. And the entire process is remarkably open. General economic targets are set by the Planning Commission, and these are sent to twenty-five or so modernization commissions composed of representatives of all economic groups. There the sector targets are discussed and modified, and the paper is passed upward through the Economic and Social Council to Parliament. The quality of staff analysis seems high, and French capitalists are said to be influenced in their decisions merely by the plan's projections. Apart from selective wage-price controls, the existence of a sizable nationalized sector, and an important degree of state influence over investment funds, the French government has an arsenal of compulsion roughly similiar to that of our own. Tax policy in France is, however, much more flexible than ours; administrators have a range of tax favors to extend to innovative firms which cooperate with the plan. In all of this no formal econometric model is used; the planners work more from experience than theory. The main influence of the plan seems disarmingly simple: industrialists see projections of demand and production which they have come to trust, and are led to make bolder investments than they otherwise might. The government, for its part, attempts to offer relatively stable policies, and encourages investors toward technological innovations and managerial improvements they might otherwise delay. Can it really be "government arousing capitalism from its lethargy?", ask the authors of a recent comparative study of French and British planning.[36] The world watches capitalist Planning in France and elsewhere with interest, and a natural skepticism.

French indicative Planning attracted attention because French capitalists seemed so comfortable with it, and some observers linked Planning with the nation's economic resurgence. The French Left does not like Planning as it is done there, complaining that it fails to address disparities in wealth and income, and has narrow social objectives. Planning that is warmly received on the Right and complained about on the Left is an international development which shakes a number of assumptions. Moderates and even conservatives in other capitalist societies wonder if they have not misjudged the potentialities of Planning. Elsewhere in Europe there are other models of ongoing Planning to which some degree of success is often attributed. In the Netherlands a formal econometric model with 36 equations and as many variables has been utilized by the Central Planning Bureau. The model guides the government in year-by-year stabilization, but there is no binding Plan. In Sweden, ad hoc planning commissions launch each Planning period, instead of a permanent and central Planning ministry. These countries are often cited as examples deserving respectful study,

even though the internal problems of both—especially Sweden—
remain acute.

Other Western European examples tend to leave traditional
American suspicions of Planning pretty much intact. In Belgium
and Italy, Planning is very perfunctory, and opinion about it is
quite divided. West Germany, far from the citadel of laissez-
faire that it is sometimes called, is developing an extensive set of
guidance institutions along American lines, with a growing
tendency to budget for long periods; but there is no Plan or
Planning. Across the channel from France there has been an
experience with Planning that is as chastening to Planners as
the French experience has been exciting.

Planning in Britain lacks the French reputation for effectiveness, to put the best face on it, and it is difficult to determine
whether the problem has been chiefly in the Planning process
adopted there, or in the economy and culture of Britain, or in
the Planning idea itself, as anti-Planners insist. Interestingly
enough, Planning was launched in Britain in the early 1960s
(for the second time; there had been a brief trial of Planning
in the late 1940s) by the Tories, who were alarmed by Britain's
sluggish growth, her balance of payments problems, and the
looming entry into the Common Market. Industrialists, especially from the Iron and Steel Board, urged the experiment. A
National Economic Development Board ("Neddie") was established, with regional "little Neddies" for various industries;
the Treasury was reorganized; a Plan was published in 1962.

Then Labour came to power in 1964, the scope of Planning
was expanded and a second Plan came out in 1965. Economic
problems intensified in the late 1960s, and the government practiced crisis management, ignoring the Plan, which was in any
event indicative. Britain's economic woes are now worse than
ever, and Planning appears simply to have lapsed. Anti-Planners
triumphantly comb the period since 1961 for lessons reinforcing
their argument. Planners think that Planning was half tried,
and in a poor environment. British Planning was weak and
infirm from the start. The French consult interest groups at two
lower levels, but preserve the Planning Commission as a body

292 · Toward a Planned Society

representing national perspectives and apolitical expertise. They respect expertise in a special way, commentators say, whereas the British expect rational decisions to come from the inter-action of interest groups and assume that their civil servants will defer to representatives from the private sector. Thus in Britain the influence of organized labor and industrialists is relatively greater, and the influence of the Planning ministry less, than across the channel. In Britain also the State has less leverage over investment funds, and no tradition of discretionary taxation as an adjunct to economic management. Whatever the reasons, British Planning, with the same general goals of eco-nomic growth, price stability, low unemployment, balance of payments equilibrium, and balanced regional development that are the general goals of Planning elsewhere, has disappointed its backers and so far not shaken the American suspicion of Planning by its example.

Around the world Planning is in a state of ferment, failing, half-succeeding, yet irresistibly expanding its geographical and cultural influence. The literature on Planning is now enormous, most of it either on the developing nations or the Soviet bloc, much of it highly technical in nature. Economists build and criticize models, adapt Wassily Leontief's input-output analysis, devise applications of linear programming. Americans in search of ideas for the renovation of their political economy are not drawn to these studies. In familiar, capitalist-democratic Europe, France attracts the Planners, Britain the skeptics. Another inter-esting experience with Planning has recently caught American eyes, in an industrial-capitalist-democratic society somewhat like our own but one with quite different cultural antecedents. This is Japan.

The first socialist government in Japan drafted a national plan in 1947, with elaborate economic projections but not a word about implementation. Since American occupation au-thorities were hostile to Planning and Prime Minister Yoshida (1949–54) was an outspoken friend of free enterprise, little was done to forward the idea of planning Japan's reconstruction. After Yoshida's fall in 1954 the Economic Counsel Board was renamed the Economic Planning Agency so that it could produce a plan for Japanese development to satisfy officials of the world bank. *A Five Year Plan for Economic Self-Support* was duly produced in 1956; nobody paid much attention to it. The next year's *New Long Range Economic Plan* paid tribute to free enterprise, and offered various alternative economic projections, with no suggestion of coercion. Economic growth during these years continued to outstrip projections found in the plans, and so they were easily ignored. In 1960 the new Ikeda government brought out the *Plan for Doubling National Income in Ten Years,* with alternative projections that obviously urged the government to invest in social overhead capital and human resources. The agency writing these plans, the Economic Planning Agency, still had no administrative authority within the Japanese system, but its informal influence was growing.

Within the public sector the plan may have led to more rational and better-timed public investment. The private sector was under no obligation to respect the plan's projections, but we are led to believe by students of the subject that a combination of high patriotism, capitalist involvement in fashioning the plan, and respect for the expertise of the planners has led the plan to have an "announcement effect" similar to that of the French plan. Japan, also, works with indicative rather than imperative Planning. Behind the announcement effect the government has a string of financial institutions through which it virtually controls private investment funds. In most descriptions of the Japanese system, capitalists themselves plan to allocate their resources along lines generally suggested by the government plan, and this has contributed to both orderly and dynamic growth. Critics have found Japanese Planning, in Victor Lippit's words, "largely decorative," and question whether the Planning process can promote other social goals—environmental protection, price stability, or "a stable civil life"—as well as it has promoted growth. Whatever the contribution of Japan's Planning, the Japanese economy has grown more spectacularly since World War II than anyone believed possible, and her GNP is now second in the non-communist world. Few people know how Japanese Planning works, but many American policy-makers and analysts, like Herbert Stein, know that Japan has some kind of Planning and that there is a strong possibility that this has given the nation an important economic advantage. Franklin Roosevelt could point to no such examples forty years ago.

American interest in forms of social management abroad, especially in industrialized, capitalist democracies like our own, has continued to increase since John F. Kennedy sent Walter Heller to Europe in the early 1960s to report to him on planning. The literature in English on French and Japanese Planning especially is now large and rapidly growing. These societies are particularly interesting to leaders of a cautious, conservative country like our own. Unlike the Scandinavian countries, which are often pointed to as illuminating social laboratories, France and Japan are not particularly "socialist." They have large and vital economies, and many problems similar to our own. Planning abroad is a subject that ranges geographically and socially from the U.S.S.R. to China, Tanzania to Israel. Of all these ongoing experiments in social control, France and Japan now exert by far the most influence toward a more receptive American attitude regarding Planning. Nixon's last chairman of the CEA, Herbert Stein, told a public gathering in December 1973:

> I think there will be a question at some point . . . whether we don't need to follow the example of the Japanese, who have an economic planning agency, or the French, who have a Commissariat Général au Plan.[37]

Stein mentioned "economic" Planning. People who are not sure that they are in favor of Planning often make it a more comfortable idea by prefacing it with the word "economic." The public, presumably, is ready to accept almost any degree of governmental manipulation of the baffling system that gives them jobs and income. If they were told that Planning required social influence rather beyond the narrow confines of employment totals and gross national product, they might become alarmed, thinking the government was about to match up their daughters with suitable mates. "Economic Planning" is now an acceptable term; "Social Planning" is not.

I read not long ago that the declension of the word "planning" is, I plan, you pseudo-plan, he does not plan at all. Similarly, it will be seen upon reflection that economic Planning is not Planning at all, but merely planning. It is a way-station on the road to social Planning; many societies have rested there for years, even indefinitely. When the momentous step is taken to finally set up a national economic Planning apparatus with that explicit function, it is usually some time before leading economic and political groups are comfortable with the presence of a planning commitment, staff, and process. Yet before long the logic of planning thrusts against barriers, and it is seen that Planned social management must be broadly social, not merely economic in the narrow sense. Everything relates to everything. Thus public authority must explicitly encompass questions of population growth and distribution. A nation without a national growth policy may have a national planning staff in a building all their own, turning out five-year plans full of impregnable equations. But there is not yet Planning.

In the last ten years every Western European nation has adopted a national growth policy, one of the prerequisites to a Planned society. This happened not because of ideology, but in response to the metropolitanization of mankind which is worldwide. Some 350 million people will become city residents between 1970 and 1980, placing cities like Calcutta, Caracas, Rio, Mexico City, Lagos, Tripoli, and Djkarta under veritable siege. The problem is less acute for Rome, London, or Paris, but the European population distribution problem is serious enough to have produced a policy response which the nations of the less-developed world could not manage. The French government has devised a set of comprehensive and coordinated policies to stabilize the size of Paris, the British have the same goal for London, the Italians for Milan-Turin-Genoa, the Swedes for their relatively crowded Southern regions. France and Britain are zoned into areas of development with varying priorities and needs, and the government uses direct controls, construction grants, tax incentives and operating subsidies to remove industrial and commercial facilities to the provinces. These are in addition to its own investment in infrastructure. In Sweden, a government department will consult with firms willing to relocate out of the metropolitan areas of the South, and recommend appropriate incentives. Many of these countries are decentralizing their government offices. There is some interest in effective NGP in the communist countries of Eastern Europe, particularly in Finland, Poland, and in Hungary where the stabilization of the growth of Budapest is a recent goal. But growth policies in the West appear to be producing the intended results. James Sundquist's recent study of European growth policies reports a net out-migration from the London and Paris regions for the first time in modern history, and the first absolute decline in population of Stockholm since the influenza epidemic of 1918. For the first time these societies have achieved some rudimentary social control over population distribution, without the barbarities that attended this sort of intervention in population distribution by Stalin and Hitler. Again Europe explores the intricacies of a planned future, writing lessons for American readers.

5

Thus the forty years that have passed since Roosevelt failed to introduce Planning have weakened many of the barriers he faced, and increased the cultural receptivity to the managerial thrust that his planning ideas represented. One or two other fundamental changes should be noted. In the grip of economic depression and grave social unrest, the untried Planning idea of the 1930s had a major and also untried rival which proved in the end more attractive. This was the Broker State, a middle course between laissez-faire capitalism and socialism, broad social intervention without a Planning capacity. This, in the end, was what the reforms of the 1930s produced. Roosevelt, despite his desire for a different system with a strong

Planning element, ultimately went along with the practice of referring to the system that came out of the 1930s as the New Deal. I have preferred to call it the post-New Deal Broker State, a compromise system that contained the social programs demanded by contemporary liberalism but without the institutional capacity or political commitment required for coherent social management. Liberal Planning was the other New Deal that was rejected and forgotten, in part because Roosevelt and his planning-minded associates did not know exactly how to design it and made errors, in part because their opportunity was narrow and brief.

The Broker State political economy had many merits. Otherwise it could not have lasted so long. It gave the appearance of competent social management for many years. No major depression occurred; economic stability and growth came together under its regime. Perhaps the government and the way it operated were responsible for this; certainly credit was claimed by people on government payroll. The post-New Deal system maximized the freedom of organized groups to pursue their own welfare through political channels. It did not impede, indeed was said to have released the dynamism of American culture. The lubricant of the system was abundance, economic growth to ease social tensions and to provide a large margin of error to accommodate the economic irrationalities that were characteristic of a system of ad hoc, short-term solutions. Along with material abundance, the Cold War also served to mask the flaws of post-New Deal arrangements. Sufficient unto the day are the institutions thereof. At least this was true of the political economy of the United States for a long generation after World War II. In a brilliant book which recounted the virtues of our system, Robert A. Dahl and Charles Lindblom's *Politics, Economics and Welfare* (1953), the future was only briefly glimpsed:

> If the security of this country should ever come to depend upon squeezing the utmost from resources, and hence on reducing conflicting policies to a minimum, the stark alternatives would be failure—or a drastic change in the policy process.[38]

Now the future is here, and the conditions that made the Broker State historically appropriate have altered. In the 1960s the anti-communist ideology eased its grip upon American emotions, and the threat to national security was seen to come primarily from domestic sources—from racial discord, generational alienation, inflation, environmental pollution, abuse of the powers of government, material shortages. When historian William O'Neill wrote a history of the 1960s he aptly entitled it *Coming Apart.* Most revolutionary in its impact was surely the realization that resources and space were finite, that planet Earth was reaching its limit for humanity and its garbage. Like Gatsby we had "believed in the green light, the orgiastic future." Growth had been expected to solve our internal problems, as well as bring mounting delights. Now it had to be accepted that growth was producing more problems than it solved, and it would have to be controlled. Some citizens learned this by reading books written by alarmed demographers and biologists; others by enduring traffic jams, air pollution, power failures, commodity and energy shortages.

To cope with these by-products of uncontrolled growth we would clearly have to rely to a great extent upon the national government. It was in no position to dodge the assignment, having annually assured the public that the rising state of the union was mostly to the credit of wise public managers. These claims of national politicians were believable in 1965, perhaps, the second year of a long economic boom, with the worst part of the 1960s ahead. Ten years later the failures of social management by public officials were all around us. The revenue system does not redistribute income or wealth to any significant degree, is riddled with exceptions which have no rational justification. No economist defends it, no citizen entirely understands it. Farm programs failed to control surpluses for thirty years, shifted income from consumers to large farmers, drove small farmers from the land. Tariff schedules are found to contribute to a substantial misallocation of resources. Housing programs fall so short of announced goals that in 1970 only 2 per cent of the urban population lived in public housing, which was nonetheless criticized for shoddy construction. Immigration laws supposedly regulate the flow of aliens, yet a wave of illegal foreign immigration washed across American borders beginning in the mid-1960s. Federal highway, mortgage insurance, and tax policies intensified the problems of center urban centers, encourage suburban sprawl, reinforced segregation, produced air pollution, and entirely canceled the efforts of the Economic Development Administration or the Department of Agriculture to shift growth to rural areas. One branch of government reclaimed land for agricultural production, another paid farmers not to produce. Regulatory agencies operated without clear policy direction, and their post-war economic record had far more critics than defenders. Everywhere one looked, public policy could be found falling short of its goals, or producing side-effects it had not intended. "A reign of error," said disillusioned ex-planner Edward Banfield.[39]

The pattern of incoherence should be no surprise to those who reflect upon the *modus operandi* of brokerism, so ably described by Tugwell and Banfield (1950), Henry Kariel (1961), Michael D. Reagan (1963), Grant McConnell (1965), Andrew Shonfield (1966), Theodore Lowi (1969). A social problem reaches critical proportions and is brought to the attention of legislators or presidents; vague national goals are legislated in a preface to a new program, which is given to some nearly autonomous agency whose activities are never meshed with activities anywhere else in the government, and oversight is minimal and episodic. Citizens' advisory committees are formed from organized constituencies, a process of bargaining goes on between administrators and organized interest groups, and the policy result, in Lowi's words, is that "any institution large enough to be a significant factor in the community shall have its existence underwritten."[40] A haven from competition is arranged for every group strong and persistent enough to arrange it. Finding discipline unpopular, the government arranges to dispense favors; no one is perceived to lose. As Lowi added, we have not social-

ized medicine or industry in this country, but "we have socialized risk."[41]

John Kenneth Galbraith as long ago as 1952 wrote of the inflationary bias built into the Broker system, so well positioned
were organized interest groups and so atomized and amorphous
the national interest. And from what source could necessary readjustments come? There was and is no central place from which
readjustments could be considered and recommended, no disposition to look to the health and functioning of the system.
Broker government took care of complaining parts, and hoped
the many policies it hatched would add up to the greatest good
for the greatest number.

The record of governmental irrationalities, Banfield's "reign
of error," was not suddenly uncovered in the late 1960s. Problems in the government's managerial performance had been
exposed periodically. Some error in policy, some internal contradiction is expected and will be forgiven. But by the late 1960s
the intellectual community was strongly critical of the system,
anxious, restless for fundamental change, and unsure of the
formula. The public as a whole, judging from opinion surveys,
shares in the rapid erosion of confidence in basic institutions.
Most people do not know the messy details of governmental
ineptitude in transportation regulation, or agricultural policy,
or resource management. They do know the general state of the
economy, where the government has long acknowledged a special
responsibility. And here the news for some time has been not
only bad, but incomprehensible. We have both inflation and
depression-stagnation, a condition which pundits have labeled
stagflation but cannot explain. Inflation reached an incredible
14.4 per cent for the last quarter of 1974, and the GNP over
that period fell by 9 per cent. Unemployment should have been
no large problem under inflationary circumstances, yet it
reached 8.2 per cent in the winter, and some predicted that it
would rise to 10 per cent by summer. The President had to admit
in January that the state of the union was "not good." And
Henry Ford II told the Joint Economic Committee: "In my
thirty years as a businessman I have never before felt so uncer-

tain and so troubled about the future of both my country and my company."⁴⁰

Not since the 1930s have there been such doubts about the fundamental workability of the political economy. The doubts are sound. The Broker State system cannot pilot this or any complex modern society through straits permanently narrowed by population pressures, material shortages, international interdependence, and recurrent war. This understanding broadens every day, and the 1970s are taking form as the decade of a searching national debate over alternative forms of organization for our government and economy. We are quite ready for the introspective assignment brought by the bicentennial.

Where do we go from here? In the 1930s, people argued for five systems: communism, socialism, Broker State liberalism (even if they did not call it that), Planning, laissez-faire capitalism. Forty years later, having made our decision and run the Broker State non-Planning system out to the end, we are narrowed to four. Although nations do not often fit themselves into any model of political economy in its textbook form, toward which of the four will America move as the post-New Deal system founders?

Many people are impressed with the evidence that America is moving toward the laissez-faire alternative. They point to the traditional individualism of the people, the enduring political and social power of capitalist elites. And the laissez-faire view enjoys better-positioned national leadership than at any time since Coolidge and Mellon. Allan Greenspan, the Ayn Rand disciple, is chairman of the President's CEA, and other men of influence, Seidman-Simon et al. openly criticize the managerial capacities of the government they head.⁴³ President Ford, it is clear, shares these views. He has no identifiable social objectives as yet, but talks periodically of deregulation and decontrol.

Such sentiments are not confined to the minority party, or to the Right. Leading liberals like Senator Proxmire talk of deregulation, as do young liberals just coming into national life, Senator Gary Hart of Colorado, Governor Jerry Brown of California; so does Ralph Nader, and most of the young radical activists one can find on the campuses or in the environmental movement. The Left as well as the Right seems irritated with government. In this setting, a let-it-alone system appears to have advantages not enjoyed since the Great Depression ruined its reputation.

The mood of deregulation, of post-Watergate hostility to the national government, is nonetheless misleading. Despite Greenspan's hopes, we will not see the laissez-faire system given another historic opportunity. So many signs point to this conclusion that I mention only the most compelling. Ford, though he has stood up for decontrol of oil pricing and commended decontrol elsewhere in the economy, has not pushed the idea with anything like the intensity required to build programmatic momentum. In part this is because he is simply not a man who is an agent of change. He is a conservative, in a word, who can bring himself to suggest modifications of the dying Broker system, but will not dare the risks of systemic transformation. Even if Ford had counter-revolutionary gifts, his political position is too weak to permit success. He is the unelected head of the minority party, facing an obstructive political minefield of Democrats who do not want him to do much of anything and entrenched interest groups who are not quite alarmed enough to risk what they have for what they know not.

These circumstances will not be altered even if Ford is re-elected. However long he is there, spasms of deregulation may and will occur. But they do not systematically address the mix of problems we face. Beneficial results may occasionally obtain, but will be random, as is always the case when ideology is the guide. In the end, a Planning system has impressive advantages over the other alternatives, two of which are still quite premature, while laissez-faire capitalism is buried too deep under layers of history to be retrieved. For the Planning idea offers a system which may accommodate both the desire for some deregulation and the need for national public control of destabilizing change. It allows America still to remain capitalist, which at the moment still seems to be the general preference. It may be designed to suit the tastes of the Left, near or far, or to honor the values of conservatives, as Richard Nixon almost figured out.

The Right Wingers, after all, were correct in one thing. The post-New Deal system *was* the anteroom of Planning. As Gunnar Myrdal wrote:

> When it turned out to have been an illusion that the need for a particular intervention was only temporary; when the acts of intervention proved to have disturbing effects, often far outside the field where they were applied . . . ; when their lack of compatibility with each other and with other aims and policies . . . stood out as irrational and damaging; and when they created serious administrative difficulties,

then

> attempts at coordination were forced on the State. . . . This is the road we have travelled toward economic Planning.[44]

Or, in the superb summary of Andrew Shonfield:

> . . . Once the state has accepted the obligation to intervene intermittently, in order to secure some desirable condition for society, it soon discovers that its actions exert a powerful influence. . . . A responsible government cannot opt out of the duty of assessing the long-term consequences of these intermittent interventions. Once it begins to make such an assessment, there is a strong inducement to examine the nature of the more fundamental objectives that it would in any case pursue, in default of these short-term pressures. The next stage is an attempt to organize these objectives into a coherent design, in which the various parts are consistent with one another, and then to put them inside the framework of a timetable. Introduce a periodic check on how far events are keeping pace with the timetable—and the main instruments of modern economic planning are in position.[45]

So Planning irresistibly presses forward, here at the end of America's second century. The way back to non-intervention is blocked by political realities and by the steady increases of the cultural influence of collectivism. The managerial instinct in contemporary society is stronger with every turn of the calendar. The tools that put a human on the moon are ready at hand, the Enlightenment confidence in human rationality runs strong again after the pessimistic years dominated by Hitler and Stalin. And the idea of systems penetrates deeply into contemporary intellectual life, carried for a time by operations research and the quasi-science of systems analysis, now more broadly by the common encounter with the concept of ecology. All the ingredients are present, and reaching critical mass. If there are no wars, if a few new oil fields are suddenly punctured, if an ideology legitimating Planning in American terms proves slow to materialize, if the accidents of leadership give us another uncomprehending President, there will be delays in the adoption of Planning. But there can be no cancellation of our appointment with the unfinished agenda of the 1930s. The liberal Left now stirs with recognition that the once-forbidden Planning idea has revived. The Socialists, more numerous than is appreciated, are eager to begin. And now, after Nixon, moderate conservatives have crossed their own Planning threshhold. It is hard to improve upon Michael Harrington's summary: "Now there is no question that the 1970s will see planning in the United States. The only really crucial questions are: what kind of planning? Planning for whom?"[46]

7

What kind of Planning? For our survival, Planning must be effective. To harmonize with our national values, it must also be democratic. We wish to drive a hard bargain if liberty must yield to security, if elites are given more responsibility for the public direction. Here on the eve of Planning we have most need of clarification of alternatives. At the May 22 conference on planning held in Washington, one heard the full range of predictions in answer to this question. It was apparent that this is a pessimistic age, that even those who call for change are troubled by its possibilities. Many of the conference participants, all of whom were people who thought some kind of Planning necessary for America, nonetheless imagined various ways that the thing might turn out badly. A few business leaders, while drawn to the idea of more predictable and rational public policies, expressed the old fears that perhaps Planning was a Trojan Horse with socialism inside. More frequently one heard predictions of the opposite outcome. Knowing that industrialists were talking of Planning, some observers grimly forecast that the new political economy would be dominated by the corporations, even the multinationals. A slide into fascism was glimpsed by a few alarmed participants, Planning by a coalition of capitalists and the military, with profits carefully nurtured, the environment despoiled, labor and consumer interests ignored, civil liberties routinely infringed, and a continuation of the Imperial Presidency.

Planning has always been somehow conducive to exaggerated expectations. Socialism will be the result, we are warned; no, Fascism. They sky will fall. Those who make such predictions will be surprised by the years just ahead. One day it will be agreed that America is Planning. A Planning law will have been enacted, the government will be officially committed to forecasting and anticipation, coherent national policy to influence basic sources of social change, social and economic reporting, a six-year Plan. The word "Planning" will be legitimized at last. It will not feel terribly different. The intense social problems that called Planning into being will not at once be solved. There will be confusion and miscalculation; projections will be made, and they will often be wrong. The habits of the past, the Broker State characteristics of our governing mode, will not be brushed aside overnight. People with advantages will not at once find them transferred to others; people free now to mistreat the earth and their neighbors will not be at once disciplined to socially responsible behavior. We are never simply Planning or not Planning in any pure sense, but moving toward or away. When some Congress legislates the nation into Planning we may then use the term and consciously begin the process. In the long run that process may, indeed must, make large differences. In the short run we will wake to the same problems, the same inadequate understanding, the same power groupings and habits and expectations in the society. Here the radical usually has a much more acute judgment than the conservative. He knows that the mere passage of a law sponsored by Hubert Humphrey will not alter the structures of power, based on possession of property and skills and position, in the country.

And one would expect conservatives to remain calmer. They normally understand that the mere passage of a Planning law will not immediately confer upon the government those masterful habits of foresight and judgment so attractive by contrast to what we must now accept. When we speculate upon the impact of Planning we need not fear a plunge toward one of the political extremes of, let us say, Portuguese politics. Those who fear ought to fear more moderately, and for the very long run. Those who hope, one reluctantly concedes, the same. And whether the long run confirms some utopian or some nightmarish prediction, that will have been worked out by the intervening generation or generations, step by step. Planning is only a mode of survival, as risky as any other, for example a republic under a written constitution in the eighteenth century. It happens to be the only mode of survival. Yet there are no guarantees.

When Planning first comes, we may be very nearly certain that it will come from one of the two established parties, fashioned by political figures who group toward the center, not the edge of those parties. Who now shows a receptivity to planning impulses? In the liberal center, Jackson and Udall push for land-use controls, Mondale for social reporting, Humphrey for national growth policy; in the conservative center, Senator Percy asks why we don't have an NGP, Senator Taft supports population policy, Senator Brock asks why the government doesn't have a central institution to display policy options, Senator Javits supports a Planning board. Planning in its first phases, for a decade or generation, will be consensual. This quite in contrast to the 1930s, when the conservative community, after a frightened dalliance with Planning in 1932–33, hardened into vigorous opposition to the idea.

Thus given the question, What kind of Planning?, we may at least anticipate that it will be centrist, accepting capitalism and the Constitution, comfortably fallible, operated by politicians whose names, faces, and vocabulary we are familiar with, proposing no instant transition to a radically different political or economic system. Within these perimeters we will choose our Planning mode. They are not so wide as in some other countries. America conducts its political struggles along a narrower spectrum than most other societies. Still our choices are wide, the conflicts ahead are real. William James liked the comment he had from an American farmer, that people are not very different, but the differences that there are, are very important. Here, Lenin and Hitler are not the models, or the prospects. We choose from American models, and so far as history presents the matter, between political traditions that have culminated in the sustained leadership of Roosevelt and Nixon.

This book has sketched in those variants of Planning, with all the rough edges and ambiguities that we have learned to expect. Now we might attempt an extrapolation of the Planning history that Roosevelt and the liberals made, Nixon and the conservatives more briefly traced in the sand.

Notice first the areas of potential agreement. Any Planning government, liberal or conservative, would have to install and operate the central cluster of institutions which provide the Planning capacity—institutions for long-range forecasting and anticipation of social issues, high-level policy coordination, technology assessment, social reporting. Any administration would be forced to continue to make powerful efforts to control and focus the activities of the Permanent Government, the bureaucracy. This would require the now familiar efforts at executive branch and congressional reorganization, some kind of performance budgeting, and reforms to reduce the independence of outlying agencies that now frustrate the desire for policy coherence—most importantly the Federal Reserve, and the regulatory agencies. Any administration of whatever political cast, once the Planning assignment is taken on, will be forced to strive for coherent national policy in all basic areas of social change: the economy in all its major facets, raw materials, energy, land-use, population distribution, and size. Nixon and some conservatives came to the edge of an acceptance of these essentials, then could not quite comprehend or accept them. Enlightened conservatism will perhaps not be long in perceiving Planning as the only long-range formula for continued social order. An important portion of liberal leadership was basically ready for these things forty years ago.

Differences in goals, tactics, and style are nonetheless marked between these two traditions. Liberal Planning may be expected to make income redistribution one of its goals; to turn more readily to nationalization; to tilt toward consumers, rather than producers. Conservative Planning would leave redistribution to the workings of natural selection, prefer competition to nationalization, tilt toward producers rather than consumers. Both accepting the necessity for national land-use controls, the liberals would be emotionally with the environmentalists, the conservatives emotionally with far-sighted developers. Accepting the need for a national energy policy, liberals would curb consumption by controls to protect lower-income groups, conservatives would rely upon the price mechanism. Accepting the need for some kind of Incomes Policy, liberals hope to curb profits, conservatives to curb wages. Both liberal and conservative presidents have a poor record at meshing domestic and foreign policy. Indeed, Eisenhower of all recent presidents probably best understood that military needs could not be considered entirely apart from civilian, Lyndon Johnson and Gerald Ford separating the two policy areas in the most total isolation. The World War II Planning experience shows the importance of forcing the military into an overall framework of priorities, and one assumes that liberals would be more likely to appreciate this in the future.

The differences in approach to national growth policy, to population curbs, to technology assessment, are not necessarily substantial, I think, when the issues are joined; liberals are more eager to pass a law, conservatives more wary. National manpower policy does not seem very important to conservatives, even conservatives with strong planning instincts. Nixon was content to shift manpower programs as much as possible to the states, and opposed the public employment program passed by a Democratic Congress. On this issue only the liberals have a strong sense of urgency, possibly because their natural constituency benefits from occupational retraining. Liberal Democrats enacted the public employment program which began in 1971, and in early 1975 two Democratic legislators introduced the Humphrey-Hawkins bill to finally commit the government to the full employment goal of 1946.

Conservatives have less interest, also, in social reporting. The Nixon administration saw the need for better federal statistics, appointing a national commission which reported in 1971, but its chief interest was in economic data. Social indicators seemed a squashy field, a happy hunting ground for professors of sociology and other cranks. The 1973 publication *Social Indicators* carried on the pioneering work of the 1968 document *Toward a Social Report,* but it came out of the HEW bureaucracy and the White House neither supported nor noticed it. This too was an interest of liberal Democrats, who knew that the social deprivations of their special constituency, the poor and racial minorities, were obscured by the traditional reliance on economic data.

On the role of the market, the attitudes of those mainly in the liberal or conservative tradition are not as sharply differentiated as is widely assumed. Commitment to competition is historically associated with both sides of the American political spectrum. The liberal and the populist traditions both contain a strong defense of competition and a suspicion of bureaucracy, running prominently from Wilson and Brandeis through Paul Douglas and Estes Kefauver to William Proxmire. Increasingly this has become a minor strain in the social outlook of the American Left. Conservatives are thought to be the special friends of the marketplace. Their record, of course, is quite inconsistent. Business leaders of conservative outlook have had a large hand in building the regulatory state, even while they honored competition on ceremonial occasions. The market gets its best defense from conservatives where the increase in competition is farthest removed from the speaker's own area of sales.

People who hold the market in high regard, whatever their political philosophy, have an important contribution to make in the discussion of Planning techniques. They will insist that shifts from market to bureaucratic guidance be soundly justified, and remind us that the market is an administrative system which allocates resources and encourages disciplined performance at no cost in public bureaucracy. It must have its place in Planning. It is not hard to imagine, in fact, that under Planning the market will govern more of human affairs than is now the case under our meddlesome leviathan in Washington. The market will be especially important in the early years of the Planning experiment, when required skills, techniques, and institutions are immature and erratic. Reliance in selected places upon the market would allow Planners to follow Gunnar Myrdal's advice not to make peace with bureaucracy, to concentrate managerial energies upon the commanding heights. George Peek, first head of Roosevelt's AAA, commented on the proliferation of New Deal programs in late 1933, saying: "The government has got more hay down now than it will get up before it rains."[47] Retrospect strongly suggests that New Deal Planning would have been much more effective if that insight had been more respected. It is no monopoly of either party, or any one political tradition.

No one interested in Planning, not even the most ardent centralizer, believes that everything can be directed from Washington. Everyone favors decentralization, and this has always included Planners. Praise for decentralization is of course partly a reflex in standard American political discourse, and partly a ritualistic gesture to calm the nerves of that multitude of Americans with a personal or ideological stake in local government. But one also hears it because it is obvious that many decisions must be made and information gathered far down in the provinces. Centralization vs. decentralization—it is a perennial conundrum, a complex and fascinating subject. Entire books only nibble at its edges, with a very few, such as James Sundquist's *Making Federalism work,* offering a comprehensive grasp. I will not make such an effort here. But we might summarize the main elements of the record of public policy in the matter.

Decentralization seems intrinsically antipathetic to Planning, which has a centripetal tendency, and can tolerate independence of outlying units only in matters of relative unimportance. In theory. But the first generation of American Planners, the Roosevelt generation, assumed that some accommodation could be arranged. Paul Appleby stated the New Dealers' first premise: "Nothing can be decentralized properly which has not first been centralized. The basic essential is national controllability."[48] If this was assured, decentralization of certain functions should be vigorously pursued. This was the heart of democracy.

But exactly what did decentralization mean? New Dealers talked of power to the people, but this did not imply the devolving of national assignments upon existing state and local governments. These, enlightened people in the 1930s knew, were unrepresentative and dominated by narrow economic, social, and racial interests. Some New Deal programs had to be implemented through local governments—relief, public housing— but there were many efforts to bypass those governments and set up new local institutions through which citizens could participate in decision-making. This was called "grassroots democracy," in TVA director David Lilienthal's phrase. Many federal agencies pioneered in this. TVA gathered farmers in Farm Improvement Associations for education and explanation, the AAA organized county committees of farmers to make acreage allocations, REA organized local cooperatives to receive electricity, the SEC organized over-the-counter brokers so that they could be reached with regulation, the FSA organized tenant farmers into little groups for self-education and even political action. This was often more democracy—more power—than many people had known before. Farmers, black and white, voted on cotton and wheat programs, Indians voted on tribal charters, all at Washington's request. Organization gave channels of expression to formerly unorganized groups. But this was an imperfect democracy. Federal agencies claimed to be consulting, but mostly they were manipulating, and recruiting constituencies. Yet the idea of organizing the unorganized and encouraging participation was full of potential for new adventures in self-government. One decendant was the community action thrust of OEO, maximum feasible participation.

Grassroots democracy was one liberal idea for countering the elitist implications of Planning. It was not pressed to the point of making a major difference, but its direction was toward the awakening of dormant participatory desires, and the spread of public education. A second meaning of decentralization was the establishment of new governmental entities at local levels which would be more adequate for delivery of services than the antiquated system of towns, counties, states. Running water was the great educator of the 1930s, and to a lesser extent, dust. States could not hope to control erosion, floods, or dust storms, acting alone. The New Deal allied itself passionately with the regional idea, dreamed of eight valley authorities and only got one. Henry Wallace hoped for fewer than one hundred Soil Conservation Districts to unify all conservation activities. These new entities would take a generalist perspective, meshing all special programs shipped out from Washington to address discrete problems.

But regionalism foundered. Valley authorities were blocked, SC districts were fragmented and given narrow purposes, and every federal agency set up a different regional division of the country. Indeed, a major assault upon the federal system was not made during the 1930s. States and counties, of all American institutions most in need of revolutionary revision, retained their place in the intergovernmental system. Unable to establish regional tiers above local governments, the New Deal made equally unsuccessful efforts to reform them by installing a planning capacity. State planning agencies were funded in 46 states, and county planning commissions in most counties by 1942.

Almost none of these survived the war. American local government escaped significant modernization in an era of reform. The threat was raised, but was rebuffed.

It is deeply unfortunate that the reform ferment of the 1930s did not seriously address itself to the structure of state/local government. Despite the complexity of the issue, what needed to be done was not all that obscure. Below the federal level, governments were frequently too small, overlapping in jurisdiction and function, inadequate in revenue-raising capacity, with weak administrative organization and weak executives. Understandably, voter interest was low. Consolidation was the principal key to improvement, with jurisdictions redrawn along more rational geographical, economic, and demographic lines. William Anderson in 1942 thought that an 80 per cent cut in the units of local government would be about right. In 1966 a CED committee came to the same conclusion. "Most American communities," said the report *Modernizing Local Government,* "lack any instrumentality of government with legal powers, geographical jurisdiction, and independent revenue sources necessary to conduct local self-government in any valid sense."[49] Yet on this structure the federal government piled layers of responsibility and influence in the years after World War II. From 1946 to 1972, federal spending grew by a multiple of 5.9, but state and local spending by 13.5. In 1952, the federal government had spent 75 per cent of governmental revenues, state and local governments spending 25 per cent by 1972, the proportions were 56 per cent and 44 per cent. In 1973 State and local governments will spend $43 billion in federal grant monies, channeled through 1200 separate programs, apart from their own selected activities.

Lyndon Johnson called this "creative federalism," and thought it a fine thing. Whether advantages outweigh disadvantages is a lively question, with the balance tilting toward the latter. Program evaluation is a backward art, compared to auto racing for example, but there is much evidence that channeling federal money through local governments doesn't produce the results that had been promised. And there are other costs in addition to ineffectiveness. With the encouragement of federal authorities, state and local governments now spend nearly half the total governmental outlay in the United States, but there is no unified public sector budget and no clear federal authority to manipulate it in the interest of national economic management. The central government's ability to tune the economy through fiscal policy has been reduced by the passion to let the lower governments play a larger role.

The flaws in sub-federal governmental structure, and in federal-state/local governmental relations, have been apparent for some time, and there has been a brave and tireless effort to devise remedies. The approach of the NRPB in the 1930s was revived with section 701 of the 1954 Housing Act, granting funds to build a planning capacity at local levels. Four other major laws took the same approach, so that by 1970 the federal government had spurred the creation of 401 law enforcement planning districts, 957 community action agencies, 419 area manpower programs, 419 health and area planning agencies, 129 air quality regional agencies, 232 local development districts, 58 coastal zone management agencies—and this does not exhaust the list of special purpose sub-state or regional districts created because cities, counties, states were not designed to handle the problems.

A lot of planning money went out in this way, $350 million through 24 grant programs in 1973 alone. Confusion and fragmentation forced other remedies. One solution, arrived at locally and written into a 1968 law, was to set up Councils of Government, clearinghouses for many local jurisdictions to channel grant applications up and money back downward. In the jargon, these are general purpose sub-state districts. Involved people are very hopeful that they will make a difference. Another hopeful idea was the 1969 establishment of Federal Regional Councils, multi-state committees of representatives from seven major federal agencies, where coordination is attempted. On top of this series of layers in the American federalist jungle are proliferating regional agencies and state compacts which Washington had no hand in devising. Everyone is trying very hard. But the result is more layers and circles of authority, more overlap and complexity, than the participatory urge of the citizenry can surmount. A very encouraging development is the spreading reform movement at work at state and local levels—new constitutions, reorganization of bureaucracies, improved staff services, a promising modernization of America's most backward political institutions. There is a long way to go.

Nixon knew a mess when he saw one, but the only idea he had was for the federal government to send more money and fewer instructions—to the existing system of local and state governments. The rule was, the best governments were those "closer to the people." This, for him, was decentralization. He called it a New American Revolution, but it was merely simplification and reinforcement of the going system. Did Nixon really believe that Americans got more responsive, enlightened, and effective government from city than county, county than state than federal, merely because of physical proximity? Nobody else thought so who had given the matter sustained attention. The Nixon approach would preserve and strengthen the arrangement of local institutions that makes decentralization almost impossible. The efforts taken by liberal administrations from FDR to Johnson have created area-wide and regional institutions above the jungle of local governments, but order has not come out of the traffic jam. "As the nation approaches the bicentennial," writes a leading student of intergovernmental relations,

> the condition of American federalism . . . roughly resembles that of the British constitution and of mother country-Colonial relations of 200 years ago. Conceptually, the so-called system is in ferment. Fiscally, it is in a state of flux and some fear. Managerially, it is in considerable confusion.[50]

A fitting way to commemorate the bicentennial, a congressional committee was recently told, would be to redesign American federalism.[51] A real New American Revolution would mean a decision to send power only down to governments and juridictions redesigned to match their responsibilities. Consolidation, goodbye to the 80 per cent. Then after modernization of local government, decentralization of appropriate functions. Until this is done, decentralization will continue to be a much-honored word which in theory stands for public participation and in reality stands for the frustration of national majoritarian purpose.

8

These issues have mostly to do with technique. How does the government best organize itself for Planning, how far and how fast must it go in the effort to intervene to shape the future? A rather wide range of differences distinguish liberal from conservative Planning, judging by experience. The anxiety that some people feel over the arrival of Planning is not justified by issues of this sort. Some errors may be repaired. If, in the Roosevelt fashion, some liberal government undertakes to regulate where the free market would have produced more socially desirable adjustments, if in the Nixon manner some conservative government impedes the advances that could be made in social accounting, the opposition may mass to force revision.

But if we move from issues of technique to the issue of power, the choices to be made between the Roosevelt and Nixon models are fundamental, and error will be hard to reverse. Planning, people have long worried, increases governmental power and thus threatens our liberties. There is much wrong with this simple idea. Our liberties are already reduced by concentrations of economic power, and they are going to be reduced further in the future whether we Plan or not. Planning offers the best means to enlarge options and maximize freedom as we enter the age of crowding and exhausted resources. And under Planning the government will not necessarily have more power or be involved in more social manipulation than it is now.

With all these qualifications, the issue of power is fundamental, and Planners cannot evade it by pointing out that freedom is now narrowed by private forces, and that it may only be maximized in the troubled future through democratic Planning. These thoughts are sound, but if we do not design a democratic Planning as well as an effective Planning the fears of anti-Planners may be validated. Planning may not look very different in the early stages, for social transitions are slow. But its inner dynamics imply the abandonment, after two centuries, of the Madisonian system of government, checked and balanced to equilibrium. After half a century, we find it necessary to compress the fragmented baronies of the Broker State toward a more unitary and resolute apparatus of public power. Delays and obstructions thrown up by minorities must now give some ground to majority rule, or orders from authorities who claim to represent majority rule. With the old safeguards weakened or destroyed, the new safeguards must be participating, informed majorities which can preserve a tolerance of harmless individual thought and behavior while pursuing the required social discipline. On the eve of the bicentennial, we approach a fundamental redesign of the political economy; like the Founders we build a stronger government than the country had known. We, too, must be determined to keep the site of effective power in the people.

In meeting this issue, contemporary conservative ideas are virtually exhausted. The conservatism Nixon learned was suspicious of majorities at the outset, and for forty years has opposed or ignored the political reforms that broadened the franchise, opened up the legislative and political process, staightened the channels of decision. During his lifetime, American conservatism was learning with the utmost reluctance to adjust its suspicion of strong national government to modern realities. Time brought enlightenment to those who were flexible, led them finally to see the need for centralized national power so that order and stability could be preserved against complex destabilizing pressures. Nixon was one of these, and as President he accepted and practiced the basic liberal doctrine which required a strong government and a strong Presidency.

Then how do we avoid arbitrary power if the Madisonian checked-and-balanced system is transformed into one in which the Chief Executive can in fact control the government he heads, and that government holds virtually unlimited social authority? Here conservative ideas were close to bankruptcy. The situation had not been anticipated, it almost seemed. Neither the administration nor the larger conservative community had a new political theory to cope with the new circumstances. The administration thus became schizophrenic, reaffirming old ideas which were contradictory to the new Planning thrust. Power, the President said on every occasion, must be sent back to the states, cities, towns. The New Federalism.

This was a gesture, perhaps even a cynical one. It did not address in a serious way the new problems of power and democracy. Local governments are controlled by local elites; conservatives proposed no changes here. And the dribble of power directed their way would not have altered the issue even had local power been democratically accountable. Overwhelming power remained in Washington, where Nixon knew it belonged. And how was that to be checked? The Nixon government produced one remedy worth more than it has been conceded. His state papers hammer at the need for simplified government, consolidated programs and fewer laws, so that people could understand where responsibilities had been deposited, and hold officials accountable. It is an important idea, and one hopes it will have much influence under Planning. This was, however, a minor contribution and not distinctively conservative. As we know, Nixon developed (he borrowed it from American liberals, and from DeGaulle) the notion of a plebiscitary Presidency. Every four years, The People could speak, selecting their leader. They were children, as he told Theodore White, and the leader would lead them. Toward the institutions that might check this presidential power, Nixon had a consistent disdain. He had given up on Congress, staffed the Court with many mediocrities, despised the press, and had no real use for the Republican party. His attitude toward party, once he was in office, was thoroughly radical in its implications. He did not see the need for it. As

Senator Robert Dole, chairman of the Republican National Committee, was reported as saying, "the Republican Party was not only not involved in Watergate, but it wasn't involved in the nomination, the convention, the campaign, the election, or the inauguration."[52]

The conservative response to the problem of power under Planning, as Nixon constructed it, has far reaching and disturbing implications. He was not, of course, the last word in conservative intellectual leadership. But no thinker of that persuasion has offered plausible answers to the new question, How does the public control a government wielding more concentrated power than ever before?

The arrival of Planning joins political theory and public administration, urgently requiring a synthesis of the forms of control and the means of accountability. At the second of these task, as with the first, the tradition of the Left presents more impressive resources. Admittedly that tradition is full of inconsistency, of uncritical enthusiasm along with hesitation when it came to devising the political and constitutional changes required to control the Planning political economy. Yet the main ideas and channels of effort of the 1930s are clear and promising enough, and they have been extended in succeeding years: political democratization to open the political process to excluded groups; decentralization to local jurisdictions larger and more rational in outline than those handed down out of the history of federalism; the organization of unorganized groups; mass political mobilization through a party realigned by ideological leadership so that choices as well as accountability may be clearer; defense of civil liberties; a powerful Presidency.

Only one of these ideas was ever given anything like full implementation—the strong Presidency. Too much faith was placed in this institution alone, as the era of Vietnam was to prove. The Left is shaken, not only in its confidence in the Presidency, but in a strong national government. Localism and withdrawal into isolated communities is a flourishing impulse, coming naturally out of the disillusioning history of forty years of what were thought to be New Deal centrist solutions. Both these

turnings away from Washington and White House are healthy
correctives; but they offer no solutions in themselves. In moving
into Planning, we return to the ground of the other New Deal,
and there is in both its administrative thought and its political
reform experience and commitments the most creative body of
ideas for the era of interdependence, crisis, and social discipline
ahead. These ideas lead toward patterns of mass democracy and
collectivism unfamiliar to Americans, except in utopian communities, local crises, or national emergency. But then, we
wanted to grow and prosper, and thus ordered up an unfamiliar
future. Some await it in dread, others in eager confidence. There
is evidence in support of both. I prefer confidence—not on the
evidence, which is mixed and anyway too difficult to assess, but
because confidence will steady our hand, and help fulfill its own
prophecy, helping to make this, in Morris Lewellyn Cooke's
phrase from the 1930s, "a permanent country."

For some reason, all America's planners and Planners have
possessed a touch of audacity rather than an air of grim necessity. No one expressed it better than Daniel Burnham, master
city planner, nearly a hundred years ago:

> Make no little plans, they have no magic to stir men's blood and
> probably themselves will not be realized. Make big plans; aim high
> in hope and work, remembering that a noble, logical diagram once
> recorded will never die. . . . Remember that our sons and grand-
> sons are going to do things that would stagger us.

Notes

Chapter 1:

The 1930s: Franklin Roosevelt and the Planning Idea

1. Robert D. Cuff, *The War Industries Board* (1973), p. 149.
2. George B. Galloway, "American Proposals for Central Planning," *Plan Age*, 2 (Dec. 1936).
3. Stuart Chase, *A New Deal* (1932), p. 252.
4. Quoted in Charles F. Roos, *NRA Economic Planning* (1940), pp. 4–5.
5. James G. Smith, *Economic Planning and the Tariff* (1934), p. 1.
6. Robert M. Crunden, *A Hero in Spite of Himself: Brand Whitlock* (1969), p. 425.
7. Franklin D. Roosevelt, "Growing up by Plan," *The Survey*, 67 (Feb. 1, 1932), p. 69.
8. Samuel I. Rosenman (ed.), *The Public Papers and Addresses of Franklin D. Roosevelt* (1938–46), vol. I, p. 632.
9. Rosenman, vol. IV, p. 338.
10. Rosenman, vol. II, pp. 122–23.
11. Rosenman, vol. II, p. 11.
12. Rexford G. Tugwell, "The Principle of Planning and the Institution of Laissez-Faire," *American Economic Review*, 22 (March 1932), supplement, p. 69. When Tugwell left Columbia and emerged as Roosevelt's close adviser, both moderates and conservatives were horrified at his views. They did not call him a liberal, but "Rex the Red." And it was true that,

among other daring and irreverent statements, he had written in the
above essay that under planning "business will logically be required to
disappear. This is not an overstatement for the sake of emphasis; it is
literally meant. The essence of business is its free venture for profits in
an unregulated economy." Under planning we would "destroy it as
business and . . . make of it something else. That something else has no
name." But "the traditional incentives, hope of money-making, fear of
money-loss, will be weakened; and a kind of civil service loyalty and
fervor will need to grow gradually into acceptance." Spoken, many businessmen thought, just like a professor. Tugwell was no socialist. He was
a man much committed to order, discipline, and the virtues of a more
decentralized and pastoral civilization. And he had no respect for the
profit motive. Such a man should not have been all that frightening, but
the thought of Tugwell "in power" terrorized conservatives for years,
even after he left the government in 1937.

13. John Kenneth Galbraith, *American Capitalism* (1956), pp. 7–8.
14. U.S. Forest Service, *A National Plan for American Forestry* (March 13, 1933), p. viii.
15. Wesley Calef, *Private Grazing and Public Lands* (1960), p. 50.
16. Samuel T. Dana, *Forest and Range Policy* (1956), p. 275.
17. Sherwood Anderson, *Puzzled America* (1935), p. 71.
18. Quoted in Mel Scott, *American City Planning Since 1890* (1969), p. 302.
19. Edgar B. Nixon, ed., *Franklin D. Roosevelt and Conservation, 1911–1945* (1957), I, 256–57.
20. National Resources Planning Board, *A Plan for Planning* (1934), p. 88.
21. *Ibid.,* pp. 83–84.
22. Richard J. Kalish, "National Resource Planning, 1933–1939," Ph.D. dissertation, University of Colorado, 1963, p. 243.
23. Edward H. Hobbs, *Behind the President: A Study of Executive Office Agencies* (1954), p. 84.
24. John D. Millett, *The Process and Organization of Government Planning* (1947), p. 149.
25. President's Committee on Administrative Management, *Report with Special Studies* (1937), pp. iii, v.
26. Richard Polenberg, *Reorganizing Roosevelt's Government* (1966), p. 26.
27. *Ibid.,* p. 29.
28. *Ibid.,* p. 9.
29. Philip Funigiello, *Toward a National Power Policy* (1973), p. 69.
30. William E. Leuchtenburg, "Roosevelt, Norris and the Seven Little TVAs," *Journal of Politics,* 14 (Aug. 1952), p. 431.
31. Polenberg, *Reoganizing Roosevelt's Government,* p. 49.
32. *Ibid.,* p. 51.
33. Lindsay Rogers, "Reorganization: Post-Mortem Notes," *Political Science Quarterly,* 53 (June 1938), p. 168.

34. Quoted in George B. Galloway, ed., *Planning for America* (1941), p. 11.
35. *Ibid.*, p. 46.

Chapter 2:

From Pearl Harbor to the Employment Act, 1941-1946

1. David Novick, Melvin Anshen, and W. C. Truppner, *Wartime Production Controls* (1949), p. 6.
2. *Ibid.*, p. 401.
3. Karl Schriftgiesser, *Business Comes of Age: The Story of the Committee for Economic Development* (1960), pp. 4–5.
4. *Ibid.*, p. 14.
5. Stephen K. Bailey, *Congress Makes a Law: The Story Behind the Employment Act of 1946* (1950), pp. 243–45.
6. *Ibid.*, p. 228.
7. *The Age of Keynes* (1965), p. 174.

Chapter 3:

From the Employment Act to the 1960s

1. Quoted in Roger Garaudy, "New Goals for Socialism," *The Center Magazine* (Sept.–Oct. 1972), p. 34.
2. John Kenneth Galbraith, *The New Industrial State* (1967), pp. 33–34.
3. Seymour Harris, ed., *Saving American Capitalism: A Liberal Economic Program* (1948), p. 3.
4. *Ibid.*, p. 157.
5. R. G. Tugwell and E. Banfield, "Governmental Planning at Mid-Century," *Journal of Politics*, 13 (May 1951), pp. 146–47.
6. U.S. Congress, Senate Committee on Labor and Public Welfare, *History of Employment and Manpower Policy in the U.S.: Twenty Years of Experience Under the Employment Act of 1946* (1966), p. 63.
7. Charles Aikin and Louis Koening, "The Hoover Commission: A Symposium," *American Political Science Review*, 43 (Oct. 1949), p. 935.
8. Harold Seidman, *Politics, Position and Power* (1970), p. 19.
9. President's Materials Policy Commission, *Resources for Freedom*, I, p. 130.
10. Edwin L. Dale, Jr., *Conservatives in Power* (1960), p. 175.
11. *Ibid.*, p. 163.
12. Neil MacNeil and Harold W. Metz, *The Hoover Report, 1953–55* (1956), p. 299.

13. Emmet John Hughes, *Ordeal of Power* (1963), p. 139.
14. Peter Lyon, *Eisenhower* (1974), p. 486.
15. *Ibid.,* p. 505.
16. Patrick Anderson, *The President's Men* (1968), p. 178.
17. *Ibid.,* p. 179.

Chapter 4:

The Democrats, 1961-1969

1. James M. Landis, *Report on Regulatory Agencies to the President-Elect* (1960), p. 374.
2. Rexford G. Tugwell, *The Emerging Constitution* (1974), p. 208.
3. Quoted in William L. Cary, *Politics and the Regulatory Agencies* (1967), p. 25.
4. J. Edward Day, *My Appointed Round: 929 Days as Postmaster General* (1965), p. 97.
5. Richard F. Fenno, "The Cabinet: Index to the Kennedy Way," *New York Times Magazine* (April 22, 1962).
6. Arthur M. Schlesinger, Jr., *A Thousand Days* (1965), p. 540.
7. *Ibid.*
8. *Ibid.,* p. 541.
9. *Ibid.,* p. 567.
10. *Ibid.,* p. 568.
11. Thomas Cronin, "Everybody believes in democracy until he gets to the White House," *Law and Contemporary Problems,* 35 (Summer 1970), p. 574.
12. Garth Mangum, ed., *The Manpower Revolution* (1965), p. 491.
13. William H. Miernyk, *The Economics of Labor and Collective Bargaining* (1973), pp. 165–72.
14. William R. Monat, "The Once and Future Revolution: Manpower Policy in the U.S.," *Public Administration Review,* 30 (Jan.–Feb. 1970), p. 77.
15. Garth Mangum, *The Emergence of Manpower Policy* (1969), p. 130.
16. *Ibid.,* p. 160.
17. Phyllis Piotrow, *World Population Crisis* (1973), p. 45.
18. *Ibid.,* p. 43.
19. Dwight D. Eisenhower, "Let's Be Honest with Ourselves: II," *Saturday Evening Post,* 236 (Oct. 26, 1963), p. 27.
20. *Public Papers of the Presidents: Lyndon B. Johnson, 1965* (1966), p. 4.
21. U.S. Congress, Senate, Committee on Labor and Public Welfare, 91st Congress, 1st and 2nd Sessions, hearings, *Family Planning and Population Research, December 1969* (1970), p. 22.

22. *Ibid.*, p. 26.
23. Lyndon B. Johnson, *The Vantage Point* (1971), pp. 339–40.
24. Louis Lowe Loewenstein and Dorn McGrath, "The Planning Imperative in America's Future," in George F. Mott, ed., "Urban Change and the Planning Syndrome," *Annals of the American Academy of Political and Social Science*, 405 (Jan. 1973).
25. U.S. Department of Agriculture, *National Growth and Its Distribution: Symposium on Communities of Tomorrow* (1967), p. 75.
26. U.S. Congress, Senate, Committee on Government Operations, 91st Congress, 1st Session, Hearings on S 2701, *A Bill To Establish a Commission on Population Growth and the American Future* (1969), p. 38.
27. Thomas Cronin, "Presidents as Chief Executives," in R. G. Tugwell and Thomas Cronin, eds., *The Presidency Reappraised* (1974), p. 239.
28. Charles Dawes, *The First Year of the Budget of the United States* (1923), p. ii.
29. Arthur Maass and Lawrence Radway, "Gauging Administrative Responsibility," in Dwight Waldo, ed., *Ideas and Issues in Public Administration* (1953), p. 451.
30. Elizabeth Drew, "HEW Grapples with PPBS," *The Public Interest*, 8 (Summer 1967), p. 9.
31. Charles Jacob, "The Question for Presidential Control: Innovation and Institutionalization in the Executive Branch," paper delivered at the 1973 annual meeting of the American Political Science Association, copy in author's possession, p. 10.
32. U.S. Congress, Senate, Committee on Government Operations, *Planning Programming Budgeting: Official Documents* (1967), p. 2.
33. *Ibid.*, p. 4.
34. Edwin L. Harper et al., "Implementation and Use of PPB in Sixteen Federal Agencies," *Public Administration Review*, 29 (Nov.–Dec. 1969), p. 623.
35. Aaron Wildavsky, *The Politics of the Budgetary Process* (1974, rev.), p. 206.
36. U.S. Congress, Joint Economic Committee, *The Analysis and Evaluation of Public Expenditures: The PPB System* (3 vols., 1969), I, p. 6.
37. *Ibid.*, III, 922.
38. Cronin, *The Presidency Reappraised*, p. 238.
39. Heineman, President's Task Force on Government Organization, *Final Report* (June 15, 1967), pp. 2–10.
40. Raymond A. Bauer, ed., *Social Indicators* (1966), p. xii.
41. U.S. Department of Health, Education and Welfare, *Toward a Social Report* (1960), p. iii.
42. Melvin R. Levin, *Community and Regional Planning* (1972), p. 69.
43. David Broder, *The Party's Over* (1971), p. 68.

Chapter 5:

Richard Nixon, 1969-1974

1. Congressional Quarterly, *Nixon: The First Year of the Presidency* (1970), p. 72-A.
2. *Ibid.*, pp. 107A–109A.
3. Quoted in Lowdon Wingo, "Issues in a National Urban Development Strategy for the U.S.," *Urban Studies*, 9 (1972), p. 6.
4. National Commission on Urban Problems, *Building the American City* (1969), p. 9.
5. U.S. Advisory Commission on Intergovernmental Relations, *Urban and Rural America: Policies for Future Growth* (1968), pp. 125–27.
6. Daniel P. Moynihan, *Coping* (1973), p. 276.
7. Executive Order #11,452, 34 *Federal Register 1223* (1969).
8. See, for example, Moynihan's "Toward a National Urban Policy," *The Public Interest* (Fall 1969), *The Politics of Guaranteed Income* (1973), and *Coping* (1973).
9. U.S. National Goals Research Staff, *Toward Balanced Growth: Quantity with Quality* (1970), p. 6.
10. *Ibid.*, p. 223.
11. Letter from NGRS staff member to author, Feb. 25, 1975.
12. *Toward Balanced Growth*, p. 51.
13. *Public Papers of the Presidents: Richard M. Nixon, 1970* (1971), p. 14.
14. Quoted in R. Gordon Hoxie, ed., *The Presidency of the 1970s*, II (1972), pp. 49–50.
15. Allen Drury and Fred Maroon, *Courage and Hesitation: Notes and Photographs of the Nixon Administration* (1971), p. 58.
16. *The New York Times* (July 18, 1968), p. 21.
17. John Osborne, *The Second Year of the Nixon Watch* (1971), p. 69.
18. Charles E. Jacob, "The Quest for Presidential Control," unpublished paper (1973), author's possession.
19. U.S. Congress, House Committee on Government Operations, *Hearings on Reorganization Plan #2 of 1970* (91st Congress, 2nd Session, April-May 1970), p. 61.
20. Jacob, "Quest for Presidential Control," p. 15.
21. John Kessel, "The Domestic Council," unpublished manuscript (1974), p. 39.
22. U.S. Congress, House Committee on Government Operations, *Reorganization of Executive Departments*, I (92nd Congress, 1st Session, June-July 1971), p. 69.

23. Office of Management and Budget, *Papers Relating to the President's Departmental Reorganization Program* (Feb. 1972), pp. 5–6.

24. U.S. Congress, House Committee on Government Operations, *Reorganization of Executive Departments: Department of Community Development,* II (92nd Congress, 1st and 2nd Sessions, Jan.–April 1972), p. 761.

25. *Ibid.,* p. 41.

26. *Ibid.,* p. 212.

27. *Weekly Compilation of Presidential Documents,* 8 (April 3, 1972), p. 708.

28. The comparisons were drawn up by Arnold Reitze, *Environmental Law,* I (1972), pp. 61–63.

29. Rowland Evans and Robert Novak, *Nixon in the White House* (1971), p. 401.

30. C. Jackson Grayson and Louis Neeb, *Confessions of a Price Controller* (1974), pp. 197, 199.

31. *The National Journal,* (May 5, 1973), p. 637.

32. *Congressional Record* (October 30, 1973), p. 519675.

33. News release from Senator Jackson's office, n.d., p. 3.

34. *Santa Barbara News-Press* (July 30, 1972), p. B-3.

35. *Los Angeles Times* (May 2, 1972), p. 3.

36. *The National Journal* (May 5, 1973), p. 641.

37. U.S. Domestic Council, *Report on National Growth: 1972,* pp. xi ff.

38. U.S. Congress, House Committee on Banking and Currency, Subcommittee on Housing (92nd Congress, 2nd Session), *National Growth Policy,* I (1972), pp. 86, 376, 385, 488, 740; II, p. 656; I, p. 890.

39. *Ibid.,* I, p. 87.

40. U.S. Congress, Senate Document 93–19 (93rd Congress, 1st Session), *Toward a National Growth Policy* (1973), p. 5.

41. Claude Barfield, "Nixon Reorganization Raises Questions About Role of Science in Federal Policy Making," *National Journal* (March 24, 1973), p. 410.

42. *Ibid.,* p. 410.

43. U.S. Commission on Population Growth and the American Future, *Population and the American Future* (1972), p. 1.

44. *Ibid.,* p. 192.

45. U.S. Congress, House Committee on Public Works, *A National Public Works Investment Policy* (93rd Congress, 1st Session) (Nov.–Dec. 1973), p. 24.

46. Interview with John Ehrlichman, Dec. 17, 1974.

47. Moynihan to author, Jan. 2, 1975.

48. *The New York Times* (Dec. 12, 1971), p. 1.

49. John C. Donovan, "The Domestic Council and the Politics of Presidential Leadership," address to the American Society of Public Administration (March 23, 1972). See also Douglas Hallett, "A Low-Level Memoir of the

Nixon White House," *The New York Times Magazine* (Oct. 20, 1974).
50. Quoted in David Broder, "The Domestic Legacy," in Staff of the *Washington Post, The Fall of a President* (1974), p. 121.
51. *Congressional Record*, v. 120, #21 (Feb. 25, 1974), p. 52116.
52. *Ibid.*, p. 52117.
53. *Congressional Record*, vol. 120, #84 (93rd Congress, 2nd Session), pp. H5021, H5024.
54. *Ibid.*, p. H5028.
55. *The National Journal* (July 14, 1973), p. 1029.
56. U.S. Government Printing Office, *Weekly Compilation of Presidential Documents*, 9 (April 23, 1973), p. 401.
57. *Ibid.*, p. 404.
58. *Congressional Quarterly Almanac* (1973), p. 698.
59. *Los Angeles Times* (Dec. 26, 1972), p. 6 (II).
60. U.S. Congress, Senate Committee on Interior and Insular Affairs, *Federal Energy Organization: A Staff Analysis* (1973), p. 3.
61. U.S. Comptroller General, *United States Actions Needed To Cope with Commodity Shortages* (April 29, 1974), pp. 1–154.
62. R. Gordon Hoxie, ed., *The Presidency of the 1970s*, II (1972), p. 49.
63. Simon Lazarus, *The Genteel Populists* (1974), p. 1.
64. Dan Rather, *The Palace Guard* (1974), p. 8.
65. Edward R. Fried et al., *Setting National Priorities: The 1974 Budget* (1973), p. 6.
66. *Weekly Compilation of Presidential Documents*, 9 (Feb. 5, 1973), p. 86.
67. Evans and Novak, *Nixon in the White House*, p. 241.
68. *Ibid.*, p. 359.
69. Drury and Maroon, *Courage and Hesitation*, p. 368. William Safire, in his interesting memoir *Before the Fall* (1975), likened Nixon to a layer cake. I counted ten layers when Safire wearied of the metaphor (pp. 97–99). Nixon's speech writer Patrick Buchanan lamented in a memo that Nixon "is seen as a textbook political transient, here today, gone tomorrow, shuttling back and forth, as weather permits, between liberal programs and conservative rhetoric" (in Jonathan Schell, "Reflections: The Nixon Years, III," *The New Yorker* (June 16, 1975, p. 56).
70. Richard J. Whalen, *Catch the Falling Flag* (1972), p. 18.
71. Evans and Novak, p. 40.
72. Theodore H. White, *The Making of the President: 1972* (1973), p. 147.
73. *Los Angeles Times* (Aug. 6, 1974), p. 12.
74. James Reston, *The New York Times* (Nov. 9, 1962), p. 34.
75. Walter Lippmann, *The New Imperative* (1935), p. 50.
76. Evans and Novak, p. 189.
77. Jeb Stuart Magruder, *An American Life: One Man's Road to Watergate* (1974), p. 146.

Chapter 6:

Crossroads

1. *The Los Angeles Times* (Aug. 23, 1974), p. 10.
2. *Ibid.*
3. John Herbers, "In Six Months, Ford's Style Is Set," *The New York Times* (Feb. 23, 1975), pp. 1, 36.
4. *The New Republic* (March 1, 1975), p. 9.
5. *The New York Times* (Sept. 28, 1974), p. 69.
6. *Weekly Compilation of Presidential Documents,* 10 (1974), #41, p. 1241.
7. *Newsweek* (Dec. 30, 1974), p. 9.
8. U.S. Domestic Council, *Report on National Growth and Development: 1974* (Dec. 1974), p. 85.
9. *Ibid.,* p. 43.
10. *Ibid.,* p. 63.
11. Interview with John Ehrlichman, Dec. 17, 1974.
12. *The New York Times* (Feb. 23, 1975), p. 69.
13. *The New York Times* (Feb. 28, 1975), pp. 43, 48.
14. Wassily Leontief, "Maybe We Need an Economic Planning Agency," *Current* (May 1974), p. 27.
15. Lynton Caldwell, "Environment and Administration" in William Murdoch, ed., *Environment: Resources, Pollution and Society* (1971), pp. 392–93.
16. Soma Golden, "The Economy: Next 25 Years," *The New York Times* (Dec. 29, 1974), p. III-1.
17. C. Jackson Grayson, "Beating Inflation Without Controls," *Santa Barbara News Press* (Oct. 27, 1974), pp. E-6-E-7.
18. Herbert Stein, "Better Planning of Less," *Wall Street Journal* (May 14, 1975), p. 18.
19. Gerhard Colm and Luther Gulick, *Program Planning for National Goals* (1968), p. 18.
20. John Kenneth Galbraith, *Economics and the Public Purpose* (1973), p. 319.
21. Quoted in William R. Ewald, ed., *Environment and Change* (1968), p. 249.
22. Jack Friedman, "A Planned Economy in the U.S.?" *The New York Times* (May 18, 1975), p. 11.
23. Walter J. Hickel, *Who Owns America?* (1971), p. 129.
24. Neil Chamberlain, *Private and Public Planning* (1965), p. 3.
25. Neil H. Jacoby, *Corporate Power and Social Responsibility* (1973), p. 56.
26. Galbraith, *Economics and the Public Purpose.*

27. *The 1974 American National Bank Annual Report* (1975), pp. 5–6.
28. The University of California, *The University in the Seventies* (1974), p. 20.
29. *Ibid.*, p. 69.
30. James P. McGrath, Congressional Research Service, Library of Congress, to the Honorable Jerry Litton, July 19, 1974. I cannot resist quoting the response of Mr. John Davis, assistant to the chairman of the Council of Economic Advisors: "While much of CEA's work could retrospectively be viewed as long term, i.e. concern with inflation, etc., the Office is far too concerned with ongoing annual economic concerns to get involved in projections or plans in excess of one year" (p. 4). Here moves either that albino in bureaucratic ranks, utter candor, or the spirit of post-Moynihan Nixon.
31. *Report on National Growth: 1974*, pp. 63–84.
32. Quoted in J. J. Servan-Schreiber, *The American Challenge* (1968), pp. 79–80.
33. Michael Kaser and Janusz Zielinski, *Planning in East Europe: Industrial Management by the State* (1970).
34. Charles E. Lindblom, "Economics and the Administration of National Planning," *Public Administration Review*, 25 (Dec. 1965), p. 281.
35. Kaser and Zielinski, p. 47.
36. Everett Hagen and Stephanie White, *Great Britain: Quiet Revolution in Planning* (1966), p. 143.
37. Stein's comment was made at a meeting in New York, Dec. 29, 1973, and was reported in *Challenge* (March–April 1974), p. 42.
38. Robert A. Dahl and Charles E. Lindblom, *Politics, Economics and Welfare* (1953), p. 348.
39. Edward Banfield, *The Unheavenly City* (1968), p. 260.
40. Theodore Lowi, "Permanent Receivership," *The Center Magazine*, 7 (March–April 1974), p. 36.
41. *Ibid.*, p. 37.
42. *The New York Times* (Feb. 23, 1975), p. 69.
43. Mr. Ford probably doesn't know it, but there is at least one subversive among his "advisers." Arthur Burns, taciturn head of the Federal Reserve Board, wrote an article extolling Planning in 1957!
44. Gunnar Myrdal, *Beyond the Welfare State* (1960), p. 22.
45. Andrew Shonfield, *Modern Capitalism* (1965), p. 122.
46. Michael Harrington, "American Society: Burdens, Problems, Solutions," in Irving Howe and Michael Harrington, eds., *The Seventies* (1972), p. 9.
47. Gilbert Fite, *George N. Peek and the Fight for Farm Parity* (1954), p. 254.
48. Paul Appleby, *Big Democracy* (1940), p. 104.
49. Committee for Economic Development, *Modernizing Local Government* (1966), p. 15.

50. David B. Walker, "How Fares Federalism in the Mid-Seventies?," *Annals of the American Society of Political and Social Science*, 416 (Nov. 1974), p. 18.

51. U.S. Congress, House Committee on Banking and Currency, *National Growth Policy*, II, p. 703.

52. Quoted in Charles Roberts, ed., *Has the President Too Much Power?* (1974), p. 58.

Bibliography

To list the important literature on the subjects touched upon in this book would require another volume of this size. What follows is a selective bibliography of only the essential works, those to which my own debt is especially heavy. The footnotes, perhaps, indicate my reliance upon certain serials: *The Congressional Record, Public Papers of the Presidents of the United States, Weekly Compilation of Presidential Documents, Congressional Quarterly Weekly Reports, National Journal Reports,* the various annual reports of federal agencies, especially the annual economic report of the President, and two journals of special interest to planners (and anti-planners) of all types, *The Journal of the American Institute of Planners,* and *The Public Administration Review.*

Chapter 1:

Baldwin, Sidney. *Poverty and Politics: The Rise and Decline of the Farm Security Administration* (1968).
Banfield, Edward C., ed. "Then Years of the Farm Tenant Purchase Program," *Journal of Farm Economics,* 31 (Aug. 1949).
Beard, Charles A. *An Open Door at Home* (1935).
Bennett, Hugh H. *Soil Conservation* (1939).

Calef, Wesley. *Private Grazing and Public Lands: Studies of the Local Management of the Taylor Grazing Act* (1960).

Chase, Stuart. *The Economy of Abundance* (1934).

Christie, Jean. "The Mississippi Valley Committee: Conservation and Planning in the Early New Deal," *The Historian*, 32 (May 1970).

Clawson, Marion, and Burnell Held. *The Federal Lands* (1957).

Cooney, Ralph B. "Planning by the States," *New Republic*, 95 (July 30, 1938).

Corey, Lewis, *The Unfinished Task: Economic Reconstruction for Democracy* (1942).

Cuff, Robert D. *The War Industries Board* (1973).

Dewey, John. *Liberalism and Social Action* (1935).

Dorfman, Joseph. *The Economic Mind in American Civilization*, Vol. 5: *1918–1933* (1959).

Emmerich, Herbert. *Essays on Federal Reorganization* (1951), esp. Ch. 3.

———. *Federal Organization and Administrative Management* (1971).

Ezekiel, Mordekai. *Jobs for All Through Industrial Expansion* (1939).

———. *$2500 A YEAR* (1936).

Fusfeld, Daniel R. *The Economic Thought of Franklin D. Roosevelt and the Origins of the New Deal* (1956).

Galloway, George B. *Planning for America* (1941).

Graham, Otis L., Jr. "The Planning Ideal and American Reality: The 1930's," in Stanley Elkins and Eric McKitrick, eds., *The Hofstadter Aegis* (1974).

Gross, Neal C. "A Post Mortem on County Planning," *Journal of Farm Economics*, 25 (Aug. 1943).

Hardin, Charles M. *The Politics of Agriculture: Soil Conservation and the Struggle for Power in Rural America* (1952).

Hawley, Ellis W. "Herbert Hoover, the Commerce Secretariat, and the Vision of an 'Associative State,' 1921–1928," *Journal of American History*, 61 (June 1974).

———. *The New Deal and the Problem of Monopoly* (1965).

Heermance, Edgar L. *Can Business Govern Itself?* (1933).

Herring, E. Pendleton. *Public Administration and the Public Interest* (1936).

Himmelberg, Robert F. "Business, Antitrust Policy, and the Industrial Board of the Department of Commerce, 1919," *Business History Review*, 42 (Spring 1968).

Hobbs, Edward H. *Behind the President: A Study of Executive Agencies* (1954).

Howenstine, E. Jay. "The Industrial Board, Precursor of the N.R.A.: The Price-Reduction Movement After World War I," *Journal of Political Economy*, 51 (July 1943).

Jacob, Charles E. *Leadership in the New Deal* (1964).

Johnston, Frontis W. "The Evolution of the American Concept of National Planning: 1865–1917," Ph.D. dissertation, Yale, 1938.

Jones, Byrd. "A Plan for Planning in the New Deal," *Social Science Quarterly*, 50 (Dec. 1969).

Jones, Jesse, with Edward Angly, *Fifty Billion Dollars* (1951).

Kalish, Richard J. "National Resource Planning 1933–1939," Ph.D. dissertation, University of Colorado, 1963.

Karl, Barry D. *Executive Reorganization and Reform in the New Deal* (1963).

———. "Presidential Planning and Social Science Research: Mr. Hoover's Experts," *Perspectives in American History*, 3 (1969).

Kirkendall, Richard S. *Social Scientists and Farm Politics in the Age of Roosevelt* (1966).

Koenig, Louis W. *The Invisible Presidency* (1960).

Laidler, Harry W., ed. *Socialist Planning and a Socialist Program* (1932).

Lange, Oscar. *On the Economic Theory of Socialism* (1938).

Leiserson, Avery. *Administrative Regulation* (1942).

Lerner, Max. *It Is Later Than You Think* (1939).

Leuchtenburg, W. E. *Franklin D. Roosevelt and the New Deal* (1963).

Leuchtenburg, William E. "The New Deal and the Analogue of War," in John Braeman et al., eds., *Change and Continuity in 20th Century America* (1964).

Lewis, John D. "Democratic Planning in Agriculture," *American Political Science Review*, 35 (April 1941).

Lynch, David. *The Concentration of Economic Power* (1946).

Maass, Arthur. *Muddy Waters: The Army Engineers and the Nation's Rivers* (1951).

Machlup, Fritz. *The Political Economy of Monopoly* (1952).

Mackenzie, Findlay, ed. *Planned Society* (1937).

Mansfield, Harvey C. "Federal Executive Reorganization: Thirty Years of Experience," *Public Administration Review*, 29 (July–Aug. 1969).

Marshall, Robert. *The People's Forests* (1933).

Marx, Fritz M., ed. *Public Management in the New Democracy* (1940).

Merriam, Charles E. "The National Resources Planning Board: A Chapter in American Planning Experience," *American Political Science Review*, 38 (Dec. 1944).

———, *On The Agenda of Democracy* (1941).

Millett, John D. *The Process and Organization of Government Planning* (1947).

Morgan, Robert J. *Governing Soil Conservation: 30 Years of the New Decentralization* (1965).

Mumford, Lewis. *The Culture of Cities* (1938); esp. for regional planning.

National Resources Board. *A Plan for Planning* (Dec. 1, 1934).

Neustadt, Richard. *Presidential Power* (1960).

Nixon, Edgar B., ed. *Franklin D. Roosevelt and Conservation, 1911–1945*, I and II (1957).

Odum, Howard W. *Southern Regions of the U.S.* (1936).

Pinkett, Harold T. "The Keep Commission, 1905–1909: A Rooseveltian

Effort for Administrative Reform," *Journal of American History,* 52 (Sept. 1965).

Polenberg, Richard. *Reorganizing Roosevelt's Government: the Controversy Over Executive Reorganization, 1936–1939* (1966).

President's Committee on Administrative Management. *Report with Special Studies* (1937).

President's Research Committee on Social Trends. *Report Social Trends* (2 vols., 1933).

Reese, John H. "The Role of the Bureau of the Budget in the Legislative Process," *Journal of Public Law,* 15 (1966).

Roosevelt, Franklin D. "Growing Up By Plan," *Forum,* 67 (Feb. 1, 1932).

Rosenman, Samuel I. *The Public Papers and Addresses of Franklin D. Roosevelt,* 8 vols. (1938–46).

Schlesinger, Arthur M., Jr. *The Coming of the New Deal* (1959).

———. *The Politics of Upheaval* (1960).

Schwarz, Jordan A. *The Interregnum of Despair: Hoover, Congress and the Depression* (1970).

Scott, Mel. *American City Planning* (1971).

Seligman, Lester G., and Elmer E. Cornwall. *New Deal Mosaic: Roosevelt Confers with His National Emergency Council* (1965).

Soule, George. *A Planning Society* (1932).

Sternsher, Bernard. *Rexford G. Tugwell and the New Deal* (1963).

Swope, Gerard. *The Swope Plan* (1931).

Thomas, Norman. *After the New Deal: What?* (1936).

Thompson, Warren S. *Research Memorandum on Internal Migration in the Depression* (1937).

Tugwell, Rexford G. *The Brains Trust* (1968).

———. *The Democratic Roosevelt* (1957).

———. *The Industrial Discipline and the Governmental Arts* (1933).

———. *Industry's Coming of Age* (1927).

Tugwell, Rexford G., and Edward C. Banfield. "Grass Roots Democracy— Myth or Reality?" *Public Administration Review,* 10 (Winter 1950).

U.S. Department of Agriculture. *The Land Utilization Program: 1934 to 1964* (1965).

U.S. Forest Service. *A National Plan for American Forestry* (1933).

U.S. National Resources Committee. *Drainage Basin Problems and Programs: 1937* (Feb. 1938).

U.S. National Resources Planning Board. *National Resources Development Report for 1932* (Jan. 1942).

Vance, Rupert. *Research Memorandum on Population Redistribution Within the U.S.* (1938).

Wann, A. J. *The President as Chief Administrator: A Study of Franklin D. Roosevelt* (1968).

Warken, Philip W. "A History of the National Resources Planning Board, 1933–43," Ph.D. dissertation, Ohio State University, 1969.

Weinstein, James. *The Corporate Ideal in the Liberal State: 1900–1918* (1968).
Wilson, Joan Hoff. *Herbert Hoover* (1975).
Wooton, Barbara. *Plan or No Plan* (1935).

Chapter 2:

Bailey, Stephen K. *Congress Makes a Law: The Story Behind the Employment Act of 1946* (1950).
Bernstein, Barton J. "The Debate on Industrial Reconversion," *American Journal of Economics and Sociology*, 26 (April 1967).
Burns, James M. *Roosevelt: Soldier of Freedom* (1972).
Chase, Stuart. *Democracy Under Pressure* (1945).
Corey, Lewis. *The Unfinished Task: Economic Reconstruction for Democracy* (1942).
Dahl, Robert A., and Charles E. Lindblom. *Politics, Economics and Welfare* (1953).
Eakins, David W. "Business Planners and America's Postwar Expansion," in David Horowitz, ed., *Corporations and the Cold War* (1969).
———. "Policy Planning for the Establishment," in Ron Radosh and Murray Rothbard, eds., *A New History of Leviathan* (1972).
Fitch, Lyle, and Horace Taylor. *Planning for Jobs: Proposals Submitted in the Pabst Postwar Employment Awards* (1946).
Flash, Edward S., Jr., *Economic Advice and Presidential Leadership: The Council of Economic Advisers* (1965).
Galloway, George B. *Postwar Planning in the U.S.* (1942).
Gaus, John M. "The Planning Process in Government," in T.C.T. McCormick, ed., *Problems of the Postwar World* (1945).
Gross, Neal C. "A Post Mortem on County Planning," *Journal of Farm Economics*, 25 (Aug. 1943).
Gulick, Luther. "War Organization of the Federal Government," *American Political Science Review*, 38 (Dec. 1944).
Gulick, Luther, *Administrative Reflections from World War II* (1948).
Hamby, Alonzo. "Sixty Million Jobs and the People's Revolution: The Liberals, the New Deal, and World War II," *The Historian* (Aug. 1968).
———. "The Vital Center, the Fair Deal, and the Quest for a Liberal Political Economy," *American Historical Review*, 77 (June 1972).
Hansen, Alvin. "Social Planning for Tomorrow," In A. Hansen, ed., *The U.S. After the War* (1945).
Hinchey, Mary H. "The Frustration of the New Deal Revival 1944–1946," Ph.D. dissertation, University of Missouri, 1965.
Lekachman, Robert. *The Age of Keynes* (1965).
Lerner, Abba P. *The Economics of Control* (1944).
Lorwin, Lewis. *Time for Planning* (1945).

Millis, Walter, Harvey Mansfield, and Harold Stein. *Arms and the State: Civil Military Elements in National Policy* (1958).

National Resources Planning Board. *National Resources Development Report for 1943*, I and II (1943).

National Resources Planning Board. *Progress Report* (1942).

Nelson, Donald M. *Arsenal of Democracy* (1946).

Novick, David, Melvin Anshen, and W. C. Truppner. *Wartime Production Controls* (1949).

Polenberg, Richard. *War and Society: The U.S., 1941–1945* (1972).

Rosenfarb, Joseph. *Freedom and the Administrative State* (1948).

Schriftgeisser, Karl. *Business Comes of Age: The Story of the Committee for Economic Development* (1960).

Smith, Harold D. *The Management of Your Government* (1945).

Somer, Herman M. *Presidential Agency: The Office of War Mobilization and Reconversion* (1950).

Stone, I. F. *Business as Usual: The First Year of Defense* (1941).

Tugwell, Rexford G. *The Stricken Land* (1947).

U.S. Bureau of the Budget, *The United States at War* (1957).

U.S. Civilian Production Administration, *Industrial Mobilization for War: History of the War Production Board* (1947).

U.S. Congress, House of Representatives, Special Committee on Post-War Economic Policy and Planning. *Hearings* (78th Congress, 2nd Session), May 18–June 6, 1944.

———, *Hearings* (79th Congress, 1st and 2nd sessions), April 24–May 31. 1945.

Chapter 3:

Adams, Sherman. *Firsthand Report: The Story of the Eisenhower Administration* (1961).

Aikin, Charles, and Louis Koenig. "The Hoover Commission: A Symposium," *American Political Science Quarterly*, 43 (Oct. 1949).

Anderson, Patrick. *The President's Men* (1968).

Bach, George L. *Making Monetary and Fiscal Policy* (1971).

Banfield, Edward C. "Congress and the Budget: A Planner's Criticism," *American Political Science Review*, 43 (Dec. 1949).

Burns, James MacGregor. *Congress on Trial* (1949).

Dale, Edwin L. *Conservatives in Power: A Study in Frustration* (1960).

Eisenhower, Dwight D. *Mandate for Change, 1953–56* (1963).

———. *Waging Peace, 1957–1960* (1965).

Emmerich, Herbert. *Federal Organization and Administrative Management* (1971).

Falk, Stanley L. "The National Security Council Under Truman, Eisenhower and Kennedy," *Political Science Quarterly,* 79 (Sept. 1964).

Finer, Herman. "The Hoover Commission Reports," *Political Science Quarterly,* 64 (Sept. 1949).

Flash, Edward S., Jr. *Economic Advice and Presidential Leadership: The Council of Economic Advisors* (1965).

Graves, W. Brooke. *Reorganization of the Executive Branch of the Government of the U.S.: A Compilation of Basic Information, 1912–1948* (1949).

Hamby, Alonzo. *Beyond the New Deal: Harry S. Truman and American Liberalism* (1973).

Hammond, Paul Y. "The National Security Council as a Device for Interdepartmental Coordination," *American Political Science Review,* 54 (1960).

Harris, Seymour, ed. *Saving American Capitalism: A Liberal Economic Program* (1948).

Howard, John T. "The Role of the Federal Government in Urban Land Use Planning," *Fordham Law Review,* 29 (April 1961).

Hughes, Emmet John. *The Ordeal of Power* (1963).

Keyserling, Leon. "The Middle Way for America," *The Progressive* (May 1949).

Lyon, Peter. *Eisenhower: Portrait of the Hero* (1974).

MacNeil, Neil, and Harold W. Metz. *The Hoover Report, 1953–1955* (1956).

Mansfield, Harvey C. "Federal Executive Reorganization: Thirty Years of Experience," *Public Administration Review,* 29 (July–Aug. 1969).

————. "Reorganizing the Federal Executive Branch," *Law and Contemporary Problems,* 35 (Summer 1970).

Miller, Merle. *Plain Speaking: An Oral Biography of Harry S. Truman* (1973).

Morgan, D. A. "Improvement of Management in the Federal Government: Report to the President of the President's Advisory Committee on Management," *Public Administration Review,* 13 (Winter 1953).

Norton, Hugh S. *The Role of the Economist in Government* (1969).

Nourse, Edwin G. *Economics in the Public Service* (1953).

Parmet, Herbert S. *Eisenhower and the American Crusades* (1973).

President's Water Resources Policy Commission. *A Water Policy for the American People* (1950).

Rostow, Eugene V. *Planning for Freedom: The Public Law of American Capitalism* (1959).

Rovere, Richard. "Eisenhower Over the Shoulder," *The American Scholar,* 31 (Spring 1962).

Schriftgeisser, Karl. *Business Comes of Age* (1960).

Shannon, William V. "Eisenhower as President: A Critical Appraisal," *Commentary,* 26 (Nov. 1958).

Slesinger, Reuben E., ed. *National Economic Policy: The Presidential Reports* (1968).

Smith, Harold D. *The Management of Your Government* (1945).

Sundquist, James L. *Politics and Policy: The Eisenhower, Kennedy, and Johnson Years* (1968).

Truman, Harry S. *Memoirs by Harry S. Truman: Year of Decisions*, I (1955); *Years of Trial and Hope*, II (1956).

U.S. Commission on Intergovernmental Relations. *A Report to the President* (June 1955).

U.S. Commission on the Organization of the Executive Branch of the Government. *Concluding Report to Congress* (May 1949).

U.S. President's Materials Policy Commission. *Resources for Freedom*, I–IV (1952).

Chapter 4:

Bakke, E. Wight. *The Mission of Manpower Policy* (1969).

Bauer, Raymond A., ed. *Social Indicators* (1966).

Bell, Daniel. "Toward a Social Report: The Idea of a Social Report," *The Public Interest*, 15 (Spring 1969).

Blake, Judith. "Population Policy for Americans: Is the Government Being Misled?" *Science*, 164 (May 2, 1969).

Burns, James M., ed. *To Heal and To Build: The Programs of President Lyndon B. Johnson* (1968).

Carr, Donald E. *Death of the Sweet Waters* (1971).

Cary, William L. *Politics and the Regulatory Agencies* (1967).

Cronin, Thomas E. "Everybody Believes in Democracy Until He Gets to the White House . . .": An Examination of White House-Departmental Relations," in *Papers on the Institutionalized Presidency* (1971).

Cronin, Thomas E. and Sanford Greenberg, ed. *The Presidential Advisory System* (1969).

Day, J. Edward. *My Appointed Round: 929 Days a Postmaster General* (1965).

Dienes, C. Thomas. *Law, Politics and Birth Control* (1972).

Dorfman, Robert and Nancy, eds. *Economics of the Environment* (1972).

Drew, Elizabeth. "HEW Grapples with PPBS," *The Public Interest*, 8 (Summer 1967).

Driver, Edwin D. *Essays on Population Policy* (1972).

Duncan, Otis Dudley. "Social Forecasting—The State of the Art," *The Public Interest*, 17 (Fall 1969).

Enthoven, Alain C., and K. Wayne Smith. *How Much Is Enough: Shaping the Defense Program, 1961–1969* (1971).

Evans, Rowland, and Robert D. Novak. "Nixonomics: How the Game Plan Went Wrong," *The Atlantic Monthly* (July 1971).

Ewald, William R., Jr. *Environment and Change* (1968).

Fairlie, Henry. *The Kennedy Promise* (1973).

Fenno, Richard F., Jr. "The Cabinet: Index to the Kennedy Way," *The New York Times Magazine* (April 22, 1962).

Gawthrop, Louis C. *The Administrative Process and Democratic Theory* (1970).

Goldman, Eric. *The Tragedy of Lyndon Johnson* (1968).

Gordon, Kermit, ed. *Agenda for the Nation* (1968).

Gordon, Robert A. ed. *Toward A Manpower Policy* (1967).

Gorham, William. "PPBS: Its Scope and Limits: Notes of a Practitioner," *The Public Interest*, 8 (Summer 1967).

Gross, Bertram. "The New Systems Budgeting," *Public Administration Review*, 29 (March–April 1969).

———. *Social Intelligence for America's Future* (1969).

Harkavy, Oscar et al. "Family Planning and Public Policy: Who Is Misleading Who?" *Science,* 165 (July 1969).

Harper, Edwin L. et al. "Implementation and Use of PPB in Sixteen Federal Agencies," *Public Administration Review*, 29 (Nov.–Dec. 1969).

Hartke, Vance. "Toward a National Growth Policy," *Catholic University Law Review*, 22 (Winter 1973).

Jacob, Charles E. "The Quest for Presidential Control: Innovation and Institutionalization in the Executive Branch," unpublished paper delivered at annual meeting of American Political Science Association, 1973.

Kaysen, Carl. "Data Banks and Dossiers," *The Public Interest*, 7 (Spring 1967).

Kelly, Katie. *Garbage* (1973).

Lester, Richard A. *Manpower Planning in a Free Society* (1966).

Levin, Melvin R. *Community and Regional Planning* (1972).

Levitan, Sar A. *Federal Manpower Policies and Programs to Combat Unemployment* (1964).

Levitan, Sar A., and Garth L. Mangum. *Making Sense of Federal Manpower Policy* (1967).

Levitan, Sar A., and Irving Siegel, eds. *Dimensions of Manpower Policy* (1966).

MacMahon, Arthur W. *Administering Federalism in a Democracy* (1972).

Mangum, Garth L. *The Emergency of Manpower Policy* (1969).

———, ed. *The Manpower Revolution* (1965).

McFarland, Carl. "Landis' Report: The Voice of One Crying in the Wilderness," *Virginia Law Review*, 47 (April 1961).

Miernyk, William H. *The Economics of Labor and Collective Bargaining* (1973).

Mondale, Walter F. "Reporting on the Social State of the Union," *Transaction,* 5 (June 1968).

Mott, George G., ed. "Urban Change and the Planning Syndrome," *Annals of the American Academy of Political and Social Science,* 405 (Jan. 1973).

Neustadt, Richard E. "Approaches to Staffing the Presidency: Notes on FDR and JFK," *American Political Science Review,* 57 (Dec. 1963).

Piotrow, Phyllis T. *World Population Crisis: The U.S. Response* (1973).

Reilly, William K., ed. *The Use of Land: A Citizens' Policy Guide to Urban Growth* (1973).

Revelle, Roger. "What Must We Do To Avoid a Population Catastrophe?" *Harvard Magazine* (Dec. 1973).

Schick, Allen. "The Road to PPB: The Stages of Budget Reform," *Public Administration Review,* 26 (Dec. 1966).

Schlesinger, Arthur M., Jr. *A Thousand Days: John F. Kennedy In the White House* (1965).

Schultze, Charles L. *The Politics and Economics of Public Spending* (1968).

Servan-Schreiber, Jean-Jacques. *The American Challenge* (1968).

Sidey, Hugh. *A Very Personal Presidency: Lyndon Johnson in the White House* (1968).

Tugwell, Rexford G. *The Emerging Constitution* (1974).

Tugwell, Rexford G., and Thomas E. Cronin, eds. *The Presidency Reappraised* (1974).

U.S. Advisory Commission on Intergovernmental Relations. *Urban and Rural America: Policies for Future Growth* (1968).

U.S. Congress, House of Representatives, Committee on Government Operations, Subcommittee on Conservation and Natural Resources, Hearings. *Effects of Population Growth on Natural Resources and the Environment* (Sept. 1969).

U.S. Congress, Joint Economic Committee. *The Analysis and Evaluation of Public Expenditures: The PPB System* (3 vols., 1969).

U.S. Congress, Senate Committee on Government Operations, 91st Congress, 1st Session, Hearings on S-2701. *A Bill To Establish a Commission on Population Growth and the American Future* (Sept. 15, 1969).

U.S. Congress, Senate Committee on Government Operations. *Planning-Programming-Budgeting: Official Documents* (1967).

U.S. Congress, Senate Committee on Labor and Public Welfare. *Family Planning and Population Research.* Hearings, 91st Congress, 1st and 2nd Sessions (Dec. 1969 and Feb. 1970) (1970).

U.S. Congress, Senate Committee on Labor and Public Welfare, Special Subcommittee on Evaluation and Planning of Social Programs, 92nd Congress, 1st Session. *Full Opportunity and National Goals and Priorities Act* (1971).

U.S. Congressional Research Service. *The Technology Assessment Act of 1972* (Feb. 6, 1972).

U.S. Department of Agriculture. *National Growth and Its Distribution: Symposium on Communities of Tomorrow* (Dec. 11–12, 1967).

U.S. Department of Health, Education and Welfare. *Toward a Social Report* (1969).

U.S. Department of Labor. *Manpower Report of the President* (1963–1968).

U.S. National Commission on Urban Problems. *Building the American City* (1969).

U.S. News and World Report. "Solve U.S. Domestic Ills with Defense Billions? That's Clifford's New Idea," 65 (Oct. 7, 1968).

U.S. President's Task Force on Government Organization (Ben W. Heineman, Chairman). *Final Report,* June 15, 1967.

Chapter 5:

Agena, Kathleen. "The Implications of Nixon's Non-Policy Toward Urban Growth," *Planning,* 38 (June 1972).

Barfield, Claude. "Nixon Reorganization Raises Questions about Role of Science in Federal Policy Making," *National Journal* (March 24, 1973).

Beckman, Norman. "National Growth Policy: 1972," *Urban Land* (Nov. 1973).

———. "National Urban Growth Policy: 1973 Congressional and Executive Action," *American Institute of Planners Journal* (July 1974).

———. "Toward Development of a National Urban Growth Policy: Legislative Review 1971." *American Institute of Planners Journal* (July 1972).

Beyle, Thad et al. "New Directions in State Planning," *American Institute of Planners Journal,* 35 (Sept. 1969).

Blechman, Barry M. et al. *Setting National Priorities: The 1975 Budget* (1974).

Congressional Quarterly. *Nixon: The First Year of His Presidency* (1970).

Council on Environmental Quality. First Annual Report, *Environmental Quality* (1970). Second Annual Report, *Environmental Quality* (1971).

Cronin, Thomas E. "Everybody Believes in Democracy Until He Gets To The White House . . .": An Examination of White House–Departmental Relations," in *Papers on the Institutionalized Presidency* (1971).

Cronin, Thomas E. "The Swelling of the Presidency," *Saturday Review of the Society* (Feb. 1973).

Davidson, Roger H. *The Politics of Comprehensive Manpower Legislation* (1972).

Donovan, John C. "The Domestic Council and the Politics of Presidential Leadership," paper read at the Annual Meeting, American Society of Public Administration, March 23, 1972.

Drury, Allen, and Fred Maroon. *Courage and Hesitation: Notes and Photographs of the Nixon Administration* (1971).

Evans, Rowland, and Robert Novak. *Nixon in the White House: The Frustrations of Power* (1971).

Fried, Edward R., et al. *Setting National Priorities: The 1974 Budget* (1973).

Goodwin, Irwin, ed. *Energy and Environment* (1974).

Grayson, C. Jackson and Louis Neeb. *Confessions of a Price Controller* (1974).

Greenberg, Daniel S. "Science and Richard Nixon," *The New York Times Magazine* (June 17, 1973).

Hartke, Vance. "Toward a National Growth Policy," *Catholic University Law Review*, 22 (Winter 1973).

Haveman, Roby H., and Julius Margolis, eds. *Public Expenditures and Policy Analysis* (1970).

Havemann, Joel. "OMB's 'Management-by-Objective' Produces Goals of Uneven Quality," *National Journal Reports* (Aug. 18, 1973).

Herbers, John. "The Other Presidency," *The New York Times Magazine* (March 3, 1974).

Hickel, Walter J. *Who Owns America?* (1971).

Hoxie, R. Gordon, ed. *The Presidency of the 1970s*, Vol. II (1972).

Ink, Dwight and Alan Dean. "A Concept of Decentralization," *Public Administration Review*, 30 (Jan.–Feb. 1970).

Jacob, Charles E. "The Quest for Presidential Control: Innovation and Institutionalization in the Executive Branch," paper read at the 1973 Annual Meeting of the American Political Science Association.

Jaffe, Frederick. "Public Policy on Fertility Control," *Scientific American*, 229 (July 1973).

James, Dorothy B. *The Contemporary Presidency* (1973).

Johnson, Richard T. *Managing the White House: An Intimate Study of the Presidency* (1974).

Kessel, John. *The Domestic Presidency: Decision-Making in the White House* (1975).

Kolodziej, Edward A. "The National Security Council: Innovations and Implications," *Public Administration Review*, 29 (Nov.–Dec. 1969).

Kraft, Joseph. "Who's Running the Country?" *The Atlantic Monthly* (April 1974).

Levitan, Sar A., and Robert Taggart. *Social Experimentation and Manpower Policy* (1971).

Magruder, Jeb Stuart. *An American Life* (1974).

Maisel, Sherman J. *Managing the Dollar* (1973).

Miernyk, William H. *The Economics of Labor and Collective Bargaining* (1973).

Miller, Roger L., and Raburn M. Williams. *The New Economics of Richard Nixon* (1972).

Monat, William R. "The Once and Future Revolution: Manpower Policy in the U.S.," *Public Administration Review*, 30 (Jan.–Feb. 1970).

Morrison, Rodney J. *Expectations and Inflation: Nixon, Politics and Economics* (1973).

Moynihan, Daniel P. *Coping* (1973).

————. *The Politics of a Guaranteed Income: The Nixon Administration and the Family Assistance Plan* (1973).

————. "Toward a National Urban Policy," *The Public Interest,* 17 (Fall 1969).

Noll, Roger G. *Reforming Regulation: An Evaluation of the Ash Council Proposals* (1971).

Osborne, John. *The Nixon Watch* (1970).

————. *The Second Year of the Nixon Watch* (1971).

————. *The Third Year of the Nixon Watch* (1972).

————. *The Fourth Year of The Nixon Watch* (1973).

President's Commission on Population Growth and the American Future. *Population and the American Future* (1972).

Rather, Dan, with Gary P. Gates. *The Palace Guard* (1974).

Reilly, William K., ed. *The Use of Land* (1973).

Reitze, Arnold W. *Environmental Planning: Law of Land and Resources,* Vol. I (1972), Vol. II (1974).

Rose, David J. "Energy Policy in the U.S.," *Scientific American,* 230 (Jan. 1974).

Rosenbaum, Walter A. *The Politics of Environmental Concern* (1973).

Rourke, Francis E. "The Domestic Scene: The President Ascendant," in Robert E. Osgood et al., *Retreat from Empire: The First Nixon Administration* (1973).

Safire, William. *Before the Fall* (1975).

Schell, Jonathan. "Reflections: The Nixon Years," *The New Yorker* (May–July 1975).

Schick, Allen. "The Budget Bureau That Was," in The Brookings Institution, *Papers on the Institutionalized Presidency,* Reprint #213 (1971).

————. "A Death in the Bureaucracy: The Demise of Federal PPB," *Public Administration Review,* 33 (March–April 1973).

Schlesinger, Arthur M., Jr. *The Imperial Presidency* (1973).

Schultze, Charles L., et al. *Setting National Priorities: The 1971 Budget* (1970).

————. *Setting National Priorities: The 1972 Budget* (1971).

————. *Setting National Priorities: The 1973 Budget* (1972).

Silk, Leonard. *Nixonomics* (1972).

Surrey, Stanley. *Pathways to Tax Reform: The Concept of Tax Expenditures* (1973).

Thomas, N. C. and H. W. Baade, eds. "The Institutionalized Presidency," *Law and Contemporary Problems,* 35 (Summer 1970).

Tugwell, Rexford G., and Thomas E. Cronin, eds. *The Presidency Reappraised* (1974).

U.S. Comptroller General. *U.S. Actions Needed To Cope with Commodity Shortages* (April 29, 1974).

U.S. Congress, House Committee on Banking and Currency. 91st Congress, 2nd Session. *Hearings on HR 17880: To Extend the Defense Production Act of 1950* (June–July 1970).

U.S. Congress, House Committee on Banking and Currency. 92nd Congress, 2nd Session. *National Growth Policy: Hearings,* Part I (1972).

U.S. Congress, House Committee on Government Operations. 91st Congress, 2nd Session. *Hearings on Reorganization Plan #2 of 1970* (April–May 1970).

U.S. Congress, House Committee on Government Operations. 92nd Congress, 1st Session. *Reorganization of Executive Departments:* Part I, Overview (June–July 1971).

U.S. Congress, House Committee on Government Operations. 92nd Congress, 2nd Session. *Hearings on Reorganization of Executive Departments:* Part II, Department of Community Development (1972).

U.S. Congress, House Committee on Interior and Insular Affairs. *Land Use Planning Act of 1974,* Report #93-798 (Feb. 1974).

U.S. Congress, House Committee on Interstate and Foreign Commerce. 91st Congress, 2nd Session. *Family Planning Services* (Aug. 1970).

U.S. Congress, House Committee on Public Works. *Hearings: A National Public Works Investment Policy: A Strategy for Balanced Population Growth and Economic Development* (Nov.–Dec. 1973).

U.S. Congress, Joint Economic Committee. 92nd Congress, 1st Session. *Hearings on Phase II of the President's New Economic Program* (Nov. 1971).

U.S. Congress, Joint Economic Committee. 92nd Congress, 2nd Session. *National Priorities—The Next Five Years* (May–June 1972).

U.S. Congress, Joint Economic Committee. *A Proposal for Achieving Balanced National Growth and Development,* Senator Hubert H. Humphrey (Feb. 1973).

U.S. Congress, Senate Committee on Banking, Housing, and Urban Affairs. 93rd Congress, 2nd Session. *Hearing: Oversight on Economic Stabilization* (Jan.–Feb. 1974).

U.S. Congress, Senate Committee on Government Operations. 91st Congress, 1st Session. *Hearing on S-2701: A Bill To Establish a Commission on Population Growth and the American Future* (Sept. 1969).

U.S. Congress, Senate Committee on Interior and Insular Affairs. 91st Congress, 1st Session. *National Environmental Policy: Hearings on S-1075* (April 1969).

U.S. Congress, Senate Committee on Interior and Insular Affairs. *Federal Energy Organization: A Staff Analysis* (1973).

U.S. Congress, Senate Committee on Labor and Public Welfare. 91st Congress, 1st and 2nd Sessions. *Family Planning and Population Research* (1970).

U.S. Congress, Senate Committee on Labor and Public Welfare. *Family Planning Services and Population Research Amendments of 1973* (May 1973).

U.S. Congress, Senate Committee on Rules and Administration. 92nd Congress, 2nd Session. *Technology Assessment for the Congress* (Nov. 1972).

U.S. Congress, Senate Document #93–19, 93rd Congress, 1st Session. *Toward a National Growth Policy: Federal and State Developments in 1972* (1973).

U.S. Congressional Research Service. *The Technology Assessment Act of 1972* (Feb. 6, 1972).

U.S. Council on International Economic Policy. *International Economic Report of the President* (Feb. 1974).

U.S. Department of Labour. *Manpower Report of the President* (Jan. 1969).

U.S. Department of Labor. *Manpower Report of the President* (April 1971).

U.S. Domestic Council. *Report on National Growth: 1972* (1972).

U.S. Environmental Policy Division, Congressional Research Service. *Congress and the Nation's Environment* (Jan. 20, 1973).

U.S. Environmental Protection Agency. *Final Conference Report for the National Conference on Managing the Environment* (1973).

U.S. National Commission on Materials Policy. *Material Needs and the Environment Today and Tomorrow* (June 1973).

U.S. National Goals Research Staff. *Toward Balanced Growth: Quantity with Quality* (July 4, 1970).

U.S. News and World Report. "Nixon's Top Command: Expanding in Size and Power" (April 24, 1972).

U.S. Office of Management and Budget. *Papers Relating to the President's Departmental Reorganization Program* (Feb. 1972).

U.S. President's Commission on Federal Statistics. *Federal Statistics*, I and II (1971).

Whalen, Richard J. *Catch the Falling Flag: A Republican's Challenge to His Party* (1972).

Chapter 6:

Arrow, Kenneth J. *Social Choice and Individual Values* (1951).

Banfield, Edward C. *The Unheavenly City* (1968).

Bell, Daniel, ed. *Toward the Year 2000* (1968).

Bieda, K. *The Structure and Operation of the Japanese Economy* (1970).

Bollens, John C. *Special District Governments in the U.S.* (1957).

Braybrooke, David and Charles E. Lindblom. *A Strategy of Decision: Policy Evaluation as a Social Process* (1963).

Broder, David S. *The Party's Over: The Failure of Politics in America* (1971).

Brown, Lester R. *World Without Borders* (1972).

Bundy, McGeorge. *The Strength of Government* (1968).

Burns, James Macgregor. *Uncommon Sense* (1972).

Burnsnall, William J. et al., eds. *Planning Challenges of the 1970s in the Public Domain* (1970).

Caldwell, Lynton K. "Environment and Administration," in William Murdoch, ed., *Environment: Resources, Pollution and Society* (1971).

Chamberlain, Neil W. *Private and Public Planning* (1965).

Clawson, Marion, and Peter Hall. *Planning and Urban Growth: An Anglo American Comparison* (1973).

Cohen, Stephen S. *Modern Capitalist Planning: The French Experience* (1971).

Colm, Gerhard, and Luther Gulick. *Program Planning for National Goals* (1968).

Committee for Economic Development, *Modernizing Local Government* (1966).

Crozier, Michael. *The Bureaucratic Phenomenon* (1964).

Dahl, Robert A., and Charles E. Lindblom. *Politics, Economics and Welfare* (1953).

Devons, Ely. *Planning in Practice* (1950).

Faber, Mike, and Dudley Seers, eds. *The Crisis in Planning*, I and II (1972).

Frankel, Charles. "The Specter of Eugenics," *Commentary* (March 1974).

Frankel, Max. "Revenue Sharing is Counter Revolution," *New York Times Magazine* (April 25, 1971).

Friedmann, John. *Retracking America: A Theory of Transactive Planning* (1973).

Friedmann, John and Barclay Hudson. "Knowledge and Action: A Guide to Planning Theory," *American Institute of Planners Journal* (Jan. 1974).

Friss, I. "Planning and Economic Reform in Hungary," in Zoltan Roman, ed., *Progress and Planning in Industry* (1972).

Galbraith, John Kenneth. *Economics and the Public Purpose* (1973).

———. *The New Industrial State* (1967).

Grodzins, Morton. *The American System* (1966), ed. by Daniel J. Elazar.

Grosenick, Leigh H., ed. *The Administration of the New Federalism* (1973).

Gross, Bertram, ed. *Action Under Planning* (1967).

———. "The Managers of National Economic Change," in Roscoe C. Martin, ed., *Public Administration and Democracy: Essays in Honor of Paul Appleby* (1965).

———. "National Planning: Findings and Fallacies," *Public Administration Review*, 25 (Dec. 1965).

Grossman, Gregory. *Economic Systems* (1972).

———, ed. *Essays in Socialism and Planning in Honor of Carl Landauer* (1970).

Hackett, John, and Anne-Marie. *Economic Planning in France* (1963).

Hagen, Everett, and Stephanie White. *Great Britain: Quiet Revolution in Planning* (1966).

Hansen, Niles M. "French Indicative Planning and the New Industrial State," *Journal of Economic Issues*, 3 (1969).

Hardin, Charles M. *Presidential Power and Accountability: Toward a New Constitution* (1974).

Hardin, Garret. "The Tragedy of the Commons," *Science*, 162 (Dec. 13, 1968).

Harlow, John S. *French Economic Planning* (1963).

Harrington, Michael. *Socialism* (1972).

―――. *Toward a Democratic Left* (1968).

Heilbroner, Robert L. *An Inquiry into the Human Prospect* (1974).

Herbers, John. "In Six Months, Ford's Style is Set," *The New York Times* (Feb. 23, 1975).

Howe, Irving, and Michael Harrington, eds. *The Seventies* (1972).

Initiative Committee for National Economic Planning. "The Cace for Government Planning," *The New York Times* (March 16, 1975).

Jacoby, Henry. *The Bureaucratization of the World* (1973).

Jacoby, Neil H. *Corporate Power and Social Responsibility* (1973).

Jewkes, John. *The New Ordeal by Planning: The Experience of the Forties and the Sixties* (1968).

Kahn, Alfred J. *Studies in Social Policy and Planning* (1969).

―――. *Theory and Practice of Social Planning* (1969).

Kariel, Henry. *The Decline of American Pluralism* (1961).

Kaser, Michael, and Janusz Zielinski. *Planning in East Europe* (1970).

Kaufman, Herbert. "Administrative Decentralization and Political Power," *Public Administration Review*, 29 (Jan.–Feb. 1969).

Keiser, Norman F. "Public Responsibility and Federal Advisory Groups: A Case Study," *Western Political Quarterly*, 11 (June 1958).

Klein, Philip A. *The Management of Market-Oriented Economies* (1973).

Kolodziej. Edward A. "The National Security Council: Innovations and Implications," *Public Administration Review*, 29 (Nov.–Dec. 1969).

Komiya, Ryutaro, "Economic Planning in Japan," *Challenge*, 18 (May–June, 1975).

Landauer, Carl. *Theory of National Economic Planning* (1947).

Leach, Richard H., ed. "Intergovernmental Relations in America Today," *Annals*, 416 (Nov. 1974).

Levine, Robert A. *Public Planning: Failure and Redirection* (1973).

Lindblom, Charles E. "Economics and the Administration of National Planning," *Public Administration Review*, 25 (Dec. 1965).

―――. *The Intelligence of Democracy: Decision-Making Through Mutual Adjustment* (1965).

―――. "The Science of Muddling Through," *Public Administration Review*, 19 (Spring 1959).

Lippit, Victor. "Economic Planning in Japan," *Journal of Economic Issues,* 9 (Mar., 1975).

Loewenstein, Louis and Dorn McGrath. "The Planning Imperative in America's Future." *Annals of the American Academy of Political and Social Science,* 405 (Jan. 1973).

Lowi, "Decentralization—To Whom? For What?" *Midway,* 9 (Winter 1969).

———. *The End of Liberalism* (1969).

———. "Permanent Receivership," *The Center Magazine,* 7 (March–April 1974).

———. "The Public Philosophy: Interest-Group Liberalism," *American Political Science Review,* 61 (March 1967).

MacAvoy, Paul, ed. *The Crisis of the Regulatory Commissions* (1970).

Mannheim, Karl. *Man and Society in an Age of Reconstruction* (1935; English version, 1949).

March, James G. and Herbert A. Simon. *Organizations* (1958).

McConnell, Grant. *Private Power and American Democracy* (1965).

Meade, James E. *Planning and the Price Mechanism* (1949).

Meadows, Donella H. et al. *The Limits to Growth* (1972).

Mertins, Herman and Bertram Gross, eds. "Symposium on Changing Styles of Planning in Post-Industrial America," *Public Administration Review,* 31 (May–June 1971).

Millikan, Max F., ed. *National Economic Planning* (1967).

Mullaney, Thomas E. "A Look at Economic Planning," *The New York Times* (March 9, 1975).

Myrdal, Gunnar. *Beyond the Welfare State* (1960).

———. *Challenge to Affluence* (1963).

Ophyls, William. "The Scarcity Society," *Harper's Magazine,* 248 (April 1974).

Patton, H. Milton and Janet W. "Harbingers of State Growth Policies," *State Government,* 47 (Spring 1974).

Peterson, Norman V. "A National Plan for Century III," *Journal of the American Institute of Planners,* 33 (July 1967).

Peterson, Wallace. "Planning the Market Economy," *Journal of Economic Issues,* 3 (March 1969).

Reagan, Michael D. *The Managed Economy* (1963).

———. *The New Federalism* (1972).

Reagan, Michael D. "Toward Improving National Policy Planning," *Public Administration Review,* 23 (March 1963).

Reitze, Arnold W., Jr. *Environmental Law:* I (1972) and II (1974).

Rose, David J. "Energy Policy in the U.S.," *Scientific American,* 230 (Jan. 1974).

Seloma, John, and Frederick H. Sontag. *Parties* (1972).

Seidman, Harold. *Politics, Position, and Power: The Dynamics of Federal Organization* (1970).

Shultz, George P., and Robert Z. Aliber, eds. *Guidelines, Informal Controls, and the Market Place* (1966).

Shonfield, Andrew. *Modern Capitalism* (1965).

Sirkin, Gerald. *The Visible Hand: The Fundamentals of Economic Planning* (1968).

Skinner, B. F. *Beyond Freedom and Dignity* (1971).

SoLo, Robert A. "Organizational Structure, Technological Advance, and the New Tasks of Government," *Journal of Economic Issues,* 6 (Dec. 1972).

Sundquist, James. *Dispersing Population: What America Can Learn from Europe* (1975).

Sundquist, James L. "Europe Stops the Urban Swarm," *The Nation,* 219 (July 20, 1974).

Sundquist, James L., and David W. Davis. *Making Federalism Work* (1969).

Sundquist, James L., David B. Walker, and Ralph R. Widner. *Metropolitanization and National Policies for Growth: A European Reconnaissance and Its Relevance to the U.S.* (1972).

Thayer, Fred C. "Presidential Policy Processes and the 'New Administration,'" *Public Administration Review,* 31 (Sept.–Oct. 1971).

Tsuru, Shigeto. *Essays on Economic Development* (1968).

Tugwell, Rexford G. *The Emerging Constitution* (1974).

———. *A Model Constitution for a United Republic of America* (1970).

U.S. Congress, House Committee on Banking and Currency, Subcommittee on Housing. 92nd Congress, 2nd Session. *National Growth Policy:* Hearings, I and II (June 6–7, 1972).

U.S. Congress, Senate Committee on Labor and Public Welfare, Special Subcommittee on the National Science Foundation. 93rd Congress, 2nd Session. *National Policy and Priorities for Science and Technology Act, 1974* (Oct. 8, 1974).

Westin, Alan F. *Privacy and Freedom* (1967).

Wildavsky, Aaron. *The Politics of the Budgetary Process* (1964).

———. "The Political Economy of Efficiency," *The Public Interest,* 8 (Summer 1967).

———. "Does Planning Work?" *The Public Interest,* 24 (Summer 1971).

Wilson, James Q. "The Bureaucracy Problem," *The Public Interest,* 6 (Winter 1967).

Wooton, Barbara. *Freedom Under Planning* (1945).

Index

Housing Act of 1954, and "701" grants, 124, 162
Housing and Urban Development Act of 1970, 218
Humphrey, Hubert H., and planning bill of 1973, 236-37; and planning bill of 1975, 278-79, 95, 228

Ickes, Harold, 52-53, 60-61
Initiative Committee for National Economic Planning, 277

Jackson, Senator Henry, 219-24, 238-40, 245-46, 278
Javits, Senator Jacob, 278
Johnson, Hugh, quoted, 15, 30
Johnson, Lyndon B., becomes President, 139-41; and the Great Society, 141-87; and political reform, 185-86
Jones, Jesse, and the RFC, 47-49

Kennedy, John F., becomes President, 126-27; his administration, 127-29; relationship to Planning, 130-39; and the business community, 137; and the population issue, 152-53; and political reform, 183-84, 141, 189, 294
Kennedy, Senator Ted, 230
Kestnbaum, Meyer, chairman of Commission on Intergovernmental Relations, of 1953-1955, 115-16
Keynes, John Maynard, 22
Keyserling, Leon, 93-94, 104-5

Land-use planning, during New Deal, 36-44; in the 1960s, 219-24; under Nixon, 238-40
Landis, James M., 132-33
Lekachman, Robert, quoted, 90
Leontief, Wassily, 277
Liberalism, as of 1932, 7-8; at end of the 1930s, 64-68; post-war, 92-98; and the Broker State system, 296-

303; the liberal Planning model, 307-20, 12
Lilienthal, David E., 311
Lippmann, Walter, 260, 279
Litton, Congressman Jerry, 284
Lorwin, Lewis, 95
Love, Governor John A., 245
Lowi, Theodore, quoted, 299-300

McNamara, Robert S., and the PPBS system, 171-74, 286
Magruder, Jeb Stuart, 261
Management by Objectives (MBO), 207
Mangum, Garth, 147-48
Manpower policy, 142-49
Marketplace, advocates of, 309-10
Marshall, Robert, 38
Merriam, Charles, 52
Mineta, Norman, 227
Mitchell, John, 254
Mitchell, Wesley, 52
Mondale, Senator Walter F., 182
Moore, Hugh, 150-51
Morgan, Arthur E., 40
Morton, Rogers C., quoted, 265, 224
Moynihan, Daniel P., influence on Richard Nixon, 193-94, 180, 182, 191, 197-98, 199, 200, 203, 225, 232, 255, 258
Muskie, Senator Edward, 222-23, 213
Myrdal, Gunnar, 303, 310

National Economic Council (NEC), 50-52
National Environmental Protection Act, 213-14
National Goals Research Staff (NGRS), 200-201; publishes *Toward Balanced Growth*, 201
National Growth Policy (NGP), origins in the 1960s, 159-66; New Deal precursors, 160-61, 195; in 1969 and early Nixon years, 194-203; biennial